THE POLITICS OF HISTORICAL VISION

CRITICAL PE R

A GUILFOR D

EDITE D

DOUGLAS K

IINIVERSITY OF T E

The Politics
of Historical Vision:
Marx, Foucault,
Habermas

STEVEN BEST

THE GUILFORD PRESS
NEW YORK   LONDON

©1995 The Guilford Press
A Division of Guilford Publications, Inc.
72 Spring Street, New York, NY 10012

Printed in the United States of America

This book is printed on acid-free paper.

Last digit is print number: 9 8 7 6 5 4 3 2 1

Library of Congress Cataloging-in-Publication Data

Best, Steven.
    The politics of historical vision : Marx, Foucault, Habermas / by Steven Best.
        p.   cm. — (Critical perspectives)
    Includes bibliographical references and index.
    ISBN 0-89862-851-2
    1. Postmodernism—Political aspects.   2. Political science— Philosophy.   3. History—Philosophy.   4. Marx, Karl, 1818–1883—Contributions in political science.   5. Foucault, Michel—Contributions in political science.   6. Habermas, Jürgen—Contributions in political science.   I. Title.
    II. Series: Critical perspectives (New York, N.Y.)
JA74.B474   1995
320′.01′1—dc20   94-44894
                                                               CIP

For Billie
my funny valentine

ACKNOWLEDGMENTS

This book would not have been possible without the support and encouragement of many people. For critical readings of specific chapters I wish to thank Harry Cleaver, Kathy Higgins, Kelly Oliver, and Bob Solomon. David Hall, Mark Poster, and Richard Wolin generously read the entire manuscript in its last stages and offered extremely helpful critical remarks. For their patience with my interminable delays in publication I am grateful to Peter Wissoker and Guilford Press. My friendship with Ruth Andersen, Briankle Chang, John Coker, Tom Derr, Ali Hossaini, Joe Pendergast, Renan Rápalo, Keith Hay-Roe, and Tina and Jason have been invaluable. Murray Bookchin's work and friendship has stimulated me to go in new directions that I will follow in my next book on his theory of social ecology. There were numerous occasions that I would have had to abandon this project to bartend or pump gas if it had not been for the help of Noah Khosbin and Ali Hossaini. As always, Keith Hay-Roe pulled me out of numerous computer quagmires. Jack Haddox and other colleagues rescued me from a trying three-year stint in the surplus reserve army of Ph.D.'s. Joe Pendergast, currently working in Seattle, created the eerie image for the front cover. The soulful vocals and trumpet of Chet Baker provided a soothing background for the writing of much of this manuscript, as my cat Dos kept me constant company amid piles of papers and books. I owe an immense debt to my two closest friends, Bob ("Ralph") Antonio and Doug Kellner. Without Bob's unflagging moral support, my eyes would have strayed from the prize. I will never forget our great times together in Austin and our tequila-laden respites from the performance principle of academia. Bob scrupulously read every page of this manuscript numerous times, and each of his critiques immensely improved the final product. I owe even more to Doug Kellner, my mentor and friend, who also carefully read this entire book in various drafts. Doug has helped me through various crises in recent times and his work has been a constant source of inspiration. I have learned a great deal about teaching and writing from his example. My best piece of luck of the last decade has been to know and work with him. His merciless ("Kellneri-an") critiques forced me to restructure this project numerous times; whatever readability and cogency it has owes much to him. But there is one person who has been there for me from the start; to her I dedicate this book.

PREFACE

Never before has it been more necessary to recover the
past, to deepen our knowledge of history, to demystify
the origins of our problems, to regain our memory of
forms of freedom and advances that were made in liberating humanity of its superstitions, irrationalities, and,
above all, a loss of faith in humanity's potentialities.
                                        —MURRAY BOOKCHIN

Human beings have never been without history. In the paradoxical formulation of phenomenology, the only unchanging structure of human existence is its capacity to change and evolve—its "historicity." According
to philosophical anthropology, human beings differ from "merely" natural
beings because their existence is not limited only to instinct and passive
adaptation to the natural environment. Rather, human existence is socially and linguistically mediated, consciously created and defined, and
changes throughout time. For existentialists, human beings have a history but no nature; they constitute not an essence but an open-ended existence defined by their choices and actions.

First and foremost, history is ontological or pretheoretical; it is not
primarily a narrative, but a concrete reality that is lived. History is the
temporal context of human evolution within socionatural conditions; it
is the continuous present that instantly recedes into the past and from which
we project the future. Nor is history only "what hurts," as Fredric Jameson reminds us in a statement against idealist hermeneutics: it is the structure of life itself. Secondarily and derivatively, history is a reflexive study
on human events and their causes and consequences. As Sartre's character Roquentin discovered in *Nausea,* history is lived before it is written
about and the historian engaged in narrative and biography cannot in good
faith escape the flow of time and the anguish of autobiography. As a discipline, history begins when human beings first differentiate "now" from
"then" in oral or written accounts, when they realize they have a past

that is useful to know, interpret, relate, study, and maintain, a past preserved in various forms that have included songs, poems, verse, prose, chronicles, and "science."

Yet, in the 1980s, both Jean Baudrillard, a radical postmodernist, and Francis Fukuyama, a neoconservative State Department intellectual, declared that we have reached "the end of history"—the point at which the engines of historical change allegedly have run out of steam. For Baudrillard (1987, 1988), the modern dynamics of incessant change are over, as are modern hopes for enlightenment, progress, and reform or revolution. There is still movement and flux in history, but it is random, repetitive, and meaningless. Nothing new can happen and all we can do is accomodate ourselves to the frozen emptiness of time. Fukuyama (1992) claims that we have reached the final stage in the evolution of human thought. The end of history occurred with the collapse of Communism and the alleged triumph of capitalism as the only viable form of social organization. Unlike Baudrillard, Fukuyama believes there still may be wars, real events, and economic and political change, but he claims the main dynamics of social and political thought have run their course. The direction of future evolution is toward a steady increase in the tradition of "democratic egalitarianism" inaugurated by capitalism.

Such theories of the end of history point more to the decline in historical imagination than to history itself. The smug claims of Baudrillard were instantly refuted, appropriately, not by intellectuals removed from history, but rather by the masses making it. As Baudrillard was delivering his world-weary diatribes of doom and gloom before his black-clothed laity, the citizens of Europe had taken to the streets to tear down the Berlin Wall, to overthrow oppressive communist systems and gain sovereignty from the Soviet Union, and to wage bloody ethnic and nationalist wars. While some of these events in fact confirm Fukuyama's version of the end of history thesis, since communism is collapsing and free market structures are being universalized, ideological consensus on the meaning of freedom and the good life is nowhere at hand, and the ideals of democracy are far from secure. Fukuyama is blind to the decline of liberalism; the persistence of economic crisis; the increasingly perilous nature of egalitarian norms with the rise of neoconservativism, neofascism, and technocratic–authoritarian ideology; and the bitter historical conflicts still raging.

Besides presupposing God-like powers of omniscient retrospection and projection, concepts of the end of history are inherently conservative. If we are truly at the end of history, we need not bother with historical criticism or political activism, since there's nothing fundamental to change. However Marx's original ideals were discredited by the work of Lenin, Stalin, and their successors, it does not follow that if communism (or at least one version of it) has lost, then capitalism has won. Fukuyama's claim that history has ended with late capitalism is as ludicrous and reactionary as Hegel's earlier claim that the history of freedom culminates with the Prussian bureaucracy. It is yet another example of the Eurocentric arrogance that the modern West is the center and summit of history, even now as the fulcrum of global power shifts from the West to the East.

Contemporary appeals to the end of history are part of the postmodern apocalyptic mindset that pronounces the death of the fundamental values and referents of modern thought. Appearing at the fin-de-millennium and after three centuries of explosive growth and transformation in Western society, the postmodern scene is marked by an "inverted millenarianism in which premonitions of the future, catastrophic or redemptive, have been replaced by senses of the end of this or that" (Jameson 1991: 1). Recent decades have seen obituaries for ideology, history, philosophy, normative epistemology, "Man," universal values, Marxism, literature, and the avant garde. Even reality itself, allegedly buried under the profusion of signs, images, and simulacra of consumer capitalism, is said to have vanished.[1] The postmodern sensibility feels the dissolution of old certainties; it senses that the boundaries of the modern world are collapsing, not expanding. Few still believe, for instance, in the Enlightenment equation of reason and freedom.[2] The horizon of a liberatory future is increasingly clouded by a growing sense that the fundamental dynamics of change, transformation, progress, and emancipation are over.

For all their hyperbole, postmodern visions of the end of history capture an important aspect of advanced capitalist societies—the decline of historical knowledge, consciousness, and imagination. If we are not literally at the end of history, in the last stretches of a culturally and ecologically viable existence, we are certainly in the midst of a deteriorating ability to situate the present within a larger system of historical references and to envisage an alternative future. The various forms of the rejection of history—from the avant-garde attack on narrative, memory, and the past to the neoconservative longing for a preindustrial time, from ahistorical forms of deconstruction to poststructuralist definitions of history as an undecideable text to the fragmentary and momentary consciousness of the video generation—affirm Henry Ford's claim that "History is bunk," or perhaps Voltaire's cynical jest that "History is only a pack of tricks we play on the dead."

Increasingly, we are witnessing a world without memory where, to use Guy Debord's metaphor, mere images of reality flow and merge randomly like reflections on water. In his own eulogy to History, Debord says,

> History's domain was the memorable, the totality of events whose consequences would be lastingly apparent. And thus, inseparably, history was knowledge that should endure and aid in understanding, at least in part, what

was to come: "an everlasting possession," according to Thucydides. In this way history was the *measure* of genuine novelty. It is in the interests of those who sell novelty at any price to eradicate the means of measuring it. When social significance is attributed only to what is immediate, and to what will be immediate immediately afterwards, always replacing another, identical immediacy, it can be seen that the uses of the media guarantee a kind of eternity of noisy insignificance. (1990: 15)

With the erasure of historical memory and knowledge, Debord argues, the cascade of images and events instantly recedes to the remote realm of the forgotten or unverifiable. The function of the society of the spectacle, the social system organized around the production of images and diversions that depoliticize and pacify social actors, is *"to make history forgotten within culture"* (Debord 1983: #192). Rather than concretizing history in narrative and popular memory, culture, in its degraded, commodified form, serves to induce amnesia and thwart collective action.

From cyberspace and virtual reality to infotainment, MTV, and docudramas, it is clear that today we are in something like Debord's spectacle or Baudrillard's hyperreality governed by the play of images and simulations. Under such conditions, history is little more than a sign, stereotype, or pastiched text, represented as a costume drama and consumed as a sound bite. Typically, as in so many retrospectives, the history of the past is represented as the history of popular culture, thereby erasing elements of the world not directly spawned by the culture industries. In the age of instant history, where events are reported as they unfold, where almost nothing escapes the electronic panopticon, where everything is forced into the glare of media lights, social reality is speeded up, decontextualized, and reassembled into a pastiche of representations, where it is trivialized in its juxtaposition to the advertisements that sponsor our worldviews. The paradox is that as history accelerates, historical consciousness deteriorates; change speeds up to the point where the events of last week drop into a time warp and we are nostalgic even for yesterday.

Demagogues, tyrants, and mythmakers well understand the political utility of history, and exploit it for their own purposes. They know that the ability to define the meaning of the past grants the power to define the meaning of the present and future; they understand that a people without a historical memory are easily manipulated through myths of the present. To lack a narrative of one's own past, from the personal to the national level, is to fall victim to the pseudohistorical representations of others. Each culture needs to see the present as history and to create its own narratives that secure their meaning and identities within time.

The efforts to rewrite history as fictionalized in Orwell's *1984* are now practiced on a daily basis in high-tech "democracies" where electronic media are the "fourth pillar" of government. Bureaucrats of the image plan the staged events, the photo opportunities, the press reports, and information "leaks" for the orchestration of reality. From the *CBS Evening News* to the *New York Times* to *The McNeil-Lehrer News Hour,* corporate media powers control the parameters of political discourse and establish the codes and frames for understanding history and social reality.[3] Where history is represented at all, it is decontextualized and reduced to easily consumable sound bites. In their capitalist appropriation, the technologies of film and television generally have undermined historical consciousness.[4] As is clear from the insipid fare of magazines and talk shows, the American public generally is not interested in history, politics, or social analysis; rather, their passions—themselves induced by the media—are largely for trivia, entertainment, and Hollywood gossip. When television, our dominant "communication" medium, references history, it typically does so in the form of docudramas that conflate fact and fiction, or in the form of narratives that equate the changing fashions of popular culture with the determinant forces of history. If, as Lowenthal has said, "the past is a foreign country," then it is most readily accessible through *Lifestyles of the Rich and Famous.*

One of the key strategies of social control is to divorce the present from the past and to display it as timeless and eternal. The naturalization of the present obviates social criticism and change and induces a fatalistic sense: if things have always been this way, how could they ever change? In the beginning, capitalist ideology says, there was exchange-value and all human beings were warring competitors for profit. Ignorance of a time when work had profound social and individual meaning, when people were deeply connected to the land and their community, when social values emphasized cooperation rather than competition, and when the concept of the public good restrained the unleashing of private interests, serves to legitimate capitalism and its specific mechanisms of exploitation as eternal, necessary, or the best of all possible worlds. This legitimation is all the more powerful with the ideological conflation of capitalism and nature. We find this in Social Darwinism, which transforms a historical form of aggressive competition into a law of nature, or in the mechanistic worldview of modern science, which extends the operations of an emerging factory civilization into the entire cosmos, so that nature too becomes a lifeless machine.

The myth of the eternal present has been a hallmark of Western philosophy. Traditionally, philosophy has defined itself in opposition to history, which it considered to be an inferior mode of knowledge. As early as Plato, philosophers separated themselves from historians by claiming that the philosopher's task was to discover Truth in the eternal and universal aspects of reality, while historians labored in the illusory world of the contingent and emphemeral. From Hellenic to modern culture, history has been divorced from truth and associated with rhetoric, narrative form, and the study of mere appearances of reality, while philosophers set out to grasp the nature of the True, the Good, and the Beautiful. Descartes spoke for the Western philosophical tradition when he said, "History is like foreign travel. It broadens the mind but does not deepen it."

With the rise of the natural sciences, however, philosophy was dethroned from its role as "queen of the sciences." Under the spell of Newton and the triumphs of the natural sciences, positivist historians in the nineteenth century overturned philosophy's traditional claim to superiority by renouncing metaphysical speculation, limiting knowledge to the realm of the visible, and insisting that history was an empirical science grounded in observation of facts. With the methods of the natural sciences promoted as the only valid form of knowledge, positivists demoted philosophy to the role of conceptual handmaiden of empirical methodology (a position first voiced by an obliging philosopher, John Locke). Yet both philosophy and science were subject to a forceful critique in the nineteenth century with the emergence of a new evolutionary outlook that began with the geographers Hutton and Lyell and continued with Hegel, Darwin, Marx, and others. With the rise of historicism, the view that all forms of human understanding are temporally situated and shaped, both philosophy and science were resolved into history and interpreted as historically produced modes of knowledge.

Since human beings, their cultures, and their social institutions are nowhere the same and are constantly changing, they can only be understood through history and historical knowledge. Dilthey argued correctly against Descartes that "Man knows himself only in history, never through introspection" (1962: 138). To foist positivist models onto the study of human beings and to search for the invariable laws governing human behavior and social change is to distort the dynamic, contingent, mutable, and indeterminate character of social action. The historicist insight into the local, time-bound, and variable nature of social phenomena is the basis for genuine knowledge of human beings and for a critical theory of society. The impulse to think, to question, and to challenge the current state of affairs begins with awareness that social reality is historical and contingent in nature, with the knowledge that things have not always been this way and therefore could be otherwise, with the realization that what has been constituted can be deconstituted and reconstituted. Historical memory and historical knowledge therefore are potential forms of empowerment, which threaten the legitimacy of political rule that tries to maintain itself as eternal or necessary: "Forgetfulness closes history whereas remembrance keeps open both the past and the utopian future of man. Remembrance is the womb of freedom and justice and must be cultivated long before men are able to name their slavery within the discourse of rational freedom and consensus" (O'Neill 1976: 4).

The three theorists I have selected to study—Marx, Foucault, and Habermas—all uphold the importance of historical knowledge for social criticism and political change. As interdisciplinary social theorists, they employ historical methods and analysis to gain critical perspectives on capitalist modernity, to grasp its continuities and discontinuities with the past, and to develop political resources to change its various aspects. In quite different ways, each develops a critical theory with liberatory intent, and their historical work is directly informed by political values and goals—hence my title "The Politics of Historical Vision."[5]

As Sheldon Wolin (1960) has analyzed it, the term "vision" has two different meanings: an empirical, descriptive sense that refers to the phenomenon of the eye transmitting sense data from the world to the brain; and a normative, prescriptive sense that refers to the act whereby the imagination constructs a particular reality that may or may not accord with the "objective world." These meanings articulate two fundamentally different approaches to history: a "traditional" or positivist approach that claims to represent historical reality through theory-free observation sentences without intending to change it, and a "critical" approach that denies the possibility of purely objective theory and uses theory to promote social change.

In this latter sense, "historical vision" refers not to a cold and detached description of the past, but to a theoretical analysis of history and social reality informed by an imaginative vision of an alternative future that is grounded in knowledge of real historical dynamics. To have such a vision of history is to look beyond the given and obvious; to challenge the ideas, values, and institutions of the dominant social powers; and to envisage new possibilities for the future. As William Blake insisted, vision is the active force that shatters the limitations of mere sense perception, such as is enforced by the Lockean reflection theory of knowledge, in order to see higher realities. Vision is the precondition for imaginative creation. In the dialectical tradition from Aristotle to Hegel to Marx, Marcuse, and Bookchin, the "is" of given reality must be distinguished from what should or could be. But just as history without vision is blind, so vision without history is empty, devoid of concrete grounding, merely romantic and utopian.

Critical theories therefore have strong normative underpinnings which involve commitments to human freedom from forms of oppression and domination. The political vision of critical theorists relates to their understanding of what domination is, how different power systems have emerged, how they can be challenged, and how a different social world can be brought about that creates the conditions of human freedom. Marx, Foucault, and Habermas all write a history of the past to challenge the legitimacy of the present and help envision and create a different future. All three theorists break from the positivist historiographical tradition that is based on a rigid separation of fact and value. Avowedly political in approach, they analyze history not for the sheer sake of historical knowledge, but rather to advance critiques of the present era, to show the historical constitution of present modes of social domination, and to further the cause of human freedom.[6] Their historical vision, inextricably linked to their political vision, seeks to identify historical continuities and discontinuities, progressive and regressive features of history, and forces of domination and liberation. The critical power of their theories is dependent on their ability to contextualize historically present values and practices, to point to possibilities for change, and to stimulate new modes of thought and action. While each theorist gives methodological issues their due (to varying degrees), there is nevertheless a primacy of the political insofar as their historical analyses are informed by practical commitments to freedom from domination.[7]

Thus, the difference is not between critical theory that is political and "objective" theory that is not, but between overt and covert politics, between open and suppressed normative–political commitments. The distinguishing feature of a critical theory is that it can unapologetically bring out its normative commitments and avoid a false separation of theory and practice, whereas positivist theories fail to clarify, and thus necessarily to defend, their own normative assumptions.[8] Ultimately, the phrase "politics of historical vision" points to the specific theoretical and political visions that inform social theory and history. It is meant to underline the now generally accepted belief that no understanding of history is innocent; that all historians impose an intelligibility on history that is not inherent in human actions themselves; that all "facts" are selected and interpreted from a specific point of view; and that each interpretation of history is inevitably political in its representation of events, in its stance toward the present social reality, and in the practical implications of its narrative, method, and vision.

NOTES

1. For the most eloquent dirges for the death of the Real, see Baudrillard (1983a, 1983b); and Kroker and Cook (1986).

2. See, for example, "On Reason and Freedom" in Mills (1959).

3. For an analysis of the media's orchestration of reality, see Hertsgaard (1989); for a study of how this process was employed during the Gulf War, see Kellner (1992).

4. There have been a few notable exceptions to this rule, as when the U.S.

television miniseries *Holocaust* precipitated a national debate on Nazism in West Germany in 1979. More recently, *Schindler's List* has played an important role in reviving historical memory and promoting critical debate. Such contributions are invaluable in the midst of the attempts by historical revisionists to whitewash or deny Nazi genocide.

5. Throughout this book, I use the term "critical theory" in the most general sense, designating simply a critical social theory, that is, a social theory critical of present forms of domination, injustice, coercion, and inequality. I do not therefore limit the term to refer only to the Frankfurt School, an obvious absurdity if the term also includes Marx and Foucault. Despite his crypto-positivism (see Chapters 2 and 4), I still read Foucault as an engaged social critic, rather than, as Richard Rorty claims, a "stoic, a dispassionate observer of the present social order" (1985: 172). The whole purpose of historical analysis for Foucault is to loosen the grip of established reality and to open up a "space of concrete freedom, i.e., of possible transformation" (Foucault 1988d: 36). As will be shown, Foucault is certainly not practicing "critique" as something that unmasks falsehood or "repression" in the name of truth, universal values, and "emancipation," but rather as a critical historical study that problematizes the present and is judged according to its political utility rather than being grounded in a universal set of normative values (Dean 1994).

6. See, for example, Diderot's praise for Voltaire's philosophical history: "Other historians relate facts to inform us of facts. You [Voltaire] relate them to excite in our hearts an intense hatred of lying, ignorance, hypocrisy, superstition, tyranny; and this anger remains even after the memory of the facts has disappeared" (cited in Becker 1964: 91–92). Renier, by contrast, provides an example of a noncritical history: "The task of the historian is simply and exclusively to keep available for social use the knowledge of the past experiences of human societies" (1965). For historians like Renier, the "social use" of history is limited to the acquisition of knowledge, independent of its strategic use in social struggles.

7. I hold this to be true even of Habermas, whose work frequently bogs down in metatheoretical issues, but also has been engaged in numerous political debates and struggles (see Chapter 4).

8. As I show in the chapters below, however, Marx and Foucault do not state and defend the normative assumptions of their theories and this creates difficulties for their projects.

CONTENTS

MODERNITY AND HISTORICAL VISION

Modern historiography originates in the fifteenth century with the Italian Renaissance and the break from Christian-influenced medieval historiography. Before (and sometimes into) the modern era, historians gave largely haphazard accounts of political events and figures or dogmatic Christian interpretations of a universal history whose meaning was the salvation of humankind. In Christian historiography, "truth" was found in biblical revelation, and the role of the historian was to show how divine law informed secular events, to periodize history according to major stages in God's plan, and to glorify his will. St. Augustine drew a sharp distinction between the earthly city and the City of God, between profane and sacred time, and he located truth, meaning, and stablity only in the divine kingdom. In such schemes, human actions and events were reduced to a religious meaning. It was still possible in the seventeenth century for historian Jacques Bossuet to claim that the "long sequence of particular causes which make and break empires, depends on the secret commands of divine Providence" (quoted in Hampson 1968: 22).

The new "humanist" approach to writing history that began in the fifteenth century situated itself in opposition to the "dark ages" of historiography and in alignment with the classical past. Contradicting the Christian tradition, humanist historians believed that human beings were makers of their own history and not mere pawns of God's design. Humanists generally acknowledged God as the first cause of history, but they believed his will was unknowable and his direct interventions into history too few to have major significance. While the basic tenets of the Christian faith were still accepted by humanist historians and even by many subsequent Enlightenment figures, history was now oriented toward identifying human actions and their causes and consequences, rather than trying to discern the operations of a divine plan.

With the emergence of humanism and the secularization of

knowledge, historiography was established on a critical rather than a dogmatic basis. As early as the beginning of the fifteenth century, historians worked to overcome a "scissors and paste" history (Collingwood) that uncritically combined diverse historical accounts into a patchwork narrative (see Breisach 1983; Collingwood 1956). On the lookout for biased reports and false documents, historians began to interrogate the credibility of their sources. New standards of historical accuracy appeared, conventional accounts of the past were rejected, and scholars tried to build new interpretations based on original research of primary documents and the use of "textual criticism." As evident in the work of Voltaire, who proposed a critical secular history that depicted numerous facets of human existence, historians also widened the scope of historical inquiry, away from the drum and trumpet history of kings and their armies to include a study of culture, economics, the arts and sciences, and various social institutions.

The full purview of human activity, unavailable to the blind eye of religion, was coming into focus in the modern historian's sight. By the nineteenth century, history had severed ties with literature and moral philosophy to become an autonomous discipline, and by midcentury it had widely conferred on itself scientific status. The role of history was defined as organizing facts into laws, rather than as educating through narratives. The modern historian's vision was considerably sharpened by a growing methodological sophistication, which led to the understanding that the role of the historian was to reconstruct objectively the past *wie es eigentlich gewesen*, as it actually occurred (Ranke). But as historical method became more rigorous, historical vision became more narrow and history became a highly specialized and fragmented field of study. Critical and interdisciplinary visions of history were abandoned in the name of science.

Yet it was developments within history itself that greatly affected historiography and sparked the emergence of classical sociology and modern social theory. By the time of the French Revolution, the secularization and modernization processes that produced humanism, democracy, individualism, technologically advanced industry, capitalism, and the nation-state also created a powerful sense of rupture in history, of a present fundamentally different from the past, of a new era based on incessant change and innovation, a modernity that shattered all forms of tradition and stability. A new time consciousness was emerging that pervaded everyday life, the arts, and eventually science and philosophy. Nearly all modern social and political theorists, beginning with Machievelli, More, and Hobbes, laid claim to a new vision of a new world.[1] They tried to assess or criticize the novel social conditions and intended their theories to intervene in social reality for the improvement of humanity.

As is explored in detail below, modernity generated a proliferation of conflicting historical visions that in turn yielded competing political ideologies and strategies. Yet the historicist vision unleashed in modernity—the modern tendency to see things as changing rather than eternal, as evolving rather than static—all too often was realized in partial, contradictory form that reproduced the ahistorical, metaphysical elements of medieval thought. It is the metaphysical themes that haunt modern thought, and the dubious political programs these have informed, that provoke new postmodern visions and politics.

FROM PROVIDENCE TO PROGRESS: THE FUTURE'S SO BRIGHT

Enlightenment is man's emergence from his self-incurred immaturity.

—KANT

The moment will come . . . when the sun will shine only on free men on this earth, on men who recognize no master but their reason; when tyrants and slaves, priests and their stupid or hypocritical instruments will exist only in history or on the stage; when men will study the efforts and sufferings that characterized the past only to guard vigilantly against any recurrence of superstition and tyranny.

—CONDORCET

A central vision of modern social and historical theory is that of a novel present that realizes the forces of historical progress and freedom. Under the secularizing influences of modern rationality, Enlightenment philosophers interpreted historical events in terms of improvement in the human condition rather than the realization of a divine plan. History was thereafter understood in terms of progress, rather than providence, where progress signified cumulative advances in human learning, morals, happiness, and freedom. The belief that the modern mind was becoming liberated from dogma, ignorance, prejudice, and superstition, in conjunction with new discourses of liberty and equality and immense advances in science, technology, and medicine, allowed Enlightenment thinkers to compare favorably their own era with all past history.

As asserted in the famous *querelle des anciens et des modernes,* French *philosophes* declared their age and culture a historical advance over all others. Typical of the movement, Voltaire confidently declared the modern world to be "the most enlightened age of all time." For Voltaire, the primary use of history was to recover the immense lineage of human crime, cruelty, and ignorance in order to prevent the repetition of such folly in the future. With d'Alembert, Diderot, d'Holbach, and others, he applied norms of rational analysis to society and claimed that the task of human beings was to develop their critical powers. The *philosophes* attacked the *ancien régime,* despotism, privilege, religious dogmatism, and superstition; they championed individualism, tolerance, reason, reform, cosmopolitanism, and in some cases democracy as liberating forces.[2] Kant answered the question, "What is Enlightenment?" by defining it as having the courage to think for oneself. In the optimistic spirit of the time, Rousseau, Kant, Condorcet, Leibniz, and others adhered to the Christian ideal of the perfectability of human beings, and believed that advances in reason, science, and technology could bring proportionate moral dividends as well as increases in freedom, material well-being, social stability, and universal harmony among nations. The key assumptions of Western thought since Plato and Aristotle have been that reality is rational in nature, that reason can discover the fundamental principles or laws on which to base human behavior, that these principles are timeless and universal in nature, and that, if followed, society can be peaceful and orderly and all moral conflicts can be resolved. Through obedience to the voice of Reason, Enlightenment figures believed that a social order could be born that would reflect the order and harmony of Newton's heavens.[3]

As Rotenstreich holds, the modern doctrine of progress implies "a cumulative advance [in human knowledge], throughout all regions of history, toward an all-encompassing encounter with a universal norm and its realization" (1971: 197). There are two major assumptions that typically inform modern concepts of progress. First, the structure of human time is unified and continuous; different cultures and nations ultimately belong to one and the same historical process. Rather than separate, diverging histories, there is only one grand, or universal History that encompasses all human beings and is represented by a single theory.[4] Thus, Comte speaks of a "necessary identical development" of all humanity and Spengler states that "there are not several kinds of Evolution having traits in common, but one evolution going on everywhere after the same manner" (quoted in Manicas 1987: 68).

Second, the continuity of historical time is governed by a purpose, by a teleological movement where human beings advance from a state of potentiality to a state of actuality. History is seen to be the process of the civilization and education of the human species, of the realization of universal norms such as freedom, equality, and reason. This process is motivated and defined by cumulative advances in science, economics, morality, and politics, which occur through the gradual rationalization of social and personal existence. For Kant and Hegel, history is determined by underlying forces that use human will and conflict to achieve the goal of rational freedom. Kant sees the entire history of the human race as the realization of a hidden plan of nature to bring about a peaceful cosmopolitan order wherein human capacities can be developed, while Hegel's more violent vision regards the slaughterbench of history as the sacrificial site where Reason produces a universal order of freedom. Such progressivist accounts employ a stage theory of history that traces the evolution of human knowledge, charting a trajectory from "primitive" or "savage" cultures to modern society. Each era advances the progressive movement of history more than the preceding one and the whole process culminates in European modernity with the moral improvement or perfection of human beings. For some modern thinkers, moral progress is a necessary and inevitable effect of the march of reason and science. To cite Spengler again, "Progress . . . is not an accident, but a necessity. . . . As surely as the tree becomes bulky when it stands alone, and slender if one of a group . . . so surely must evil and immortality disappear; so surely must man become perfect" (quoted in Manicas 1987: 70).

The speculative nature of the progressivist vision has earned it the title of a "philosophy of history." For Voltaire, one of the first to use the term, it simply meant critical, non-Christian history. The term later assumed a more general meaning and designated those philosophies of the modern tradition—from Kant, Hegel, and Marx to Comte, Toynbee, and Sartre—which sought to grasp the meaning, dynamics, and goals of history. As defined by Löwith, a philosophy of history seeks "a systematic interpretation of universal history in accord with a principle in which historical events and successions are unified and directed toward an ultimate meaning" or end state (1949: 1). Whether history is viewed as linear, cyclical, or a hybrid of both, philosophies of history seek a unifying principle that unravels the mystery of human time. All such theories posit a teleology, or at least a developmental tendency, of history toward reason and freedom. Generally, they are purely philosophical and speculative in nature, although speculation can be conjoined with empirical or "scientific" reasoning, as in the case of Marx.

Although Enlightenment thinkers rejected the Christian narrative in content, substituting human agency for divine fiat, progress for providence, and the values of dignity and autonomy for humility and sin, they appropriated and transcoded the religious form and poetic force of Christian historiography into a secularized framework. In their speculative nature, their attribution of meaning and purpose in history, their positing of a final stage of history, and their appeal to natural law and a timeless rational structure of reality, such Enlightenment narratives are deeply religious and metaphysical in character. In Becker's words, "the *Philosophes* demolished the Heavenly City of St. Augustine only to rebuild it with more up-to-date materials" (1964: 31).[5] The religious vision of much modern theory is most explicit in the case of Comte, who, while rejecting all forms of theologism and religious authority, set out to construct "the true Providence" through "the renascent Priesthood of Positivism" and "its true disciples" (in particular, women and the working class, those least harmed by the "vicious system" of modern education). Together the new Priests and their laity will bring a new "Religion of Humanity," "a true spiritual power" of science that will allow "human regeneration."

The very attempt to distinguish among past, present, and future and to construct a stage theory of history is the product of the Jewish and Christian historiographical tradition. Instead of cycles of misery and happiness to be borne in a tragic manner, the historical view of ancient culture conveyed in the Judeo-Christian narrative posits a forward-moving direction in history, beginning with the Fall, continued in the nonrepeatable death and resurrection of Christ, and culminating in a future state of human redemption. History moved forward in linear fashion, directed toward a goal and informed by a purpose. Universal histories that posit the unity of humanity ultimately stem from the Christian emphasis that all human beings are equal before the eyes of God and belong to the same divine community and plan.

In both Christian and Enlightenment narratives, history thereby acquires a meaning that transcends specific events and local contexts, culminates in a universal framework, has a rational structure, and is informed by a basic principle or teleological impetus. This is not, of course, to deny significant discontinuities between modern and medieval thought. Enlightenment thinkers, for example, rejected the Christian doctrine of original sin and saw human beings as inherently good, or at least as malleable enough to be morally educated. Moreover, the religious halos of modern thought would not have been possible without the secular reality of advances in scientific knowledge and technology. As Blumenberg (1983) insists against Löwith, the modern notion of progress is derived not only from the Judeo-Christian tradition, but also has an empirical basis in the growing ability of the modern world to control external reality. This was an important component in the self-consciousness of the modern mind, for, as Buckle says, "the measure of civilization is the triumph of the mind over external agents" (1973: 132).

Still, the optimistic outlook of the Enlightenment has been greatly exaggerated (Gay 1969: 98–122). Kant's claim that his was an age of Enlightenment rather than an enlightened age helps to recover some of the skepticism and even pessimism that pervaded the eighteenth century. No one thought that human powers of reason were unlimited, in either the ethical task of influencing human action or the epistemological project of grasping the nature of reality. Voltaire ridiculed Leibniz's doctrine of the best of all possible worlds and claimed that evil was a pervasive force in the world. Rousseau thought the natural goodness of humanity declined as social institutions advanced.[6] Reactionaries like De Maistre claimed that human beings were aggressive and evil by nature and were not fit for freedom. Materialist *philosophes* such as La Mettrie, Holbach, and Helvitus denied the existence of free will and progress in history. Even the most ardent proponents of progress such as Condorcet saw progress as a mixed blessing and displayed ambivalence about human nature. Linear models of history as the progression of the rational mind frequently contained within them a cyclical vision of history as an endless battle of progressive and regressive forces whose oscillations could potentially cease in a genuinely enlightened era. But faith in the masses to become educated and rational was very limited. Despite great scientific progress, few Enlightenment thinkers saw evidence of significant moral progress beyond the fact that witches and heretics were no longer burned at the stake.

No sooner had Enlightenment ideology began to develop than there emerged critical reactions against it, precipitated by the debacle of the French Revolution and gathering tremendous force by the end of the eighteenth century. An initial and formidable challenge came from the German counter-Enlightenment, originally connected with the Lutheran Reformation, which adopted a hostile, defensive stance against the political and cultural hegemony of France and its modernizing influences (Berlin 1982, 1992).[7] Led by Hamann, who had a major influence on later German Romantics like Fichte and Schelling, the counter-Enlightenment waged war against scientific materialism, utilitarianism, ethical naturalism, secularism, and universalism. It stood every core tenet of the Enlightenment on its head and championed the particular over the general; the national over the cosmopolitan; the concrete over the abstract; direct sensation and lived experience over the construction of conceptual systems; imagination, instinct, and intuition over logic, reason, mathematics, and the natural sciences; the genius and free individual over community and social conformity; and traditional religion and faith over agnosticism, deism, or atheism.

From various critical quarters, including Enlightenment thinkers themselves, Enlightenment principles were attacked on three different grounds. First, a philosophical argument questioned assumptions concerning the existence of an immanent logic in history, historical laws, and the unified nature of history and humankind. Vico, Herder, Spengler, Nietzsche, Weber, Marx, and others in the modern tradition subjected totalizing and teleological visions of history to sharp critique, advocating countervisions of historical plurality, nonevolutionism, or cyclical theories of history. More vehemently than anyone, Schopenhauer advanced a vision of the world as blind, purposeless, aimless will. Second, an existential argument denied the supremacy of reason over the emotions, will, imagination, and intuitive insight. Romantics like Schelling, Fichte, Wordsworth, Coleridge, as well as existentialists like Dostoyevsky, Schopenhauer, Nietzsche, and Kierkegaard argued that human beings are not primarily rational beings but rather are governed by more powerful emotional, instinctual, volitional, and unconscious urges. The French archreactionary De Maistre saw reason as a feeble instrument incapable of managing the primal human instinct for violence and self-immolation. Both romantics and existentialists alike deplored the decline of emotions, imagination, vitality, spontaneity, individuality, and freedom that resulted from the rise of rationality, technology, scientific calculation, and mass society. They denied that reason could construct conceptual systems that reflected the nature of reality. Romantics held that artists and poets, not scientists, had privileged access to reality through intuitive insight and direct imaginative apprehension. Thus, Hamann proclaimed, "God is a poet, not a mathematician," and Herder cried, "I am not here to think, but to be, feel, live!"[8]

Third, there was the empirical argument that Enlightenment principles and institutions have led to historical regression rather than progression.[9] While liberal theorists like Locke, Smith, and Spencer championed the emerging capitalist order with its property rights and free markets as convergent with both human nature (defined in terms of competitive instincts) and the general welfare, empirical critiques of the Enlightenment came mainly from the Right or Left. French conservatives such as Burke, Tain, and Tocqueville decried the secularism, liberalism, and individualism of the modern era as a loss of order, and called for a return to religion, family, tradition, community, and heredity-based rights.[10] De Maistre— whose reactionary stance is so extreme he makes Hobbes look like an anarchist and Schopenhauer seem more sanguine than Dr. Pangloss— resurrected the doctrine of original sin, professed hatred for all intellectuals, called for the total subordination of the individual to the state whose central authority was the executioner, and celebrated the ubiquity of suffering and violence as deserved punishment for the corrupt human species. As Berlin notes (1992), he stands in a league all by himself and should be seen not merely as a conservative, but rather as the founder of twentieth-century fascism.

On the other hand, anarchists, socialists, and other critics railed against the brutality and inhumanity of the modern world and the coercive nature of modern reason. In a critical tradition stretching from Nietzsche and Weber through the Frankfurt School to postmodern theory, nineteenth- and twentieth-century critics linked advances in modern rationalization processes and "instrumental reason" to increases in domination rather than freedom. Hence, we find accounts of modernity as an "iron cage," a "one-dimensional society," or a "disciplinary archipelago."

While such critiques sometimes focused exclusively on the repressive and exploitative aspects of capitalism, Marx, Habermas, and others seek more dialectical arguments, arguing that capitalism has also brought advances in democracy and freedom that can be appropriated and advanced in a new social context (see Chapters 2 and 4). This dialectical vision of history mediates between the conservative negation and liberal celebration of capitalism to criticize its core features while appropriating other features and seeking to advance them in a "higher" stage of history.

The Enlightenment also has been attacked for its racist, Eurocentric, and ahistorical positions. Where some thinkers like Hobbes, Condorcet, or Rousseau posited a natural equality among human beings, and Diderot, Voltaire, and Rousseau saw features of non-European cultures (such as Tahitian sexual freedom or Chinese tolerance) as superior to their own, others denigrated premodern and non-Western cultures as inferior to the "civilized" cultures of the modern West. With few exceptions such as Wallace and Darwin, racist arguments dominated nineteenth-century evolutionary theory such that "savages" and "Negroes" were considered closer to apes than Europeans (Eiseley 1958). In Kantian terms, premodern cultures belong to the ontogenetically equivalent stage of childhood, while only modern Europe matured into rational adulthood. "Enlightened" figures such as Locke, Hume, and Kant, even while recognizing cultural diversity, believed in the superiority of the West and defended slavery and genetic racism. Despite his sympathetic remarks about Chinese, Indian, Persian, and Islamic cultures, Voltaire privileged the rational norms of the West. Leopold Von Ranke thought philosophers of history would "very wisely restrict their views to only a few [European] nations in the history of the world, while regarding the lives of all the others as naught, as a mere supplement" (1973: 58). Comte claimed that Europe was "the theatre of the preponderant evolution of humanity" (1974: 205), and that there France stood center stage. History, Comte believed, should focus only on "the development of the most advanced peoples" and avoid those cultures "whose evolution has so far been, for some cause or another, arrested at a more imperfect stage" (1974: 199). For Comte, "the West alone is charged with the glorious and difficult mission of laying the foundations of human regeneration" (1973: 3).

In their equation of "higher" with "more rational," such evolutionary schemes are inherently racist. Ironically, Eurocentric theories of historical progress are rooted in ahistorical assumptions. From Descartes to Kant, modern philosophers constructed theories of knowledge informed by a static view of human nature that converted different culturally shaped modes of knowledge and experience into a predetermined, universally given form. This assumption was given its classic form in Hume, who grounded his empiricist epistemology in a science of human nature that sought to grasp the "secret springs" of all human knowledge and belief: "Mankind are so much the same, in all times and places, that history informs us of nothing new or strange in this particular. Its chief use is only to discover the constant and universal principles of human nature" (1955: 83). Like Descartes and Kant, Hume took the ahistorical paradigm of the natural sciences as the proper model for philosophy and psychology.

As Collingwood observes, the search for a theory of human nature necessarily obscures historical diversity and is possible "only to a person who mistakes the transient conditions of a certain age for the permanent conditions of human life" (1956: 224). Collingwood thinks this was an easy mistake for Enlightenment thinkers to make, given their limited knowledge of cultures other than their own. The result of such historical ignorance was that Enlightenment thinkers "could cheerfully identify the intellectual habits of a western European in their own day with the in-tellectual faculties bestowed by God upon Adam and all his progeny" (Col-lingwood 1956: 224).

The proclivity of the white middle classes of European descent to proclaim themselves the representatives of all humanity and to project their own values and interests onto other cultures is aptly described by Solo-mon (1988, 1993) as the "transcendental pretense." Through appeal to universal principles, above all to the idea of human nature, many in the modern tradition sought to represent their ideas as the only valid ones, as grounded in nature itself. Knowledge of nature provided the means to distinguish between good and bad, right and wrong, the natural and the artificial, and thereby to bring society into harmony with the universal natural order. Whatever differences divided camps like rationalists and romantics, they were one in their appeal to nature, human nature, and universal values. On the occasions when modern theorists analyzed cul-tures outside of the temporal and spatial boundaries of central Europe, they typically came armed with a host of ready-made, a priori assump-tions that sought universal conditions and characteristics of "man in gener-al." They thereby found in the mirror of history only their own reflections. "The seemingly simple ideal of 'humanity' turned out to be a simplemind-ed gloss over irreconcilable differences between people, and a denial of real historical change" (Solomon 1993: xvi). Far from innocent, the modern universalist vision of history disguised personal interests, devalued other cultures, and "became an aggressive intellectual and cultural platform meant to pound alternative conceptions of human nature into submission" (xi).[11] Where Eurocentrism is the theory, imperialism is the practice.[12]

Thus, although the modern world unleashed new historical impulses, they often were limited in their scope and ahistorical in approach. In the new naturalist discourse — the appeals to human nature, natural law, natur-al sentiment, natural philosophy, and so on — modern theory preserved the foundationalist fervor of providential history.[13] It was not until the end of the eighteenth century, as a result of evolutionary thinking in geology and biology, that such static schemes would be overturned in favor of evolutionist outlooks.[14] But despite the ideas of development, change, and evolution that pervaded the nineteenth century, some modern theorists found it necessary to appeal to ahistorical and teleological grounds to anchor their descriptive and normative claims. The ahistorical bias behind eighteenth century theory took a more extreme form in the oxymoronically titled "science of history" that emerged in the nineteenth century.

POSITIVISM AND ITS DISCONTENTS

> History is not entertainment, but science. . . . Its aim is
> not to have us make a pleasant acquaintance with such
> and such a period of our choice but to have us know
> man completely in all the phases of his existence.
> —FUSTEL DE CULANGES

One of the most important running debates in historiography is the question of whether history is merely a literary or narrative form, designed for political and moral edification, or a science, designed for explanation of the past and prediction of the future. Beginning with the Greek historians Herodotus and Thucydides, and continuing through the recent work of narrativists and analytic philosophers of history, theorists have distinguished between truth and fiction and have placed historical writing on one side or the other. For positivists, history is distinct from fiction in its concern for empirical facts, objective truth, deductive logic, and lawlike forms of explanation. Narrativists deny that history can have an objective basis and see it primarily as literary form, a poetic interpretation of the past imaginatively reconstructed in the form of narrative. Still others, like Ricoeur (1984), seek a middle ground by arguing that all historical writing is informed by pretheoretical narrative and poetic structures, but nevertheless can attain legitimate objectivity and explanatory status.

Positivism, of course, derives its name from its founder, Auguste Comte, who developed a "positive philosophy" that broke with the "critical" and "negative" mode of modern thought. This new "science" sought to grasp the laws structuring social phenomena, to construct a positive system of knowledge, and to order society on that basis. Comte claims to have identified the general law of history—"the actual march of the human intellect," "the final bent of the human mind toward positive studies"—in the gradual liberation of reason from the darkness of myth and fiction. The postmetaphysical, postcritical stage of knowledge designated as "positive" is the end result of a three-stage evolutionary process where the mind learns to overcome theological and metaphysical schemes in order to become strictly rational, factual, and empirical in its outlook. As Comte says, in the final, positive state of knowledge,

> the human mind, recognizing the impossibility of obtaining absolute truth, gives up the search after the origin and hidden causes of the universe and a knowledge of the final causes of phenomena. It endeavours now only to discover, by a well-combined use of reasoning and observation, the actual laws of phenomena—that is to say, their invariable relations of succession and likeness. The explanation of facts, thus reduced to real terms, consists henceforth only in the connection established between different particular phenomena and some general facts, the number of which the progress of science tends more and more to diminish. (1988: 2)

This passage demonstrates Comte's debt to Hume, the father of modern positivism, and succinctly summarizes the positivist approach to social theory and historiography. Inspired by the stunning triumphs of the natural sciences, Comte and his successors, such as nineteenth-century historians Buckle and Bury, sought the same order and rigor of knowledge in the social realm. In their drive to overcome metaphysics and close "the wide and dreary chasm" (Buckle) between the natural and social sciences, positivists broke with the philosophy of history, narrativist theories, and the literary and hermeneutic traditions. They tried to ground the study of society and history in the norms and methods of science, and set out in search of historical laws.[15]

With Comte's contribution still too recent, Buckle lamented the primitive state of historiography compared to the advanced state of the natural sciences: "The most celebrated historians are manifestly inferior to the most successful cultivators of physical science: no one having devoted himself to history who in point of intellect is at all to be compared with Kepler, Newton, or many others that might be named" (1973: 125). Yet, Buckle thought the lack of such a state of knowledge need not be cause for despair: "Whoever is at all acquainted with what has been done during the last two centuries, must be aware that every generation demonstrates some events to be regular and predictable, which the preceding generation had declared to be irregular and unpredictable: so that the marked tendency of advancing civilization is to strengthen our belief in the universality of order, of method, and of law" (125).

Buckle's work evinces the drive of much modern theory for order and science, for reconstructing reality into tidy conceptual systems. Human actions, he believed, are never chaotic or capricious, but rather "form part of one vast scheme of universal order" (1973: 127). Buckle thought the historian's task was not simply to write volumes replete with "the most trifling and miserable details" of anecdotes and unrelated events, but to collect the most relevant historical facts and discover the physical laws, such as those relating to climate, food, and soil, informing them. With such an approach, Buckle held "little doubt that before another century has elapsed, the chain of evidence [for constructing historical laws] will be complete, and it will be as rare to find an historian who denies the undeviating regularity of the moral world, as it now is to find a philosopher who denies the regularity of the material world" (127).

Thus defined, the historian's enterprise, like that of the natural scientist, is the "explanation" of history, which means the subsumption of facts and events to more general determining laws—what Popper and Hempel later termed the "covering law model."[16] The natural and social worlds are governed by the same mathematical and quantifiable logic. The belief that the science of history deals with invariables and universals repudiates the Aristotelian theory that history deals only with particulars. Since explanations restrict the knowable to the observable, they also renounce appeal to origins or causes of phenomena.[17] Following Hume, positivists claim that causality, material or final, entails appeal to occult phenomena ("power, force, energy, or necessary connection" [Hume]) and mysterious essences hidden from the empirical gaze. Since causes are unknowable, historical laws are constructed from observable relations among facts or events; they are linked together in general laws by identifying universal relations of "succession and resemblance" and "constant conjunction" (Hume). As Comte says, "We do not pretend to explain the real causes of phenomena . . . we try only to analyze correctly the circumstances of their production, and to connect them by normal relations of succession and similarity" (1988: 8). The denial of causality requires the rejection of psychologism and idealism (employed by Collingwood and others) and the categories of motive and intention that these traditions employ to explain human behavior. Since the interior processes of mental life are nonobservable, explanatory appeals to them would be metaphysical. Rather, intentionality is subsumed to the general, invariable, objective laws of history.

Like the natural sciences, the goal of historical explanation is prediction: given a true statement about empirical conditions, an event is logically deducible from a law. Assuming knowledge of initial conditions, we can say that the event *had to* occur. Contingency and indeterminancy are erased from social action; the appeal to the irregularity or variability of events is merely a sign of impoverishment, of the historian's inability to identify deeper, underlying laws. From the *philosophes* to scientific Marxists, many modern theorists believed in the necessity and inevitability of history, a determinism in logical continuity with the providential theory of history. Such a vision of history unavoidably entailed the self-aggrandizement of elites and the depoliticization of the masses, for "science" is the rightful property of the cognoscenti.

As we shall see, in quite different ways, Marx, Foucault, and Habermas all reject the positivist program of seeking timeless, universal laws of history and assimilating social phenomena to the explanatory logic of natural events. But the rejection of modern determinism and scientism comes from within early quarters of modern theory itself, pointing to a deeply divided tradition over the possibility and desirability of a science of history. The first modern argument that social disciplines have their own logic was developed by Vico in the early eighteenth century. In his *New Science* (1968, orig. 1725) Vico challenged the first scientistic doctrine — not Comtean positivism, but Cartesian rationalism — that saw the entire world as mathematical in nature, that upheld geometry as the model for all forms of knowledge, and that attempted to deduce true principles from clear and distinct ideas expressed in rational terms. Vico argued not only that this model did not apply to the realm of history, but that historical reality can be known with more certainty than natural reality since only history is created by human beings. In fact, he argued, since nature is a divine creation, only God can know it. Vico's argument is based on the epistemological doctrine *verum et factum convertuntur* ("truth and fact are interchangeable"), which claims that the condition of knowing something truly is that the knower itself has made it. Since only history is a human invention, it alone remains the proper object of human knowledge and it cannot be illuminated using models imported from the natural sciences, being an entirely different ontological and epistemological domain.

The thesis that the social sciences have their own logic was further advanced by neo-Kantians and the German hermeneutic tradition. Kant's distinction between the realm of freedom and the realm of necessity served to bifurcate the inner life of the human being itself and, by extension, the natural and social sciences. The methodological dualism between the natural and social sciences was a given not only for neo-Kantians of the nineteenth century, but also for early figures of the German hermeneutic tradition such as Wolff, Rickert, Schleiermacher, and Dilthey, as well as for key twentieth-century figures like Collingwood, Dray, Gallie, and Winch.

Appropriating Mill's concept of the "moral sciences," Dilthey distinguished between the *Geisteswissenschaften,* which were based on a logic of interpretation or understanding (*Verstehen*), and the *Naturwissenschaften,* which were based on a logic of explanation (*Erklären*). Like positivists, Dilthey rejected all metaphysical interpretations of universal history and insisted that history is an empirical discipline: "Hegel constructed metaphysically, we analyse the given" (1962: 125). While both the natural scientist and the historian deal with facts, regularities, and even forms of prediction, Dilthey insisted that history has a distinct logic, method, and subject matter that cannot be assimilated to those of the hard sciences. For Dilthey, events in the human realm are the result of will, intention, and volition and are not subject to laws, whereas events in the natural realm are strictly physical, nonconscious, and determined in character. Unlike the natural world, the human world is "mind-affected"; it is suffused with values and meaning that the historian can reconstruct in its general patterns of intelligibility: "Though there is nothing like 'the meaning' of history, the situations with which the historian deals are already meaningful, that is, they have received interpretations from the people involved in them" (65). The task of the historian is to grasp the meaning of actions from the standpoint of historical subjects themselves; to discover how this meaning is embedded in institutions, communities, and historical processes; and to discern the patterns of meaning underlying historical diversity made possible by "the regularity and structure of general human nature" (112).[18]

Thus, the historian is concerned with meaningful relationships, not causal relations. The natural world is to be explained, while the human world is to be understood. Dilthey believed that the proper way to understand human action was through an imaginative and empathetic reinvention of the thoughts and motivations of a historical person, accessible in the forms of texts and documents, while situating this person within his or her society. Similar to Vico, Dilthey argued that we can know the human world better than the natural world because the data of consciousness can be known directly. Whereas scientific explanation deals with sense perception of external data, historical understanding seeks a subjective standpoint. The norms of pure rationality and objectivity impede the emotional and imaginative contact required of the historian; whatever objectivity is possible in historical understanding, it requires a subjective standpoint and a dialectic of facts and imagination, in which imagination allows us to determine relevant facts and in turn itself is based on facts. Later hermeneutic thinkers like Husserl, Heidegger, Gadamer, and Ricoeur would argue that the "lifeworld" of beliefs, values, and meaning existed prior to any reflexive operation or explanatory logic.

In his 1903 essay, "Clio Rediscovered," George Trevelyan issued a powerful critique of Bury's A Science of History that anticipated later postmodern notions. For Trevelyan, facts do not exist independently of the imagination, which selects and arranges them in general patterns or narrative order. With Dilthey, he insists that no historian devoid of emotion or understanding could understand the lives and culture of past peoples. The notion of scientific history "is due to a misapplication of the analogy to physical science" (Trevelyan 1973: 230). This is so primarily because history is too complex, irregular, and contingent for the construction of universally applicable causal laws. "The law of gravitation may be scientifically proved because it is universal and simple. But the historical law that starvation brings on revolt is not proved; indeed the opposite statement, that starvation leads to abject submission, is equally true in the light of past events. You cannot so completely isolate any historical event from its circumstances as to be able to deduce from it a law of general application. . . . An event is itself nothing but a set of circumstances, none of which will ever recur" (231). Writing against the grain of modern determinism, Trevelyan argued that a "true conception of history" is one that realizes "that the history of mankind is not simple but complex, that history never repeats itself but ever creates new forms differing according to time and place" (241).

Besides being context bound, Trevelyan claimed that historical interpretation is incomplete and perspective bound. No one interpretation of a historical event like the French Revolution is exhaustive; several perspectives, all imperfect, are necessary, and the best interpretation will be informed by emotional understanding and acute imaginative powers. As postmodernists would later do, Trevelyan privileges the literary over the scientific aspect of history. There is science in the collecting and weighing of evidence and facts, but there is art in their imaginative arrangement and literary presentation: "It is the business of the historian to generalize and to guess cause and effect, but he should do it modestly and not call it 'science,' and he should not regard it as his first duty, which is to tell the story" (1973: 233). The ultimate purpose of history is educative, not scientific, the moral and political training of the mind of the citizen. It is the narrative itself, "the tale of the thing done," not technical cause and effect relations, that educates minds and trains political judgment. Trevelyan draws an important political consequence from the two different visions of history: where scientific history issues from an elitist concern for specialized knowledge, literary history seeks to promote public enlightenment and is therefore more democratic in character and result.

In the debate over the methodological status of the social sciences, two polarized positions emerged. At one pole, the reductionist, positivist, or "naturalist" tradition tries to subsume the social sciences to the logic and methodology of the natural sciences; it denies the historical and subjective constitution of knowledge in order to construct abstract nomological models. At the opposite pole, the autonomy, *Verstehen,* or "antinaturalist" tradition posits an irreducible gulf between the two fields of inquiry; it rejects the validity of causal explanations, laws, and observational techniques for the study of human reality. This tradition claims that the social world is open and contingent, while the natural world is determined. Since human events are such that they could *not* have happened, that other actions and outcomes are always possible, there is indeterminacy in history. Where nature is governed by unchanging laws, human beings and social dynamics change throughout time. Unlike natural events, historical events are unique and nonrepeatable. The predictions made in the natural sciences have the character of necessity, while those in the social sciences can be at best merely probable.

Where positivists claim that the purpose of history is scientific, providing explanations and predictions, hermeneutic theorists and others argue that the primary purpose of history is educative, providing moral or political knowledge. Activist uses of history reject the allegedly disinterested perspective of the positivist and seek to use the past to improve present and future life. As Habermas notes (1971), the different emphases on explanation, understanding, and critique entail different "interests" and practical strategies: the control of reality, the search for consensual dialogue, and the goal of human emancipation.[19] The positivist vision of an orderly, controlled, and predictable social reality entails the suppression of diversity, dissent, and personal spontaneity. These implications were fully present in the frightening visions of Saint Simon and Comte, who both attacked democracy and dissent as anarchic forces that had to be supressed in favor a social order maintained by an elite group of scientists, engineers, and industrialists (Comte's new "Priests of Humanity"). The unavoidable conclusion to be drawn from Comte's call for "Order and Progress" is that the rational society is best organized like a military barracks, that enlightenment is not the courage to criticize but the need to submit, both to the laws of Fact and the facts of Law. As Habermas notes (1973), positivism effaced the moral and critical aspects of Enlightenment rationality to reduce it to mere technical rationality allegedly purified of any subjective taint.[20]

In contrast, the hermeneutic or pragmatist vision of a social reality constructed in dialogue and interpretation promises to yield more liberty and democracy in its abandonment of a privileged position for truth and its emphasis on intersubjective communication and mutual understanding. But, as the critical interest points out, one cannot accept cultural traditions at face value or see forms of communication as free of distortion; rather, theory must locate the forces of ideology and domination that block communication and understanding and inform a politics that seeks the elimination of such distorting influences.

We see that the dynamic forces of modernity generated a plethora of conflicting historical visions and political programs. There were sharp divisions between positivist and antipositivist approaches to history and society; between those clinging to tradition, religion, and community, and those favoring reason, secularism, and individualism; between those embracing modernity as progress and those rejecting it as regress; between those endorsing pluralism and relativism and those defending universalism and foundationalism; between those advocating democracy and those espousing monarchy, aristocracy, or technocracy; between those championing egalitarianism and those proclaiming natural inequality; between those who pessimistically denied the freedom and value of human beings and those who optimistically envisaged their potential perfection.

Very simplistically, the different visions of history and politics can be divided among conservative, liberal, and radical approaches: the first approach, which comes out of Burke and is realized most extremely in De Maistre and Bonald, rejects modernity and seeks the renewal of tradition. The second approach, which stems from the *philosophes,* utilitarians, and political economists, embraces modernity and promotes Enlightenment ideas, individualism, and capitalism. The third approach represented by socialists and anarchists also embraces the Enlightenment and individualism as historically progressive, but argues that capitalism develops them in dangerous and incomplete ways, and that the liberatory aspects of modernity must be developed in a noncapitalist form. Seeking neither to remain within the present order, nor to go backward in time to a mythical Golden Age, the radical vision foresees a liberatory postcapitalist modernity of the future. This alternative, dialectical vision must also be distinguished from a vision of a postmodernity that is not always progressive or emancipatory in nature (see below).

Hence, one needs to use caution when using terms such as "the Enlightenment" or "the modern era," insofar as these labels imply a homogeneous worldview or movement that never existed. Although Enlightenment thinkers shared certain general tenets—such as embracing freedom, secularism, and critical reason over dogma, superstition, tyranny, and tradition—they differed greatly over specific issues. Holbach rejected the existence of the divine rule of nature, while Voltaire insisted on it; Kant championed reason as the ground of moral judgment, but Hume made it the slave to the passions; where Diderot limited enlightenment to an elite, Rousseau favored the education of the majority; Jefferson and Paine believed in self-evident natural principles, while Bentham ridiculed them as "nonsense on stilts" and advanced an empirically based utilitarian ethics. As analyzed by Hawthorn (1990), Enlightenment philosophies assumed different forms in France, England, and Germany, and among and within these countries there was wide disagreement over the nature of history, society, and theory. As Marx saw, the Enlightenment produced abstract philosophy in Germany, but fomented revolution in France.

Similarly, there is great diversity within "modern social theory." Not all modern social theorists, for example, adhered to a positivist program or a realist epistemology. Following Antonio and Kellner (1994) one can distinguish between two opposing traditions: a "critical" tradition (e.g.,

Marx, Weber, and Dewey) that qualifies the modernist faith in rationality, attends to the complexities of historical generalizations, rejects the belief in theory-free knowledge, complicates the linear vision of progress, and situates the subject within history; and a "dogmatic" tradition (e.g., Comte and Spencer) that uncritically champions science and rationality, produces overly totalizing theories, seeks purely objective "facts" and knowledge, posits an essentialist model of the subject, and formulates elitist political programs.

One needs to keep in mind that the first substantive critiques of the Enlightenment and modern social theory came from within the modern tradition itself, from both its conservative and its progressive wings. Just as the *philosophes* rejected the extreme claims of Cartesian rationalism, arguing that reason is not the only or fundamental motive of action and is limited in its ability to grasp reality (Gay 1966), classical social theory sought to reconstruct key Enlightenment concepts and ideals (Antonio and Kellner 1994). A key "performative contradiction" (Habermas) of postmodern theorists is that their rhetorical celebration of difference, plurality, discontinuity, and incommensurability is not put into practice methodologically when they analyze modern theorists. Rather, they construct a straw model of "modern theory" as a unified movement informed by a host of naive and erroneous assumptions; they fail to examine the historical context (the reaction against feudalism and Christianity) that led to the excesses of rationalism; and they typically do not refer to specific figures or texts. While many modern theorists do articulate the themes attacked by postmodernists, others were critical of these tendencies and sought more complex positions. Where a thinker like Descartes thought he could reconstruct the universe given matter and motion, Hume, Kant, Voltaire, Gibbon, Wieland, and others rejected totalizing claims of reason and, anticipating a favorite postmodern thesis, advocated philosophical modesty. As Holbach claimed, "It is not given man to know everything; it is not given him to know his origins; it is not given him to penetrate the essence of things or to go back to first principles" (cited in Gay 1966: 144–145).

As we turn now to the postmodern theories themselves, we see that they too are highly diverse in nature. Although some theorists, like Foucault or Laclau and Mouffe (1985; Laclau 1988; Mouffe 1988) can be read as still working within the modern tradition, others, like Baudrillard or Lyotard have burned any bridges connecting them to modern theory and have crossed over into a radical postmodern territory. In general, postmodern social theories are predicated on visions of history alternative to those typically found in modern theory, and these visions generate quite different political responses to modernizing processes.

DARKNESS ON THE EDGE OF TOWN:
POSTMODERN COUNTERVISIONS

> One may say almost anything one likes about history
> except that it is rational. The very word sticks in one's
> throat.
> — DOSTOYEVSKY

> No universal history leads from savagery to humanitari-
> anism, but there is one that leads from the slingshot to
> the megaton bomb.
> — ADORNO

> The ancients have stolen all our best ideas.
> — TWAIN

The connection between postmodern discourse and history is direct insofar as the very identity of the postmodern is premised on a historical break
with preceding modern movements. The sharp historical consciousness
of postmodern theory informs its methodological attack on universalist,
foundationalist, and essentialist theories that abstract from changing sociohistorical conditions to ground theory in a timeless norm or standpoint.
Moreover, the first major discourses of the postmodern emerged in the
field of historiography, where Somerville and Toynbee posited a new discontinuity in history, a post-modern era that was said to differ significantly from the modern era.

The prefix "post" is ambiguous to the extent that it has temporal and
philosophical meanings, signifying both a movement after and rejection
of modern movements in theory and the arts. We also need to distinguish
among "postmodernism," a critical movement within theory and the arts;
"postmodern theory," a theoretical development within philosophy and
social theory that breaks from core tenets of modern theory; and "postmodernity," a term that implies a larger, more systematic claim that we
are in a new historical era (see Featherstone 1988; Best and Kellner 1991).
The argument of Jameson (1991) that we are in a new postmodern culture but not a new postmodernity that allegedly has superseded the main
dynamics of "modernity" demonstrates that these claims are independent.
Yet the accumulation of so many postmodern discourses in fields ranging
from architecture and anthropology to philosophy and social theory leads
one to wonder if indeed we are not in a new "post-culture" (Steiner 1971),
a "post-modern period" (Mills 1959), or a "postmodernity" (Baudrillard
1984), where the hallmarks of the modern world—humanism, rationalism, progressivist theories of history, discrete nation states, and so on—
are historically obsolete or philosophically bankrupt.[21]

Still, it is important to realize that "postmodern" tenets are not wholly new or original. Indeed, new theoretical developments always have important anticipations in earlier times. The "new science" of the seventeenth century, for example, was not a total break with the past but a continuation of twelfth-century Greco–Arabic natural science (Randall 1976) and of some fertile ideas of fourteenth-century European medievalism (Butterfield 1957). Similarly, many "postmodern" moves replay long-standing dissatisfaction with Enlightenment concepts and values. Long before Foucault and Lyotard, Burke and other conservatives attacked the Enlightenment for its alleged superficial rationalism, naive optimism, and reckless utopianism, and some of these critiques were first voiced within the *philosophe* community itself (Gay 1966). From Toulmin's account (1990), we see that many key postmodern themes, such as the emphasis on particularity, rhetoric, and the context-bound nature of theory were already present in sixteenth-century Renaissance humanism. Voltaire, Condillac, Hume, Kant, Comte, and Spencer assailed rationalist faith in the unlimited powers of "pure reason" to know the world. Critical quarters of modern social theory and art issued further challenges to the universalism, foundationalism, and realism, as Nietzsche did in the nineteenth century and Dewey, Heidegger, Rorty, and others have done in the twentieth century. Nearly every major tenet of postmodernism, such as the embrace of diversity over uniformity and desire over thought, was powerfully prefigured by existentialism and Romanticism. In fact, one could find anticipations of postmodern theory with the first appearance of relativism and skepticism in the arguments of the sophists or Pyrrhonists, or with the Heraclitean critique of the static Parmenidean ontology.

Thus, postmodern theory should be understood not as an absolute rupture or break with modern theory, but rather as a continuation of the critical aspects of modern thought itself and the skeptical, relativist, pluralist, and pragmatist underground tradition of Western philosophy. As a prefix, "post" has more meaning as a philosophical than a temporal designator, pointing to an attitude skeptical of the powers of reason that appears throughout both Western and Eastern history. Thus, the postmodern belief that nothing is new and everything has been done can be applied to postmodernism itself. Advocates of the postmodern tend to exaggerate the novelty of their theories and to dehistoricize their work in relation to preceding traditions of thought. Such hyperbole leads Gerald Graff, for one, to puncture "the myth of the postmodernist breakthrough" (1973).[22] In social theory and historiography, we can point to the critique of totalizing, universal histories by Von Ranke, Herder, and Weber; the denunciation of radical and utopian schemes of change by Burke; the rejection of foundationalism and timeless truths in favor of relativism by Montesquieu, Herzen, and Dilthey; the attack on the notion of a fixed human nature by Vico, Rousseau, and Marx; the abandonment of metaphysical theories of history by Dilthey; the disavowal of grand narrative schemes as illusory or dangerous in favor of a strict empiricism by Hume and Popper; the celebration of incommensureable cultural differences by Machiavelli, Vico, Montesquieu, Montaigne, and Herder; the adoption of a multicausal model that analyzes a complex interrelationship of numerous social forces by Montesquieu and Marx; and the emphasis on the literary nature of historiography by Trevelyan. The list is hardly exhaustive.

What is new in postmodern theory, therefore, is not so much specific tenets or claims, but the coalescence of various issues in one discourse and the emergence of a *zeitgeist,* mainly confined to certain intellectual and artistic circles to be sure, that is skeptical toward claims that reason can bring freedom or truth. Despite the various continuities one can find between postmodern and modern theories, the term "postmodern theory" is not necessarily wrong or superfluous because the critical elements in modern theory that were marginalized in relation to the dominant models have become increasingly strong and prominent in recent theory. This is not necessarily to agree with Jameson's claim (1991) that the tenets defining postmodern thought are now primary and dominant rather than secondary and emergent (in philosophy, for instance, the modern Anglo-American tradition still prevails), but these tenets have taken on greater cohesion, force, and influence in contemporary times. The keystones of Western rationalism are simply no longer tenable for an increasing number of contemporary thinkers in various fields, and the "modern period" in culture and thought appears to be ending in significant ways. Nevertheless, any discussion of postmodern theory has to grasp both continuity and discontinuity with previous modes of thought. The alleged "rupture" of postmodern with modern discourse is not incompatible with continuities with prior theories, since what is at issue is not any specific tenet but a whole family of concepts, issues, styles, and methods that align themselves in a new conceptual framework. It is in this light that we can understand Lyotard's cryptic remark that "the postmodern is undoubtedly a part of the modern" (1984: 79).

In the fields of social theory, philosophy, and historiography, postmodern theorists break with any attempt to situate reason outside of history. Many modern theorists seek to ground epistemological and normative claims in timeless, universal foundations rooted in clear and distinct ideas, *a priori* categories of the mind, purified structures of consciousness, human nature, or the laws of history or nature. Postmodern theorists deny that such foundations exist and seek to complete the break with premodern essentialism and foundationalism that many modern theorists failed to accomplish. The "quest for certainty" (Dewey 1979) such foundationalism validates is overturned in the certainty that such a quest is groundless.

Rejecting all static, ahistorical conceptions of phenomena, postmodern theorists—following Hegel, Marx, Weber, Dewey, and others—adopt historicizing, contextualizing approaches to culture, literature, philosophy, and other "texts," reading them as artifacts produced within specific social, historical, and linguistic conditions. For postmodern theorists, everything is historically constituted, even desire and the body, dimensions of human life that typically have been considered pregiven and invariable.[23] In particular, postmodern theorists abandon essentialist and idealist analyses of the subject as a unified consciousness that projects its intentions onto the field of social action. They reject not only simplistic Enlightenment models of a rationally motivated subject, but also the more general ideal of a conscious, autonomous self. By extension, they break with the notion of humanity as an evolving, unified macrosubject. There is no collective agent of history in the form of Hegel's Spirit or Lukács' Proletariat, only different historical groups and individuals.

This detotalizing move informs the postmodern critique of evolutionism and the philosophy of history. Postmodern theorists argue that history is not a continuous, linear path of development that encompasses all cultures within one great movement and culminates in universal harmony at the impetus of teleological laws. Rather, history is a discontinuous, fractured plurality of micronarratives governed by an indeterminant play of contingent forces devoid of purposes, immanent logic, or coherent direction. The deconstruction of history follows the same movement as the dismantling of the subject, author, and text. Rather than seeking a universal history that subsumes disparate peoples into the abstraction of "humanity," postmodern theorists acknowledge temporal discontinuity and celebrate cultural diversity. Lyotard's (1984) declaration of war against totalizing metanarratives that reduce difference to uniformity is the battle cry of the postmodern movement that seeks to liberate the full plurality of historical and cultural voices. Thus, following the lead of Rousseau, Herder, Weber, and other modern dissenters from Eurocentric progressivism, postmodern theorists reject the devaluation of premodern cultures, sometimes—as is true of the early work of Baudrillard and Foucault—going so far as to evince nostalgia for past eras uncorrupted by instrumental reason. The core political vision of postmodern theorists is that of the liberation of difference and plurality from the oppressive and homogenizing effects of modern theory.

In their critique of speculative, metaphysical conceptions of history, postmodern theorists have ironic similarities to the positivist tradition, but they depart radically from positivism in their rejection of the unity of the sciences, the search for historical laws, and the belief in truth, objectivity, and determinist models of cause–effect relations. Renouncing the possibility of a science of society or history, postmodern theorists claim that historical theory is nothing but rhetoric and narrative "with moral intent" (Seidman 1991). Where the scientistic versions of modern historiography emphasize universal laws, order, necessary causal connections, and the continuity of history, postmodern accounts of history emphasize chance, contingency, plurality, and indeterminancy, and firmly oppose the *a priori* reduction of change to regularity and universal law, such as is evident in the work of Buckle. Postmodern theorists reject both idealist emphases on history as the outcome of human intentionality as well as determinist emphases on the inevitablity of actions and events. Frequently, this circle is squared by granting chance and indeterminancy for social and linguistic structures, while seeing the subject as determined by these forces.

Postmodern theorists abandon the modern sociological belief in society as an ordered whole that can be grasped through systemic theory. They believe society is too dispersed, fragmented, differentiated, and complex to be adequately represented or mapped in a coherent theory, and they therefore produce partial and fragmented accounts of the world. They reject Marxian dialectics as a totalizing device and instead, with Hume, tend to see things as "entirely loose and separate." Like Toynbee, they tend to see history as merely "one damn thing after another." Ironically, while they reject modern foundationalism, they retain modern individualism, both epistemologically (the isolated knowing self) and politically (the desiring monad). For Perry Anderson (1984), the postmodern emphasis on discontinuity, indeterminancy, and contingency results in "the randomization of history." Postmodern theorists, he claims, fail to grasp important continuities, developmental trajectories, and underlying causal mechanisms behind historical change—such as Marx and Habermas both attempt to theorize.

Postmodern theorists also deny the modern norms of truth and objectivity and claim that knowledge is unavoidably subjective and partial. Embracing a skeptical, ironic, and relativist viewpoint, they see all interpretations as equally good or bad, relevant or irrelevant, and they reduce historical "facts" to fictional constructions. Some postmodern theorists speak as though historical events have no independent status beyond the linguistic fictions of writers. Influenced by the Nietzschean–Foucauldian critique of the modern will to truth, postmodernists regard the real significance of truth and objectivity as their political function of legitimating scientific and political authority. Where many modern theorists have championed science and Enlightenment rationality as emancipatory, postmodern theorists attack these forces as repressive, pointing to the disastrous consequences of the rationalization of the social world, such as the production of new modes of destruction, violence, and social control.

Thus, the modern linkage between reason and freedom comes undone in the postmodern description of rationalized domination. Rather than rethinking this relationship, as do critical modern theorists, many postmodern theorists reject the ideals of both reason and freedom and find nothing but the seeds of a totalitarian order in modern utopian schemes of a rational transformation of society and humanity. The realization of the ideals of the French slogan "Liberty! Equality! Fraternity!" in the Reign of Terror and Napoleanic invasions, the social engineering scenarios of St. Simon and Comte, or the catastrophic outcome of the Bolshevik revolution are precisely the kind of examples postmodern theorists have in mind when they refuse modern activist programs based on abstract, utopian, global, or elitist visions of change. Accordingly, Lyotard (1984) finds the main characteristic of the "postmodern condition" to be "incredulity toward metanarratives." For Lyotard, a "metanarrative" is similar to the narratives produced by the philosophy of history tradition. It is a modernist vision of history as progress, as a linear, teleological movement of events toward the confluence of reason and freedom, grounded in foundationalist principles. For Lyotard and others, the metanarratives articulated by Leibniz, Kant, Turgot, Condorcet, St. Simon, Comte, Hegel, Marx, and Habermas are no longer credible in the wake of the deformation of reason in history and the philosophical critique of assumptions concerning the unity of history, the perfectibility of humankind, and the teleology of reason and freedom.

While they may reject metanarratives and lack positive normative conceptions of freedom, many postmodern theorists nevertheless use historical analyses to historicize modernity and promote political resistance to domination. Thus, Deleuze and Guattari and Lyotard in his early work analyze how capitalism tries to colonize desire and the libido, and they seek ways of escaping psychological and bodily repression. The early work of Baudrillard studies modern rationalization processes, which he thinks reduce the individual and forms of communication and exchange to crude utilitarian functions. Foucault's genealogies seek to expose how our identities have been constituted by normalizing powers so that they may be recreated in less coercive forms. Postmodern feminists attack essentialist theories of gender identity in order to free subjects for new social roles and psychological identities.

Postmodern critiques generally focus on the oppressive effects of modern rationalization processes, particularly as they constrain individual identities. Socially conscious and politically radical postmodernists, belonging to what Foster (1983) calls a "postmodernism of resistance," are interested more in changing society than playing with language. Where Foucault serves as a model, such theorists use postmodern categories to overcome the deficiencies of modern theory, to eliminate the idealist and metaphysical aspects, to politicize historical theory and knowledge, and to help create new political forms. While postmodern theorists like Baudrillard and Kroker/Cook lapse into nihilism and break all links between theory and practice, and Rorty limits the role of the intellectual to being a private ironist, Foucault and others stand within the modern activist tradition, while renouncing the specific forms it has adopted.

We see that postmodern theories are predicated on a rejection of the cardinal features of the modern traditions of historiography, philosophy, and social and political theory. Modern theory in various forms has come under attack for the allegiance to narratives of historical progress; the embrace of science, determinism, and objective laws of history; the search for necessary and universal foundations for theory; the humanist belief in free, creative agency; the ahistorical appeal to human nature; the equation of freedom and rationality; totalizing forms of theorizing; and global and elitist models of social change. In place of such claims and tenets, postmodern visions of history typically see no progress or directional tendencies in history, deny the authority of science and validity of facts and causal and objective analysis, reject foundationalism and universal values, decenter the subject to determining social or linguistic forces, link rationalization to domination, reject global, utopian, or systemic forms of theorizing and politics, and abandon normative language and epistemology.

Today, the core concerns of the modern era—rationality, freedom, progress, individualism, truth, and objectivity—are being challenged by postmodern theorists. Amidst the bloody turmoil of the Middle East and Bosnia–Herzagovina, the resurfacing of global tensions in areas such as North and South Korea, and the spectacle of suffering in places such as Rwanda, Kant's and Condorcet's visions of a future marked by universal reason, peace, and happiness seem hopelessly naive. There is no doubt that modern values have received problematic philosophical formulation and political embodiment, and therefore that postmodern critiques can—as they have—contribute toward the revaluation and reinvigoration of modern values and theory (Best and Kellner 1991). Yet, all too often, the aim of postmodern critiques has been to destroy the modern intellectual and political traditions, with the result that they have failed to redeem its important resources and have offered little or no positive alternatives to modern theory and politics. Rather, postmodern theories have done much to disarm effective social critique, while contributing to a climate of pessimism, skepticism, relativism, and a loss of faith in human potential to organize social and individual existence on a free, rational, and peaceful basis. The postmodern countervision sees modern history as the bearer of a new dark age, rather than the harbinger of progress and enlightenment. In postmodern culture, the modern sense of change, novelty, dynamism, and unrealized possibilities of the future gives way to a gloomy pronouncement of stasis and exhaustion of historical energies. The end of history thereby signifies the end of liberatory visions and struggles or, voiced differently, the eternity of capitalism.

In the shadows of the Enlightenment, can the notions of progress, freedom, rationality, selfhood, truth, and objectivity be reconstructed and salvaged, in a politically progressive rather than conservative orientation, or are we truly moving toward the dystopian visions of Orwell, Huxley, and the cyberpunks? The contrasting theories and politics we find represented by Marx, Foucault, and Habermas point to competing responses to the secular forces of science, technology, individualism, and Enlightenment that define the modern world. At least since the French Revolution, battle lines have been drawn between enemies and champions of the revolutionary forces of modernity and the crucial issues that arose there are still hotly debated and far from resolved. Marx and Habermas represent quite different positions on the side of those who wish to advance liberatory aspects of modernity, while Foucault represents a "postmodern" approach that seeks to construct theoretical and political alternatives to modernity and modern theory. Yet, as is detailed in subsequent chapters, these lines of distinction cannot be drawn so simply: Marx and Habermas represent competing positions within the modern framework; and Foucault, in addition to offering postmodern alternatives to both Marx and Habermas, also draws from many of the same modern elements that inform their work. He straddles the borderline between modern and postmodern theory, rather than taking the leap of unfaith into the extreme postmodernism of Baudrillard, Lyotard, and others.

The question, therefore, is not what we can create *ex nihilo* in our allegedly new postmodern epoch in order to produce wholly new models of theory and politics, but which resources remain within the modern tradition that are useful for conceptualizing our historical present and creating an alternative future, and which elements are obsolete or problematic, and can be improved on by the postmodern critiques. This is precisely what is at stake in the modern/postmodern debates, and a critical comparison of Marx, Foucault, and Habermas promises to yield valuable insights into the important theoretical and political issues and conditions that confront us today.

NOTES

1. As Germino notes, "Machiavelli wrote of charting a 'new way not yet travelled by anyone'; both Luther and Bodin propounded concepts related to temporal government which they claimed could be found nowhere in the political thought of the past; Hobbes modestly insisted that 'civil philosophy' was 'no older' than his book *De cive;* Vico entitled his major work *The New Science;* and a long line of writers — Condorcet, Comte, Mazzini, Marx — presented themselves as har-

bingers of a new age of enlightenment and progress about to dawn for mankind" (1972: 8).

2. Of course, modern thinkers retained many traditional and conservative elements in their new theories. As is obvious in the case of Descartes, "radical" methods of doubt only served to better secure prevailing customs and belief. Few broke with Christianity, and many like Kant and even Voltaire continued to curry the favor of the old regime.

3. The idea that the social order mirrors the natural order and that the social body can be governed with the same precision as natural bodies leads to the vision of a "cosmopolis," of a society governed by natural laws (see Toulmin 1990). Although this idea was held by ancient Greece and China, and other premodern cultures, it held a special attraction for modern thinkers obsessed with the problem of social order. Hence we find Machievelli's notion of a science of government, Hobbes' vision of a social physics, Condorcet's plan for a social mathematics, and Comte's goal of a positive science or sociology. All four theorists demonstrate the powerful influence of modern mechanistic philosophy and the natural sciences on social theory.

4. Not all modern universal histories are insensitive to cultural and historical differences. Leopold Von Ranke, for example, sought a universal history that represents "the human race in all its variety" (1973: 59). While Ranke searches for a universal order and continuity in historical development, he claims that "history can never possess the unity of a philosophical system" (1973: 60). Each nation and stage of history has its own character, but they are linked in a universal history characterized by the struggle between freedom and necessity. Ranke's Eurocentrism, however (see below), casts serious doubt on his success in representing a dialectic of unity and diversity.

5. Becker's account is helpful for identifying key continuities between modern and medieval history, but it does not also analyze their fundamental discontinuities.

6. Rousseau is a wonderfully ambivalent thinker whose tensions reflect the dialectic of the Western civilization he analyzed. Where Rousseau the Romantic and author of the *Discourse on the Origins of Inequality* saw civilization as the corruption of the natural goodness of man, Rousseau the *philosophe* and writer of *The Social Contract* saw the gradual refinement of the human animal through social institutions.

7. It is an interesting historical irony that today it is Germans like Apel and Habermas who are trying to defend the Enlightenment, while French theorists like Foucault, Derrida, Lyotard, and Baudrillard are the most aggressive proponents of the postmodern attack on the Enlightenment. There are, of course, countertendencies in each national tradition, both then and now, for French thinkers like De Maistre spearheaded attacks on the Enlightenment, and German conservativism, led by the Christian Democrats, is currently seeking to dismantle its progressive heritage.

8. Another false stereotype of the *philosophes* is the claim that they reserved no place for art or the imagination in human life. As noted by Gay (1969), many emphasized the value of imagination and the arts. Thinkers like Lessing and Mendelssohn cautioned that reason could deaden emotions and self-awareness. Hume was not the only Enlightenment figure who understood that reason was not neces-

sarily lord over life, for as Diderot said far before Freud, "There is a bit of testical at the bottom of our most sublime sentiments and most refined tenderness" (cited in Gay 1969: 189-190).

9. Many critics point out that the modern era is not a simple linear progression of knowledge. As Toulmin (1990) has shown, the seventeenth century did not represent a time of peace, prosperity, and tolerance compared to all preceding eras. He claims that there was less, not more, toleration of rational viewpoints compared to earlier periods in the seventeenth century, as is evident in the different receptions of the work of Copernicus and Galileo. Toulmin holds that the relative peace and prosperity of sixteenth-century Europe came to an end in the seventeenth century, which was scarred by economic depression, social illness, and the social, political, and intellectual chaos created by the Thirty Years War. He also argues that seventeenth-century thinkers produced a considerably more narrow and truncated version of rationality than employed by earlier humanists. Where sixteenth-century humanism merged theory and practice and grounded rational inquiry in local, particular, and concrete contexts, philosophers, beginning in the seventeenth century, severed reason from any contact with rhetoric, poetics, ambiguity, paradox, diversity, regionalism, skepticism, and relativism. Thinkers like Descartes and Kant inaugurated the modern project of abstracting reason from these contexts and seeking timeless, universal foundations for truth. The question remains, however, whether the ideal of progress can be reconstructed in a more viable form (see Chapter 4).

10. As Gay notes (1969), many Romantics rejected the standard Enlightenment view of the medieval era as the dark ages and emphasized positive qualities such as community they found to be lacking in modernity. Gay observes that some Enlightenment thinkers like Voltaire and Gibbon also rejected a strictly negative view of the medieval era.

11. Hampson argues that the Eurocentric construction of history, based on ignorance of other cultures, began to change in the sixteenth century, with increasing colonial contact with other peoples and published accounts of these cultures (1968: 25ff.). Before such accounts, European knowledge of other cultures was limited to classical antiquity and stereotyped images of non-Western savages. As cosmologists reduced the earth to one planet among many, and anthropologists brought Europe and its Western heritage into a larger family of diverse cultures, "*Homo Europeenis* came gradually to believe that neither the world nor the universe revolved entirely round his collective person" (27). The European fascination with the exotic led some like Rousseau to exhalt early or foreign cultures as more pure and closer to nature. But knowledge of extra-European cultures did not spell the end of Eurocentrism; thinkers like Hume attempted to assimilate differences into a universal sameness that reflected the image of modern Europe.

12. Certainly not all modern thinkers adopted the transcendental pretence that seemed mainly a temptation for philosophers. Against the imperialist implications of universalist visions, Gay (1969: 461–462) notes that many Enlightenment thinkers like Voltaire and Bentham were political relativists who thought that different countries at different stages of development required different social institutions. The Enlightenment belief in tolerance and self-determination must also qualify Solomon's idea of a "bully culture."

13. As Becker notes, "Most eighteenth-century minds were too accustomed to a stable society with fixed ranks, too habituated to an orderly code of manners and a highly conventionalized art, to be at all happy in a disordered universe. It seemed safer, therefore, even for the enlightened ones, to retain God, or some plausible substitute, as a kind of dialectical guarantee that all was well in the most comfortable of commonsense worlds" (1964: 49–50). This marks an important point of difference with the postmodern outlook, which goes so far as to celebrate chance and contingency. The search for order and foundations in the modern tradition unites otherwise opposing viewpoints. Whether guided by rationalist or empiricist frameworks, or a Kantian hybrid of both, the hallmark of modern philosophy, even in skepticist form such as Hume's, was to find the rational foundations for knowledge that were universally valid and were grounded in the isolated subject. It didn't matter whether modern philosophers appealed to innate ideas, experience, human nature, or *a priori* categories, since in each case the goal was to ground knowledge in universal principles—a move possible only through an erasure of social and historical determinants of knowledge.

14. As well described by Eiseley (1958), the seventeenth and eighteenth centuries were dominated by the medieval notion of a Chain of Being that posited a fixed, immovable hierarchy of life ascending from minerals through human beings to angels. Evolutionary thinking began in the late eighteenth century with James Hutton's theory of uniformitarianism, which claimed that the earth was not the product of a singular Divine creation, but rather the long, steady outcome of natural forces such as wind and water. The evolutionary outlook of geology carried over into biology where it influenced Cuvier, Lyell, Wallace, Darwin, and others. The age of the earth was dated in million rather than thousands of years and life forms were seen to be the products of change and evolution. In the *Origin of the Species,* Darwin argued that animal species themselves change as a result of "descent through modification." In *The Descent of Man,* he claimed that human beings too have evolved from other animal species and as a result of the same forces such as natural and sexual selection. The new evolutionary *zeitgeist* clearly influenced the work of Spencer, Hegel, Marx, and others.

15. Needless to say, the Comtean vision of history was itself pervaded by narrativist, speculative, and metaphysical elements. Comte's three-fold stage of mental evolution and social emancipation—following the lead of Vico, Turgot, d'Alembert, and Hegel—is one of the great metanarratives of modern theory. This scheme is as speculative and metaphysical as that of Condorcet, from whom Comte tried to break. As I show below, it was hardly an "objective" analysis in its deeply partisan stance against democracy in favor of technocracy.

16. For the classic account of this model, see Hempel (1942).

17. There is an important distinction to be drawn between a strict positivism, which rejects all appeals to nonobservable phenomena, such as "causes," and realism, which allows such appeal (e.g., to "gravity" or "quarks") as potentially legitimate principles of explanation, or "transdiction." On this distinction, see Manicas (1987).

18. Despite his acute historicist outlook, Dilthey makes numerous references to "human nature." The tension lessens according to his definition of human nature: "Man is only given to us at all in terms of his realized possibilities. In the

cultural systems, too, we seek an anthropologically determined structure in which an 'X' realizes himself. We call this human nature but this is only a word for a conceptual system constituted by an intellectual method. The possibilities of man are not exhausted by this either" (1962: 138). Thus, Dilthey appears, like Marx (see Chapter 1) to have a historical concept of a human nature defined in terms of general possibilities, but which are realized or not only in specific historical forms.

19. All historical writing is predetermined by distinct aesthetic and political values. Brown (1992) notes that historical visions are typically informed by a guiding metaphor, such as that of society as an organism, machine, or cybernetic system. Rorty's work, for example, is shaped by the metaphor of social interaction as a conversation; Foucault sees society as a war or battlefield. In his magisterial analysis, White (1973) undertakes a formalist study of the "deep structure of the historical imagination." In exhaustive detail White shows that historical writing is determined by a poetic act that prefigures the historical field and how it will be represented. A given historical "style" represents a combination of modes of emplotment (such as tragic), argument (such as mechanistic), and ideology (such as radical).

20. By the disastrous fiat of positivism, "interest and inclination are banished from the court of knowledge as subjective factors. The spontaneity of hope, the act of taking a position, the experience of relevance or indifference, and above all, the response to suffering and oppression, the desire for adult autonomy, the will to emancipation, and the happiness of discovering one's identity—all these are dismissed for all time from the obligating interest of reason. A disinfected reason is purged of all moments of enlightened volition" (Habermas 1973: 262–263).

21. For a more detailed genealogy and discussion of postmodern discourse, see Best and Kellner (1991).

22. See also the analysis of Huyssen, who defines postmodernism as the "the search for tradition" while pretending toward innovation. "Despite its radical and legitimate critique of the gospel of modernism, postmodernism, which in its artistic practices and its theory was a product of the 1960s, must be seen as the endgame of the avantgarde and not as the radical breakthrough it often claimed to be" (Huyssen 1986: 168).

23. Some poststructuralist interpretations of history are extreme idealist reductions of real events to language. The classic case of the textualization of history is Hindess and Hirst's claim that "by definition, all that is past does not exist. To be accurate, the object of history is whatever is *represented* as having hitherto existed" (1975: 308).

1

MARX AND THE ENGINES OF HISTORY

The first premise of all human history is, of course, the
existence of living human individuals. Thus the first fact
to be established is the physical organisation of these
individuals and their consequent relation to the rest of
nature. . . . The writing of history must always set out
from these natural bases and their modification in the
course of history through the action of men.
— MARX AND ENGELS (1978: 149–150)

Karl Marx lived and wrote during what he understood to be the most
momentous social transformation in the history of humanity — the emergence of capitalist modernity. Marx was one of the first social theorists
to analyze systematically the capitalist mode of production and to see it
as constituting a modern world radically different from all previous social forms. Marx noted that although capitalism produced a massive rupture in the fabric of history, knowledge of the origins and nature of the
new social system transforming the entire globe was occluded. This was
the result of the sheer novelty and complexity of the wage and market
system, of the oppressiveness of its effects on human beings, and of an
ideology that obscures underlying social relations, presenting the movement of commodities and the hegemony of exchange value as if governed
by natural laws.

The underlying motivations of Marx's work were to understand
thoroughly the nature of the capitalist mode of production, to analyze
it as a radically new form of society, and to lay bare its fundamental
mechanisms of operation. These analytic aims were subordinated to the
political goals of exposing these operations as mechanisms of domination,
of tearing off the veils that clouded the political vision of the working class,
of organizing the working class into a unified international body, and

of abolishing capitalism as a system based on exploitation, dehumanization, and class antagonism. In order to accomplish these tasks, Marx required immense historical knowledge, a historical method that treats all social and cultural phenomena as socially constituted, a social theory informed by this assumption, and a theory of history that grasps the basic outlines and mechanisms of historical change. Such modes of understanding allowed Marx to contextualize capitalism and understand its origins, trajectories, and seemingly impending demise.

Marx's critical outlook was developed by assimilating numerous theoretical and political influences. Most importantly, these included French utopian socialism, English political economy, and German idealism. Marx shared many political sentiments with the utopian socialists, but he condemned their lack of theoretical rigor and developed a "scientific socialism" (Engels) based on empirical analysis rather than moralizing rhetoric. Through a scientific account of human activity, Marx sought to grasp the dynamics of social and historical change, to uncover the constituting forces of the present, and to predict the probability of future events.

Although Marx uncritically embraced the positivist attitude that elevated scientific knowledge and method over all other forms of knowledge (1978: 155), he rejected the positivist search for ahistorial "laws" of development and its pretension to value neutrality. For Marx, the whole point of science was to help the working class overthrow forces of oppression. In *Capital,* Marx alternated passages of dense empirical analysis of capitalism with stinging attacks on its "vampire-like" thirst for the blood of living labor (see Kellner 1983). Marx's scientific attitude was informed by a strong moral sense, by a *"categorical imperative to overthrow all those conditions* in which man is an abased, enslaved, abandoned, contemptible being" (Marx 1978: 60). But Marx saw no contradiction between the "scientific" and moral–political character of his theory. Most theorists simply interpreted the world, but Marx maintained that the time had come to change it, by merging science and critique, theory and practice. Marx thus sought a theory of history and society that was both endowed "with the precision of natural science" (1978: 5) and also was "in its very essence critical and revolutionary" (1977: 103).

Marx believed that dialectics grants this revolutionary character to social and historical analysis.[1] Marx's version of science was radically different from what later emerged as "scientific Marxism," and the differences stemmed principally from Marx's more supple appropriation of Hegelian dialectics.[2] Against the ahistorical methods of Western philosophy, Hegel developed a dialectical vision of reality that treats all phenomena as historically and socially produced, and sees conflict and contradiction as the driving forces behind historical change. The dialectical method made it possible for Marx to overcome the reifying approach of positivist science that sees social reality as static and given. Marx's emphasis on the historical constitution of all things was evident in his critique of Feuerbach's materialism. According to Marx, Feuerbach grasped the reality of the sensuous empirical world, but failed to see that it was "not a thing given direct from all eternity, remaining ever the same, but the product of industry and of the state of society . . . an historical product" (1978: 170).

Hegel's dialectical method had revolutionary implications because, according to Marx, it helped to overcome fatalistic resignation to "the way things are," and shifted focus to how they have been constituted and can be changed. In Marx's hands, dialectical method revealed the changing forms of conflict and crisis that operate in society, undermine its stability, and create new social dynamics. Dialectics also enabled Marx to move beyond the positivist method of treating phenomena as external and separate from one another by grasping the movement of things in their interrelationship, as different aspects of the same structure or system, as "opposites" united in the same relation. This allowed Marx, for example, to see gross wealth and poverty as inseparable effects of the capitalist market.

Of course, Marx argued that Hegel, by emphasizing the causal primacy of consciousness over social activity and relationships, understood dialectics in a mystified, inverted manner; consequently, Marx redefined dialectics in a materialist context. For Marx, the contradictions that propel history forward are not, as for Hegel, logical contradictions among opposing ideas, but conflicting material forces rooted within a particular social system. Marx shared Hegel's view that human beings transform themselves and their societies through the activity of production, but Marx saw this activity as the work of human beings rather than "Spirit."[3] In his call for a "real history" of human beings in their changing forms of productive labor, Marx developed the "materialist interpretation of history" and was one of the first modern social theorists to interpret history as the product of human beings in their concrete, productive activity.

For Marx, the primary forces of history were not ideas, political machinations, or war, but rather production, commerce, and industry: "In the whole conception of history up to the present this real basis of history has either been totally neglected or else considered as a minor matter quite irrelevant to the course of history" (1978: 165). Marx's materialist standpoint placed him in opposition to the idealism of Dilthey, Collingwood, and others who understood historical explanation to consist of identifying and sympathetically reconstructing the thoughts and motives of past historical agents. Where humanist historians like Vico anticipated Marx in their analysis of history as a human product, and theorists such as Aristotle, Locke, Hobbes, Machiavelli, and St. Simon understood economics to be a central human activity, it was Marx who developed these ideas most forcefully and consistently. Against Carlyle and others who exalted the determinant role of great men in history, Marx, following Michelet and Vico, emphasized the crucial role of common people and the "masses" in shaping history.

On Marx's conception, dialectics is neither an immanent historical force, nor a totalizing worldview that subsumes all differences into an undifferentiated whole; rather, it is a supple empirical method, "a way of thinking that brings into focus the full range of changes and interactions that occur in the world" (Ollman 1993: 10). Theorists such as Lenin, Trotsky, Gramsci, and Lukács rightly emphasized dialectics as the heart of Marx's methodology, but dialectics must also be understood as a theoretical and political vision that projects future emancipatory possibilities based on the analysis of existing society and past history. Where dialectical *method* relates to analysis of the present and past, dialectical *vision* is future oriented and grounds the norm of human emancipation in actual historical possibilities disclosed by dialectical method, while seeking to overcome debilitating oppositions in social and personal life.

In order to carry out a materialist analysis of modern capitalism, Marx, beginning in 1844, immersed himself in the study of political economy. While he drew from Ricardo, Smith, Mill, and others, Marx developed a sharp critique of political economy and shifted its analytic and political perspective. He showed that political economy was not a science, but rather an ideology that analyzed rent, profit, and other categories apart from the exploitation of the working class. Where political economy operated from the hidden point of view of capital, Marx analyzed social and economic phenomena from the perspective of the working class and its struggles for autonomy from capitalist exploitation (see Cleaver 1979, 1992).

Marx was decisively influenced by the Enlightenment movement and was very much a "modernist" in his basic temperment. He personified the Enlightenment emphasis on critique and its demand for rational social reconstruction and universal values. Early in his life, he called for a "ruthless criticism of everything existing" and carried through sharp but fragmentary attacks on religion, philosophy, property, law, money, the state, and Hegel. It is no accident that Marx entitled a later work, in the spirit of Kant, *Critique of Political Economy*. "Critique" for Marx, however, did not involve an analysis of autonomous forms of knowledge and their limits, but rather of the sociohistorical conditions underlying knowledge and the crisis tendencies that threaten the stability of capitalist society. Marx also embraced the modernist celebration of change and innovation as liberating forces (see Berman 1982). Far from advocating a return to simple communal life, Marx's historical vision was oriented toward the future. He emphasized the limitations of static, isolated social forms and praised the dynamic qualities of capitalism that overturned tradition and provincial boundaries to unleash new social forces and establish new universal human relations. Marx praised the "revolutionary" bourgeoisie for accomplishing "wonders far surpassing Egyptian pyramids, Roman aqueducts, and Gothic cathedrals" (1978: 476); for liberating the productive forces that "slumbered in the lap of social labour" (477); for creating new wants, international interdependency, and the urban environment; and for rescuing much of the population from the "idiocy of rural life" (477).

Despite its empirical and "scientific" character, Marx's theory belongs to the "philosophy of history" tradition. While rejecting the theological interpretation of history, Marx nevertheless retained the narrative codes of salvation within the secular context of progress. With Condorcet, Comte, and other Enlightenment thinkers, Marx developed a metanarrative that linked advances in science, technology, and rationality with advances in freedom and progress. Marx thus accepted the Enlightenment view that history, in however a tortured or indirect way, represents a progressive development toward a rational society and free individuality. But unlike apologists for the modern world, Marx was acutely aware of the negative side of modernity, and he condemned capitalism as a system of exploitation that thwarts the very possibilities for progress and emancipation that it calls into being. Moroever, unlike Habermas (see Chapter 3), Marx did not accept the rationalist faith in the power of reason and lofty moral principles to dissolve social conflict and self-interest. Marx believed instead that those who abuse power can only be removed through force, and he derided all liberal attempts to reconcile antagonisms without changing their fundamental sources rooted in class domination. Marx was rationalist enough, however, to believe that the proletariat would break its capitalist chains once it attained a rational understanding of the material conditions of its oppression.

While Marx analyzed the emergence of a universal history, he saw this as the result of real historical developments, of an increasingly global form of capitalism, rather than as a manifest destiny or the autonomous march of reason. The idea of a universal history, of a common social goal and international form of association, was fundamental to Marx's vision of history and concept of human liberation. From the beginning to the end of his career, Marx was decisively influenced by the Hegelian–Romantic vision of a social and individual being no longer divided against itself, of a harmonious and unalienated mode of human existence that overcomes the forms of antagonism and fragmentation created by the historical process. Marx's vision of emancipation foresaw the possibility of a future communist society where the conflicts among human beings and between humanity and nature can be overcome, where the human species can join in a rational and democratic association that reconciles particular and general interests, where national differences are eliminated in an international social order, and where the contradiction between "human essence" and human existence is abolished so that human beings develop rather than mutilate themselves in their activity.

Following Hegel, Marx interpreted history as a process of differentiation, driven by conflicts and contradictions. In its historical development, an original unity, be it a concept or a communal clan, is sundered apart, alienated from itself, differentiated into various aspects, and eventually returns to itself in a climactic moment that signals the end of history, at least as hitherto known. For Marx, history involves the alienation of a subject — not Reason, but humanity — from its creative powers. But the movement of history allows for an eventual recuperation of these powers in a higher, more developed form. Marx's theory of history traced the historical process of domination and alienation, but it analyzed the tendencies whereby this same process ultimately can lead to human liberation.

Marx's historical vision, as I show below, is a materialist translation of Hegel's notion of a "concrete identity," of a differentiated unity that can become whole again after protracted alienation through historical movement.[4] Since Marx's unity, unlike Hegel's, is not guaranteed by history, but has to be produced out of tendencies and possibilities within the present, his emancipatory norm requires a political vision of how the working class can collectively transform present possibilities of freedom into a social reality and thereby win the emancipation of all humanity. Throughout his life, Marx sought a viable theory and practice that would empower workers all over the globe to seize the reins of history. Once this was accomplished, he believed, the movement of communism would bring the end of one history, the hitherto existing history of human alienation, and inaugurate the beginning of a new history of human freedom. This vision of a future communist society is an apocalyptic vision of a rupture in history as great as capitalism, yet which also builds on the achievements of the entire historical past.

Marx's dialectical method and vision of history is the focus of this chapter. Against all readings that essentialize Marx as a particular kind of theorist, such as a humanist or a positivist, or that claim he developed a crudely reductionist method, I present Marx as a supple and complex, but not always consistent, theorist of historical change and revolution. As Adamson (1985) forcefully demonstrated, we cannot speak of "*the* Marxist theory of history" since Marx developed various models and visions, and frequently changed his mind on fundamental issues. Although Marx advances a forceful, monoperspectival interpretation of history as determined by the dynamics of production and class struggle, he employs, within this context, various theoretical and political models to examine social reality from numerous standpoints. I undertake a "contextualist" reading of Marx, which maintains that he adopts different theoretical and political models in different contexts according to different analytical and political intentions and shifting historical conditions. This reading brings out the various tensions in Marx's work, such as have been resolved falsely one way or another by many of his interpreters and followers.

I begin with an analysis of Marx's concept of alienation and vision of human emancipation as it develops in his early and later texts. I show that Marx examines history from the standpoints of both continuity and discontinuity. Against some of Marx's critics, I argue that these models are complementary rather than contradictory, and consider their different political implications. I then turn to the argument, recently revived by analytic Marxists, that Marx is a technological determinist. I counter this thesis by showing that he employs a multicausal model of historical change which privileges forces or relations of production in different contexts. I then consider some of the key methodological assumptions and problems of Marx's work that relate to his use of "rational abstraction." Examining some of the critiques of Marx's analysis of precapitalist societies, I describe the tension between his continuity models—which treat all history as determined by economic, technological, and political dynamics, and so as amenable to a historical materialist analysis—and his discontinuity model, which argues for a fundamental rift between precapitalist and capitalist societies and calls into question the applicability of historical materialism to precapitalist modes of production. This chapter raises numerous issues and debates that are important for understanding the post-Marxist theories of Foucault and Habermas. As I argue throughout the book, Marx commits certain theoretical errors that Foucault and Habermas help to overcome, but he contributes a wealth of important insights and values that need to be retained and developed in our own historical context.

MODELS OF HISTORICAL CONTINUITY

Throughout all of his works, Marx advances a Hegelian vision of history as a continuous evolutionary process driven by the dynamic of "objectification." In their interaction with nature through productive activity, human beings concretize and embody their personality and creative powers in their objects. As they shape and change their world, they simultaneously shape and change themselves. The development of the individual follows the evolution of its social forms of interaction, which themselves are determined by the dynamics of production.

This evolutionary view emphasizes lines of continuity from tribal to communist society. Marx employs three different continuity models in different stages of his work: (1) the humanist model, which interprets history as both the alienation and realization of the "human essence"; (2) the productive forces model, which interprets history as the progressive augmentation of the productive forces, a movement governed by the contradiction between the forces and relations of production; and (3) the class struggle model, which interprets historical change as resulting from the struggles between contending classes.[5] While these are logically distinct models, Marx frequently combines them in his concrete historical analyses.

The humanist model is developed mainly in the early stage of Marx's work, but remnants of it turn up frequently in his later works. Following Hegel, Marx sees history as the progressive development of human freedom throughout various stages of history. But this is a double movement where freedom emerges only through the advance of alienation. For Hegel, alienation involves the separation of Reason from itself in the process of its objectification in history. Marx, in contrast, understands alienation as the separation of human producers from the "objective conditions of production," the communal context of their labor, and their own "species-being" and "human essence." These later two phrases derive from Feuerbach and designate sociality, historicity, and creative activity as fundamental attributes of a distinctly human, rather than "merely" animal, nature.

Like Hegel's Spirit, Marx's "human essence" unfolds in the process of historical development and is realized in a final stage of history. Marx views history as a continuous movement of a two-sided process: the humanization of nature and the naturalization of humanity. The humanization of nature is the process whereby human beings progressively enlarge the field of their objectification and gain increasing control over nature; the naturalization of humanity involves the evolution of the human being from a limited to a universal being and the consequent realization of its sensuous, natural powers in a free social context. Both aspects of the historical process result from the human interaction with nature through productive activity. As Marx says, "for the socialist man *the whole of what is called world history* is nothing more than the creation of man through human labor, and the development of nature for man" (1975a: 357). Unlike Habermas, therefore (see Chapter 3), Marx sees history strictly in terms of labor and production, excluding analysis of language and moral development as important dynamics of their own.

Marx grasps the totality of history not only as the alienation of the laboring subject from the process and products of production, but also as the "reintegration or return of man into himself" (1975a: 347), a movement that culminates in communism. While presented as the "negation of the negation," communism is nonetheless defined as a *positive* movement, insofar as it appropriates the whole "wealth" of history, both human wealth (which Marx interprets in terms of human individuation and the formation of the senses) and technological–economic wealth (the development of the productive forces). The early Marx sees communism as "the *positive* supersession of *private property,* as *human self-estrangement,* and hence the true *appropriation of the human* essence through and for man; it is the complete restoration of man to himself as a *social,* i.e., human, being, a restoration which has become conscious and which takes place within the entire wealth of previous periods of development" (84).

Usurping the place of Absolute Knowledge in Marx's materialist rewriting of the Hegelian narrative, communism is the practical movement that overcomes the conflicts, contradictions, and disunities produced in history. Communism reunites individuals with the material conditions of their existence, with nature, with one another, and with their own human essence: "it is the *genuine* resolution of the conflict between man and nature, and between man and man, the true resolution of the conflict between existence and being, between objectification and self-affirmation, between freedom and necessity, between individual and species. It is the solution to the riddle of history and knows itself to be the solution" (348). The riddle of history is that freedom is contained in alienation and cannot be attained without the entire process of social differentiation: " 'Liberation' is a historical and not a mental act, and it is brought about by historical conditions, the [development] of industry, commerce, [agri]culture, [and] the [conditions of intercourse]" (Marx and Engels 1978: 169). Marx believes the movement of history, the dynamic of differentiation/recuperation, leads toward the emergence of communism. The "very difficult and protracted process" of communism is "the goal of . . . historical movement" (Marx 1975a: 365). While communism represents the next stage of history, it does not create itself; rather, Marx believes that communism requires a conscious and practical act of appropriation.

Thus, Marx's initial vision of history is thoroughly inspired by Hegel and Feuerbach. It deploys a metaphysical concept of a human essence whose inner nature is realized in the process of history. History is the single, totalizable story of the realization and universalization of human freedom. The self-actualization of humanity unfolds through a teleology. Like Hegel, Marx sees nature as completing itself through human freedom and self-awareness. "History itself is a *real* part of *natural history*—and of nature's becoming man" (1975a: 355). The main difference is that Marx took nature to be primary and originary rather than as the objectification of a preexisting Spirit or Reason. Yet, in his vision of history—as determined by the logic of production and objectification, as constituted by a single "transsubjective" agent, as expressing the unfolding of its capacities, and as involving its emancipation through a conscious appropriation of the past—Marx adopts the standpoint of the "philosophy of the subject" that has been rejected by Foucault and (not altogether successfully) Habermas (see Benhabib 1986).[6]

The productive forces model first appears in *The German Ideology*. Just one year after completing the *Economic and Philosophic Manuscripts,* influenced by Engels' work on political economy, Marx attained a much more detailed and empirical understanding of the material forces behind historical change. He abandoned Feuerbach's terminology and much of his Hegelian baggage. The essentialist view of the *Economic and Philosophic Manuscripts* whereby a historical subject expresses its nature is relinquished in favor of a "pragmatological" view (Fleischer 1973) that stresses the active role of human beings in shaping their history. This view posits a dialectic between needs and productive activity, where the existence of needs requires production and production creates new needs.[7] In place of a nondifferentiated account of the "universal meaning" of history, Marx, with Engels, now divides history into a series of "modes of production"—tribal, ancient, feudal, capitalist, and communist—each of which represents a different form of social interaction with nature and creates different modes of life. Once again, we find a single, universal narrative of history, this time interpreted as the evolution of human activity through successive historical generations.

Despite a periodization scheme in which both capitalism and communism are represented as historical ruptures, Marx and Engels underline the fundamental continuity in history across successive modes of production. From this standpoint, continuity is understood not in terms of the realization of the human essence, but rather the cumulative development of the productive forces themselves: "at each stage [of history] there is found a material result: a sum of productive forces, a historically created relation of individuals to nature and to one another, which is handed down to each generation from its predecessor; a mass of productive forces, capital funds and conditions" (Marx and Engels 1978: 164). Each historical product is "the result of the activity of a whole succession of generations, each standing on the shoulders of the preceding one, developing its [i.e., the former's] industry and its intercourse, modifying its social system according to the changed needs [of the new system]" (170).

Marx and Engels find "the whole evolution of history" to be "a coherent series of forms of intercourse, the coherence of which consists in this: in the place of an earlier form of intercourse, which has become a fetter, a new one is put, corresponding to the more developed productive forces and, hence, to the advanced mode of the self-activity of individuals—a form that in its turn becomes a fetter and is then replaced by another" (Marx and Engels 1978: 194–195). For the first time, they make the claim that spawned technological determinist readings of their work: "all collisions in history have their origin . . . in the contradiction between the productive forces and the form of [social] intercourse (196).

This and other statements made by Marx in subsequent works points to the following (seemingly universal) dynamic of historical change: the technical basis of a given society calls into being certain relations of production that serve optimally to promote the continued development of the productive forces. Relations of production "correspond to" forces when they further the growth of the productive forces, and they become a conservative "fetter" to this growth when a particular social class tries to retain its social power rather than promote technological development that threatens this power. At this stage there is a "contradiction" rather than a correspondence between the forces and relations of production; a new set of relations (and hence a new economic base and a new superstructure) will emerge in order to better promote technological advance. The relations of production are subordinate to forces of production insofar as their function merely is to promote technological development.[8] The contradiction between forces and relations is described as the fundamental "motor" of historical change. Thus, on this model, the development of the productive forces is the main impetus behind the ever-expanding division of labor and the process of social differentiation. Appearing first in the individual family, the division of labor, spurred on by technological advance, results in the formation of various social classes, of industrial, commercial, and agricultural forms of labor, as well as in divisions between town and country and mental and manual labor.

The third continuity model, the class struggle model, is anticipated both in *The Holy Family* and *The German Ideology,* but makes its first explicit appearance with the publication of *The Communist Manifesto.* It also turns up in the 1859 Preface to *A Contribution to the Critique of Political Economy,* and is the privileged model of *Capital.* On this perspective, the unity of all (written) history is interpreted from the standpoint of class struggle: "Freeman and slave, patrician and plebian, lord and serf, guild-master and journeyman, in a word, oppressor and oppressed, stood in constant opposition to one another, carried on an uninterrupted, now hidden, now open fight, a fight that each time ended, either in a revolutionary re-constitution of society at large, or in the common ruin of the contending classes" (Marx and Engels 1978: 473–474). Although capitalism is again represented as a break in history, it is also seen as "the product of a long course of development, of a series of revolutions in the modes of production and of exchange" (475). As a form of class society, capitalism stands in continuity with all past societies; it is "the last antagonistic form of the social process of production" and prepares to bring "the prehistory of human society" to a close (Marx 1978: 5). Communism inaugurates both the end of (alienated) history and the beginning of (nonalienated, free) history.

Thus, one can identify various continuity models that Marx develops in different stages of his thought. Rather than seeing these models as incompatible, or as discontinuous formulations divided by an "epistemological break" (Althusser 1979; Fleischer 1973; Adamson 1985), I suggest they stand as different perspectives on history, each articulating a different yet related aspect of continuity, and that Marx employs all of them together in his later work. To be sure, there are incompatible elements in these various models; the determinism of the anthropological and nomological models, for example, contradicts the emphasis on a humanly shaped history in the pragmatological model.

But there are also fundamental lines of coherence that link these models together in a multiperspectival vision of history. While after 1844 Marx abandoned the metaphysical concept of human essence, along with the anthropological model of history, the problematic of alienation is integral to later writings (e.g., the *Grundrisse, Capital,* and *Theories of Surplus Value*) where terms such as "alienation" and "objectification" still appear frequently (see Schaff 1970; Rosdolsky 1977). The humanist model is presupposed in both the productive forces and class struggle model insofar as the development of productive forces involves a progressive separation of labor from the process and products of production, and alienation is a motivating force of class struggle. There is a direct link, moreover, between the productive forces model, and the class struggle model since Marx sometimes interprets class struggle as the active political expression of the contradiction between the forces and relations of production. This contradiction "necessarily on each occasion burst[s] out in revolution" and the "collisions of various classes" (Marx and Engels 1978: 197). On the technological determinist model (see below), this involves a struggle between ascending and descending classes, between those classes that advance the development of the productive forces and those that impede it.

Underlying all three continuity models are the constant themes of the mutual transformation of human beings and nature through production; economics, technology, and class struggle as the decisive causal forces of social change; the evolution of individuals and society by means of the evolution of the productive forces and the division of labor; and the progressive advance of history toward communism and human emancipation. From the *Economic and Philosophic Manuscripts* to *Capital,* one finds the same Hegelian vision of a collective subject of history realizing its potentiality through a process of objectification whereby the estranged products of its labor can be regained. Although Marx interchanges human beings for Spirit, he retains the Hegelian motif of a Subject behind history that emerges through a process of externalization in its conscious objectifications. Marx's "Subject," however, is unified only in the abstract, in the name of the praxis of humanity; specified more concretely, the subject of world history is fragmented into warring classes. This specification, nevertheless, leaves intact the assimilation of different social groups and activities to the logic of production.

Moreover, Marx never abandons the metanarrative of progress and emancipation, whether phrased in terms of the formation of the five senses or the transition from "necessity to freedom." Marx's vision of emancipation as reconciliation of alienated divisions of life is most pronounced in his early text, *The Jewish Question.* Here, following Hegel, Marx represents capitalism as a structure where differentiation assumes the form of dualistic separation and mutual antagonism. Capitalism is organized around the division between state and civil society, where civil society is the economic sphere of private interests at war with one another and the state is the political sphere where individuals are integrated with one another in theory but not in practice.[9] For Marx, this social division leads to a fractured existence of the human individual itself since it is divided into a public and private being, into an abstract citizen and a concrete producer or worker.

Under these conditions, the social nature of the human being appears as something accidental or extraneous; it is degraded into a mere means for the realization of private, egoistic ends. To recover the true social nature and integrity of human beings, Marx calls for the overthrow of private interests, the recuperation of species-being, and the return of the individual to itself as a coherent totality: "Only when real, individual man resumes the abstract citizen into himself and as an individual man has become a *species-being* in his empirical life, his individual work and his individual relationships, only when man has recognized and organized his *forces propres* as *social forces* so that social force is no longer separated from him in the form of *political force,* only then will human emancipation be completed" (Marx 1975a: 234). A key opposition communism overcomes, therefore, is between society and the individual. Within the mediated unity of communism, as Marx envisages it, the communal integration of precapitalist societies exists, as does the individual element of capitalism, but the two elements are no longer in contradiction to one another; rather, communism creates the free, *social individual* whose rich inner being is dependent upon conditions of social equality where the freedom of each requires the freedom of all.

DISCONTINUITY IN HISTORY

We have just examined the various continuity models Marx employed. In addition to mapping the progressive development of the objective and subjective forces of history, Marx employs a vision of historical discontinuity to mark a rupture in history with the advent of capitalism and to project an emancipatory break with capitalism through the norm of a possible future communist society.

Marx's most sustained vision of historical discontinuity can be found in the long historical section of the *Grundrisse*, "Pre-capitalist Economic Formations." In this text, Marx tries to establish the historical originality of the capital–wage–labor relationship. His intention is not a theory of precapitalist modes of production, but rather a genealogy of capitalist forms and categories. Marx attempts to grasp the historical preconditions of capitalism, "the evolutionary history of both capital and wage-labour . . . the historic origin of the bourgeois economy" (Marx 1965: 86). The relationship of labor to capital, where the worker finds the conditions of production external to him or her as capital and the capitalist finds the worker as a propertyless being, "presupposes a historic process which dissolves the different [precapitalist property] forms, in which the labourer is an owner and the owner labours" (97), with the result that the laborer owns nothing and the owners do not labor.

This genealogy has immediate political motivations and implications, for Marx is concerned to demystify the fetishized ideology of capitalism as an eternally present form of society and to underline it as a break from more organic types of society. Rather than seeing the "worker" as a universal category, as does bourgeois political economy, Marx insists that the worker is a specific historical creation. "The establishment of the individual as a worker . . . is itself a production of *history*" (1965: 68). The "worker" is precisely that abstract, laboring being who is divorced from the socionatural context of production, from both (1) the "objective conditions" of his production, and (2) its communal context. I shall briefly address each of these factors.

In his description of the various precapitalist societies, Marx argues that all are *relatively continuous modifications* of the basic tribal mode of production and its direct communal property form. He says, for instance, "*Where the fundamental relationship is the same* [in precapitalist societies], this [tribal property] form can realise itself in a variety of ways" (1965: 69, my emphasis). Thus, ancient society "is the product of a more dynamic historical life, of the fate and modification of the original tribes" (71), and "Slavery and serfdom are . . . simply further developments of property based on tribalism" (91).

Whatever their differences—which amount to a gradually evolving differentiation of the tribal form and hence emergent forms of private property—these historical mutations are always, until capitalism, *confined within the basic structural limits of tribal society*. The "original" definition of property, as Marx states throughout the *Formen*, articulates a symbiotic relation of the producing individual to the land and the community.

"*Property*—and this applies to its Asiatic, Slavonic, ancient classical and Germanic forms—. . . originally signifies a relation of the working (producing) subject . . . to the conditions of his production or reproduction as his own" (1965: 95). In all precapitalist societies, producers are integrated with the materials of labor that constitute their objective conditions of production, and which they relate to as their property. "The individual is related to himself as a proprietor, as master of the conditions of his reality" (67) and these become his condition of "realisation," where the earth itself is his "natural laboratory" (67) and is understood as an extension of his very being. The purpose of production in these precapitalist societies is not the creation of exchange value, but of simple use value, of the maintenance of the individual, family, and the community as a whole. Each individual is related to the other, therefore, as a coproprietor, as a co-owner of common property.

Producers in these social formations are owners only insofar as they are members of the community that is the crucial mediating context of their relation to the land. Marx speaks, therefore, of the social "preconditions" of production, or the "communal character" of production, which is maintained throughout *all* precapitalist social formations: "Only in so far as the individual is a member—in the literal and figurative sense—of such a community, does he regard himself as an owner or possessor. In reality *appropriation* by means of the process of labour takes place under these *preconditions,* which are not the *product* of labour but appear as its natural or *divine* preconditions" (1965: 69). The fact that the "communal ties of blood, language, custom, etc." (68) are the preconditions of all appropriation explains Marx's remark that in precapitalist society labor is not the origin of property, rather, property is the origin of labor—property, that is, as a communal form and concept.[10]

Thus, in precapitalist societies producing individuals are tied to the land and immersed in the community. Individuals produce only insofar as they participate in the community, and communal property mediates all relations to the land. Community and land constitute a primordial bond in the unity of conditions of production in precapitalist society. Although Marx is concerned to grasp the specific differences of each precapitalist mode of production, the emphasis in the *Formen* is on *what they have in common:* the natural and communal character of production. Here, Marx wishes to underline their *continuity with one another* (as "precapitalist economic formations") and their *collective discontinuity from capitalism:* "What requires explanation is not the *unity* of living and active human beings with the natural, inorganic conditions of their metabolism with nature, and therefore their appropriation of nature . . . what we must explain is the *separation* of these inorganic conditions of human existence from their active existence, a separation which is only

fully completed in the relationship between wage-labour and capital"
(1965: 86–87).

While each new property form is a gradually emerging mode of alienation (in the most narrow sense of the separation of producers from the
objective conditions of production), all property formations are confined
within the structural limits of the tribal form and none represent the complete "dissolution" of the production–land–community triad that capitalism alone represents. While there are socially significant changes in the
passage from one mode of production to another and an ever-growing
division of labor and development of technology, the basic production–
land–community triad and the "objective relation" of producers to the earth
is preserved. It is only with capitalist society that this rupture occurs and
we find, for the first time, "the total isolation of the mere free labourer"
(1965: 82).

Capitalism is a radical negation of all precapitalist societies, of the
basic tribal property form. It involves "the *dissolution*" (1965: 97) of the
socionatural character of all prior forms of production, and fully alienates
these individuals. It severs their relations to the land and community and
renders them propertyless and divided; it destroys the organic "*attitude*
to the land, to the earth as the property of the working individual" (81),
who now appears as a mere abstraction, the "worker." Capitalism overturns the simple priorities of production in use value and self-preservation
in order to establish the hegemony of exchange value, production, and
work for their own sake. Only in capitalist society do "the productive forces
appear as a world for themselves, quite independent of and divorced from
the [producing] individuals. . . . *Never,* in *any* earlier period, have the
productive forces taken on a form so indifferent to the intercourse of individuals *as* individuals" (Marx and Engels 1978: 190, first two emphases
mine).[11]

Capitalism shatters the inert ballast of tradition to generate modernity and its unique form of temporality, which is based on rapid and cease-
less change. All societies change and develop throughout history, but none
as rapidly and drastically as capitalist societies, where crisis and insta-
bility are structural norms and constants. In Marx and Engels' famous
words:

> The bourgeoisie cannot exist without constantly revolutionizing the instru-
> ments of production, and thereby the relations of production, and with them
> the whole relations of society. Conservation of the old modes of production
> in unaltered form, was, on the contrary, the first condition of existence for
> *all* earlier industrial classes. Constant revolutionizing of production, unin-
> terrupted disturbance of all social conditions, everlasting uncertainty and agi-
> tation distinguish the bourgeois epoch from *all* earlier ones. All fixed,
> fast-frozen relations, with their train of ancient and venerable prejudices and

opinions, are swept away, all new-formed ones become antiquated before they can ossify. All that is solid melts into air, all that is holy is profaned, and man is at last compelled to face with sober senses, his real conditions of life, and his relations with his kind. (1978: 476, my emphases)

Thus, capitalism is not simply unique or specific, as one might say of any mode of production; it is radically different from all preceding modes of production. To employ Althusser's distinction—which is implicit in Marx—capitalism is the first society where the economic level of the mode of production is both dominant and determinant, rather than simply ("ultimately") determinant.[12] This perspective of discontinuity, which sees capitalism as a break from rather than a summation of history, is an independent one and should not be subsumed under a generalized continuity model. What we find are not two conflicting models of historical development, capitalism as summation of and break from all preceding history, but rather two different perspectives on the same historical transition.[13] Marx views *one and the same transition* to capitalism from *two different analytic levels:* a highly abstract level that seeks the lines of historical continuity at the level of the productive forces, and a more concrete and historical perspective that delves beneath this abstraction to see the radical changes that this development effects at the level of economic and social relations of production. These perspectives form two inseparable, complementary strands in the larger web of Marx's theory of history.

POLITICAL INTERLUDE: MARX'S CHANGING POLITICAL VISION

Our task is to drag the old world into the light of day and give positive, true shape to the new one.
—MARX (1975a: 206)

The emancipation of the working classes must be conquered by the working classes themselves.
—MARX

Just as Marx has multiple models of history, so he has various models of politics and different conceptions of the relation between theory and practice.[14] As incisively analyzed by Adamson (1985), Marx's changing interpretations of the relationship between theory and practice were informed by changing political realities. During the period from 1843–1844, Marx believed the role of the radical theorist was to stimulate critical consciousness and clarify mystified social conditions. In his early, Hegelian outlook, the world was tending toward the realization of freedom, and

Marx thought the task of the theorist was to facilitate what already was coming into being by awakening the world to itself.[15] While Marx rejected any dogmatic or authoritarian concept of the intellectual, he saw social subjects to be passive in nature and in need of the outside assistance of theory that has already grasped the nature of the real.

This conception of the role of theory changed, Adamson claims, in the summer of 1844 as a result of the Silesian workers' struggles in Germany and the influence of Engels. Abandoning his Hegelian vision of history as tending toward its realization, Marx saw the working class (now identified as the main agent of social change) as active, critical, and capable of producing its own education and theory without the need for intellectuals. Criticism is still understood to be an active historical force, but it is no longer the only one. This shift is registered in the 1845 *Theses on Feuerbach*, where Marx recognizes that educators themselves need educating and rejects a hierarchical division between intellectual and worker. In *The German Ideology*, moreover, Marx claimed revolution, not criticism, was the driving force of history and he reduced the role of philosophy from the Hegelian task of grasping the nature of reality to the positivist task of merely summing up the results of science. Consequently, Marx privileged practice over theory and saw theory as emerging organically from the proletariat's experience in the workplace and in revolutionary practice. As the workers were gaining class consciousness they were assisted by the bourgeoisie itself, which Marx now thought to be demystifying social reality by reducing it to immediately visible social forces and relations.

As a result of political defeats for the working class in the period between 1848 and 1851, Adamson claims that Marx began to doubt the ability of the working class to gain critical consciousness on its own. He arrived in revolutionary Paris in March 1848 confident in the predictions of the recently written *Communist Manifesto,* but subsequent events greatly disappointed him. In this period, "Marx's strategic ideas shifted frequently — from 'democratic revolution,' to 'social-republican revolution,' to a Blanquist minoritarian coup d'état — and reflected his increasing frustration" (Adamson 1985: 54). Not wanting to abandon the model of an active proletariat, however, Marx came to emphasize the patience revolutionaries need for workers to train themselves adequately for the exercise of political power, insisting that it may take decades more for the working class to be prepared to seize power.[16]

But the break with the 1845 model that privileged practice over theory first appeared in *The Eighteenth Brumaire of Louis Bonaparte,* in which Marx recognized that bourgeois society was quickly remystifying what it was demystifying. Ideology proved to be a more potent force than Marx had previously thought, leading him to develop the notion of commodity fetishism in 1857. He then concluded that it would take severe economic crisis for the proletariat to become politically galvanized. Reversing ground, Marx argued that theory could not be subordinated to practice and he returned to his initial view that the working class was passive and needed the leadership of intellectuals such as Marx himself. This is the model, Adamson claims, that dominates Marx's political writings of the 1860s and 1870s. Works such as the *Grundrisse* and *Capital* depict workers increasingly subordinated to the process of production and distant from an adequate apprehension of social reality. Finally, pessimistic about any praxis-oriented tactic, Adamson claims that Marx could find possibility for social change only by positing objective laws independent of proletariat consciousness. "Nomological history is an antidote to . . . pessimism, in the obvious sense that it proffers the hope of a favorable historical resolution arising automatically out of capitalism's institutional working" (Adamson 1985: 71).

Although I disagree that Marx embraced this determinist position (see below), Adamson's account is valuable for pointing to some of twists and turns in Marx's political thinking.[17] In 1848 Germany, Marx advocated mass, armed insurrection; in the 1870s, he envisioned the possibility of a peaceful road to socialism in America, England, and Holland. At the onset of the 1848 revolutions, Marx sought to forge alliances between the proletariat and bourgeoisie on the assumption that they shared common interests in overthrowing absolutism. But the ruthless counterrevolutionary actions of the bourgeoisie led him to insist on the need for a communist-led, worker–peasant alliance that fought against the bourgeoisie for an immediately red republic. It was natural that in situations where class struggle was sharp and the proletariat strong, Marx would advocate the primacy of practice over theory. In situations where the proletariat were weak, he would abandon the tactic of armed insurrection, focus more on the need for theory and the guidance of intellectuals, and prepare for a long-range political battle.

Rather than seeing Marx's philosophical and tactical shifts as "inconsistencies," it is better to understand them as contextualist responses to complex historical situations where the dynamics of class struggle were constantly changing and required a flexible mode of response.[18] The various changes in Marx's political views and tactics show that he modified theory to adapt to changing political reality rather than trying to make the reality fit the theory. They demonstrate that historical materialism, as Marx insisted, is not a master theory or recipe for absolute knowledge, but a supple guide for studying political reality that does not predetermine its results.

Despite the various changes in Marx's political perspective, there are also important continuities. Once he became a communist, Marx always rejected the possibility that capitalism could be adequately changed through reform, and he tirelessly denounced liberal, pragmatic, and gradualist visions of change, as well as merely utopian perspectives that had no understanding of the dynamics of class struggle. On the other hand, except for a very brief flirtation with Blanquism in the spring of 1850, Marx also rejected premature attempts to force change through a revolution putsch led by a tiny band of radical cognoscenti whom he denounced as "professional conspirators" and self-appointed "alchemists of revolution." Marx was always cautious and skeptical about the actual possibilities for revolution and he argued that no elite group could gain power or force change if the working class itself was not sufficiently developed and capable of supporting a revolutionary struggle. Against hotter heads among revolutionists, Marx advocated the careful, patient building of a revolutionary movement in difficult times. Marx subsequently rejected any firm distinction between reform and revolution, and supported reform measures such as universal suffrage and free education not only for the immediate gains they would bring but more importantly for their pedagogical value in training proletariat consciousness.

Marx' political focus was always on ways of organizing the working class into a unified, ultimately international organization. The dominant tendency in his work was to advocate an independent, self-organizing proletariat, but in his later years he increasingly insisted on the need for discipline, centralization, and intellectual leadership. Although there is a significant tension between emphases on leadership and working class independence that in later historical experiences such as the Bolshevik revolution was resolved in favor of apotheosis of the party, these values are not incompatible.[19] At no time did Marx evince elitist attitudes; his advocation of intellectual leadership was designed to bring about proletarian independence, not impede it. As late as 1879, during a period Adamson characterizes as pessimistic and deterministic, Marx, in a letter to the German Social-Democratic Workers' Party, denounced the idea that "the working class is incapable of liberating itself by its own efforts" and must therefore "accept the leadership of 'educated and propertied' bourgeois, who also have 'opportunity and time' to acquaint themselves with what is good for the workers" (Marx, quoted in Miliband 1977: 120). However difficult the political situations of his time, Marx never lost sight of the possibility for human emancipation, of a future society based on human self-realization rather than exploitation and alienation. Political vision could never rely on moral outrage and critique alone, nor on predetermined "laws." Rather, it required a firm empirical analysis of shifting forces of class struggle and a practical commitment to social change on the part of the masses.

Contrary to common belief, Marx did not only focus on the proletarat; until the end of his career he worked to bring into a revolutionary alliance, artisans and peasants (whom he did not see merely as a regressive social class). Nor did he envisage socialism as occuring only in advanced industrial nations, recognizing revolutionary possibilities in less developed countries such as Russia. This also means it is false that Marx always insisted on the need for a bourgeois revolution before a socialist revolution, a tactic that has disastrous political implications if it requires building capitalism where the possibilities for a socialist revolution are directly at hand.[20]

Marx's visions of historical continuity and discontinuity have different political implications that form complementary perspectives. The various continuity models and the use of Hegel's term "appropriation" imply a politics that advances the progressive achievements of history, particularly as explosively developed by capitalism. Rather than a total negation of the past and present, Marx seeks to retain and build on the wealth of history in a process of *Aufhebung* (overcoming). In Benhabib's terms (1986), Marx's visions of historical continuity entail a politics of "fulfillment" rather than a politics of "transfiguration" that aims to create qualitatively new needs and relations. But these two politics, as Benhabib understands, are inseparable. Marx believes that the wealth of history cannot be appropriated and realized without being transfigured, since capitalism blocks the realization of the forces it creates. What distinguishes Marxian politics from mere liberalism is the understanding that the "rational kernal" of the old can be genuinely preserved only within fundamentally different historical conditions. The politics of transfiguration envisages communism as a second major rupture in history, as the "negation of the [capitalist] negation" of all past history. Politically, therefore, Marx privileged the discontinuity model; he always subordinated reforms to the goal of revolution and his varying political tactics were simply different experimental means to the end of revolution. Let us now consider what Marx takes to be the main causal forces in history and examine his alleged determinist positions.

ECONOMIC AND TECHNOLOGICAL DETERMINISM

> In the social production of their life, men enter into definite relations that are indispensible and independent of their will, relations of production which correspond to a definite stage of development of their material productive forces. The sum total of these relations of production constitutes the economic structure of society, the real basis, on which rises a legal and political superstructure, and to which correspond definite forms of so-

> cial consciousness. The mode of production of material
> life conditions the social, political and intellectual life
> process in general. It is not the consciousness of men
> that determines their being, but, on the contrary, their
> social being that determines their consciousness.
> —MARX (1978: 4)

This passage from the Preface to *A Contribution to the Critique of Political Economy* is one of the most cited in Marx's work, but it is also one of the most misunderstood. As the main source of economic and technological deterministic misreadings, it is a bad place to begin understanding Marx. From reading this and other general statements of Marx's method, many interpreters have argued that Marx adheres to the following model of history: (1) all human history is a unified and coherent whole; (2) each mode of production, from tribal to communist society, succeeds the other through an invariable law of internal change; (3) this mechanism involves a progressively evolving state of productive forces bursting through a series of social fetters that thwart and "contradict" its motion; (4) history therefore unfolds with strict necessity and inexorably advances toward communist society.

According to this model, Marxism is a dogmatic, *a priori* system that deduces historical reality from application of a universal law of social constitution and change. From passages like this, theorists have drawn various absurd conclusions, such as that Marx denies human freedom and moral responsibility (Berlin 1957; Tucker 1961), or is committed to predictions about inevitable historical outcomes (Popper 1966). Such deterministic and scientist interpretations of Marx's theory of history are caricatures of his actual analyses and political activities, although they have some textual support and Marx himself is partly responsible for these readings. In one oft-cited passage in *Capital,* for example, Marx refers to "the natural laws of capitalist production . . . working themselves out with iron necessity" (1977: 91). Similarly, Marx seems to hold a crude copy-theory of knowledge that denies human agency when he says "the ideal is nothing but the material world reflected in the mind of man, and translated into forms of thought" (102).

The problem with all reductionist and determinist readings of Marx's work is not that they lack a textual basis, but that they focus only on one aspect or passage of his work to the exclusion of others and ignore Marx's concrete political activities. In his *Theses on Feuerbach,* for example, Marx rejects a reflection theory of knowledge by praising idealism for grasping the active character of the mind. In *The Holy Family,* he and Engels explicitly repudiate the kind of Hegelian teleology found in the *Economic and Philosphic Manuscripts* and implied in other statements by Marx: "*History* does *nothing,* it posesses '*no* immense wealth,' it 'makes *no* battle.' It is *man,* real, living man who does all that, who possesses and fights; history is not, as it were, a person apart, using man as a means to achieve *its own* aims; history is *nothing but* the activity of man pursuing his aims" (Marx and Engels 1975: 110). Although Marx sees communism as the "goal of history," he is referring to a historically created potential that requires human intervention to be actualized. "Marx sharply rejects every school of thought which would subject history to some lawfulness *or* purposiveness . . . external and alien to the content of activities of concrete historical individuals" (Markus 1978: 54).

Such tensions in Marx's work can be resolved in a number of ways; the differences in interpretation of Marx, such as we find between Plekhanov and Lukács, result from the ambiguities and inconsistencies in his texts. There is therefore no "authentic" Marx, but a careful reading will avoid simple and dogmatic positions of any kind and bring out the tensions and changes in his work. The problem with relying on Marx's methodological reflections is that they often grossly oversimplify and misrepresent the complexity of his actual analyses.

Perhaps the most fundamental tension in Marx's work is the discrepancy between what he says in his theoretical summaries and what he does in his concrete studies. Here a key problem relates to the issue of whether or not Marx was a technological determinist, whether he privileged forces of production (technology, knowledge, work relations) over relations of production (social classes) as the fundamental causal dynamic of history. The crucial interpretative problems in the "Preface" concern the strength of the causal force behind the "determining" operations of the economic base, the meaning of the "correspondence" between forces and relations of production, and what elements constitute the economic base of society and its mode of production.[21] Deterministic readings of Marx in large part emerge from different answers to these questions.

On the economic determinist reading, the base comprises both the forces and relations of production, both technology and economic classes, and it "determines" the superstructure in the strong sense of a one-way, mechanical causal force that prevents any reciprocal interaction between the base and superstructure. While many of Marx's critics still hold to this reading, orthodox Marxists such as Kautsky and Plekhanov rejected it and emphasized the reciprocal interaction between base and superstructure. Yet they and many others adopt a technological determinist reading of Marx.[22] Like economic determinism, the technological determinist reading holds that the base determines the superstructure, but it adds that the most important factor determining the base itself is technology. In other words, a more fundamental rung is added to the causal hierarchy of society: the growth of technology determines the nature of economic activity and relations, which in turn determine the superstructure of social life.[23]

On the technological determinist reading, Marx holds that the ultimate driving force in history is technological development and that class relations are to be explained according to their function in promoting or retarding this growth. This thesis need not argue for a one-way causal determination of forces over relations of production; it need only maintain that the productive forces ultimately determine the relations of production, that relations of production are ultimately to be explained by the development of the forces of production.[24] Thus, although "analytic Marxists" Cohen (1978) and Shaw (1978) criticize a nondialectical version of technological determinism that recognizes only one-way causality between forces and relations of production, and claim that Marx saw reciprocal influence on both sides, they remain technological determinists insofar as they functionally subordinate the relations to the forces of production and assert that the main role of social relations is to develop technology.[25] Cohen attempts to support his "primacy [of the productive forces] thesis" with the "developmental thesis" that human beings, fundamentally rational in nature and living in constant conditions of scarcity, seek to acquire ever greater control over nature and therefore strive constantly to develop the forces of production. The relations of production that best develop the forces of production become the ruling social classes and survive as long as they serve the role of advancing technological growth.

For all their analytic sophistication, the major flaw of Cohen and Shaw's interpretations is their failure to emphasize the distinctly political character of Marx's historical explanations and the complex political–economic dialectic he develops — a problem that stems from their false separation of productive forces and work relations (see below). They transform a revolutionary political vision intended for the working class into an academic theory of history designed for historians. It is precisely this functionalist subordination of the relations to the forces of production that prompts other theorists to decry determinism and to insist on the primacy of the relations of production. As early as 1933, theorists such as Sidney Hook had begun to argue against the technological determinist claims made by Kautsky and Plekhanov and to champion the primacy of the relations of production. This argument was most ambitiously developed by Hindess and Hirst (1975) who reject the primacy of the productive forces, however qualified or reciprocal in nature, as a "technicism," as a functionalist subordination of consciousness, politics, and class struggle to technology. For Hindess and Hirst, the primacy of the forces of production thesis "renders inexplicable any operation of the relations of production which has the effect of not [merely] distributing the conditions of production so as to reproduce the forces" (1977: 54).

Hindess and Hirst claim that for Marx, "it is the relations of production which are the crucial element in any concept of the economic level"

(1975: 230). Unlike Cohen and Shaw, they privilege class struggle as the fundamental motor of history: "It is the forms of class struggle and their outcomes which determine the specific forms of the forces of production" (247). To support their reading, they point to quotes ignored by Cohen and Shaw where Marx defines class relations as "the specific economic form in which unpaid surplus-labor is pumped out of the direct producers," which suggests that the relations of production determine the forces of production.

The opposing claims of these theorists each provide only a partially correct and one-sided reading of Marx. The technological determinist reading rightly emphasizes that Marx grants fundamental importance to the role of technology in human life. For Marx, "Technology discloses man's mode of dealing with nature, the process of production by which he sustains his life, and thereby also lays bare the mode of formation of his social relations, and of the mental conceptions that flow from them" (quoted in Shaw 1978: 53). Marx does indeed claim that technology and the productive forces are key to explaining social change: "In acquiring new forces of production men change their mode of production; and in changing their mode of production, in changing the way of earning their living, they change all their social relations. The handmill gives you society with the feudal lord; the steam-mill, society with the industrial capitalist" (1963: 109). He also argues elsewhere that "The (economic) relations and consequently the social, moral, and political state of nations changes with the *change* in the material powers of production" (1972: 430). These emphases are conveniently glossed over in Hindess and Hirst's interpretation of Marx and they wrongly deny the forces of production any significant determining power in history.[26] But they correctly point to counteremphases on the role of class struggle in history as an independent causal force that cannot be adequately captured by technological determinism. Neither position grasps the tensions and ambiguities in Marx's analyses. The one-sidedness of the readings of Cohen and Shaw and Hindess and Hirst need to be rejected in favor of a more nuanced, contextualist approach.

THE MODE OF PRODUCTION INTERPRETATION

In his book *Analyzing Marx* (1984), Richard Miller criticizes both economic and technological determinist readings of Marx, while also trying to preserve Marx's unique emphasis on the importance of economic relations and technology in structuring society. Miller develops forceful arguments against every major aspect of the technological determinist interpretation of Marx: "Economic structures do not endure because they provide maximum productivity. Productive forces do not develop autonomously. Change in productive forces, in the narrowly technological sense that excludes work relations, is not the basic sources of change in society at large" (1984: 188).

Arguing that Marx grants causal priority in an *a priori* way to neither forces nor relations of production, Miller develops a "mode of production" thesis which holds that, for Marx,

> basic, internal economic change arises (whenever it does, in fact, take place) on account of a self-transforming tendency of the mode of production *as a whole,* that is, the relations of production, the forms of cooperation [work relations] and the technology through which material goods are produced. . . . Change may be based on developments in the forms of cooperation or in technology, giving access to enhanced productive power to an initially subordinate group, and motivating their resistance to old relations of production because the latter come to inhibit the further development of that new productive power (1984: 172, my emphasis).

Like technological determinists, Miller claims that Marx always rooted social change within the dynamics of a given mode of production, but Miller argues for a broader and nonreductionist understanding of the causal forces comprising a mode of production. This argument makes the important claim that elements within a mode of production are inseparable and so it is impossible to isolate forces or relations as primacy. Miller makes two key moves in granting a broader context of causal factors in Marx's work. First, he argues that Marx included work relations, or "modes of cooperation," among forces of production, thereby denying causal priority to technological factors as in any way autonomous from social relations. This crucial move was blocked by Cohen and Shaw with a nondialectical logic that forces a categorical separation between social and material logics that is entirely foreign to Marx's method. If we undo this dichotomy to claim, with Marx himself, that work relations are integral aspects of the forces of production, then technological determinism becomes untenable.[27]

Second, Miller claims that Marx believed social change frequently came about due to internal contradictions within a given economic structure, independent of its relation with forces of production. On Miller's interpretation, Marx holds that social change can be stimulated as much by economic relations as by technological development; economic structures can select productive forces as much as productive forces can select economic structures. Miller rejects Cohen and Shaw's functionalist subordination of relations to forces of production as well as Hindess and Hirst's voluntarism to argue in favor of a "zig-zag dialectic" between forces and relations, "with priority on neither side" (1984: 190). Miller therefore adopts a symmetrical thesis is as much to be explained as due to structure

and the processes to which they give rise as the nature of changes in structures is due to forces" (213). Forces and relations of production, in other
words, are too interdependent to raise any causal priority claim.

Miller also rejects the schizophrenic reading that Marx is a technological determinist in his general statements but not in his concrete analyses; the possibility for symmetrical causation "is left open by Marx's
general theory and realized in his specific explanations" (1984: 212).
Marx's general statement that relations correspond to forces is only "a
synopsis of a specific scenario for change in structure" and not "an assessment of the balance of ultimate causal influences" (213). Rather than sub-
scribing to a monolithic model privileging forces or relations of production,
"Marx treats primacy as relative to the questions being asked" (207). In
my own terms, Marx is a contextualist who privileges different causal factors in different contexts.

If we open the pages of *Capital,* it is hard to resist the conclusion
that in his most important and definitive work, Marx privileges relations
over forces of production. In a sustained analysis (1977: 455–491), he
describes the shift from feudalism to capitalism as a shift from a mode
of production based on handicrafts to one initially based on manufacturing. Capitalism develops by appropriating and extending the cooperative
form of labor employed in handicrafts within a new context of manufacturing whose aim is the maximization of surplus value. The "starting point"
of capitalism involves assembling in one place and one labor process a
number of workers under the control of a capitalist. Formerly independent and specialized craftsworkers engaged in a variety of tasks now oc-
cupy positions within a more complex division of labor that is indifferent
to needs and creative abilities, appropriating human beings as sheer labor
power. In the transition from feudal handicrafts to capitalist manufacturing, before the era of large-scale industry, there is no basic change in the
technical basis of production since "handicraft skill is the foundation of
manufacturing" (489). Rather, the change leading to a new mode of
production occurs at the level of work and ownership relations through
a political struggle between classes. The productive forces of feudal society are put to new use in a different social context. Newly established
capitalist work relations and production relations, in turn, condition subsequent technological developments in the form of machine production
and large-scale industry.

If this change is interpreted as a change in productive forces, it has
to be understood in the broad sense that includes work relations. It is clear,
however, that Marx believes that capitalism does not arise through a technological revolution, but rather through "the revolution in the relations
of production" (1977: 879). In fact, for Marx, it is the relations of production that are most crucial in explaining the transition to capitalism. The

incredible unleashing and development of the productive forces characteristic of capitalism can only occur after a revolution in relations of production. Before the technological basis of industrial capitalism could be developed, the proletariat first had to be formed as a class. The mass of newly created proletarians thrown onto the labor market resulted from the dissolution of bands of feudal retainers and the forced expropriation of peasants from the land. The motivation behind this was economic: through a rapid expansion in wool manufacturing and a rise in the price of wool, the new nobility found it most profitiable to drive the peasantry off the land in order to raise sheep. The desire here was to acquire money, not to develop technology (878–879).

Marx says that "the revolution in property relations on the land were accompanied [n.b., not determined] by improved methods of cultivation, greater co-operation, a higher concentration of the means of production and so on" (1977: 908). Newly emerging bourgeois property relations also led to the destruction of subsidiary trades in the countryside and to the creation of a home market (910–911). Hence, Marx speaks of "the productive forces resulting from co-operation and the division of labour" (508). He states that "the expansion of industries carried on by means of machinery and the invasion of fresh branches of production by machinery were dependent upon the growth of a class of workers who, owing to the semi-artistic nature of their employment, could increase their numbers only gradually, and not by leaps and bounds" (504).

Of course, as Hindess and Hirst fail to see, the productive forces have their own influence and effect the nature of work and ownership relations. In Chapter 15 of *Capital,* Marx shows how the machinery employed in large-scale industry had great consequences on further developments in technology and on the social mode of production as a whole.[28] It forced a mechanization of all aspects of production, transforming workshops, domestic industry, and agriculture. Initially machinery increased the demand for workers, intensively exploiting women, children, and all forms of unskilled labor. Sunsequently, however, it displaced manual labor, allowed greater capitalist domination over the working class, and heightened class struggle (1977: 590ff.). The impact of large-scale industry was most pronounced in agriculture, where machines displaced a multitude of workers, overturned the economic foundation of the old familial system, and substituted the wage-laborer for the peasant (636–639). Yet the development of machinery cannot be understood apart from a legal and political context. Marx analyzes how the implementation of the Factory Acts, beginning in 1835, transformed the character of technical, work, and capital composition (599ff.).

Thus, we find a dialectic of influence between forces and relations of production, base and superstructure, where the relations of production are most crucial in the transition to capitalist and the forces of production become crucial in subsequent developments. *Capital* is an excellent text for showing how Marx examines historical change from a number of perspectives. In his analysis of the accumulation of capital Marx concentrates on the proletarianization of the agricultural population that removed the main fetters on the accumulation of capital. Yet among the number of other significant factors for capital accumulation, Marx lists the "discovery of gold and silver in America, the extirpation, enslavement and entombment in mines of the indigenous population of that continent, the beginnings of the conquest and plunder of India, and the conversion of Africa into a preserve for the commercial hunting of blackskins" (1977: 915). Commerical wars, conflicts among nations, methods of brute force and colonization, but *not* technological development, are described as the key factors in the transition to capitalism. Nor is there any textual evidence that Marx intended all of these factors to be "ultimately" determined by the development of technology.

While Marx always discusses social change in terms of contradictions within a given mode of production, he rarely analyzes these in terms of a contradiction between forces and relations of production as he and Engels do, for example, in *The German Ideology*. More often, Marx sees contradictions that arise within the economic structure itself, apart from any antagonistic relation to the productive forces. In the *Grundrisse,* a text that makes constant rhetorical reference to the primacy of the productive forces (1965: 96, 97, 105), Marx shows how relations of production may be self-transforming. As the population of early Roman society expanded, for example, new households were given farms obtained through colonization. The expansion process, however, increased the power of the rich farmers who controlled the army and administration of public resources. These farmers used their increased power over land, slaves, and the political apparatus to become a new ruling class of large-scale absentee owners who exploited and dispossessed other farmers (92–93). Changes in the nature of productive labor, the shift from agriculture to manufacturing, "arises from intercourse with strangers, from slaves, the desire to exchange the surplus product, etc." (94) and these changes dissolve the mode of production.

In one passage, Marx describes war as the basic source of change; war is "the great all-embracing task, the great communal labour, and it is required either for the occupation of the objective conditions for living existence or for the protection and perpetuation of such occupation" (1965: 71). The ancient community "is therefore in the first instance organised on military lines" (71–72). The tendency toward war in societies like ancient Greece and Rome, or the communities of Jews "drives [them] beyond these limits" of simple reproduction (92). Marx shows how (mainly military) interaction with other communities can affect the basic nature of a given society and undermine its reproduction (71, 72, 89).[29]

In this and other accounts, Marx explains change in terms of population increase, war and colonization, class struggle, and commercial activity, rather than technological development and a contradiction between forces and relations of production. The primacy of the productive forces thesis makes its appearance only in passages that sum up Marx's general views and never in the context of concrete analysis. In fact, this thesis conflicts with Marx's concrete analyses. (Significantly, the forces/relations of production dialectic is nowhere mentioned in the thousand pages of *Capital*.) Where Marx does employ the forces/relations schema, he typically means forces in the broad sense that includes work relations, and he points to other determining factors in social change, sometimes privileging relations of production. Thus, the expansion of productive powers "is not primarily based on an autonomous drive toward technological progress" and enhanced productive power "usually results from changed forms of cooperation, not new technology" (Miller 1984: 173). Even when Marx limited himself to a rather narrow consideration of productive forces alone, "productive enhancement still lacks the particular primacy and the technological character assigned to it by technological determinism" (173).

According to Miller, technological determinism is wrong on other crucial counts. Frequently, changes in technology occur not to improve efficiency, but rather to develop wealth. In his analysis of ancient and feudal society, Marx does not suggest that slavery and feudal economic forms survive because they are the most productive economic structures at the time, but because of the relative strengths and weaknesses of different classes. In the case of feudalism, for example, "so far as productivity is concerned, a structure dominated by peasants and artisans would have been at least as effective as the feudal economic structure. But sustained unity and collective discipline over large geographic areas would have been required to break the bonds that the overlords forged from the surplus they controlled. The social relations of peasants, by focusing loyalties on the family and the village, guaranteed that the needed class solidarity would not arise" (Miller 1984: 209).

Nor is the technological determinist explanation of social stability correct. According to this thesis, an economic structure remains stable so long as it continues to promote growth of the productive forces. In his analysis of slavery and feudalism, however, Marx describes both as structures maintained by the power of an economically dominant class in the face of alternatives at least as productive (Miller 1984: 191). Feudalism and slavery persist because farmers and artisans lack the economic or political means to overturn the aristocratic ruling class.

Moreover, if technological determinism is true, how do we account for societies that seem consciously to reject technological advance or exist for long periods of time without substantial technological progress? In his numerous analyses of various non-European societies (which he lumped together under the concept of "Asiatic mode of production"), Marx emphasizes the static character of their productive forces. Beneath the constant change of political empires, the mode of production remained unaltered and changed only under the influence of colonization from dynamic Western countries. These analyses suggest that the primacy of the productive forces, when valid at all, applies for Marx only to Western countries and is not a universal principle applicable to all human societies—a key point on which Marx insisted (see below). Nowhere in his analyses of precaptialist societies does Marx apply the forces/relations couplet to understand the mechanisms of historical change. Rather, in the *Grundrisse,* Marx argues that ancient and feudal societies are variations on the basic tribal form of property and do not "dialectically" succeed one another. Far from a universal law of social transformation, Marx only applies this scheme to the transition from feudalism to capitalism. This suggests that Cohen's "developmental thesis" is wrong, or seriously restricted, insofar as many societies exist where people do not consciously seek technological progress and may even suppress it in order to preserve tradition.[30]

Given the complexity of Marx's writings, his own summary statements and the innumerable parrotings they have given rise to are grotesque simplifications and parodies of his actual method. These statements suggest a universal, *a priori,* deductive method that Marx frequently railed against and never employed. They are false and misleading because they isolate and emphasize one factor, technological innovation, out of a broad context of many relevant factors that are nonreducible to technology and are frequently privileged over it. Marx never appealed specifically to economic or technological factors of change, but rather to a broad complex of forces including political, legal, and ideological elements.[31]

The discrepency between Marx's general statements and his concrete analyses raises the question of why Marx embraces a technological determinism in his abstract statements that he abandons in practice. If, as Miller claims, Marx includes work relations within the productive forces, then even Marx's summary statements have to be read in a broad and non-technological determinist way and the problem dissolves itself. But this may not fully explain Marx's rhetorical emphasis on technology over social relations. Miller therefore suggests that Marx's emphasis on the productive forces, especially those created by modern capitalist society, was influenced by his polemics with anarchists who condemned industrial technology (1984: 219–220). Miller claims that in response to the anarchists Marx felt compelled to argue for the progressive effects of technological development and to insist that human needs could only be met through advanced technology. Miller speculates that given his broad definition of productive forces, Marx "may well have hoped that explanations that seemed to depart from the narrower mode of production theory could be reconciled with it, on further analysis" (219–220).

Perhaps more plausibly, Larrain (1986: 88) suggests that Marx's summary privileging of technology is the result of his uncritical appropriation of positivist scientism and the Enlightenment dogma that human progress is won through science and technology. On this hypothesis, Marx felt a need to legitimate his work through scientific credentials and the progressivist strain of his own thought led him to overemphasize the productive forces as the source of change. Possibly, the ideological pull of positivist and Enlightenment concepts was strong enough to lead Marx to contradict his concrete analyses. Or, finally, it is possible that Marx, as Sorel would do later, invented a myth of immanent social change in order to foster hope among the working class. But, as mentioned above, Adamson (1985: 70–71) suggests that Marx invented a teleological myth as an antidote to his own pessimism, that as social reality become increasingly mystified by bourgeois ideology, Marx turned to forces of history that guaranteed revolution independent of the consciousness of the working class.[32] I find this an implausible claim because it requires that Marx completely abandon the acute sense of contingency that informs his concrete analyses.

If Marx's own motivations for adopting scientistic rhetoric are ultimately uncertain, it is much easier to understand why technological determinism has been embraced by communist governments, for it diverts attention way from democratization of social relations toward the development of technology under bureaucratic command and justifies the use of domination and force to achieve "progress" (see Reinfelder 1980). On the narrow sense, technological determinism denies the need and efficacy of political struggle, since the outcome of history is preordained and guaranteed. The broader interpretation of Cohen and Shaw may not in theory deny the need of political struggle, but the implications of their version of technological determinism suggest it in practice. As an example of how Marx himself can overstate his case, consider his claim that "No social order ever perishes before all the productive forces for which there is room in it have developed" (1978: 5). This has the troubling political implication that social change must wait until such a point is reached. Aside from the difficulty of knowing exactly when this time arrives, a system like twentieth-century capitalism seems capable of developing its productive forces indefinitely and along highly destructive paths, while containing all progressive potential for change. Except for his early metaphysical determinism and his later nomological rhetoric, the dominant tendency in Marx himself is to insist that conscious, collective action is necessary for social transformation and that this action must be the product of a self-determining proletariat.

RATIONAL ABSTRACTION AS METHODOLOGY

> Learning how to abstract is the first step in learning how to think.
> — MARX

> Viewed apart from real history, these abstractions have in themselves no value whatsoever.
> — MARX AND ENGELS (1978: 155)

The fundamental tension in Marx's use of different historical models does not involve incompatible continuity and discontinuity perspectives, but rather ambivalent attitudes toward the applicability of his materialist categories to precapitalist and non-Western forms of production. On the one hand, Marx feels that history is continuous enough to legitimate extending an analysis that took shape in modern capitalist society to all of history. Marx's implicit argument is this: (1) in all societies, human beings have to produce to survive; (2) production is the ultimately determining activity of any society; therefore (3) the materialist theory of production is applicable to any and all societies.[33]

Yet, on the other hand, Marx is acutely aware of the specificity of different forms of production and believes that there are serious qualifications to be placed on the applicability of the materialist theory of history to precapitalist and non-Western social forms. Thus, there is tension between the diachronic and synchronic perspectives in Marx's work, between the attempts to shed some light on the dynamics of human history in general and the belief that precapitalist and non-Western societies are radically different from capitalist society and Western societies in general. The problem is: can a continuous (diachronic) model of history be applied legitimately throughout discontinuous historical formations? Can one situate an analysis of the originality of capitalism and Western society within a larger historical narrative or does this uniqueness disrupt any attempt to comprehend "the whole of history"? Can all human history be understood adequately from the standpoint of material production?

To address this problem, I begin with Marx's metatheoretical reflections on the nature and limitations of his historical method as pursued in the dense opening sections of the *Grundrisse*. Here, Marx is preoccupied with a representation of history that would grasp both the specificity of each mode of production and the general features each shares in common within one historical narrative. Marx wants to employ production as the basic category to speak of *any and all* social formations. As such, "production" is an abstraction, but not of the same order as employed by political economists. In his critique of political economy (1978: 222ff.), Marx condemns the use of *ahistorical* abstractions which are applied indiscriminantly and without regard for concrete historical differences—the bourgeois search for "general preconditions of all production" (225), which does nothing but produce "flat tautologies" and reductionist formulations. Political economists such as Mill mistakenly read the bourgeois articulation of production throughout all history, transforming precapitalist societies into a mirror image of capitalism.[34]

As the example of political economy shows, it is "possible to confound or to extinguish all historic differences under *general human* laws" (1978: 225). For Marx, abstractions are not bad or wrong, rather they are a necessary analytic device; they allow one to draw comparisons between social epochs and to make helpful generalizations across and within different social formations. It is only ahistorical and overgeneralizing uses of abstraction that Marx attacks. The issue then is a methodological problem of how to make one's abstractions valid, or "rational," such that two negative results are avoided: lapsing into tautology and obscuring historical differences. In Marx's statement of the issue:

> Whenever we speak of production, then, what is meant is always production at a definite stage of social development — production by social individuals. It might seem, therefore, that in order to talk about production at all we must either pursue the process of historic development through its different phases, or declare beforehand that we are dealing with a specific historic epoch such as, e.g., modern bourgeois production, which is indeed our particular theme. However, all epochs of production have certain common traits, common characteristics. *Production in general* is an abstraction, but a rational abstraction in so far as it really brings out and fixes the common element and saves us repetition. Still, this *general* category, this common element sifted out by comparison, is itself segmented many times and split into different determinations. Some determinatins belong to all epochs, others only to a few. [Some] determinations will be shared by the most modern epoch and the most ancient. No production will be thinkable without them; however, even though the most developed languages have laws and characteristics in common with the least developed, nevertheless, just those things which determine their development, i.e., the elements which are not general and common, must be separated out from the determinations valid for production as such, so that in their unity—which arises already from the identity of the subject, humanity, and of the object, nature—their essential difference is not forgotten (1978: 223–227).

We see that however different modes of production are, they retain essential elements in common that can and must be grasped in order to produce a theory of production as a general theory of history and to understand fully the nature of any one mode of production. Diachronically, while specific social modes of relating to nature differ, all societies are organized around production and class dynamics. Synchronically, while Marx's analytic focus is on the most developed capitalist mode of production of his time, that of modern England, he believes he can legitimately abstract from that context to speak of the "capitalist mode of production" in general.

Abstractions are rational to the extent that they incorporate change, interaction, and the concrete social relations from which they derive. In a key section of the *Grundrisse* ("The Method of Political Economy," 1978: pp. 236–244) we see Marx reducing abstractions to ever greater concreteness. He resolves, for instance, the standard sociological abstraction "population" into classes, which in turn is resolved into an even more concrete analysis based on the constitutive elements of capital and wage labor. But in the dialectic of the concrete and the abstract, all these categories require recontextualization within the whole to which they belong—which, in this case, is the synchronic category of the "capitalist mode of production." Similarly, each mode of production is itself related to its larger whole, the process of history itself.

An abstraction such as "production"—*provided that* "essential difference is not forgotten," provided that it returns to the concrete—is a meaningful and helpful category. Without some way to register not only the differences between modes of production, but also their essential similarities, we would "fall back," as Fredric Jameson says, "into a [nominalist or postmodern] view of present history as sheer heterogeneity, random difference, a coexistence of a host of distinct forces whose effectivity is undecideable" (1991: 6). Marx's use of rational abstraction allows him to avoid both an abstract universalism that seeks ahistorical laws of social movement and obscures complex differences, as well as a nominalism that claims there are only specific events and irreducible particulars of history and that denies the validity of any generalization or cross-historical comparison. For Marx, "production" is a needed and valuable abstract category, but there is "no production in general" (1978: 234), that is, no form of production exists that is not historically mediated and constituted by specific social relations of production. Hence, Marx's definition of production states: "*All* production is appropriation of nature on the part of an individual within and through *a specific form of society*" (226, my emphasis).

If the abstract bears within it the determinations of the concrete, then the most abstract process, the capitalist mode of production, bears within it a host of historical forces. In the *Grundrisse,* Marx argues that the continuous development of the productive forces throughout history makes possible a retrospective comprehension of the entire historical process from the standpoint of capitalist society:

> Bourgeois society is the most developed and the most complex historic organization of production. The categories which express its relations, the comprehension of its structure, thereby also allow insights into the structure and the relations of production of all the vanished social formations out of whose ruins and elements it built itself up, whose partly still unconquered remnants are carried along with it, whose mere nuances have developed explicit significance within it, etc. Human anatomy contains a key to the anatomy of the ape. The intimations of higher development among the subordinate animal species, however, can be understood only after the highest development is already known. (1978: 241)

On the assumption, therefore, that capitalist society is the "most developed and the most complex historic organization" of the productive activities that structure all societies, an understanding of capitalism provides the key to understanding all historical societies. Earlier societies express *in incubo* what is fully clear only in the most advanced societies. Unlike the approach that studies events in the order in which they occur, Marx's retrospective method moves from result to precondition. It attempts to deduce what was required for social phenomena to appear and function as they did, but without assuming events had to unfold in a predetermined way or that societies have to pass through a circumscribed path of development (Ollman 1993). This later model of historical explanation also breaks with the forward-looking models in his 1844–1845 period of an unfolding human essence or evolution of modes of production. With Hegel, Marx believes that history can only be understood retrospectively, only after its most essential dynamics have unfolded and matured, although he does not follow Hegel in thinking that science arrives too late to change the world. If one accepts Marx's premise that there is a strong continuity throughout history in terms of evolving productive forces, then it seems plausible to conclude (1) that this dynamic can only be fully understood at the end (or maturation) of its development, and (2) that capitalist society therefore provides "a key" for the comprehension of all history. In this later retrospective model, Marx develops the hermeneutical insights that all understanding is dependent upon one's historical and theoretical standpoint. In Adamson's words (1985: 26), "There is no starting point for gaining knowledge about genesis and development other than what currently exists."

Yet the danger of such an approach is that one might read capitalist social relations throughout all of history and thereby falsify the specificity of precapitalist societies. Marx is highly sensitive to this problem and thinks he avoids it through qualifications about the applicability of his method to precapitalist societies. His qualifications concerning his use of abstractions and his warnings against their dangers and misuse is dramatically evident in a key correspondence (1975b) regarding the application of historical materialism to non-Western countries.[35] Railing against a critic who misinterpreted his views concerning the question of what path of development Russia should pursue, Marx takes pains to emphasize Russia as a unique social and historical formation that cannot fit unqualifiably into the context of his theory. Referring to his chapter on primitive accumulation in *Capital,* Marx claims that his intention is only to chart the emergence in Western Europe of the evolution of capitalism feudal society. Thus, he says, the critic wrongly "insists on transforming my historical sketch of the genesis of capitalism in Western Europe into an historic-philosophic theory of the general path of development prescribed by fate to all nations, whatever the historical circumstances in which they find themselves, in order that they may ultimately arrive at the economic system which ensures, together with the greatest expansion of the productive powers of social labour, the most complete development of man" (1975b: 293–294). Marx then offers a comparison between subjugation of labor and "big money capital" in Roman and modern times and concludes: "Thus events strikingly analogous but taking place in different historical surroundings led to totally different results. By studying each of these forms of evolution separately and then comparing them one can easily find the clue to this phenomenon, but one will never arrive there by using as one's master key a general historico-philosophical theory, the supreme virtue of which consists in being supra-historical" (294).

Marx places similar qualifications on his method in the third section of the introduction to the *Grundrisse.* Regarding exchange, for instance, he says it is only of marginal importance in early Peruvian and Slavian societies and appears in significant form outside the boundaries of simple communities. Money exists in the most advanced part of the ancient world, but does not become a major consituting force of society until the birth of modern capitalism. "This very simple category [money], then, makes a historic appearance in its full intensity only in the most developed conditions of society. By no means does it wade its way through all economic relations" (1978: 239).

Similarly, the concept of labor is "immeasureably old," but it is also "as modern a category as are the relations which create this simple abstraction" (1978: 239–240). Labor

> has here become the means of creating wealth in general, and has ceased to be organically linked with particular individuals in any specific form. Such a state of affairs is at its most developed in the most modern form of existence of bourgeois society — in the United States. Here, then, for the first time,

the point of departure of modern economics, namely the abstraction of the category "labour," "labour as such," labour pure and simple, becomes true in practice. The simplest abstraction,then, which modern economics places at the head of its discussions, and which expresses an immeasurably ancient relation valid in all forms of society, nevertheless achieves practical truth as an abstraction only as a category of the most modern society. (240–241)

The example of labor, Marx argues, shows how even the most abstract categories are a historical product and possess their full validity only within historical relations. Finally, summarizing, Marx says: "Although it is true, therefore, that the categories of bourgeois economics possess a truth for all other forms of society, this is to be taken only with a grain of salt. They can contain them in a developed, or stunted, or caricatured form etc., but always with an essential difference" (1978: 242).

PRECAPITALISM AND THE LIMITS OF HISTORICAL MATERIALISM

We see that Marx struggles against a Eurocentric, universal history that reduces all historical cultures and dynamics to that of the modern West. Against critics like Leff, Marx does not unqualifiably treat his own categories "as timeless, of universal application to all social phenomena" (1969: xii). While in the most general and abstract sense, all societies are organized around production, Marx insists that the forms such production take are very different and that the categories applied to modern bourgeois society cannot be applied unqualifiably to precapitalist societies.

Yet, there are profound ahistorical, Eurocentric, and totalizing dimensions to Marx's analyses. For many critics, Marx's qualifications represent the logical self-destruction of his theory and reveal an inherent reductionist drive to totalize beyond and despite perceived limitations on its historical range. Initiating his categorical rejection of Marxism, Baudrillard asks, "What does it mean to say 'valid for all epochs' but 'fully applicable only for some'?" (1975: 84). Similarly, Balbus asks: "How can the category [of production] be both historically specific and transhistorical?" (1982: 16) and he concludes, "Marx clearly wants to have it both ways: the concept of a mode of production both is and is not a transhistorical category" (31). How is it possible, in other words, that Marx's *historically specific* categories provide the means to grasp the fundamental dynamics of *all* societies? And does this mean that historical materialism *itself* is only "fully valid" in capitalist society and only *partially* valid in all preceeding epochs? What sense does it make to say that such a theory is both a general theory of history and of partial applicability to all but a small fraction of that history?

Contra Balbus and Baudrillard, I see no *logical* difficulties in the way Marx presents his argument. On a nondialectical logic, something is either valid or invalid and there are no mediating degrees. Yet Marx's analysis applies to a changing *history,* and not to static "facts" to which a "truth" does or does not "correspond." In this context it *does* make logical sense to speak of "degrees" of validity. To the extent that (1) the categories of historical materialism can and do apply to precapitalist societies, and (2) the material practices and relations they illuminate are not as historically developed as they are in capitalist society, then (3) these categories have less validity in more undeveloped conditions than they do in developed conditions. If we accept premises (1) and (2), then the conclusion follows and Marxism will have at least some validity in an analysis of precapitalist societies.

Marx's "inconsistencies" or "contradictions," his qualifying distinctions between different *forms* of labor, exchange, production, and so on, provide the conceptual and historical basis of his critique of political economy. They allow him to demystify the ideology of political economy that universalizes throughout history categories that apply only to capitalist society, where "labour in reality has here become the means of creating wealth in general and has ceased to be organically linked with particular individuals in any form" (Marx 1978: 240–241). It is this "indifference toward particular kinds of labour" (241) that Marx so forcefully exposes, criticizes, and negates in his own work. It is a virtue of Marx's approach that he historicizes not only the categories of political economy, but those of his own method.

When Marx states, therefore, that the categories of historical materialism are valid for all epochs, but only "fully valid" for some, he is speaking the dialectical language of continuity/discontinuity where the "full validity" of the categories of exchange, labor, and production is realized because capitalist society has abstracted production from a socionatural context and has rid itself of all elements that would hinder the reified goals of exchange value and production for private profit. Consequently, "production" is an abstraction that applies to every social epoch, but only through a "rational" analysis that identifies the specific features of each mode of production. The thrust of Marx's qualifying remarks, therefore, do not logically undermine historical materialism as a methodology, they only oppose dogmatic, *a priori* applications of the theory in abstraction from specific historical contexts.

The problem that arises with Marx's theory is not that his qualifying remarks ensnare him in irresolvable logical antinomies, but that (1) they may be so serious and extensive as to undermine the explanatory power of historical materialism as a general theory of history, as opposed to a theory that applies only or mainly to modern capitalist society, and that

(2) "production" is nevertheless coded as the fundamental logic of history. Recent critical work suggests that the "partial validity" of historical materialism vis-à-vis precapitalist societies may be even more partial than Marx thought. Sahlins (1972) provides intriguing evidence that the notion of transhistorical scarcity is a myth and that many early cultures spent the bulk of their time in ritual, festival, and play. Sahlins also claims (1976) that culture and kinship relations are far more important in these societies than Marx allowed. Both Sahlins and Baudrillard argue that Marx imposes a utilitarian means–end logic on precapitalist societies in which exchange is primarily symbolic in character (e.g., the potlatch or the gift exchange as described by Marcel Mauss [1967]). Baudrillard (1975) effectively shows that Marx takes use value to be an unproblematic given, relating to innate human needs, when it fact it is a historical construction of societies that have rationalized both subjects and objects.

Giddens argues that materialist categories do not have the structural primacy Marx granted them and he draws a distinction between "class-divided societies" and "class societies." The former category refers to precapitalist societies where classes indeed exist, but "class analysis does not serve as a basis for identifying the basic structural principle of organisation of that society" (Giddens 1981: 108). "Class society," in contrast, refers to capitalist society where classes are of fundamental importance in the structuring of society. Habermas argues that Marx conflates material production with symbolic interaction and subsequently misses the fundamental importance of language, commmunication, and moral development as determinants of historical change (see Chapter 3). Perry Anderson (1979) claims that the forces of production in Asiatic societies were more developed and dynamic than Marx allowed and that Marx's remarks about "peoples with history" suggest a Eurocentric ideology. Bookchin (1991) convincingly argues that domination and hierarchy ultimately stem from institutionalized differences of age and sex rather than surplus production and economic classes. Bookchin also claims that Marx has internalized the Western view of nature as stingy inert matter and reproduces the myth of scarcity that requires an antiecological outlook and justifies domination as necessary for social development.

All of these critiques point to the same underlying problem: Marx has falsely universalized categories specific to modern society. Despite his seemingly cautious use of rational abstractions, Marx's theory has reductive and bourgeois dimensions. While Marx analyzes the specificity of different forms of labor and production, he reduces all forms of human interaction and practice to the model of work. Though he is right that all human societies produce the means of their subsistence, he wrongly foists an economistic logic on precapitalist social forms by subsuming a diversity of cultural practices and logics under the concept "mode of production" which *a priori* assigns a primacy to economic values and relationships. His privileging of production over other forms of action and interaction is arbitrary. If, as Lukács argues (1971: 55, 57), precapitalist societies are an organic whole where "economic elements are *inextricably* joined to political and religous factors" and "economic and legal categories are objectively and *substantively so interwoven as to be inseparable*" (Lukács' emphasis) then it is impossible to justify the claim that material production is primary, "the first historical act" (Marx and Engels 1978: 156), and that the economic is "ultimately" or in "the last instance" the most decisive factor in history. Echoing Lukács' point, Seidman states that "economic laboring practices always are embedded in a sociocultural and political context that involves normative and legal regulation and structures of institutional and political authority as well as gendered identities and relations" (1992: 57). Hence, to privilege economic activity as the "first premise of all human history," as Marx and Engels do, is to succumb to ethnocentric and androcentric prejudices.

If the universal history described by historical materialism is more fragmented and localized than Marx thought, then his abstractions are in fact not "rational." His attempts at a retrospective reading of the past from the standpoint of present dynamics projects a false line of continuity throughout history, organized around the primacy of production, despite his awareness of the historical discontinuities created by capitalism. Marx appears to be in a double bind: if he is too totalizing in his materialism, he becomes, like the political economists he criticizes, reductive and ahistorical; if, on the other hand, he burdens his theory with substantive qualifications about its limited applicability in precapitalist societies, he undermines its explanatory power as an alleged general theory of history. As it stands, Marx has not escaped the "mirror of production" (Baudrillard) that sees the past too much merely as a paler image of present dynamics. Historical materialism may be a, but not *the,* perspective for understanding past cultures.

VISIONS OF RECONCILIATION

Bifurcation is the origin of the need for philosophy.
— HEGEL

Throughout this chapter I have tried to show that determinist readings of Marx's theory of history are one-sided and false. Although there are deterministic and teleological tendencies in Marx's work, these occur mainly in the abstract summaries or presentations of his method. The thrust of his concrete analyses, in contrast, points in nondeterministic and nonteleological directions. From his texts, it is clear that Marx does not posit a linear development of modes of production leading from tribal to communist society, does not see history as a seamless narrative of progress, does not believe in an immanent law of motion leading inevitably toward communism, and does not embrace an economic or technological determinist account of social change. Rather, he sees discontinuities between Western and non-Western social forms and, within Western history, between precapitalist and capitalist societies; he holds that human beings shape, and are shaped by, their social and natural environment; he claims that history is a human product; and he believes that the "unfolding" of the contradictions of capitalism guarantee nothing but what conscious political subjects can make of them.

I have also argued that the dominant view of Marx as a facile reductionist and totalizer is wrong. Although he treats all social practices as derivative of labor and is too economistic in his analysis of precapitalist societies, Marx is opposed to any universal method that attempts to substitute deduction of historical laws for concrete analysis of specific social situations. Within the framework of historical materialism, Marx adopts a rich, complex, and multicausal analysis of social change. Diachronically, he analyzes continuities and discontinuities; synchronically, he analyzes social change from the standpoints of economics, politics, technology, work relations, war, and other factors. As Daniel Little has argued, the methodology of *Capital* is "irreducibly pluralistic" in its "variety of different forms of analysis and descriptive matter" (1986: 20). These include economic, historical, political, and sociological arguments and modes of description, along with moral critiques of exploitation and alienation. "The variety displayed in these different elements in Marx's analysis in *Capital* shows that his treatment of capitalism does not take the form of a unified deductive system from which all relevant particulars can be deduced. Instead, Marx's account is a family of related explanatory arguments, bits of analysis, historical comments, and descriptive efforts loosely organized by a common perspective. No general theory akin to atomic theory permits Marx to unify all his material into a single deductive system" (18).

The fact that Marx adopts a pluralist, multicausal mode of analysis does not mean that he is an eclectic who vacuously believes everything determines everything else. As Althusser insisted (1979: 215), the logic of overdetermination Marx employs rejects both economistic monism and the "theoretical void" of epistemological pluralism, which asserts that all perspectives and explanatory frameworks are equally valid and which fails to specify ultimately determining causes in society. Marx believes that only a materialist analysis can represent real social dynamics, and yet within this framework he specifies numerous factors of determination as they interrelate within a "structure in dominance" (Althusser). Despite the different models, standpoints, and tensions in Marx's works, there is also a good deal of coherence and consistency. Marx always tries to account for change in terms of dynamic developments within a society that lead to internal contradictions, but he does not limit this to a simple contradiction between forces and relations of production. He consistently roots the basic factors of social change in the mode of production of social life, appealing to technology, economics, work relations, and political forces.

My argument has been that Marx adopts a contextualist approach that sees historical change as the result of a complex interaction of social phenomena, all of which must be analyzed in concrete empirical contexts, where no *a priori* rules determine the results beyond the general principle that it is the mode of production of a given society that determines its mode of life. The usual practice of distinguishing between an "early" and "late" Marx does not begin to do justice to the complexity of his different views of history, politics, culture, and ideology. A contextualist reading of this contextualist method allows us to look beyond surface contradictions in Marx's works and to see deeper continuities within a broad materialist framework. A contextualist approach does not try to absolve Marx of all inconsistencies or contradictions; rather, *as* contextualist, it examines each theoretical issue independently. When a complex and prolific writer like Marx analyzes a rapidly changing social world from different vantage points over a long period of time, contradictions and inconsistencies will certainly occur, but along many lines one also finds a great deal of continuity and coherence to Marx's work.

One such line of continuity and coherence is the Hegelian vision of history as a dialectic of alienation and freedom, differentiation and unification, loss and recuperation. On this vision, human emancipation, just like the freedom of Spirit, cannot be achieved in pure, abstract, and unmediated form; rather, freedom is a historical product that requires a process of differentiation and alienation. Against Rousseau, Marx does not believe that humanity is born free and then placed in chains. It is only when there is established a complex social division of labor, an advanced development of technology, a creation of universal forms of human association, and the evolution of individuals beyond "sheep-like or tribal consciousness" (Marx and Engels 1978: 158) into beings rich in abilities and needs that the historical preconditions of human freedom exist. But since differentiation unfolds as alienation, the process reaches a point where the divisions and antagonisms that dynamically drive history forward are no longer needed and become an impediment to further progress; emancipation can be attained only through the abolition of conflicts, contradictions, and oppositions.

For Marx, this stage in history is reached in nineteenth-century capitalist society. Marx praises capitalism for its powerful development of the productive forces, for establishing universal social relations, and for producing complex individuals, but he condemns it for organizing these dynamics around the imperatives of production for private profit and thereby blocking the historical movement of democracy, equality, and freedom. Only through the abolition of capitalism and the creation of communism can the historically accumulated powers of humanity be realized in conditions of freedom.

Through analysis of actual historical possibilities, Marx foresees the end of human need (as privation) and greed and envisages a transition from the realm of necessity to the realm of freedom. "Freedom . . . can only consist in socialized man, the associated producers, rationally regulating their interchange with Nature, bringing it under their common control, instead of being ruled by it as by the blind forces of Nature" (Marx 1978: 441). In Marx's vision, the task of communism is to overturn all forces of alienation in order to allow human beings to gain control over the conditions of their practical existence, to appropriate the objective and subjective wealth of history, and to overcome all debilitating oppositions. This requires the abolition of the capitalist state, private property, religion, money, and all other alienating forces that mediate the direct relationship among freely interacting human beings and between each individual and its own nature.

By abolishing all false mediations and oppositions, Marx believes that communism can resolve the most fundamental contradiction, that between (human) essence and existence, between potentiality and actuality, such that objectification (productive activity) is no longer alienation but self-actualization. By abolishing the division of labor in the form of the "fixation of social activity," communism is the movement of human beings developing their multifaceted abilities in various ways without being restricted to any one mode of activity. "Only at this stage [of history] does self-activity coincide with material life, which corresponds to the development of individuals into complete individuals" (Marx 1975a: 192). The ultimate goal of communism is to return to the individual the most important possession he or she can have, the free time needed to develop one's personality and creative abilities.[36] Communism is defined therefore as a "fresh confirmation of *human* powers and a fresh enrichment of *human* nature" (358); it is designed to render it "impossible that anything should exist independently of individuals" as an alien power (Marx and Engels 1978: 193).

Human progress from now on is to be measured in terms of the degree of the all-around development of human individuals themselves; the social imperative shifts from development of objective to subjective forces. The social whole that Marx envisages is not an abstract or homogenous whole that erases all distinctions and levels individuality, but rather a concrete or mediated unity that allows for the genuine flourishing of differences in an unantagonistic way. Where precapitalist societies produced sociality without sufficient individuality, and capitalism produced individuality without sufficient sociality, Marx sees the goal of communism to be the overcoming of this opposition through the creation of the social individual, of free and creative individuals interacting harmoniously in solidarity with one another. To borrow Adorno's phrase, Marx's vision of history is informed by a "negative dialectics" that eschews oppressive homogeneity without abandoning the norm of unity and community.

Turning to Foucault and Habermas, we encounter two different critical assessments of Marx's theory of history and society. While both have been influenced by Marxian concepts, each seeks to move beyond Marxism to develop new critical theories relevant to contemporary capitalist conditions. As detailed below, Habermas, despite his break from Marxism, remains bound to a Hegelian vision of history and, to some extent, a philosophy of the subject, that Foucault overturns in favor of a Nietzschean vision that challenges totalizing tendencies and Enlightenment premises shared by both Marx and Habermas.

NOTES

1. As first schematized by Engels, Marx's dialectics studies four kinds of relationships: identity/difference, interpenetration of opposites, quantity/quality, and contradiction. The first two relations focus on synchronic phenomena. Marx attempts to analyze various aspects of society, while understanding them as part of a single system. Within this system, seemingly "opposite" things (such as the capital/labor relation) are really contrasting aspects of the same relation. The last two relations focus on diachronic phenomena. As discussed below, the impetus of historical change is contradictions within social orders. Gradual, quantitative accumulations of change eventually lead to a qualitative rupture and a new form of society. For a more complete analysis of dialectics, see Engels (1976), Lenin (1981), Ollman (1976, 1993), and Bologh (1979).

2. However "scientific" Marx's account of history, his analysis never relinqished strong ties to Hegelian dialectics. Later texts such as *Capital* and the *Grundrisse* are dialectic in their method and mode of exposition. For elaboration of this argument, see Ollman (1976) and Rosdolsky (1977).

3. "The act of reproduction itself changes not only the objective conditions — e.g. transforming village into town, the wilderness into agricultural clearings, etc. — but the producers change with it, by the emergence of new qualities, by transforming and developing themselves in production, forming new powers and new conceptions, new modes of intercourse, new needs, and new speech" (Marx 1965: 93). Thus, Marx believes that human subjects too are throughly historical in nature, that the human being itself is a historical product.

4. For Hegel, Spirit is originally an abstract and undifferentiated identity,

an empty substance without any reality. To be actual and self-actualizing, it must undergo a process of externalization and differentiation in space and time, where it eventually becomes whole again, this time as a "concrete unity." Similarly, I am arguing, Marx recognizes that early human societies may be organically unified, but the human beings living within them cannot be free until a new unity, differentiated and "concrete," is historically produced.

5. My scheme differs in detail and substance from the valuable analyses of Rader (1979), Fleischer (1973), and Adamson (1985). Rader also identifies three different models of history in Marx — the "base/superstructure" model, the "dialectical" model, and the "organic" model — and emphasizes their logical continuity, but without seeing important points of discontinuity. Fleischer too distinguishes between three different historical models in Marx's work, which he identifies as "anthropological," "pragmatological," and "nomological." The anthropological model of the *Economic and Philosophic Manuscripts* is a form of metaphysical determinism that sees history as the realization of the human essence. Immediately after developing this model, Fleischer claims, Marx abandons it in favor of the pragmatological model of *The German Ideology* and *Theses on Feuerbach*. These texts display a nonmetaphysical, empirical analysis of history as determined by the concrete practical activities of human beings. The nomological model is another form of determinism that sees history as the movement of objective processes and laws independent of human will.

Adamson adopts Fleischer's scheme, but adds a fourth model, found in the 1857 introduction to the *Grundrisse,* which breaks from the simple realism and evolutionism of *The German Ideology.* Unlike Fleischer, Adamson focuses on the discontinuities and logical incompatibilities between Marx's different models. In particular, Adamson stresses the conflict between the pragmatological focus on human freedom and the determinism of the nomological model. Both Fleischer and Adamson, however, occlude the continuities between the *Manuscripts* and *The German Ideology.* Just as the *Manuscripts* are not simply Hegelian and speculative, but show Marx's first attempts to incorporate empirical method and political economy into his work ("I have arrived at my conclusions through an entirely empirical analysis based on an exhaustive critical study of political economy" [Marx 1975a: 281]), so *The German Ideology* has some residual speculative Hegelian and teleological aspects in the discussion of communism. As I discuss below, I use the *Grundrisse* to bring out a discontinuity model in Marx that sees ruptures rather than continuities in history. Neither Fleischer, Rader, nor Adamson identify such a model. Against Adamson and Fleischer, I find the nomological model to be more a rhetorical tendency in Marx than an analytic model in its own right.

6. As I will argue, against Benhabib, Marx breaks with the essentialism of this model after 1844 and shows that the "unitary" subject of history changes and is fragmented into competing classes. Still, because Marx reduces human activity to production, the general agent of history remains a continuous subject of production.

7. "The satisfaction of the first need (the action of satisfying, and the instrument of satisfaction which has been acquired) leads to new needs; and this production of new needs is the first historical act" (Marx and Engels 1978: 156). The productive forces model in *The German Ideology* therefore suggests two different

"motors" of history: the dialectic between needs and production and the dialectic between forces and relations of production. In Fleischer's terms, the former dynamic is the basis of the pragmatological view, while the latter became the basis of the nomological view. While these two versions of history are incompatible insofar as the former sees history as the outcome of free human practice and the later as the determined result of laws independent of human will, the causal dynamics as stated in *The German Ideology* are compatible insofar as the productive forces/relations dynamic is put into play by the existence of human needs, and together the forces/relations of production shape new needs historically.

8. In the words of Marx's orthodox followers, "a certain state of the productive forces *is the cause* of the given production relations" (Kautsky); relations of production are an "outgrowth of the system of technology" and the whole "*mental life of society is a function of the forces of production* (Bukharin); changing "*in conformity with*" the productive forces (Stalin). Ultimately, "technical progress constitutes the basis of the entire development of humankind" (Kautsky). All quotes are cited in Larrain (1986: 45–46).

9. The important difference between Hegel and Marx on this point, of course, is that Hegel argued that the state, as the universal embodiment of Reason, worked to reconcile conflicting interests, whereas Marx saw it, on one major level, as the legal and political instrument of the bourgeoisie. For a detailed analysis of Marx's varying views on the state, see Miliband (1977).

10. "Hence the tribal community, the natural common body, appears not as the consequence, but as the precondition of the joint (temporary) appropriation and use of the soil" (Marx 1965: 68).

11. Marx also employs a discontinuity model to represent communist society. "The Communist revolution is the most radical rupture with traditional property relations; no wonder that its development involves the most radical rupture with traditional ideas" (Marx and Engels 1978: 489–490). Although communism builds from previous historical accomplishments, it is the first mode of production that abolishes antagonistic divisions between social classes, and in which human producers gain a conscious and practical mastery over the material forces of social existence. "The bourgeois relations of production are the last antagonistic form of the social process of production" (Marx 1978: 5).

12. Althusser's distinction comes mainly from this key passage in *Capital:* "For our own times . . . material interests are preponderant, but not for the Middle Ages, dominated by Catholicism, nor for Athens and Rome, dominated by politics. . . . [Yet] [o]ne thing is clear: the Middle Ages could not live on Catholicism, nor could the ancient world live on politics. On the contrary, it is the manner in which they gained their livelihood which explains why on one case politics, in the other case Catholicism, played the chief part (1977: 176n.). Only in capitalism, Marx claims, is the producer separated from the means of production; in prepcapitalist forms of production, we find a nonseparation between producers and the means of production and the resulting necessity of noneconomic forms of sanctioning relations of exploitation that allow for the dominance of superstructural phenomena.

13. Anthony Giddens (1981) and Claude Lefort (1978) argue that Marx's continuity and discontinuity perspectives are contradictory and incompatible images of history. For a critique of their claims, see Best (1991a).

14. Marx's political activities consisted mainly of journalistic writing and editing and organizing existing proletarian organizations. His direct involvement with proletariat groups occured mainly during the years between 1847–1852, when he worked with the Communist League (formerly the League of the Just), and 1864–1875, when he organized the first International. Marx played a decisive role in the formation of both organizations. He began his political career at the beginning of 1842, at age 24, as a liberal democratic journalist editing the *Rheinische Zeitung* in Cologne. Through his journalistic experiences, such as his articles on the wood-theft law, Marx transformed himself into a revolutionary communist.

15. See Marx's famous letter to Ruge in Marx and Engels (1978: 12–15).

16. The 1850 split in the Communist League resulted from differences over this issue, with some advocating immediate, armed uprising, and Marx insisting on the possible need for a prolonged self-education of the working class.

17. For an excellent, detailed analysis of Marx's politics and shifting political vision, see Gilbert (1981).

18. This is also the position in Gilbert's analysis of Marx's politics. "From the *Theses on Feuerbach* on, Marx involved a continuous attention to fresh practical experience, that is, a sort of contextualism, as one of the central facets of his theory. . . . Only a contextual examination can ferret out the crucial, relatively constant elements in Marx's theory and strategy, spell out the contradictions of tensions within it, and specify Marx's own reasons for changing it" (1981: 258–259).

19. The tension between intellectual representation and education and working class independence inherent in any notion of a party is clearly evident in the *Communist Manifesto*. One the one hand, Marx and Engels insist that "The Communists do not form a separate part opposed to other working-class parties. They have no interests separate and apart from those of the proletariat as a whole (1978: 483). Yet, on the other hand, they also claim that Communists are "practically, the most advanced and resolute section of the working-class parties of every country" and "theoretically, they have over the great mass of the proletariat the advantage of clearly understanding the line of march, the conditions, and the ultimate general results of the proletarian movement" (484). As Miliband notes, historically "from the notion of a vanguard to a *vanguard party*, there was only a short step" (1977: 128). The degeneration of Marxism into scientific socialism helped to erase this distinction and to promote the view that the party alone grasped the Truth of history which it would impart to the working class *ex cathedra*.

20. Before and after 1848, Marx argued that the democratic revolution must precede the communist revolution; during 1848, however, Marx at times thought the peasants and proletariat could combine both stages of struggle to take power directly in a socialist republic. Clearly, however, socialism cannot appear at just any point in history and requires a certain level of technological, economic, and political development, if only to satisfy Marx's demand for automated production and reduction of the workday. In *The German Ideology*, Marx and Engels inveighed against premature attempts at revolution where the struggle for necessity would replicate "all the old filthy business" of a scarcity-based history. The political implications of such a view, however, are clear in Marx's 1853 analysis of British imperialism in India, where he defends the material achievements of

modern imperialism whatever their consequences for the colonized cultures and their "stagnant," superstitious, parochial, cruel, and hierarchical ways of life. Such a utilitarian logic legitimates any imperialist adventures so long as it yields technical and economic gains in the colonized country. (See Marx and Engels 1978: 653–644.)

21. Marx himself never rigorously defined the terms "forces and relations of production" and a great deal of controversy has ensued concerning what they actually mean, whether there is a valid distinction between them, how they relate to the term "mode of production," and even whether they can be defined at all. The problem is to find definitions that are not too narrow, and therefore are supple enough to include some of Marx's nuances, but that also are not too broad, and therefore conflate key distinctions that Marx wished to maintain, namely those between forces and relations of production, and base and superstructure.

The forces of production are the basic elements employed in the production process. Marx refers to them in various ways, as the "conditions," "instruments," or "means of production." In the *Grundrisse,* Marx distinguishes between objective and subjective dimensions of productive forces. The objective dimensions include raw materials and natural resources, tools and machines, and transportation and communication systems. The subjective conditions of production refer to what Marx called "labour-power," or "the aggregate of those mental and physical capacities existing in a human being, which he exercises whenever he produces a use-value of any description" (Marx quoted in Shaw 1978: 15). The physical capacities of labor power involve strength and skill, and the mental capacities involve practical and scientific knowledge. On a too narrow definition of productive forces, important factors like science are left out, despite clear indications by Marx that it was a productive force: "But the *development of science* . . . is only one aspect, one form in which the *development of the human productive forces* i.e., of wealth, appears" (Marx quoted in Shaw 1978: 21). On a too broad definition (Rader 1979) law and morality are included, thus collapsing the distinction between base and superstructure. McMurtry (1978), Cohen (1978), and Shaw (1978) all define a force of production as anything that is directly, physically, and actually *used* in the process of production, rather than something that is necessary for production to occur (see Cohen [1978: 32ff.], McMurtry [1978: 55ff.], and Shaw [1978: 10ff.]). While government, law, or morality might be a necessary precondition of productive activity, they are not directly or physically employed in production as are tools, raw materials, or even scientific knowledge. Thus, the distinction between base and superstructure, while not rigid, can nevertheless be preserved. One important point of controversy concerns whether or not productive forces include what Marx terms "modes of cooperation." I examine this below, and in note 27.

22. Not all technological determinist interpretations of Marx are the same. The earlier orthodox readings (Kautsky, Plekhanov, Bukharin, Lenin, Stalin, and others) give a considerably more mechanistic and deterministic rendering of Marx than the neo-orthodox interpretations of analytic Marxists. The more narrow account tends to see the causal relationship between forces and relations as a one-way route with little reciprocal determination of relations on forces. Moreover, it sees history as moving through immanent laws of motion independent of and

wholly determining human agency, such that the unfolding of the productive forces of history guarantee the transition from capitalism to socialism.

The crudest version of technological determinism, such as we can find in Marshall McLuhan and Jacques Ellul, sees technology as developing throughout history on its own dynamic in complete abstraction from social relations. Marx's analyses show that he did not understand technology as a self-generating process or as unfolding through some immanent rationality. For Marx, the material is social; the development of the productive forces occurs only within given social relations of production that play a crucial role in determining the development and nature of the productive forces. Social relations are built into Marx's definition of production: "All production is appropriation of nature on the part of an individual within and through a specific form of society" (Marx 1973: 87).

Marx never separated technological development from its economic and political context. He destroyed the fetishized concept of technology through a twofold contextualization: the invention, application, and development of modern technology was seen to be determined by capitalist accumulation imperatives, and these imperatives in turn were shaped by the struggles of the working class. For Marx, the existence of a given technical state of development, and the use to which technology is applied, is always conditioned by a given social context and the objectives of the class controlling the productive forces of society. "Crises," for example, do not result from a malfunction within a self-governing system, but rather are the result of the power of the working class to disrupt capitalist accumulation imperatives (see Cleaver 1979). Marx mediates between two antithetical arguments: (1) technology develops strictly on its own accord regardless of human goals or intentions, and (2) human beings have full and conscious control of technology and are self-determined in their thoughts and action. For Marx, the freedom of individuals to shape their world occurs within a pregiven history and context that conditions them; yet they are able to transform this context, altering it more or less to suit their purposes.

23. It is traditional to define the economic base as comprised of forces and relations of production. Cohen (1978) has challenged this view by arguing that Marx only meant to include relations of production within the base and that the forces of production belong outside of the base, as a sort of subfoundation of social life. The best account of the complexities in defining forces and relations of production is Shaw (1978). For an argument that there is no valid distinction between forces and relations of production see Althusser and Balibar (1970) and Leff (1969).

24. The relations of production, for example, define the nature of work (duration, intensity, means of extraction of surplus labor, etc.), the distribution of the products of labor, as well as the social division of labor. Relations of production can either promote the development of the forces of production (as the bourgeois revolution did by abolishing feudal restrictions on trade and production) or retard it (as workers can do by going on strike or as the state can do by passing proenvironmental legislation).

25. Shaw, for instance, states, "The relations of production must be understood on their own level, not as the 'effects' of the productive forces to which they correspond" (1978: 75). Cohen argues that the productive forces cannot *fully* ex-

plain the nature of the productive relations: "They might explain, for example, why the economy is self-based, without explaining the precise distribution of rights between lord and peasant" (1978: 163), which, presumably, would be specified through an account of relatively autonomous politicolegal relations and institutions. Shaw states, "Of course the productive force 'depend' on the relations of production which utilise them because production cannot take place outside production relations, but this does not imply the productive relations determine the productive forces" (1978: 64). Rather, "The productive forces both articulate and provide the foundation for the introduction of new relations [of production]" (52). "The relations change only in response to the possibilities provided by man's improving productive abilities (66). For Cohen, Marx's statement that the relations of production "correspond to" the forces of production means that the relations are "explained by" the forces (1978: 136ff.). Thus, however much the relations may condition the forces, they receive their character and function from the forces, and not vice versa. Cohen and Shaw therefore conceive the relations of production as an adaptive response to the forces of production.

26. As George Elliot observes, "In *Pre-Capitalist Modes of Production* productive forces were denied any effectivity whatsoever, dissolved as any independent variable and reduced to specifications of relations of production—from which, in any particular mode of production, could be 'deduced' " (1986: 90). Hindess and Hirst beg the question by failing to block the argument by Cohen and Shaw that the efficacy of the relations of production is simply an assigned function of the forces of production. The technological determinist can grant the relations a dominant role in a given situation, while still insisting that this dominance itself was assigned by the productive forces. Indeed, in a later "auto-critique" of *Pre-Capitalist Modes of Production,* Hindess and Hirst themselves acknowledged the one-sidedness of their position and adopted a broader explanatory framework that granted more importance to the role of forces of production. They suggested the relation between forces and relations of production should be understood in terms of "conditions of existence" where each provides a context for the existence of the other and must be specified in terms of the other (1977: 50, 54, 72). Relations of production, for instance, cannot be specified without reference to "the determinate technical functions" necessary for their existence. There is an "interdependence of the technical and social divisions of labour" (72). Hence, they move toward the symmetrical thesis, although, quite curiously, they still privilege relations of production as a theoretical concept (5–6). This move is further supported by Hirst's later claim (1985: 15) that the proper response to the privileging of the forces of production is not to switch to the primacy of the relations of production.

27. The term "work relations" refers to the technical relations between producers in the productive process, as considered in abstraction from economic and political relations of control over people and things in that process. The arguments of Cohen and Shaw contradict numerous passages where Marx clearly defined modes of cooperation as a productive force. In *The German Ideology,* for example, Marx and Engels say: "By social we understand the cooperation of several individuals, no matter under what conditions, in what manner, and to what end. It follows from this that a certain mode of production, or industrial stage, is always combined with a certain mode of co-operation, or social stage, and this

mode of co-operation is itself a 'productive force'" (1978: 157). Modes of cooper-ation fit the definition of a productive force, since, like science or a machine, they are directly employed in the production process to make use values. Marx's point is that the sheer fact of material cooperation among human beings is itself a power-ful force used in production, contrasted to the possibilities allowed by individuals working in isolation from one another.

28. "By means of machinery, chemical processes, and other methods, [large-scale industry] is continually transforming not only the technical basis of produc-tion but also the functions of the worker and the social combinations of the labour process" (Marx 1977: 617).

29. Marx develops a similar account of the self-destructive tendencies of the feudal mode of production as a result of its inherent tendency toward civil war, resulting from the extraction of surplus goods through dominance of a military force controlled by independent family groups over land and its tillers. This ac-count of transition highlights the importance of political factors. As Miller puts it, "In the feudal wars, lords did not compete in agricultural output. They killed each other in dynastic conflicts" (1984: 227). Moreover, according to Miller, Marx's discussion of the origins of the division of labor in society, an important influence on the development of tools, assigns the causal force to contact and barter among social groups, rather than than a drive for greater productivity (190–191), and his account of preclass societies emphasizes conquest and exchange among social groups (206, n. 47).

30. In capitalism, moreover, capitalists have consistently blocked the develop-ment of technology where it threatened greater profits. Just as the auto industry fought against mass transportation, and electric companies struggled to suppress solar heating and other alternative energy sources, so the American Medical As-sociation has harassed the chiropractic profession and derided viable holistic ap-proaches to health, and giant media corporations have attempted to block technologies that allow consumers access to cable and satellite TV. In all such cases, it is commercial and political interests, or the social relations of produc-tion, not an alleged rational interest in technological development, that operate. These take precedence over and determine the development, or nondevelopment, of technology.

31. For example, as Gilbert notes, "When Marx first conceived a strategy for Germany in the 1840s, he did not look mainly to the impact of the steam en-gine and the future unfolding of capitalism," but rather to lessons from the French revolution and the immediate political situation in Germany (1981: 30).

32. As Kellner suggests (1984), it is a constant temptation for radicals to seek emancipatory norms outside of history, to seek guarantees for revolution in nomological laws or dynamics independent of the contingencies of social struggle and political consciousness. Where Marx, for example, relied on the rhetoric of objective laws of history, Marcuse found the guarantee of revolution in the bio-logical dimension itself, where freedom was allegedly an ingrained need.

33. *Every* society is rooted in material production; what does differ is the *specific character* of production, the *type* of production that prevails over others: "In all forms of society there is one specific kind of production which predominates over the rest, whose relation thus assigns rank and bathes all the other colors and

modifies their particularity. It is a particular ether which determines the specific gravity of every being which has materialized within it" (Marx 1978: 242). Thus, one society will be rooted in hunting and fishing, another in settled agriculture, still another in industrial manufacture, where agriculture itself "more and more becomes a branch of industry, and is entirely dominated by capital" (243).

34. "The aim is . . . to present production—see e.g. Mill—as distinct from distribution etc. as encased in natural laws independent of history, at which opportunity *bourgeois* relations are then quietly smuggled back in as the inviolable natural laws on which society in the abstract is founded" (Marx 1978: 225).

35. See also: "The bourgeois economy thus supplies the key to the ancient, etc. But not at all in the manner of those economists who smudge over all historical differences and see bourgeois relations in all forms of society. One can understand tribute, tithe, etc. [land payments of precapitalist societies], if one is acquainted with ground rent [a land payment of capitalist society]. But one must not identify them" (Marx 1978: 241).

36. Beyond the realm of necessity "begins that development of human energy which is an end in itself, the true realm of freedom, which, however, can blossom forth only with the realm of necessity as its basis. The shortening of the working day is its basic prequisite" (Marx 1978: 441). Marx's vision of a society organized around creature leisure, rather than arduous work, was an important emancipatory norm in the nineteenth-century context of radical thought, which was shaped by scarcity and problems of toil and want. As Bookchin notes, however, Marx's vision was not lost in twentieth-century socialism, which developed its own puritanical work ethic: "Instead of focusing their message on the emancipation of man from toil, socialists tended to depict socialism as a beehive of industrial activity, humming with work for all" (1986: 115).

2

BETWEEN THE MODERN
AND THE POSTMODERN:
FOUCAULT'S ANALYTICS
OF HISTORY

> Is it not necessary to draw a line between those who
> believe that we can continue to situate our present
> discontinuities within the historical and transcendental
> tradition of the nineteenth century and those who are
> making a great effort to liberate themselves, once and
> for all, from this conceptual framework?
> —FOUCAULT (1977: 120)

After Marx's death in 1883, the complexities and tensions of his works
were resolved into a dogmatic and mechanistic science. Beginning with
Engels' *Dialectics of Nature,* written between 1872 and 1882, and continuing through the Second International and Soviet Marxism in the 1920s
and 1930s, Marxism became a universalist and monistic method. In the
form of "dialectical materialism," Marx's work was transformed into a
positivistic and teleological science of history that erased social complexity and causal contingency and promised the global victory of communism.
Marx's emphasis on the need for a mature and independent proletariat
was completely lost in the bureaucratic command of workers by the Vanguard Party. Rather than assisting workers in the abolition of classes, intellectuals established themselves as a new ruling class over workers and
peasants.

There was a strong reaction against these developments, however,
as "Western" Marxists emphasized the critical over the scientific aspects
of Marxism (see Gouldner 1980). Beginning in the early 1920s, Lukács,

Korsch, Gramsci, and members of the Frankfurt School tried to recover Marx's emphases on the importance of alienation, political consciousness, the practical will, and the critique of ideology. Against the bogus guarantees of teleological Marxism, their analyses stressed the importance of critical consciousness in directing social change. Yet when the development of capitalist forces of production led to greater forms of domination rather than to liberation, Marx's enthusiastic support of science and technology gave way to the Frankfurt School critique of instrumental and technical reason. When socialism failed to distinguish itself from barbarism and "the contradictions of capitalism" failed to "unfold," pessimism paralyzed the practical will and blinded emancipatory political vision.

In France, Marxism did not become an influential discourse until the 1930s and it arrived in fairly orthodox form (see Poster 1975; Kelly 1982). For the next three decades, stimulated by a revival of Hegel through the work of Hyppolite, Kojève, and others, Marxism was the dominant theoretical framework for French intellectuals, rivaled only by existential phenomenology. By the late 1950s, however, structuralism and (Lacanian) psychoanalysis had emerged to pose strong challenges to both of these theories. The belief of existential phenomenology in a unified subject at the center of human experience was overpowered by new arguments that the subject was produced as an effect of linguistic structures and the unconscious. At the height of the structuralist influence in the 1960s, Althusser championed Marxism as the science of history, Sartre abandoned his radical individualist outlook to proclaim Marxism the "unsurpassable philosophy of our time," and there were numerous attempts to merge Marxism with existentialism, feminism, and psychoanalysis.

Simultaneously, however, other movements were developing that led a new generation of French intellectuals away from Marxism altogether. Nietzsche had replaced Marx as the master thinker, and attention shifted from modes of production to systems of power. In the 1960s Deleuze, Derrida, and others rejected dialectics as a totalizing methodology and sought new philosophies of difference that emphasized the irreducibility of the singular and the multiple apart from any identity, system, or whole. Beginning in the mid 1950s, an unknown theorist named Michel Foucault was also beginning a path of study that would lead him out of the Marxist orbit, away from dialectics and humanism, toward original analyses of discourse and power that would make him arguably the most important French intellectual since Sartre.

Foucault's works have been extremely influential in all fields of contemporary criticism, inspiring not only the "new historicism," but also innovative research in the areas of the family, sexuality, social regulation, education, prisons, law, and the state. In a series of historical studies on madness and psychiatry, illness and medicine, the human sciences, prisons and punishment, sexuality, and ethics, Foucault redefined the nature of social theory by calling into question conventional assumptions concerning the Enlightenment, Marxism, rationality, subjectivity, power, truth, history, and the political role of the intellectual. Foucault breaks with universalist, foundationalist, dialectical, and normative standpoints and emphasizes principles of contingency, difference, and discontinuity. Adopting a nominalist stance, he dissolves abstract essences and universals such as Reason, History, Truth, or Right into a plurality of specific sociohistorical forms. He challenges traditional disciplinary boundaries between philosophy, history, psychology, and social and political theory, as well as conventional approaches to these fields. He does not do "theory" in the modern sense, which aims at clarity, consistency, comprehensiveness, objectivity, and truth; rather, he offers fragments, "fictions," "truth-games," "heterotopias," "tools," and "experiments" that he hopes will prompt his readers to think and act in new ways. Trying to blaze new intellectual and political trails, Foucault abandons both liberalism and Marxism and seeks a new kind of critical theory and politics.

This does not preclude certain similarities with Marx. Long before Foucault, Marx placed great emphasis on the importance of research and erudition to inform radical vision. In his long hours in the British Museum, Marx established his genealogical pedigree by drawing on the government's Blue Books, which were rife with factual material on British industry, trade, finance, and working-class life. Like Marx, Foucault rejects the positivist search for universal laws of history, and he seeks to reveal the historical and political forces constituting phenomena understood as given or eternal. Foucault also works to recover the importance of the "event," of points of historical specificity and rupture, while simultaneously grasping significant lines of continuity throughout history. Foucault follows Marx in rejecting idealist theories that see history as the development of thought or the expression of universal essences. Like Marx, Foucault believes that consciousness and intentionality are derivative of material and social forces, although he minimizes the role of agency far more than Marx.

Early in his academic career, Foucault, like many French intellectuals, was considerably influenced by Marxism. Believing Marxist theory to be fundamentally sound, Foucault joined the Communist Party in 1950. This decision was the result of his disagreement with French involvement in the Indochina war and the influence of his Marxist friend and teacher, Louis Althusser. Foucault was not actively involved in meetings or activities, however, and left the Party in 1953 in part because of its contempt for homosexuality (Eribon 1991) and his disgust with its fabrication of a plot to kill Stalin (Foucault 1991: 52–53). At this time Foucault was immersed in the study and practice of psychology and initially pursued this research from a Marxist perspective. His first book, *Mental Illness and Psychology,* was heavily influenced by Marxist humanism and spoke frequently of class, contradiction, alienation, and the social context of illness and madness.

But new influences came into Foucault's life in the early 1950s with the reading of Bataille, Blanchot, and Nietzsche. He took leave of Marxism in 1955 and edited Marxist references out of his book in subsequent revisions. By 1963, Foucault concluded that Marxism was a reductionistic discourse unable to analyze key forms of human experience such as sexuality and desire, and was a derivative by-product of bourgeois political economy. In the early 1970s, Foucault made a temporary alliance with French Maoists and preached revolutionary rhetoric, but in the late 1970s, he became a fervent anticommunist and embraced "New French Philosophers" such as André Glucksmann who saw direct links between Marxism and totalitarianism. At the same time, Foucault began work on a noneconomistic analysis of power that he felt was disallowed by the Marxist point of view. Foucault continued to employ some Marxian economic categories, as is clear in major works from this period like *Discipline and Punish,* but he made a decisive break from Marx's method, politics, and modes of critique.

Foucault and Marx assail forces of domination in the present and envisage the possibility of future freedom, but their visions of this future are completely different. Instead of Marx's modified linear pattern of progress that traces a coherent movement of freedom through various modes of production, Foucault sees a cyclical pattern of successive forms of power and violence that lead to ever greater forms of domination. Although both Marx and Foucault foresee a future where individuals can be free of domination, Foucault does not share Marx's vision of a communal harmony of associated producers; rather, Foucault adopts an individualist vision of persons free from all social norms, which he equates with social constraints, and champions a creative differentiation of selves from one another. Instead of Marx's dialectical notion of the social individual, Foucault merges Nietzsche's notion of the higher type with Bataille's philosophy of excess to exalt the model of a Dionysian hero exploring the intensity of "limit experiences" (sexuality, death, madness, and crime) through the creation of new pleasures, bodies, and identities beyond the "good and evil" of conventional morality. Ultimately, Foucault's vision of history is not a Hegelian vision of continuity, progress, reconciliation, and social freedom, but a Nietzschean vision that denies progressive tendencies in history and advocates the proliferation of unreconciled differences, the aesthetic transformation of the self, and a rupture with the trajectories of Western history.

In this chapter I assess Foucault's vision of history and the methods of historical writing and social analysis that he calls "archaeology" and "genealogy." I counterpose these methods to other approachs to history, including structuralism, positivism, the history of ideas, and Marxism. I examine the claims both of Foucault's detractors, who assail him for factual errors, unwarranted generalizations, and problematic textual interpretations and periodization schemes, and his apologists, who argue that he is producing a new kind of history whose function transcends modern concerns for truth and factual accuracy. I attempt to describe Foucault's work in terms of its continuities and discontinuities in its different stages of development. I argue that despite his shifts in method, emphasis, and style, there is an overall unity and coherence to his work in terms of its critique of modernity and its search for transgressive experiences that break free of coercive norms and identities. Despite his critical stance toward key modern concepts, values, and methods, I argue that Foucault retains important aspects of modern historiography and social theory and therefore cannot unqualifiably be read as a "postmodernist."[1] Rather, Foucault produces a new kind of critical theory that is somewhere between the modern and postmodern, that reworks certain modern elements in a postmodern framework. Within this new context, Foucault emphasizes principles of difference and discontinuity; rejects the optimistic and rationalistic aspects of Enlightenment thought; breaks from humanism, transcendentalism, and progressivist and utopian visions of history; and adopts an aloof posture in relation to normative language, truth, and their principles of justification. Here, and in Chapter 4, I assess the validity of Foucault's critique of Marx and ask what is gained and lost in his new form of critical theory.

THE CRITIQUE OF RATIONALITY

In his introduction to Canguilhem's *The Normal and the Pathological,* Foucault claims that there has been a fundamental division within French philosophy that begins in the nineteenth century and runs throughout the twentieth century, a division between a "philosophy of experience, of sense and of the subject, and a philosophy of knowledge, of rationality, and of concept" (1989b: 8). On the former side, Foucault places existential phenomenology and figures like Sartre and Merleu-Ponty; on the latter side he situates the history and philosophy of science, and figures like Cavailles, Koyre, Bachelard, and Canguilhem. Foucault was certainly knowledgeable of the former tradition; indeed, one finds strong influences of existentialism (in particular, Heidegger) in his early works on madness and mental illness (see Gutting 1989). Yet his main intellectual influences stem from the history and philosophy of science. While numerous intellectuals were experimenting with structuralist–Freudian–Marxist syntheses,

Foucault notes, others "did not follow this movement. I am thinking of those who were interested in the history of science—an important tradition in France, probably since the time of Comte. [This tradition formed especially] around Canguilhem, an extremely influential figure in the French university. . . . Many of his students were neither Marxists, nor Freudians, nor structuralists. And here I am speaking of myself" (1988d: 22).

Foucault was primarily interested in philosophers and historians of science insofar as their works, along with Nietzsche's, helped to develop a critical analysis of modern forms of rationality. In France, as Foucault observes (1988d: 26), the critique of rationality was developed not through the work of Weber and the Frankfurt School, very little-known figures at that time, but rather through French theorists of science. Foucault notes that the work of Koyre, Bachelard, Canguilhem, and others helped to challenge "a rationality which makes universal claims while developing in contingency" (1989b: 12). Their work analyzes "a reason whose autonomy of structures carries with itself the history of dogmatisms and despotisms—a reason which, consequently, has the effect of emancipation only on the condition that it succeeds in freeing itself of itself" (12).

For Foucault, the most important figure from this tradition was the historian of science, Georges Canguilhem, supervisor of his *doctorat d'état, Folie et deraison* (condensed and translated as *Madness and Civilization*). Canguilhem's work in turn was decisively influenced by Gaston Bachelard, a philosopher of science.[2] Bachelard believed that the best way to analyze reason was through a historical reflection on the nature of scientific rationality. He rejected the concept of unified scientific rationality and argued that science is constituted by different "regions of rationality." Bachelard did not altogether reject the concept of scientific progress, but he did renounce the prevailing view that progress is attained through a steady, continuous accumulation of knowledge towards truth, and instead emphasized that scientific knowledge develops through "epistemological breaks." For Bachelard, truth was not a Platonic form or Cartesian idea that sufficiently clear reason could attain, but rather a pragmatic outcome negotiated within a scientific community. The emergence of a new field of scientific knowledge is prevented by what Bachelard terms "epistemological obstacles," a set of unconscious and habitual resistances to theoretical change.

With Bachelard, Canguilhem emphasized the historical nature of rationality and its discontinuous development. Canguilhem, however, shifted focus from physics and chemistry to biology and medicine and emphasized that there are also important continuities between different forms of knowledge. Undertaking a history of scientific concepts, he argued that these were "theoretically polyvalent" and that the same concepts can mean different things in different theories. He also developed an analysis of science as a normative discipline and theorized scientific accounts of norms and the normal.

Like Bachelard, Foucault holds that rationality is historical in nature, that general theories of knowledge must be abandoned in favor of specific and regional theory, and that knowledge develops in discontinuous forms and is theory laden in character. Foucault also accepts many of Canguilhem's critiques of Bachelard, however—in particular the view that there are continuities as well as discontinuities between different historical forms of knowledge. Like Canguilhem, Foucault theorizes how use of the same concept can mask different underlying epistemological assumptions, and Canguilhem's concern with the distinction between the normal and abnormal in science became central to Foucault's critique of the human sciences.

Yet Foucault also transforms the work of Bachelard and Canguilhem in important ways. Like them, Foucault is interested in the historical constitution of objects of knowledge, but he shifts the focus of inquiry in three significant ways. First, where they concentrated on well-defined fields of formal science such as physics, chemistry, and biology, Foucault examines nonformal fields, the domain of the human sciences that study the human subject as a living, laboring, and speaking being. Foucault theorizes what Ian Hacking (1979) has termed the "immature sciences" in an attempt to show they too have a coherent empirical order (see Foucault 1973b: ix). Second, following Nietzsche, Foucault shifts focus from the history of rationality to the history of truth and its relation to discourse and knowledge (Foucault 1991: 62).

Finally, Foucault reorients research from the ways in which scientific objects are constituted to the ways in which human beings are constituted as subjects of knowledge, insofar as they themselves become objects of knowledge and receive moral and psychological identities through scientific discourse. In Foucault's words, "While historians of science in France were interested essentially in the problem of how a scientific object is constituted, the question I asked myself was this: how is it that the human subject took itself as the object of possible knowledge? Through what forms of rationality and historical conditions? And finally at what price?" (1988d: 29–30). By coming to know phenomena such as madness or economics, for example, Western societies have also constituted the rational subject. Through the influence of Bataille, Foucault analyzes this as a process of reducing limit experiences such as madness or sexuality into controlled objects of knowledge. Here, "the themes of Georges Bataille may be recognized, reconsidered from the point of view of a collective history, that of the West and its knowledge. The relationship between limit-experiences and the history of truth: I am more or less wrapped up in this tangle of problems" (Foucault 1991: 71).

By theorizing the connections between knowledge, truth, and power, as they emerged in the domain of the human sciences and are bound up with constitution of individuals as distinct kinds of subjects, Foucault transforms the history of science and reason, along with the concern for limit experiences, into a political critique of modernity and its various modes of power that assume the form of "normalization" or "subjectification." Foucault holds to the Nietzschean view that to be a "subject"—that is, to have a unified and coherent identity—is to be "subjugated" by social powers. This occurs through a "deployment" of discourse that divides, excludes, classifies, hierarchizes, confines, and normalizes. Hence, toward the end of his career, Foucault declares that his ultimate project has been not so much to study power, but rather the subject itself: "the goal of my work . . . has been to create a history of the different modes by which, in our [Western] culture, human beings are made subjects" (1982a: 208). But this is a misleading distinction that signals merely a shift in emphasis rather than approach, since subjectification is the means through which modern power operates. In a series of historico-theoretical studies, Foucault analyzes the formation of the modern subject from the perspectives of psychiatry, medicine, criminology, and sexuality, whereby limit experiences are transformed into objects of knowledge.

Foucault's works are strongly influenced by an anti-Enlightenment tradition that rejects the equation of reason, emancipation, and progress. Foucault argues that an interface between modern forms of power and knowledge has served to create new forms of domination. With thinkers like Sade, Nietzsche, and Bataille, Foucault valorizes transgressive forms of experience such as madness, violence, or sexuality that break from the prison of rationality. Where modern societies "problematize" such forms of experience—that is, turn them into governmental problems, into areas of life in need of control and regulation—Foucault in turn problematizes social problematizations by uncovering their political motivations and effects and by challenging their character as natural, necessary, or timeless.[3] In what he calls a "diagnostic critique" that combines philosophy and history (1989a: 38–39, 73), Foucault attempts to clarify the nature of the present historical era, to underline its radical difference from preceding eras, and to show that contemporary forms of knowledge, rationality, social institutions, and subjectivity are contingent sociohistorical constructs of power and domination, and thus are subject to change and modification.

Foucault's ultimate task, therefore, is "to produce a shift in thought so that things can really change" (quoted in O'Farrell 1989: 39). The goal of Foucault's historico-philosophical studies, as he later came to define it,

is to show how different domains of modern knowledge and practice constrain human action and how they can be transformed by alternative forms
of knowledge and practice in the service of human freedom. Foucault is
concerned, above all, to analyze various forms of the "limit experience"
by which society attempts to define and circumscribe the boundaries of
legitimate thought and action. The political vision informing Foucault's
work foresees individuals liberated from coercive social norms, transgressing all limits to experience and transvaluing values, going beyond good
and evil to promote their own creative lifestyles and affirm their bodies
and pleasures, endlessly creating and recreating themselves.

In his periodization schemes, Foucault distinguishes between two post-
Renaissance eras: the "classical" era (1660–1800) and the "modern" era
(1800–1950). In his early and middle works, he gives very little analysis
to the Renaissance and even less to the "post-modern" era that he suggests is presently forming, concentrating on the classical and modern eras.
Foucault sees the classical era as inaugurating an intense mode of domination over human beings that culminates in the modern era.

Foucault analyzes "modernity"—a term I use to refer to both the classical and modern eras as represented by Foucault—from various standpoints and different methodological perspectives.[4] Rejecting the concept
of synchronic totality, the idea that society is a unified whole, Foucault
examines the classical and modern eras from the standpoints of their key
institutions. While each institutional optic is unique, the separate analyses
have a general coherence insofar as all are concerned with a critique of
reason and the different ways in which individuals are constituted as subjects. Moreover, like Nietzsche, Foucault rejects the philosophical pretension to systematically grasp all of reality within one philosophical system
or from one central vantage point. Foucault believes that discourse "is so
complex a reality that we not only can, but should, approach it at different levels with different methods" (1973b: xiv).

No single theory or method of interpretation by itself can grasp the
plurality of discourses, institutions, and modes of power that constitute
modern society, and Foucault's belief is that methods which break with
the totalizing assumptions of modern theory are needed to analyze properly
the complex nature of discourse, history, and social reality. As I demonstrate below, Foucault inititally focuses on knowledges and discourses
(archaeology), then institutional practices (genealogy). Realizing that both
perspectives are inadequate insofar as they deny the subject any powers
of agency, he adopts a third perspective that analyzes ways in which
subjects can constitute themselves (ethics and technologies of the self).[5]
Each particular approach informs the other and all interrelate in his later
works.

ARCHAEOLOGY AS POSTMODERN HISTORIOGRAPHY

> What one is seeing . . . is the emergence of a whole field
> of questions, some of which are already familiar, by
> which this new form of history is trying to develop its
> own theory.
>
> —FOUCAULT (1972: 5)

Beginning with *Madness and Civilization,* Foucault characterizes his position as an "archaeology of knowledge" that seeks a "mapping of the enunciative field" (1972: 131), of different forms of discourse and knowledge. He rejects the idealist version of discourse theory and insists that discourse is inseparable from practices and institutional settings. Discourse "is a complex, differentiated practice, governed by analysable rules and transformations" (211). As we have seen, this archaeological approach draws from recent developments in the philosophy and history of science, such as developed by Canguilhem and Bachelard, and, as I show, it is sharply differentiated from other historical methods such as positivism, Marxism, phenomenology, hermeneutics, structuralism, and the history of ideas.[6]

Foucault's archaeological approach is suggested in his first major work, *Madness and Civilization* (1973a, orig. 1961), where he attempts to grasp madness as a discursive construct bound up with institutional practices of isolation and confinement. In his next book, *The Birth of the Clinic* (1975, orig. 1963), he analyzes the formation of modern medical discourse and how it objectifies the body through the scientific gaze. Next, in *The Order of Things* (1973b, orig. 1966), he studies the discursive foundations of the human sciences as they developed throughout the Renaissance, classical, and modern eras. Finally, in *The Archaeology of Knowledge* (1972, orig. 1969), he pauses for an autocritique and a methodological reflection on his past books before abandoning the purely archaeological stage of his work altogether.

In the *Archaeology of Knowledge,* Foucault aligns his work with new historiographical trends. Throughout this book we find Foucault trying to overcome the dogmatic slumbers of conventional theorizing, attempting to tear away the veils of theoretical self-evidence of modern historical concepts in order to free the methodological problems they hide. His main task is to employ a "systematic erasure of all given unities" of discourse (1972: 28), of terms such as author, text, *oeuvre,* and period. In the opening pages, Foucault describes the different methods, categories, and problems that characterize the "epistemological mutation of history" (11) within which he is operating. He rejects core concepts of modern social theory and historiography—subject, origin, continuity, teleology, causality, change, period, and totality—and attempts to reconstruct some of these while employing an idiosyncratic vocabulary that includes terms such as "statement," "positivity," and "discursive formation."

Unlike Hoy (1988), who claims that Foucault in his archaeological period is still a modern theorist, and does not become a postmodern theorist until his genealogical stage, my argument is that there are already salient postmodern elements present in the archaeological stage, and these are especially pronounced in *The Order of Things* and *The Archaeology of Knowledge.* The main methodological moves of archaeology, its attack on metaphysical cornerstones of modern theory and its countervalorization of difference and discontinuity, are clear postmodern moves. Moreover, in this stage of his work, Foucault marks a rupture in history that is the end of the modern era and the beginning of a new postmodern era within which he unambiguously situates his own work (see below).

A major goal of Foucault's historiography is to complicate modern accounts of society and history, which he considers to be simplistic and reductionistic. Discourse is a "highly complex domain" (1972: 146) and must be described in its various relations, interdependencies, and forms of difference and dispersion. This complication allows the historian to liberate the differences and discontinuities of discourse that are suppressed in totalizing modern theories through concepts such as subject, influence, originality, spirit, and worldview. "These pre-existing forms of continuity, all these syntheses that are accepted without question, must remain in suspense . . . we must show that they do not come about of themselves, but are always the result of a construction of rules of which must be known, and the justifications of which must be scrutinized" (25). As Foucault demonstrates most clearly in *The Order of Things,* these rules of formation of discourse emerge in the modern era, and the possibility of their critique and supersession opens up in a new postmodern space that Foucault tries to operate in and describe.

The metaphor of archaeology suggests that Foucault is attempting an excavation of knowledge, a search for its underlying conditions and determinants. As an archaeologist of Western culture, Foucault seeks to identify the fundamental codes of discourse and knowledge as they emerge and develop historically. For a structuralist like Lévi-Strauss, human speech and action is transhistorically determined by the same unconscious rules of language; all forms of cultural production are merely variations of an unchanging set of linguistic rules. Structuralists analyze language as a structure, a coherent whole of interrelating parts, that is governed by rules of intelligibility. Archaeology follows structuralism in the search for underlying rules of human thought and knowledge. Like structuralists, Foucault rejects the phenomenological theory of the subject as a conscious originator of meaning and claims that the subject is determined in and through language. The subject does not stand at the center of language synthesizing its various linguistic acts; rather, it is dispersed throughout its various modes of speaking.

Consequently, a major goal of archaeology is to free the history of thought from the problematic of subjectivity, "to define a method of analysis freed of all anthropologism" (1972: 16). Discourse is not the product of a founding, transcendental subject (Descartes, Kant, Fichte, Husserl), or even an expression of a collective consciousness (Durkheim), but rather emerges from an unconscious, anonymous system of rules that determine subjective consciousness. Foucault rejects the transcendental standpoint that appeals to universal structures of experience discerned by and grounded in a subject that constitutes meaning. The goal of archaeology is to cleanse history of all "transcendental narcissism" (203). Archaeology attempts "to explore scientific discourse not from the point of view of the individuals who are speaking, nor from the point of view of the formal structures of what they are saying, but from the point of view of the rules that come into play in the very existence of such discourse . . . the historical analysis of scientific discourse should, in the last resort, be subject, not to a theory of the knowing subject, but rather to a theory of discursive practice" (Foucault 1973b: xiv). By knocking out the constituting subject as the origin of discourse, one can analyze discourse on its own terms, in its real complexity, as it develops unevenly on multiple levels apart from any unifying operations of a transcendental consciousness.

Thus, archaeology seeks to identify the *conditions of possibility* of knowledge, the determining "rules of formation" of discursive rationality (discursive objects, concepts, statements, themes, and theories) that operate beneath the level of "thematic content" and subjective awareness and intention. These rules form the *"positive unconscious"* of all knowledge, perception, and truth. They are "the fundamental codes of a culture — those determining its language, its schemes of perception, its exchanges, its techniques, its values, the hierarchy of its practices" (Foucault 1973a: xx). As such, they constitute a whole epistemological field, what Foucault has called an *"episteme,"* "discursive formation," or "discursive practice" (a term that serves to emphasize the imbrication of words and things, speech and action). As Foucault says, "It is these rules of formation, which were never formulated in their own right, but are to be found only in widely differing theories, concepts, and objects of study, that I have tried to reveal, by isolating, as their specific locus, a level that I have called . . . archaeological" (1973b: xi).

Clearly, archaeology is antithetical to the idealism of a Collingwood who sees history as the outcome of conscious action and historiography as the reenactment of past thought. But it is opposed even to the materialist approach of Marx; where Marx claims that "circumstances make men just as much as men make circumstances" (Marx and Engels 1978: 165),

Foucault resolves this dialectic into an unqualified determinism that denies agency altogether. Archaeology is also opposed to "commentary," a hermeneutics that seeks "to uncover the deeper meaning of speech" based on the assumption that there is an implicit meaning not explicitly expressed in statements and is rooted in subjective intention. Archaeology abandons a hermeneutic analysis of the meaning of texts for a quasi-structural analysis of the codes underlying thought and speech.

But archaeology is "neither formalizing nor interpretive" (Foucault 1972: 135), neither structuralist nor hermeneutical, but "beyond" both (see Dreyfus and Rabinow 1982). Archaeology differs from structuralism of the Lévi-Straussian kind in its rejection of a universal, transhistorical unconscious rooted in human nature. Archaeology holds that the rules of discursive formation undergo dramatic changes in different historical periods, creating fundamentally different epistemic conditions. Hence, Foucault calls these rules the "historical *a priori*" of a given culture. Archaeology proceeds from the assumption that discourses and their objects are not ideal essences (Lévi-Strauss) or informed by pregiven, unchangeable rules of grammar (Chomsky), but rather are determined by historical forces. The "*a priori*" of discourse can be understood in the Kantian sense of the conditions of possibility of discourse, with the qualification that these conditions are not universal and immutable, but rather are historical and transitory.

Where some versions of structuralism privilege the synchronic over diachronic aspect of discourse, Foucault analyzes both synchronic and diachronic dimensions. At any given time, discourse has a synchronic coherence or "positivity" that allows the archaeologist to identify its governing rules, yet positivities change and mutate. The emphasis on diachrony means that archaeology is not simply another formal and ahistorical form of structuralism, as Sartre and others have charged.[7] While Foucault gives credit to traditional historians of ideas for their efforts to account for changes in conceptual fields, he breaks with their use of linear models that analyze change in terms of an evolving continuity of ideas and renounces the use of categories such as origin, influence, and progress. If he is killing history, Foucault would say, it is the History of the philosophers informed by vast continuities and the myths of emerging freedom. For Foucault, change in configurations of knowledge does not involve a steady accumulation of knowledge or the gradual progress of truth or reason, but rather a sudden and abrupt shift in the way the world is understood. Discontinuity refers to the fact that in a transition from one discursive formation or historical era to another "things are no longer perceived, described, expressed, characterized, classified, and known in the same way" (Foucault 1973b: 217). The shift from the tolerance of madness in the Renaissance to its confinement in the classical era is an example of such a break.

Thus, in defiance of the norms of modern historiography, archaeology does not see discontinuity as a blight on the historical narrative signaling a failure to find underlying continuities linking historical events; rather, for the "new history," discontinuity is a positive working concept necessary to identify real discursive ruptures. Yet archaeology does not simply reject continuity in favor of discontinuity, for it analyzes historical transformations at both levels:

> To say that one discursive formation is substituted for another is not to say that a whole world of absolutely new objects, enunciations, concepts, and theoretical choices emerges fully armed and fully organized in a text that will place that world once for all; it is to say that a general transformation of relations has occured, but that it does not necessarily alter all the elements; it is to say that all objects or concepts, all enunciations or all theoretical choices disappear. On the contrary, one can, on the basis of these new rules, describe and analyze phenomena of continuity, return, and repetition . . . One of these elements — or several of them — may remain identical (preserve the same division, the same characteristics, the same structures), yet belong to different systems of dispersion, and be governed by distinct laws of formation. (Foucault 1972: 173)

Thus, archaeology does not deny continuity, it complicates it by analyzing it in a dialectic with discontinuity, an approach, I have argued (see Introduction), that must be employed to understand the discourse of the postmodern. It is because of this qualified, dialectical position that Foucault has rejected the label of "philosopher of discontinuity" (1988d: 99–100).

Foucault opposes his new concept of a "general history" to the traditional concept of a "total history." He summarizes the difference in this way: "A total description draws all phenomena around a single centre — a principle, a meaning, a spirit, a world-view, an overall shape; a general history, on the contrary, would deploy the space of a dispersion" (1972: 10).[8] For Foucault, evolutionary history attains its narrative totalizations through the construction of illegitimate abstractions. Beneath these abstractions are complex relations and interrelations, a shifting plurality of decentered, individualized series of discourses, unable to be reduced to a single law, model, unity, or vertical arrangement. Hence, the goal of this postmodern historiography is to break up the conceptual unities of modern historiography "and then see whether they can be legitimately reaffirmed; or whether other groupings should be made" (26). The potential result of such detotalizing moves is that "an entire field is set free" — the field of discursive formations, complex systems of difference and dispersion that can be analyzed apart from totalizing prejudices.

The task of archaeology is "to *make* differences: to constitute them as objects, to analyze them, and to define their concept" (205). But archaeology is not a radical anarchism that dissolves all previous unities into a random, chaotic flux without any pattern, order, or intelligibility. If archaeology calls into question modern unities and totalities, it is to *reconstruct* them in a more concrete and differentiated form.

Hence, while Foucault attempts to map discourse in its actual complexity and heterogeneity, he also finds an underlying unity of different groups of statements. His oxymoronic characterization of a discursive formation as a "system of dispersion" suggests that he is not pulverizing discourse into a chaotic flux of unrelated fragments, but rather is analyzing a dialectic of discursive difference and identity. For Foucault, the unity of discourse is not to be found at the surface level of concepts or themes, for similar concepts and themes can be informed by quite different assumptions, but rather at the archaeological level of constituting rules. In the classical era, for example, the disciplines of medicine, natural history, and general grammar are constituted by the same underlying rules; one basic discursive *system* governs the *dispersion* of different kinds of statements in different fields.

Where, typically, the unity of discourse is related to what is given to the speaking subject, Foucault decenters the subject and finds unity in an anonymous, prereflexive system of rules that are immanent in a practice and define its specific nature. While a given discursive formation is comprised of various discourses that can be described only in their particular domains, at the archaeological level these domains can be related to one another and be found to share the same underlying conditions. But this unity is not to be confused with an abstract totality: "The horizon of archaeology . . . is not *a* science, *a* rationality, *a* mentality, *a* culture; it is a tangle of interpositivities whose limits and points of intersection cannot be fixed in a single operation. Archaeology is a comparative analysis that is not intended to reduce the diversity of discourses, and to outline the unity that must totalize them, but is intended to divide up their diversity into different figures" (1972: 160).

Thus, archaeology rejects traditional concepts of "period" and "change," substituting for them new concepts of "episteme" and "transformation." Synchronically, archaeology attempts to establish the dialectic of difference and unity within a given discursive formation and its system of dispersion; diachronically, archaeology attempts to establish discontinuity and multiple, evenly developing levels of change. Different discourses within the same positivity change at different rates.

While archaeology analyzes the transformations from one discursive formation to another, it does not "explain" the forces behind such changes. This move is opposed, first, to positivist attempts to subsume diverse events under invariant universal laws. Second, it rejects the hermeneutic attempt to discover hidden forces of history and focuses instead on shifting discursive fields. But the shift away from explanation is mainly directed against Marxism. Archaeology avoids both an idealist "symbolic analysis" that analyzes discursive practices solely in terms of linguistic expression and communication, and a Marxist "causal analysis" that analyzes the determination of consciousness by political and economic events.

Foucault does not reject causal analysis; rather, he "suspends" it (1972: 164), postponing it for work he considers more fundamental. Archaeology seeks "forms of articulation" between discursive and nondiscursive systems. The rules of formation are to be mapped first; then one can explore the "positivities" these form, their imbrication with nondiscursive elements, and the effects these have on discourse. Archaeology wishes to show, for example, not how political practice determines the meaning of medical discourse, a typical Marxist approach, but how medical discourse is a *practice* bound up with a specific field of objects, a particular group of individuals, and which exercises distinctly political functions in society (1972: 163–164).

The thrust of Foucault's displacement of causal analysis is to establish "the autonomy of discourse" (1972: 163) far beyond what he thinks Marxism allows. Archaeology refuses to see discourse either as the direct surface on which expressive symbolic projections are written or as the mechanical effect of social processes. The concept of discursive practice breaks down Marx's base/superstructure distinction by showing that discourse is always already articulated with practices and that practices are informed by discursive rules. Foucault's approach is similar to Sahlin's (1976), who argues that the economic level of society is inseparable from culture, since "production" is always constituted through a set of symbols and meanings and not merely an instrumental logic. While archaeology seeks to describe the autonomy of discourse, Foucault explicitly renounces idealism: archaeology "seeks to discover that whole domain of institutions, economic processes, and social relations on which a discursive formation can be articulated; it tries to show how the autonomy of discourse and its specificity nevertheless do not give it the status of pure ideality and total historical independence; what it wishes to uncover is the particular level in which history can give place to definite types of discourse, which have their own historicity, and which are related to a whole set of various historicities" (1972: 164–165).

THE ORDER OF THINGS:
MODERNITY AND THE DECONSTRUCTION OF MARX

One finds the purest example of the archaeological focus on discourse (largely abstracted from institutions and practices) in *The Order of Things*.

In this text, Foucault attempts to trace the emergence and development of the human sciences and the humanist–anthropological discourse of "Man." He describes the conceptual underpinnings of successive Western orders of knowledge in the Renaissance, classical, and modern eras, while signaling the end of the modern era. Through exposition of this text, I wish to show (1) what Foucault takes to be the archaeological conditions of modern discourse; (2) why he thinks Marx's work is continuous with, rather than a break from, the modern era; and (3) how Foucault anticipates the dawning of a new postmodern era in knowledge.

In the classical era, words and things were assumed to stand in a perfect, God-given correspondence and language was a translucent mirror of reality. All classical thought, not only the mathematical disciplines but also the various "purely empirical domains," attempted to provide an exhaustive systematization of the world. This was accomplished through the construction of ordered tables of identities and differences of all things as given to representation, through a *mathesis universalis*. The knowing subject grasped the totality of natural relations without itself figuring in the representing process as a representing subject or an object to be known.

At the end of the eighteenth century, this classical knowledge collapsed and gave way to the modern episteme. The modern era is characterized by a "profound upheaval" in thought whereby language, objects, and the human subject itself acquire an empirical and historical density. Where classical thought saw representation as a mere given, modern thought is preoccupied with the question of the origins and legitimacy of representation. In the modern framework, representation no longer involves the autonomous power of the mind to order reality according to analytic grids. The data of representation are now given to thought from sources outside of immediate consciousness, buried within the finite conditions of human existence, within the dimensions of its biological life, its productive activity, and its communicative processes. The static categories of the classical episteme are now overturned by the flow of time as Order gives way to History, which mediates all knowledge and experience. "History in this sense is not to be understood as the compilation of factual successions of sequences as they may have occured; it is the fundamental mode of being of empiricities" (Foucault 1973b: 219). In the modern era, Foucault claims, the data of knowledge are understood to change, evolve, and have a historical origin and nature. Thus, the very presuppositions of Foucault's own discourse emerge here, and hence there are important modern elements in Foucault's "postmodern" discourse.

With its fall from a privileged place in the natural order of things into the depths of empirical facticity and temporality, the subject is transformed into "Man." Within the new "analytic of finitude," Man is understood as a finite and historically conditioned being, subject to the laws of biology, production, and language. Man is both the subject and object of knowledge, appearing in the epistemic space carved out by the new empirical sciences (biology, economics, and philology). Abandoning the field of classical representation, the empirical sciences, and the human sciences (psychology, sociology, and literature and myth) after them, "withdraw into the [empirical] depths of things and roll up upon themselves in accordance with the laws of life, production, and language" (1973b: 313).

Where the empirical sciences withdraw from the realm of representation altogether, not taking man as an object of study, philosophy and the human sciences take up the issue of representation in a new way, focusing on the conditions of possibility of representation as a form of knowledge and being. Both philosophy and the human sciences acknowledge that the subject is a constituted being, yet each believes it is also a constituting being who can overcome the limitations on its knowledge. To square this circle, each field takes a transcendental turn. The human sciences construct a transcendental theory of the object by claiming that it precedes the conditions of knowledge and provides the foundation for the unity of subjective representations. The human sciences see Man as empirically determined in its biological, economic, and linguistic nature, but it can grasp these laws and "subject them to total clarification" (1973b: 310) through reflexive analysis.

Philosophy constructs a transcendental theory of the subject by claiming that the subject determines its relation to the object through *a priori* conditions of experience. Beginning with Kant, modern philosophy constitutes Man within a series of "doublets" that convert empirical constraints on knowledge into transcendental grounds of the possibility of knowing that are rooted in the subject's very being. These include the transcendental/empirical doublet, in which the empirical contents of knowledge speak of the conditions that make all knowledge possible; the cogito/unthought doublet, where the unconscious ground of all thought reveals itself to the conscious mind; and the doublet of retreat/return of the origin, in which the very history that precedes Man provides the pathway back to the origins of his nature.

For both philosophy and the human sciences, the immediacy and translucency of knowledge in the classical episteme gives way to the opacity and density of thought. All modern thought is preoccupied with the problem of the "unthought," whereby knowledge is gained only by grasping what eludes immediate consciousness. Philosophy seeks this unthought in a transcendental consciousness; the human sciences in a more distant region beyond the subject itself, in the realms of biological function, social conflict, and linguistic signification. Yet this epistemological deficit that threatens the certainty of knowledge and the supremacy of the knowing subject is annuled and transformed into an ontological asset. Man is the being whose limitations on its knowledge provide the basis for its total recuperation. Since Man *is* the experience given to himself, the labor whose law constrains him, and the subject of a language that determines him, he is "able to recover his integrity on the basis of what eludes him" (323). Thus, although the status of the subject as originator of knowledge becomes threatened in the new field of temporality and finitude, its sovereignty is maintained in its transcendental reconstitution. The goal of modern thought is to return the Other to the Same, to reconstruct the foundations of knowledge, in spite of history, and to recapture the identity of Man. The goal of a postmodern thought, conversely, would be to overthrow these fictions, to dissolve the subject into language, and to liberate history from metaphysical constraints.

For Foucault, Marx's works belong entirely to the modern era and are ensnared in its aporias. In contrast to Althusser and others who interpret Marx's later work as an "epistemological break" from both his earlier humanist works and bourgeois theory in general, Foucault sees Marx's ideas as wholly derivative of the modern episteme: "At the deepest level of Western knowledge, Marxism introduced no real discontinuity: it found its place without difficulty . . . within an epistemological arrangement that welcomed it gladly . . . and that it, in return, had no intention of disturbing and, above all, no power to modify, even one jot, since it rested entirely upon it. Marxism exists in nineteenth century thought like a fish in water: that is, it is unable to breath anywhere else" (1973b: 261–262). Foucault does not deny that Marxism stands in opposition to bourgeois economic theories, but he sees these disputes as family squabbles within the modern episteme and emphasizes the importance of their similarities over their differences. "Their controversies may have stirred up a few waves and caused a few surface ripples; but they are no more that storms in a children's paddling pool" (262).

Thus, it should be no surprise that Foucault's analysis of nineteenth-century political economy takes up Ricardo rather than Marx, just as he foregoes explication of Darwin to focus instead on Cuvier. Marx's fundamental economic ideas, such as labor as the source of value or the primacy of production over circulation, were already anticipated by Ricardo, Smith, and others, and were possible only in the modern episteme. Ricardo, not Marx, first introduced historicity into economics, such that "The mode of being of economics is no longer linked to a simultaneous space of differences and identities, but to the time of successive productions" (1973b: 255). Ricardo and Marx each give different answers to the problem of the immobility of history that emerges in the nineteenth century. This theme arises as a result of what some perceived as a stabilization of economic dynamics and the culmination of the sense of human finitude in modern capitalism (258–259). Where Ricardo pessimistically views history as moving gradually to a point of final stabilization, Marx optimistically sees an increase of crisis tendencies in capitalism that allow for its revolutionary transformation. Yet, Foucault regards these "options" as of no consequence, as nothing more than two different ways of combining history, economics, and anthropology, of voicing the fundamental themes of the modern era.

Thus, Foucault's deconstruction of Marx shows his thought to be bound to a framework it cannot reject, to be contaminated by the same conceptual elements as the theories he opposes, to be determined by the same linguistic rules. Consequently, Foucault claims that Marx's thought, like any other modern thinker, is fractured by the doublets of the modern episteme. Trying to negotiate the empirical and transcendental, Foucault claims, Marx acknowledges human finitude and historicity, but posits a human essence that stands beyond time and social conditioning; caught between the *cogito* and the unthought, Marx seeks to bring the unconscious forces determining thought into conscious awareness; split between the retreat and return of the origin, he sees communism as the means to recover the lost origin and essence of the human subject, as the "true appropriation of the *human* essence through and for man," and "the emancipation and recovery of mankind" (Marx 1975a: 348, 358). Like Comte, Marx's work shows that positivism and eschatology, seemingly opposite, are "archaeologically indissociable" (320) insofar as both seek a truth grounded in an empirical discourse whose historical genesis is retraced, and culminates in modern science. The eschatological themes prominent in Marx pronounce the end of history with the end of alienation: "calendar time will be able to continue, but it will be, as it were, void, for historicity will have been superimposed exactly upon the human essence" (262).

Thus, for Foucault, Marx is simply another modern thinker trapped in transcendental metaphysics. Foucault is in agreement, then, with Baudrillard, Sahlins, and others (see Chapter 1), who see Marx as ensnared in the rationalistic logic of bourgeois political economy. This critique is made not only in *The Order of Things* but also, and perhaps even more forcefully, in a key but neglected essay on Bataille, "Preface to Transgression" (1977). It is there, following the same path taken in the early 1960s by Derrida, Deleuze, and others, that Foucault seeks an alternative to humanism, anthropology, and dialectics, drawing inspiration from the works of Sade, Bataille, Blanchot, Klossowski, and Nietzsche. With the death of God, and the consequent discovery of sexuality, Foucault claims that the key phenomenon of modern times has been the experience of finitude and being, limit and transgression. Foucault counts himself among those, in particular Bataille, "seeking a language for the thought of the limit," a nondiscursive, nonrepresentational language through which one confronts eroticism, ecstasy, limit experiences, and trangression. To develop this new thinking, it is necessary to renounce not only the philosophy of the subject, but the tradition of dialectics since Kant in order to move into the "extreme forms of language" supplied by Bataille, Blanchot, and Klossowski, thinkers who "bring us closer to the possibility of a non-dialectical language" (1977: 41).

In place of the search for totality, Foucault calls for the interrogation of the limit; in place of the movement of contradictions, he envisages the act of transgression and the rupture with ordinary being. Experiences such as sexuality cannot be illuminated through dialectics and productivist anthropology. Foucault rejects Marxian anthropology as a bourgeois-inspired, utilitarian reduction of the human being to rational categories:

> In a form of thought that considers man as worker and producer—that of European culture since the end of the eighteenth century—consumption was based entirely on need, and need based itself exclusively on the model of hunger. When this element was introduced into an investigation of profit (the appetite of those who satisfied their hunger), it inserted man into a dialectic of production which had a simple anthropological meaning: if man was alienated from his real nature and immediate needs, it was nevertheless through its agency that he recaptured his essence and achieved the indefinite gratification of his needs. But it would undoubtedly be misguided to conceive of hunger as that irreducible anthropological factor in the definition of work, production, and profit; and similarly, need has an altogether different status, or it responds at the very least to a code whose laws cannot be confined to a dialectic of production." (1977: 49–50)

Thus, Foucault rejects not only dialectics, but also Marxian anthropology, as a rationalist discourse that cannot grasp the profound nonutilitarian dimensions of human existence that he links to sexuality, eroticism, forms of excess, and the sacred. While we have already registered the importance of this critique, Foucault, like so many of Marx's critics, proves himself insensitive to the complexities of Marx's analyses and fails to take note of the multiplicity of models with which Marx operates. In "Preface to Transgression," we find that he reduces Marxian dialectics to a search for abstract totalities. He does not account for the phenomenon of contradiction and conflates simple with complex wholes, failing to see the differentiating element in dialectics as well as its concern to grasp unities and interrelationships.

In *The Order of Things,* Foucault reduces Marx's theories to a simple essentialism and metaphysics of alienation, equating certain tendencies or moments in Marx's work with its complex totality. Part of his objection is to the hermeneutical dimension of Marx's thought that seeks to grasp the forces constituting the appearances of reality. For Foucault, hermeneutics belongs to an antiquated Renaissance epistemology and is bound up with an essentialism that seeks the underlying essences of reality. Clearly, the hermeneutic attempt to decipher the mystified appearances of social reality need not appeal to underlying timeless essences. This may be the case for Plato, but it is not the case for Marx and the archaeological attempt to find rules of formation that determine consciousness itself can be nothing but a type of hermeneutics (see Best 1988 and Dreyfus 1984). Only through the hermeneutic attempt to go beyond the surface appearance of social reality to its underlying "essence" (by which Marx only meant social reality adequately understood), was Marx able to grasp the social relations behind the seemingly autonomous circulation of commodities and to reveal the mode of exploitation behind the surface justice and equality of the wage.

Foucault fails to appreciate that for however brief a period in his 1844 humanist writings Marx flirted with essentialism, he decisively broke with it in the same year to emphasize the historical production of needs and subjectivity. Arguably, by "human essence," Marx meant not an ahistorical and unchanging human nature, but rather basic characteristics that distinguish human beings from animals and that evolve and change historically. Hence, Marx would insist that "the human essence is no abstraction inherent in each single individual. In its reality it is the ensemble of the social relations" that condition each individual and change historically (1975a: 423). What human beings "appropriate," then, is not a lost essence or substance à la Hegel, but their own historically created possibilities embodied in objective forms, including social knowledge, modes of technology, and their dynamically evolving humanity. Foucault equates the attempt to appropriate the continuously developing wealth of human beings with a metaphysical "return of the origin," thereby blocking a politics of transfiguration (see Chapter 1). Moreover, Foucault never acknowledges the similarities to his own approach, not recognizing that Marx broke sharply with progressivism to insist on historical discontinuities, the uneven development of different social levels, and the contingency of practical change.[9]

In *The Archaeology of Knowledge,* however, Foucault seems to reverse the view of Marx presented in *The Order of Things.* Where in *The Order of Things* he emphasizes the continuities between Marx and modern thought, in *The Archaeology of Knowledge* he sees Marx as the first theorist to initiate a decentering movement that situates the subject within larger economic forces that determine it. On this point, then, Marx escapes from the modern episteme to take the first step toward a posthumanist, postmodern historiography. Foucault's claim now is that Marx initiated "an entirely new discursive practice on the basis of political economy" (1972: 188). Apparently Foucault no longer believed that Marx is bound to the modern doublets, since belief in an abiding essence of the subject is the common factor in all doublets.

Perhaps Foucault, like Althusser, is thinking here of the Marx of *Capital*, who defines human individuals as mere bearers of social functions. Yet Marx's view of the subject tended mainly toward a dialectical view, neither determinist nor voluntarist, structuralist nor phenomenological, but rather hermeneutical — a socially situated subject who shapes the forces that shape it. Unlike Foucault, Marx sees the subject as something active and as having a positive content, a social, natural, and historical being whose creative capacities evolve through time. In his conception of the subject as an empty form that is acted on by shifting discursive formations but itself never acts, that never changes except in its forms of speech and thought, and that has no evolving practical abilities, it is Foucault's theory, not Marx's, that is essentialist and ahistorical.

POSTMODERNITY
AND THE DEATH OF MAN

Paradoxically, the modern era inaugurates both the birth and death of History and Man. In the closing pages of *The Order of Things*, Foucault describes the first indications of a new postmodern epistemic space where the subject, now interpreted as an effect of language, desire, and the unconscious, is once and for all dethroned. There are numerous apocalyptic references to the coming of a new postmodern era (1973b: 384–387).[10] The postmodern era is understood strictly in terms of shifts in discourse and knowledge, as a posthumanist era. Oscillating between the positive and the fundamental, the empirical and the transcendental, attempting to construct a solid foundation over a perilous epistemological fault line, modern efforts to construct the figure of Man necessarily failed. While the "death of Man" perhaps was initiated first by the human sciences in their appeal to a region of determination beyond consciousness, the "countersciences" (psychoanalysis, ethnology, and linguistics) abandon the standpoint of Man altogether, identify the conditions of knowledge to lie entirely outside of a representing consciousness, and thereby inaugurate a new postmodern episteme.

Clearly, archaeology itself belongs to, and is made possible by, this emerging postmodern episteme. Against modern theories like phenomenology and Marxism, Foucault wants to create a new postmodern form of thought that does not reduce difference and dispersion to a unified Same, that abandons the "problematics of origin" as well as the metaphysics of Return that seek to recuperate Man's essential identity alienated in history and thereby try to "subjugate time" (1973b: 335). Modern thought sets itself the impossible task of reconciling empirical and transcendental standpoints and resorts to metaphysical fictions in the process. It moves haltingly toward a historicist outlook, but cannot shake the hangover of metaphysics and essentialist thinking. The task of archaeology is to break from the doublets of modern thought by abandoning all transcendental and humanist standpoints. Archaeology repudiates the view of the subject as a foundation for knowledge and truth—whether conceived in static terms of an immutable nature, or in more dynamic terms of a historically unfolding human essence—and seeks to awaken thought from its "anthropological slumbers."

The demolition of Man and the modern episteme and the emergence of a new postmodern form of thought are presented in liberatory tones. Foucault believes we are just now on the verge of another historical rupture, where new forms of thinking, inaugurated by Nietzsche and the countersciences, are emerging, but where the old forms still dominate. New forms of thought can emerge once the foundations of the modern episteme erode, and it is Foucault's task to help in the process of erosion by abolishing talk about the essence or liberation of Man. By questioning the whole basis of modern thought, Foucault attempts "to renew contact in this way with the project for a general critique of reason" (1973b: 342), which is an implicit goal of his archaeological investigations. What political implications this critique would have, and what forms of thought would replace anthropology, is not specified until his genealogical and ethical works. What is clear is that Foucault finds a great deal of promise in the posthumanist, linguistic space opened up by Nietzsche and the countersciences.

Yet, in line with his emphasis on a dialectic of continuity and discontinuity, Foucault's incipient postmodern thought is not premised on a total break with the classical and modern epistemes, but on a reconfiguring of some of their key elements. Where the classical era understood the coexistence of human beings and language, Foucault sees the "most important philosophical choice of our period" to be undertaking an analysis of this coexistence that avoids "a naive return to the Classical theory of discourse" (1973b: 339, 338). Most importantly, as we have seen, Foucault draws from the historical problematic of the modern era opened up by Hutton's uniformitarianism at the close of the eighteenth century and continuing in the nineteenth century in the work of Lyell, Darwin, Hegel, Marx, and others. Where classical thought analyses reality primarily in terms of spatial categories, modern thought, through the analytic of finitude, relies fundamentally on temporal categories.

In his brief "history of History" (1973b: 367–373), Foucault concedes that History—that is, historical consciousness—has existed long before the modern era, since the beginnings of antiquity. History has fulfilled a number of functions in Western cultures, serving as "memory, myth, transmission of the Word and of Example, vehicle of tradition, critical awareness of the present, decipherment of humanity's destiny, anticipation of the future, or promise of a return" (367). Foucault capitalizes this kind of history to signal that it is a metaphysical mode of time that reduces temporality to a linear order and difference to a frozen essence or identity. This mode of time was drastically altered in the modern era, however, which discovered that rather than a single time, there were a plurality of unevenly developing times specific to different forms of life, labor, and language.[11]

Thus, beginning in the nineteenth century, within the analytic of finitude, things are understood to have their own forms of history and Man becomes a part of these. The paradoxical result is that Man is dehistoricized insofar as his history is nothing but the temporal modulation of the different empirical orders to which he is subjected. Man, on Foucault's determinist schemes, does not have his own history independent of things. Moreover, while history provides the conditions of possibility for the human sciences, it also destroys any claim they might make to universal validity, since it destabilizes and relativizes their contents. While Foucault rejects the problematic of Man constituted within the analytic of finitude, modern history provides the conditions of possibility for Foucault's work itself, and he attempts to advance the modern rejection of linear order and unified time beyond its metaphysical containment.

Thus, Foucault does not reject modern thought *en toto;* rather, he appropriates the emphasis of modern thought on the historical constitution of "Man" and breaks with the various methods and concepts that try to limit the decentering and historicizing impulses this constitution inaugurates through a subordination of the empirical to the transcendental. For Foucault, besides "myth" and "transmission of the Word and Example," history can serve as "memory" and "critical awareness of the present." These are key themes Foucault will develop in later stages of his work, in his "diagnostic critique" that continues the archaeological project of redefining historiography in nonmetaphysical form. I examine below the problems with a complete abandonment of the subject and some of the totalizing dimensions of a postmodern methodology designed to liberate difference. Let us turn now to the next major stage in Foucault's work and examine the similarities and differences between archaeology and genealogy.

GENEALOGY, HISTORICAL MATERIALISM, AND POLITICS

> [P]ower in its strategies, at once general and detailed, and its mechanisms, has never been studied. What has been studied even less is the relation between power and knowledge, the articulation of each on the other.
> —FOUCAULT (1980a: 51)

> My role—and that is too emphatic a word—is to show people that they are much freer than they feel, that people accept as truth, as evidence, some themes which have been built up at a certain moment during history, and that this so-called evidence can be criticized and destroyed. To change something in the minds of people—that's the role of an intellectual.
> —FOUCAULT

As we have seen, Foucault's archaeologies privilege analysis of discourse and knowledge over practices and institutions, but without such analysis constituting an idealist project. On Foucault's definition of discourse, language is always bound up with actions, practices, and institutional networks. Foucault never regards discourse as anything but a discursive *practice* embedded in institutional networks of power and authority. Yet while discursive practices are socially conditioned and variable, Foucault believes discourse has an autonomy from political and economic processes. He thus seeks to bracket the nondiscursive context of discourse to focus on the conditions of emergence and intelligibility of various discursive formations. Beginning in 1970, in the shift from archaeology to genealogy, Foucault removes these brackets and situates discourse within its larger social and political context, explicitly addressing the relationship between knowledge and power, and analyzing the power effects of discourse as they constitute subjects and their bodies.

Foucault's most detailed reflections on the genealogical method occurs in his essay "Nietzsche, Genealogy, History" (1977, orig. 1971). Ostensibly an exposition of Nietzschean genealogy, Foucault simultaneously articulates his own appropriation of the genealogical method—as becomes obvious halfway through the essay when Foucault shifts from "he" (Nietzsche) to "we." The key aspect of Nietzschean–Foucauldian genealogy is its attempt to break from the metaphysical assumptions informing "traditional history" and to recapture the complexity of historical time in a new *"wirkliche"* or "effective" history. Effective history rejects the view of traditional history, in which time is nothing but an accidental veneer to be peeled away in order to find the essences and identities that abide throughout the flux of history. Against this detemporalization of history, genealogy holds that there is nothing constant in history, that there are no essences or identities, that everything is historically consitituted and so has a history. Reason, sentiments, values, and the body itself are all historically variable and constituted phenomena.

Traditional history employs a metaphysics of origins and endings. The search for "origins" involves an ahistorical attempt to grasp a pure essence, a primal, undifferentiated source that abides in the face of historical change and contingency. Against this, genealogy advances the notion of an always already begun beginning, an overdetermined event that is constituted within a pregiven context, and practices that are constantly changing within historical relations. When acknowledging change at all, the search for origins valorizes the first moments of existence as pure and untainted and contrasts this with a subsequent fall and decline. Overturning the lofty pretensions of metaphysics, genealogy finds the impure and lowly grounds of values and practices in human sentiments and the will to power. Thus, it finds the "origins" of reason in unreason, of disinterested truth in scientific passion, of law in the thirst for violence, of morality in immorality, and of liberty in the machinations of elites, authorities, and ruling classes.

Genealogy is also opposed to the notion of a plan, goal, or end in history, which presupposes a purpose as established by God, Reason, or Spirit. It therefore rejects all forms of universal history, progressivism, and metanarrative. Genealogy is an attempt to "free historical chronologies and successive orderings from all forms of progressivist perspective" (Foucault 1980a: 49). For the genealogist, history is not the march of reason toward freedom, but rather a haphazard succession of various power formations: "Humanity does not gradually progress from combat to combat until it arrives at universal reciprocity, where the rule of law finally replaces warfare; humanity installs each of its violences in a system of rules and thus proceeds from domination to domination" (151).

Genealogy breaks with teleology and causal determinism to vindicate the operations of chance, accidents, contingency, discontinuities, and reversals in history. Teleological schemes are reductionistic insofar as they force all events into a predetermined meaning, treating them as mere moments of an ideal and fictitious continuity. For Foucault, "events" are singular and mark points of reversal or discontinuity. Like any historian, the genealogist tries to reconstruct historical processes, but does so neutrally "without imposing on them a positivity or a valorisation" (1980a: 50). As demonstrated in the opening pages of *Discipline and Punish* (1979), in his graphic description of the torture of Damien, the genealogist begins by finding a discontinuity in the past, an event that seems entirely foreign to the present sensibility, in order to disturb the complacency of the present, to mark its rupture with the past, and to rethink the values of the present.

The break with metaphysics and metanarrative allows for the emergence of real historical time, unfolding in its actual complexity. The first task of genealogy is deconstructive; it seeks to dismantle homogenizing narratives and identify areas of difference, discontinuity, and dislocation. Genealogy's understanding of time is informed by a glance that "distinguishes, separates, and disperses, that is capable of liberating divergence and marginal elements—the kind of disassociating view that is capable of decomposing itself, capable of shattering the unity of man's being through which it was thought that he could extend his sovereignty to the events of the past" (1977: 153). The search for descent "disturbs what was previously considered immobile; it fragments what was thought unified; it shows the heterogeneity of what was imagined consistent with itself" (147).

Genealogy also opposes the kind of progressivist view that Marx developed in *The Economic and Philosophic Manuscripts* and *The German Ideology,* but broke with in succeeding years, that sought to grasp fundamental lines of continuity in history that can be "appropriated" for future purposes:

> Genealogy does not pretend to go back in time to restore an unbroken continuity that operates beyond the dispersion of forgotten things; its duty is not to demonstrate that the past actively exists in the present, that it continues secretly to animate the present, having imposed a predetermined form to all its vicissitudes. Genealogy does not resemble the evolution of a species and does not map the destiny of a people. On the contrary, to follow the complex course of descent is to maintain passing events in their proper dispersion; it is to identify the accidents, the minute deviations—or conversely, the complete reversals—the errors, the false appraisals, and the faulty calculations that gave birth to those things that continue to exist and have value for us; it is to discover that truth or being do not lie at the root of what we know and what we are, but are the exteriority of accidents. (1977: 146)

Abandoning a "suprahistorical history" whose memory is informed by metaphysical assumptions, Foucault substitutes a "countermemory." Genealogy is a "countermemory" in two distinct senses. First, it is a *counter*memory in that it opposes the dominant forms of "memory" and historical representations created by ruling groups and presented as factual truth. Through validating the narratives and experiences of marginalized and oppressed groups, genealogy helps to awaken and create different historical memories that can help challenge and subvert forms of domination. Second, genealogy is a counter*memory* because it rejects the metaphysical model of a pure consciousness reflecting on a continuous past. Countermemory involves "a transformation of history into a totally different form of time" (1977: 160), one that breaks with universalist, evolutionist schemes and admits hitherto largely alien temporal schemes involving discontinuity, plurality, uneveness, and randomness.

It should be clear that genealogy has strong continuities with archaeology. Like archaeology, Foucault characterizes genealogy as a new mode of historical writing, calling the genealogist "the new historian" (1977: 160). Both methodologies break with metaphysical views that efface temporality from history. Using painstaking measures to reconstitute the past on the basis of dusty documents, both approaches attempt to historicize what is thought to be immutable and to find the hidden histories of present-day values, discourses, practices, and institutions. Both reexamine the social field from a micrological standpoint to enable analysis of discursive discontinuity and dispersion. Both seek to purge historical writing of humanist assumptions by decentering and dispersing the subject. Both analyze modern reason through historical researches into the beginning of the human sciences. Both reduce the individual to nothing but an effect of prepersonal forces, be they discourse or power.

Foucault does not reject archaeology in favor of genealogy since his focus is still on discourse and knowledge; rather, genealogy "concerns the effective formation of discourse, whether within the limits of [political] control, or outside them" (Foucault 1972: 233). Archaeology and genealogy now combine in the form of theory/practice where theory is immediately practical and political in character; they are two different, and complementary, perspectives in the analysis of power formations.[12] The main difference between these two perspectives is not methodological, but lies in their respective objects of study: rules, discourse, and knowledge as compared to practices, institutions, and power. But the continuity between the two different approaches is even stronger, since the emphases of genealogy were always implicit in archaeology and archaeology, was never conceived as an "idealism" to be opposed to the "materialism" of genealogy. Genealogy marks the *explicit politicization* of Foucault's work, where the goal is to analyze various power/knowledge formations and to help create new power/knowledge formations to overturn regimes of domination. The thematic of power was implied in the archaeological studies, but in genealogy it shifts from the background to the foreground. Thus, Foucault states: "When I think back now, I ask myself what else it was that I was talking about, in *Madness and Civilization* or *The Birth of the Clinic*, but power? Yet I'm perfectly aware that I scarcely used the word and never had such a field of analyses at my disposal" (1980a: 115; see also 1991: 145–146). In both works, Foucault was concerned with the social methods of regulating experience through division, classification, incarceration, and surveillance.[13]

The shift from archaeology to genealogy was accompanied by a parallel shift from aloof archivalist to impassioned militant. Foucault's remarkable political career began in 1968 and continued until the end of his life. Although formerly denounced by leftists, students, and many of his colleagues as a Gaullist technocrat, a conservative, or apolitical mandarin, after 1968 Foucault became a model of the engaged intellectual.[14] Unlike Marx, Foucault's political activities went far outside the orbit of workers' struggles, although they included these; on numerous occasions he involved himself with unions, strikes, and workers' experiences.[15] For the most part, however, Foucault worked in different areas, with the new struggles emerging in the schools, prisons, courts, and elsewhere, and he tried to respond to political events as they unfolded around him.

Foucault's most well-known and successful political intervention came in 1971, when he founded the Groupe d'Information sur les Prisons (GIP), an organization designed to protest the deplorable conditions of French prisons, to help the prisoners articulate their needs and defend their rights with their own voices, and to question the social distinction between the innocent and the guilty. As markers of the success of this group, it helped to spark prison reform and disbanded in 1972, having evolved into a new organization comprised only of prisoners themselves. In subsequent years, Foucault passionately involved himself in the struggle for the rights of French immigrants, Vietnamese boat people, Soviet dissidents, condemned Spanish militants, the solidarity movement in Poland, the Iranian revolution, and sexual politics. As with Marx, an important part of Foucault's politics was realized in journalistic activity.[16] In countless petitions, speeches, and demonstrations, Foucault spoke out against injustice wherever he found it and sought to advance the cause of human rights on an international level.[17] Never afraid of "dirty hands," he put in long hours performing the most mundane political duties, such as organizing demonstrations and keeping financial books. In 1983, Foucault planned to write a book attacking the failures of the Socialists then in power, and the French Left in general for lacking skill in the "art of government." One of his last projects was to organize a group of intellectuals interested in disseminating information and exploring new possibilties for political action.

With the turn to genealogy, Foucault follows Marx's lead in breaking with the apolitical character of positivist historiography and using historical research for leftist political goals. Like Marx, Foucault employs historical analysis in an effort to defetishize and denaturalize the present, to underline the discontinuities between the present and the past. Foucault maintains that to criticize is to specify "how the present is absolutely different from all that it is not, that is to say, from our past" (1989: 39). Genealogy thereby problematizes the present as eternal and self-evident and exposes the operations of power and domination working behind neutral or beneficent facades. In Foucault's words, "It seems to me that the real political task in a society such as ours is to criticize the working of institutions which appear to be both neutral and independent; to criticize them in such a manner that the political violence which has always exercized itself obscurely through them will be unmasked, so that one can fight them" (1984: 6). Genealogy attempts to demonstrate how objectifying forms of reason (and their regimes of truth and knowledge) have been made, treating them as historically contingent rather than eternally necessary forces. Consequently, "they can be unmade, as long as we know how it was they were made" (Foucault 1988d: 37).

Foucault claims that his genealogies owe a great, unacknowledged debt to Marxism:

> There is also a sort of game that I play . . . I often quote concepts, texts and phrases from Marx, but without feeling obliged to add the authenticating label of a footnote with a laudatory phrase to accompany the quotation. . . . It is impossible at the present time to write history without using a range of concepts directly or indirectly linked to Marx's thought and situating oneself within a horizon of thought which has been defined and described by Marx. One might even wonder what difference there could be between being a historian and being a Marxist. (1980a: 52–53)

In fact, Foucault greatly overstates his case, since the thrust of genealogy is directed away from the core assumptions of Marx's theory of history and politics.

In large part, the differences between Marx and Foucault stem from different understandings of power, of what and where it is. Foucault claims that, as a result of Marx, we have a good understanding of the mechanisms of exploitation, but we still know very little about power (1977: 212–213; 1991: 148–149). Marx understands power as the means whereby a dominant class exercizes control over society through control of the social means of production. Power is centralized in the hands of a superordinate class and wielded against all subordinate classes. Power and domination are enforced through exploitation and backed by ideology. Foucault believes the Marxist analysis of power is reductionistic. Where Marx equates power with exploitation, Foucault, like Weber, argues that exploitation is only one aspect of power, which is itself far more general in its nature, strategies, and range of effects. Power should be understood not as exploitation, but as rationalization, or rather, as a series of discursive–institutional employments of rationality that seek to "normalize" and "discipline" the social population through the liquidation of alterity and the production of docile minds and bodies.

Against the Marxist "economic subordination" of power to class, Foucault painstakingly tries to uncover the historical emergence of a disciplinary power that operates in all institutional spheres of society and not just the factory; that regulates the body itself and not just the working day; that is exercised more by means of surveillance than extraction of surplus labor, that confines subjects in a psychological straightjacket of "normal" identity; that creates discourses of truth rather than merely false consciousness; and that involves a production, not just repression, of subjects.

This analysis is undertaken primarily in *Discipline and Punish* and *The History of Sexuality*. In these works, Foucault argues that beginning in the eighteenth century, industrial society generated a disciplinary power based on regulating individuals and controlling their thoughts and movements. While disciplinary power has a coherent strategy of normalization, its mechanisms are heteromorphous and diffused throughout the various institutional networks comprising society, creating a "disciplinary archipelago." Power is ubiquitous, but it is not omnipotent. Foucault and Marx share a similar vision of society as structured around conflict and struggle. Foucault insists that power necessarily engenders resistance and to underscore this point he employs an inverted Clauswitzean model to conceive of politics as the continuation of war by other means, seeing "all problems of power in terms of relations of war" (1980a: 123).[18] In fact, to mark his break with idealist linguistic models, Foucault claims, "one's point of reference should not be to the great model of language (*langue*) and signs, but to that of war and battle. The history which bears and determines us has the form of a war rather than that of a language: relations of power, not relations of meaning" (114).

Foucault does not so much deny Marxist claims to be true as he insists they are incomplete and inadequate, that they effect a totalizing closure on other forms of analysis. In understanding the intimate connection between capitalism and normalization, Foucault shows, for example, that disciplinary power emerges within the general context of industrial capitalism and is used as a strategy by the capitalist class (1980a: 105, 188). Thus, Foucault's argument is not that disciplinary power is independent of economics and production, only that it cannot be reduced to these.

Foucault's understanding of power reorients historical research. Following Nietzsche's genealogies of morality, asceticism, justice, and punishment, Foucault seeks to write the histories of unknown, forgotten, excluded, and marginal discourses that are suppressed by Marxism and forms of traditional history alike. Genealogy "must record the singularity of events outside of any monotonous finality; it must seek them in the most uncompromising places, in what we tend to feel is without history — in sentiments, love, conscience, instincts" (Foucault 1977: 139–140). Genealogy involves the "making visible of what was previously unseen" (1980a: 50) due to a too-narrow focus on large-scale economic and political processes. This entails "addressing oneself to a layer of material which had hitherto had no pertinence for history and which had not been recognized as having any moral, esthetic, political or historical value" (50–51). Thus, Marxian history itself is too limiting in its scope; although it goes beyond a merely political history to analyze the social and historical impact of trade, commerce, and industry, it remains a reductionistic macrohistory that ignores or occludes the study of independent microhistories. Foucault complains that Marxists, subsequently, have rejected his analyses as "politically unimportant and epistemologically vulgar" (1980a: 110; 1991: 76–78).

Against the Marxist charge that genealogy writes the history of the "banal," Foucault undoes the opposition between sublime and banal history and tries to vindicate the importance of micronarratives. A macrotheory that centers analysis around production and class must give way to a series of microtheories that analyze various institutions without seeking a totalizing "theory of society." The discourses of madness, medicine, punishment, and sexuality have independent histories and institutional bases, irreducible to larger phenomenona such as the modern state and economy.

The pluralizing and detotalizing moves of the genealogical model have important political implications. Genealogy must wage a twofold struggle, within both the realm of theory and that of society at large. Within the institution of theory itself, the genealogist seeks to battle for legitimacy. Against "the tyranny of globalising discourses" (1980a: 83), Foucault calls for "an insurrection of subjugated knowledges" (81), of those "disqualified" discourses that both positivistic science and Marxism reject because they do not fit comfortably into a systematizing framework, because they are deemed marginal and incapable of being formalized, "located low down on the hierarchy, beneath the required level of cognition or scientificity" (82). Genealogies are the combined product of the erudite knowledge of the historian and the popular knowledge of chronicled struggles. The genealogist attempts to recuperate lost and forgotten histories and struggles insofar as they bear on the understanding and transformation of present-day power relations. "In the specialised areas of knowledge there lay the memory of hostile encounters which even up to this day have been confined to the margins of knowledge" (83). Genealogy attempts to make tactical use of suppressed histories and knowledges, to deploy a *counter-memory* of the past, to find the relevance of these memories and histories for contemporary struggles.

Foucault characterizes genealogies as "anti-sciences," not because they seek to "vindicate a lyrical right to ignorance or non-knowledge" and attack the concepts and methods of science per se, but rather because they contest "the [coercive] effects of the centralising powers which are linked to the institution and functioning of an organised scientific discourse" (1980a: 84). The question is not so much whether a particular theory —

Marxism, psychoanalysis, genealogy—is or is not a "science," and therefore legitimate or illegitimate, but rather what kind of aspirations to power accompany the search and demand for science. Foucault is not denying the possibility of scientific discourse, or rejecting it as oppressive per se, rather he is objecting to the exclusion of everything that is not "scientific" from the realm of legitimate knowledge. Such a rigid boundary, enforced by bourgeois and some Marxist theorists alike, automatically disqualifies local, popular forms of knowledge that Foucault believes are critical for understanding and transforming contemporary relations of power.

Hence, where productivism in theory entails a workerism in politics, genealogy in theory demands a micropolitics in practice. The detotalizing optic of genealogy allows for the analysis of a whole range of micropowers that are invisible to or clouded over by the economistic vision. If, analytically, it is discerned that power is local and decentered in form, so forms of political struggle must be of similar character in order to combat the various facets of power. The subjugated voices of history speak to hidden forms of domination; to admit their speech is necessarily to revise one's conception of what and where power is. Unlike classical Marxism, genealogy allows a pluralization of power struggles, it legitimates a multiplication of struggles that could facilitate the kind of larger (systemic) social struggles Marxists anticipate. Genealogy precludes the dismissal of sexual, racial, or cultural politics as inconsequential or secondary in relation to class politics. The struggles of students, minorities, women, homosexuals, prisoners, and other groups no longer need be subordinated to the class struggle; the "margins" move into the "center," or rather, these spatial metaphors and the oppositions they imply are dismantled.

Since power operates far beyond the confines of production, class, and exploitation, Foucault argues that simply changing the mode of production of the state is politically ineffective because it does nothing to alter the various power mechanisms that circulate throughout various social institutions. Because the state is not the source of disciplinary power, but rather its effect, a crystallization of various regional powers, power has to be analyzed not in a descending manner, from a centralized point of a king or class that moves below toward the subjects of power, but in an ascending manner, in fragmented analyses of various social institutions where disciplinary mechanisms arise and later congeal in the state. Hence, for a modern concept of macropolitics, where clashing forces struggle for control over a centralized source of power rooted in the economy and state, Foucault substitutes a postmodern concept of micropolitics where numerous local groups struggle against diffuse and decentered forms of power spreading throughout society, in the prisons, asylums, hospitals, and schools.

Foucault's concept of power/knowledge has direct implications for a critical theory of political knowledge as it is instantiated in totalizing narratives of history and society and in universal intellectuals. Genealogy voices a suspicion of Enlightenment reason that informs the Marxist tradition, along with the scientific models Marx and many of his followers have uncritically appropriated. As Foucault claims, a leftist appropriation of reason, science, and truth can be just as authoritarian as that of the Right. In place of the truth of politics Foucault analyzes a politics of truth that sees truth as a discourse that legitimates power and authority. Genealogy breaks with the elitism of hierarchical Marxist models insofar as it attempts to democratize knowledge and erode the privileges of a theoretical avant-garde. The universal intellectual who legislates the political will for all groups is replaced by the concept of the "specific intellectual" who intervenes only at the local level, on specific issues. Marx's unfortunate metaphor of the intellectual as the head of the struggle and the proletariat as its heart or body (1975a: 257) was disastrously literalized by Lenin, Stalin, and their successors in the form of the vanguard party. Yet, as I argue in Chapter 1, the thrust of Marx's politics anticipates Foucault's attack on the bureaucratic manipulation of politics by an intellectual elite.

If Marx thought the intellectual should exert a strong, but not authoritarian, role in the organization of the working class, Foucault thinks the role of the intellectual should be far more minimal, limited to critical questioning and providing instruments of analysis. As a specific intellectual, the genealogist contributes to the production of a counterknowledge and political practice that challenges dominant knowledges in the service of normalization by exposing their historical, contingent, and modifiable character. The specific intellectual makes no pretensions to speak *ex cathedra*, from the standpoint of absolute knowledge, or even to draw up manifestos and deliver inaugural addresses. The intellectual does no more than challenge existing ways of thinking and acting and offer to different groups or individuals historically based forms of knowledge. The intellectual's task is to raise questions, not provide answers; to induce skepticism, not complacency; to deconstruct, not reconstruct; to describe, not prescribe:

> The job of an intellectual does not consist in molding the political will of others. It is a matter of performing analyses in his or her own fields, of interrogating anew the evidence and postulates, of shaking up habits, ways of acting and thinking, of dispelling commonplace beliefs, of taking a new measure of rules and institutions . . . it is a matter or participating in the formation of a political will, where [the intellectual] is called to perform a role as citizen. (Foucault 1991: 12)

The intellectual participates in the creation of a political will, but does not constitute or mandate it. Like Lukács, and some tendencies in Marx,

Foucault privileges the knowing standpoint of actors directly involved in struggles, rather than that of the intellectual analyzing them from the outside.

The intellectuals should listen to the nonintellectuals and help them formulate their problems and solutions, but the former should never speak for or above the latter: "I absolutely will not play the part of one who prescribes solutions. I hold that the role of the intellectual today is not that of establishing laws proposing solutions or prophesying, since by doing that one can only contribute to the functioning of a determinate situation of power that to my mind must be criticized" (1991: 157). This attitude is crucial, as shown in Chapter 3, for understanding why Foucault refuses to specify the normative underpinnings of his analyses: he believes that normative justification is relevant only for those who make prescriptive statements, a project that he resolutely avoids.

Despite differences between the archaeological and genealogical stages of Foucault's work, a key continuity in his work to this point is his rejection of the subject, seeing it as completely determined by discourse or power. The contradiction of trying to activate politically nonexistent subjects is one of the factors that impels Foucault to reconsider his view of subjectivity and to move into a new stage of analysis.

ETHICS, FREEDOM, AND TRANSGRESSION

Develop your legitimate strangeness.
— RENE CHAR

Perhaps one day, [the idea of transgression] will seem as
decisive for our culture, as much a part of its soil, as
the experience of contradiction was at an earlier time for
dialectical thought.
— FOUCAULT (1977: 33)

In order to trace the beginnings of modern normalizing practices to deeper historical matrices, Foucault's 1980s works depart from the familiar territory of modernity to analyze Greek, Roman, and Christian cultures. Specifically, Foucault's concern with the genealogy of the modern hermeneutics of desire, the search for the "deep truth" of onself in one's sexuality through the ritual of confessional practices, leads him to the more distant beginnings of this process in premodern sources. Thus, *The History of Sexuality* (initially conceived as a six volume project) carried over into two subsequent works, *The Use of Pleasure* and *The Care of the Self,* before being cut short by his death.

This shift in the objects of historical study is accompanied by a number of important philosophical changes. Foucault now sees positive aspects of Enlightenment rationality, he rejects his deterministic view of the subject, he employs an ancient and modern discourse of freedom and autonomy, and he finds models for resistance to disciplinary power in the ethical practices of ancient culture.[19] Where he once sought a subject that disassociated itself from all forms of identity to achieve a "happy limbo of non-identity" (1980c: xiii), he now sees the necessity of producing new, positive forms of "identity," of a self's conscious relation to itself.[20] He now weaves premodern, modern, and postmodern elements into the complex layers of his thought. These changes raise numerous questions about Foucault's work: has he broken completely with his earlier concerns with power and domination? Has he abandoned politics for ethics, aestheticism, or dandyism? Has he renounced his structuralist-inspired rejection of the subject for a neohumanism?

In his works from the 1960s and 1970s, Foucault analyzed the subject as an effect of discourse and disciplinary practices and equated forms of rationality with mechanisms of domination. He now notes the one-sidedness of this view and, in an "auto-critique," rejects his prior deterministic view of the subject: "If one wants to analyze the genealogy of the subject in Western civilization, one has to take into account not only techniques of domination, but also techniques of the self. One has to show the interaction between these two types of self. When I was studying asylums, prisons, and so on, I perhaps insisted too much in techniques of dominatio. . . . I would like, in the years to come, to study power relations starting from techniques of the self" (Foucault and Sennet 1982: 10).

In *The Use of Pleasure* (1986) and *The Care of the Self* (1988a), Foucault follows through on this proposal. Using the Greeks and Romans as his model, he analyzes how they problematized their everyday practices to create a free self. In an elaborate, self-created "ethics," using "technologies of the self," men from Greek and Roman ruling classes set down rules for regulating their behavior in the realms of diet, family relations, and sexuality. The ultimate goal of ethics was aesthetic, to stylize one's life and transform it into a work of art.[21]

Foucault finds in Greco-Roman technologies of the self examples of how individuals can seek knowledge about themselves, discipline themselves, and create new identities in a space of freedom rather than domination. Technologies of the self, the care and art of the self, provide a way to break with socially imposed identities, with essentialist definitions of truth and human nature promoted by normalizing disciplines. The goal of these technologies, or ethical techniques, was not to discover or recuperate one's real "nature," a normalized construct that only appeared with Christianity and modernity, but continually to produce oneself as a free and creative agent. Where earlier (1980b) Foucault was promoting new pleasure and bodies, in a Bataillean–Dionysian vein, he now employs an Aristotelian–Apollonian element and advocates creating entirely new selves and identities rooted in self-styled ethics.

Most generally, Foucault embraces a Nietzschean–modernist project of the endless reinvention of the self, of constant self-overcoming, becoming, and transformation.[22] He calls for experimentation with all the forms of experience that Western society tolerates, when it does at all, only in the realm of literature (1977: 222). In place of the Socratic maxim, "Know thyself" and the modern injunction to grasp the truth of onself, Foucault's mandate is to get free of oneself, which means to continuously create oneself anew. Against Marxist humanism and the Frankfurt School, Foucault claims: "the problem is not to recover our 'lost' identity, to free our imprisoned nature, our deepest truth; but instead, the problem is to move toward something radically Other . . . we must produce something that doesn't yet exist and about which we cannot know what it will be" (1991: 121). Foucault seeks not a (Marxian) production of the self, but its (Bataillean) destruction and (Nietzschean) reconstruction, "the creation of something entirely different, of a total innovation" (122).

While there are important advances over Foucault's earlier works, insofar as he breaks with his deterministic view of the subject, many of his critics see these later works as a regression from his fruitful analyses of power and domination. Wolin (1986), for example, claims that Foucault adopts an amoral, apolitical aestheticism that shifts focus from the social world to the self and emphasizes beauty to the exclusion of other intellectual and moral values. Rochlitz (1992: 251) argues that the later work of Foucault holds that the "sole purpose" of the art of the self is to live a beautiful life.

These critiques have a degree of truth, but they need qualification. First, as Wolin reminds us (1992), Foucault was preoccupied with subjectivity ever since writing *Folie et déraison,* where he saw madness as an important limit experience and source of transgression of normalizing rationality. In subsequent works, he looked to language, death, and pleasure as other sources of transgression.[23] Second, as I have argued, we should see Foucault's later concern with the self as an advance over his earlier determinism, which granted no role to creative agency. Third, we know from biographical facts that during the late 1970s and early 1980s, in addition to doing drugs and frequenting the San Francisco bathhouse scene, Foucault was also intervening in numerous important political issues at an international level.

Although it is true that Foucault's later emphasis shifts from disciplinary power to the aesthetics and care of the self, we cannot rightly see his later work as purely aestheticist, since the selfhood he is valorizing has an ethical and rational component that requires moderation, reflexivity, and consciously defined relations toward others. What we find instead is Nietzsche's ideal of the "grand style," in which Dionysian passions are sublimated into a consciously controlled and stylized life. A greater mistake would be to interpret Foucault's later work as apolitical. This reproduces the orthodox Marxist dichotomy between the personal and political and stigmatizes personal concerns as merely "bourgeois." Rejecting a false dualism between ethics and politics, Foucault instead seeks a "politics as ethics" (1982b), precisely in order to overcome the deficiencies of his earlier work and to root politics in practices of the self. If power operates through discipline and normalization, struggle against it cannot be divorced from personal existence. Foucault thus joins a countercurrent within the Marxist tradition (Gramsci, Lefebvre, Debord, and others) that has emphasized the importance of a politics of everyday life for a larger social transformation. This shift was initiated out of awareness of the historical changes in capitalism that lead to the commodification of culture and colonization of previously "private" spaces of life. As Foucault has emphasized (1983), a politics of desire and everyday life is necessary in a world where fascist tendencies have burrowed deep into the core of subjectivity.

Rather than espousing a neodandyism, Foucault's intent is to employ ethics and aesthetics to reconstitute normalized subjectivity. While Foucault is not uncritically endorsing the Greeks as an "alternative" — since he rejects their sexist, hierarchical values — he finds that they nevertheless provide examples of nonnormalized identities. As Bernauer says, Foucault makes reference to Greek morality "in criticism of those models which would confine human creativity to the realm of art and replace the task of self-elaboration with the duty of a self-discovery governed by a hermeneutics of desire" (1992: 260). Against a "science of life," an "aesthetics of existence" seeks "to free us from the obligation of deciphering ourselves as a system of timeless functions which are subjected to corresponding norms" (262). The aesthetic stylization of life is more the result than the aim of a critical ethics, which includes both rational and political components. The attempt to transform oneself into a work of art is not only an aesthetic task, but also an *ethical* project that requires moderation, sublimation, and practical reasoning, in addition to a *political* project that challenges normalizing rationalities and institutions as social inventions. As O'Farrell argues, "The modification of the self . . . produces a modification of one's activity in relation to others, and hence a modification in power relations, even if only at the micro-level to begin with" (1989: 129). It is in and through ethics that individuals pursue a transformative practice that results, ideally, from critique.

Yet while there are important logical and practical connections between ethics and politics, it is undeniable that Foucault has shifted emphasis from the social to the personal, that he undertheorizes their interconnection and does not analyze how ethics or the aesthetics of existence could link to larger social struggles. The fact that Foucault only discusses struggle at a personal rather than also at a collective level, suggests that he still equates social relations with coercion, treating them as something from which individuals have to escape if they are to acquire freedom. Thus, while the later Foucault finally brings the active subject into politics, he fails to develop the dialectical notion, such as we find in Marx, of the social individual. Marx too envisioned a creative, aesthetic transformation of life, but understood the self as the developmental product of history and analyzed the social (workers democracy) and technological (advanced automation) conditions required for individuals to have the time and opportunity for creative self-actualization.

Unlike Greek and Roman ethics from which they are derived, Foucault's ethics turn out to be entirely individualized; lacking any social component of duties and obligations toward others, they concern only the transformation of the self. For McCarthy, "the aesthetics of personal existence is an inadequate ethical-political response to a world in which misery and injustice are rampant" (Hoy and McCarthy 1994: 234). Indeed, as Rochlitz notes (1992), Foucault's project of self-transformation is available only to a small minority of people who are relatively autonomous from the drudgery of work and poverty and can focus their time and energy on matters of lifestyle, rather than mere survival. Foucault's "politics as ethics," therefore has no mass relevance, is entirely cooptable by new-age movements and capitalist culture industries, and is in danger of lapsing into individualism or dandyism by inadequately stressing the dialectical connections between personal and social struggle. While Foucault's ethics as politics retain a potentially subversive force, since the cultivation of personal freedom entails a break from coercive social norms and institutions and *may* lead to radical social action, such action is not a necessary extension of his project and is not explicitly developed.

Foucault develops his final political reflections in his key essay, "What is Enlightenment?" (1984). This essay is Foucault's philosophical swan song, and provides a fitting summary of his political perspectives. It should be read not as announcing entirely new themes, although there are some, but rather as articulating his lifelong concern with limit experiences, with identifying and transgressing the lines of forbidden behavior, with experimenting with the self and moving it toward an ever greater space of freedom. The disconnected analyses on technologies of domination and technologies of the self come together somewhat in this essay, which sees the labor of freedom and the project of criticism to be intimately connected. Here, Foucault aligns his work with Kant and Enlightenment criticism and further develops a view of the subject as a potentially active and autonomous agent.[24] The model of Enlightenment criticism that Foucault now champions issues from Kant's 1784 response to the question of *Was ist Aufklärung?* According to Foucault, Kant's essay inaugurates a new tradition—stretching from Hegel to Nietzsche and Weber to Habermas—where philosophical thought reflects on the nature of the present as something fundamentally different from the past.

This emphasis on the present as difference involves what Foucault calls "the attitude of modernity" (1984: 38). Bracketing any institutional analysis of modernity, Foucault defines the modern attitude as a kind of historical and critical sensibility, as "a type of philosophical interrogation—one that simultaneously problematizes man's relation to the present, man's historical mode of being" (42). Foucault draws a sharp distinction between the Enlightenment and humanism in order to disassociate the two and reassert his repudiation of the modern humanist tradition and its universal values. Yet he now aligns his own work with the Enlightenment tradition and appropriates its critico-historical outlook. He claims that "the thread that may connect us with the Enlightenment is not faithfulness to [its] doctrinal elements, but rather the permanent reactivation of an attitude—that is, of a philosophical ethos that could be described as a permanent critique of our historical era" (42).

This endorsement of Enlightenment criticism qualifies his earlier sweeping denunciation of reason as a coercive force. No longer essentializing rationality as inherently oppressive, Foucault now analyzes it as open to various uses and possibilities. Reason can provide the tools with which to criticize and counteract its own coercive effects in the disciplinary society. In a thinly veiled and misleading gesture to Habermas, Foucault now rejects "the intellectual blackmail of 'being for or against the Enlightenment' " (1984: 45). The appropriation of the Enlightenment must itself be rational and critical, discriminating enough to separate its critical, historical attitude from modern humanism, essentialism, and foundationalism rooted in universal values.

Foucault employs the philosophical ethos of the Enlightenment in a postmodern context, in a new critical vision that abandons humanism and transcendentalism, champions difference, and is oriented toward "the 'contemporary limits of the necessary,' that is, toward what is or is no longer indispensible for the constitution of ourselves as autonomous subjects" (1984: 43). Returning to his earlier Bataillean motifs, first developed in his 1963 "Preface to Transgression," Foucault claims that critique is a departure from a "limit attitude" that attempts to define the arbitrary limits placed on thought and action, in order to transgress them and move towards greater freedom. The goal of criticism is to ask, "In what is given to us as universal, necessary, obligatory, what place is occupied by whatever is singular, contingent, and the product of arbitrary constraints? The point, in brief, is to transform the critique conducted in the form of necessary limitation into a practical critique that takes the form of a possible transgression" (45).

The Kantian project undergoes a transformation from a critique of the limits of rationality to a reflection on the limits of experience in general, from grasping the limits of the understanding beyond which knowledge must *not* transgress, to grasping the (socially imposed) "limits" of subjectivity and experience that individuals must *attempt to* transgress. This is a shift from the negative to the positive, from epistemology to a politics that departs from "a historical ontology of ourselves" (45). In Foucault's postmodern context, criticism abandons any attempt to grasp the formal, universal structures of reason in favor of problematizations of specific historical sites. Against Habermas and the Enlightenment, criticism "is no longer going to be practiced in the search for formal structures [of the mind] with universal value, but rather as a historical investigation into the events that have led us to constitute ourselves and to recognize ourselves as subjects of what we are doing, thinking, saying" (46–47).

Thus, the Kantian employment of a transcendental framework and its search for the *a priori,* universal aspects of all human experience is rejected in favor of a historical examination of the social forces constituting subjectivity. Historical critique "will not deduce from the form of what we are what it is impossible for us to do and to know; but it will separate out, from the contingency that has made us what we are, the possibility of no longer being, doing, of thinking what we are, do, or think" (1984: 46). The goal of this genealogical project, then, is human freedom; "it is seeking to give new impetus, as far and as wide as possible, to the undefined work of freedom" (46). The purpose of the reformulation of the Kantian version of Enlightenment "is to free thought from formal structures and place it in a historical field where it must confront the singular, contingent, and arbitrary which operate in what is put forward as universal, necessary, and contingent" (Bernauer 1992: 271). Subjectivity and sociality are mutually connected insofar as limits of the self point to social constraints. Freedom is conceived not in terms of a disembodied, ahistorical capacity for rationality, but rather a socially situated ability to reflect critically on and reject coercive norms, values, and practices.

The politics of limits acknowledges not only the false limits placed on subjective experience, but also the real limits on knowledge and change. It claims "we have to give up hope of ever acceding to a point of view that could give us complete access to any complete and definitive knowledge of what may constitute our historical limits" (Foucault 1984: 47). The limits of what we can know of the past are matched by what we can accomplish in the future. Foucault stresses the open-ended, partial, and experimental character of politics, based on gradual transgressive reforms rather than sudden revolutionary change. Historical inquiry cautiously tries "to grasp the points where change is possible and desireable, and to determine the precise form this change should take. This means that the historical ontology of ourselves must turn away from all projects that claim to be global or radical" (46). Reaffirming his earlier worries about radical, utopian visions of political change (1977: 230), Foucault states: "We know from experience that the claim to escape from the system of contemporary reality so as to produce the overall programs of another society, of another way of thinking, another culture, another vision of the world, has led only to the return of the most dangerous traditions" (1984: 46). Foucault embraces a program of "partial transformation" rather than programs for a "new man" (47). The emphasis is not on overturning capitalism, but regimes of normalization, not on smashing the state, but imposed identities.

Thus, Foucault substitutes an individualist politics of transgression for a revolutionary politics of liberation.[25] As Foucault understands it, the politics of liberation combines a repression model of power with a humanist–essentialist notion of the subject and an apocalyptic conception of change. Political revolution will free human nature from the shackles of alienation, so that a new humanity can blossom in the postcapitalist world. For the politics of transgression, however, there is no human essence waiting to be liberated, no state of perfect freedom to be achieved, and no promised end of power relationships. Foucault tries to avoid pessimism and fatalism, but, borrowing a Kantian metaphor, openly acknowledges, "I do not know whether we will ever reach mature adulthood" (1984: 49). Politics is a continual encounter and transgression of limits, a permanent reform of the present system based on practices of freedom and liberty, lacking any guarantee that the future can be more free than the present or past. Abandoning grand revolutionary visions, Foucault adopts a modest approach to change: "the object is to proceed a little at a time, to introduce modifications that are capable of, if not finding solutions, then at least of changing the givens of a problem" (1991: 159).

There are substantive contradictions and tensions between Foucault's theory and his practice that revolve around his failure to articulate the connections between collective and individual levels of experience. Foucault's rhetoric of radicalism has shifted from social to personal change as he seeks a "complete transformation" of the self apart from normalized identities. His awareness of the dangers of social revolution has no appropriate analogue at the personal level, where radical change can be equally as dangerous and destablizing.[26] Not only are there dangers of self-destruction and narcissistic hedonism, but also of fascism. If Foucault's own attempts at transgression are any example of the new politics, the fascination with death and violence, experiments with psychic derangement and destruction of the self, the use of drugs, and the practice of sadomasochism constitute a dubious basis for progressive social transformation. While I have argued that Wolin's charge that Foucault is an aestheticist is not entirely true, his claim that Foucault is amoralist is correct.[27] Through his lifelong refusal to specify the normative underpinnings of ethics and politics, and to employ any positive moral language, Foucault eschews the question of which forms of pleasure should be satisfied and which should not, which are healthy and which are dangerous, which further democracy and which promote fascism.

Moreover, the analytic relations Foucault sees between disciplinary power and capitalism are not carried through to a political critique of capitalist economic logic, but rather are directed only against its specific social institutions, practices, and norms. His awareness of the "global functioning of . . . a *society of normalisation*" (1980a: 107) is conjoined with an unqualified attack on global politics. Both Marx and Foucault employ a discontinuity model at the theoretical level to analyze the specificity of capitalist society, but only Marx develops a discontinuity model at the political level to envisage a postcapitalist social order.

Ultimately, Foucault lacks a vision of the future as anything but an abstract possibility that is vaguely different from the present. In a sweeping move that can only induce paralysis and acceptance of the status quo, Foucault claims that "to imagine another system is to extend our participation in the present system" (1977: 230). This critique does not discriminate between different utopian visions. While Foucault is rightly suspicious of efforts at social engineering, such as dictated by St. Simon or Pope Comte, he does not acknowledge the power of an imagination that envisages alternatives to the degraded and dehumanized present. He occludes the important difference between the attempt to *suggest* future possibilities, which stimulates creative action, and the attempt to *impose* them, which stultifies new alternatives. He does not see that the "utopian" vision of a realm of freedom, democracy, and individual creativity liberated from the drudgery of work is based on actual existing historical possibilities within the present, rather than fashioned from conjured-up fantasies. In place of "utopias" that (on his definition) offer certainties and consolation, Foucault advances "heterotopias" that attempt to disturb, shock, and shatter complacent thinking (1973b: xvii). Certainly, leftist thought can use provocations and critiques, but a strict heterotopian strategy can leave us disoriented and without social maps and positive points of reference. What Foucault in fact leaves us, however, are various ideas and "tools" for political experimentation.

Foucault's failure to specify positive alternatives forces him into vague formulations. What is entailed by terms such as "profound changes" and a "new balance of relations" (1991: 162–163)? How "profound" are the changes to be, how "new" the relations? Can proceeding "a little at a time" effect significant transformation? Can "radical" change occur without profound historical discontinuity, social upheaval, and utopian imagination? Ultimately, Foucault's vision of change is directed at the personal rather than the institutional level. Genealogy betrays the nonoppositional nature of the contemporary "critical" attitude that no longer challenges the basic imperatives of a system bent on global destruction of all life forms; it therefore foresakes a ruthless critique of the grow-or-die logic of the capitalist economy. Lacking such a systemic critique, it unavoidably lapses into a Panglossian apology that admits capitalism is, after all, the best of all possible worlds and the end of history. With Candide, Foucault, by default, embraces the position that all we can do is to cultivate our own gardens, to carve out our own personal space of freedom within a system devouring the entire planet. The emphasis on the transgression of the limits of personal experience therefore must be accompanied with a vision of transgressing social and political limits.

Thus, Foucault's final vision of the future is nondialectical and has profound apolitical dimensions; it does not grasp the relation between collective politics and individual resistance, between social liberation and personal freedom, between systemic change and meaningful local reforms. Quite unlike that of Marx, Foucault's vision is not a Hegelian vision of future integration attained through an *Aufhebung* of the past and present, but rather a Nietzschean vision of separation, of fragmented individuals in the pursuit of different lifestyles, of a future disconnected from the historical accomplishments of the past and the possibilities of the present. Foucault does not attempt to "resolve" the basic contradictions of history and capitalism, he is content to let them stand in order to retreat, at least in his writings, to the local and private spheres of existence.

PHILOSOPHER OR HISTORIAN?

> [By writing], I aim at having an experience myself—by passing through a determinate historical content—an experience of what we are today, of what is not only our past but also our present. And I invite others to share the experience. That is an experience of our modernity that might permit us to emerge from it transformed.
> —FOUCAULT (1991: 33–34)

> What I'm saying has no objective value; but perhaps it can serve to clarify the problems that I've tried to shed light on.
> —FOUCAULT

Despite the various shifts and turns in Foucault's work, one can identify a general project that at first is only implicit and later is explicitly brought out and developed. Foucault undertakes a history of Western forms of truth, knowledge, rationality, and subjectivity, and analyzes their relationship with systems of power and domination. He is concerned with the problematization of fundamental domains of experience in Western culture whereby society subjects experiences such as madness, illness, deviance, and sexuality to analysis and control. He tries to show how subjectivity is constituted in a wide range of discourses and practices, within a field of power, knowledge, and truth. He seeks a "diagnostic critique" of modernity that exposes the operations of power that limit experience and espouses a transgression of those limits in favor of a greater freedom of the self. Foucault's works articulate the surrealist goal of *depaysment*, of making experience strange and problematic so that richer forms of subjectivity can be developed.

Foucault's fundamental concern with the power mechanisms of modernity has been pursued from various methodological perspectives: first, in the 1960s, from the standpoint of archaeology; then, in the 1970s, from genealogy; finally, in the 1980s, from ethics and technologies of the self. These different standpoints should be seen not as incompatible frames of reference, but rather as complementary, overlapping perspectives that analyze the imbrication of knowledge, power, truth, and subjectivity.

While Foucault combines elements of Kant, Marx, Nietzsche, Heidegger, Bachelard, Canguilhem, Bataille, Blanchot, and others, he transforms them into an original framework of research that overturns numerous tenets of modern historiography and social theory while reconstrucing other elements. He attempts to escape from the transcendental, teleological, progressivist, and humanist assumptions of eighteenth- and nineteenth-century thought, and to advance new theoretical and political perspectives informed by detotalizing and antifoundationalist postmodern principles. Where modern theories typically assume an overarching unity and coherence to society and history, Foucault seeks to dissolve and unravel unities and universal constructs, to destroy society and history as objects of totality and identity, and to rethink them as differentiated and heterogeneous fields. He makes no attempt, therefore, to discover general causal laws to which one can reduce particular events and by which these events receive their intelligibility. Rather, he tries to recover the specificity of events, the occurence of historical breaks, lines of continuity and discontinuity, and possible points of resistance and trajectories of freedom. Where modern theorists evince predilections toward universal values rooted in natural law or a timeless human nature, Foucault sees only local, specific, changing, nongeneralizable events, discourses, and values. Where the modern mind is prone to find the progression of reason and freedom in history, Foucault sees a kaleidoscopic mélange of events with no directional tendencies except toward greater forms of domination.

Foucault's detotalizing impulse applies as well to his own works and method. While there is a general coherence to Foucault's works, they do not comprise a systematic philosophy in the manner of Kant or Hegel; rather, they constitute fragmentary analyses and often represent conflicting perspectives (see Best and Kellner 1991). Foucault claimed that his works are provisional and experimental in character, not finished systems or master keys. Hence, he saw theory as a "toolkit" that provides new instruments for research and political activity to be applied in specific situations (1980a: 145).

Foucault's works defy classification, since he freely crosses disciplinary boundaries, working at once within the fields of history, philosophy, social theory, and politics. Although he certainly rejects the "philosophy of history" as a universalist, progressive historical vision, philosophy and history converge in a philosophical critique of the present era. While there are a number of properly "philosophical" issues in his work—concerning problems of language, truth, identity, and so on, they are never analyzed abstractly and ahistorically; rather, such issues are examined in concrete, historical terms that show how these problem emerge, how they become possible in certain epistemic settings, how they change throughout time, and how they have practical implications. While Foucault has renounced the label of "philosopher," saying he is more interested in having direct experiences than in constructing theoretical systems (1991: 29), he is renouncing only a certain conception of philosophy—that concerned with an abstract and ahistorical analysis of truth and foundations of knowledge. He lays claim to the title in a different sense: that of someone who engages in critique, who attempts to "think differently, instead of legitimating what is already known" (1986: 9). Conversely, although he plays the "truth-game" of history by using dates and periodizations, by citing references, and by quoting texts, Foucault eschews the label of "historian." This is in part because he never analyzes history for its own sake, but always with certain philosophical and political problems in mind, such as the impetus behind the sudden explosion of discourse about sexuality in the modern era. Still, against the charges of Sartre and others, Foucault insists that he is not a "negator of history," and he is adamant about the need of the theorist to do his or her own original historical research to illuminate political problems, rather than relying on standard narratives (1991: 124–129).

Ultimately, we should see Foucault neither as philosopher nor historian, but as a politically engaged thinker undertaking a historico-philosophical critique of the present. Foucault reorients historical inquiry away from standard attempts to refamiliarize readers with the past in favor of forcing us to confront our real distance to the past in a process of defamiliarization (White 1978). He forcibly underlines the fact that knowledge and experience are contingent and historical in character rather than universal and eternal. Archaeology and genealogy help to overcome essentialist definitions of human experience and practices by analyzing them in a historical context characterized by discontinuity. After reading Foucault, it is difficult to analyze phenomena such as "madness" and "sexuality" from the ahistorical and essentialistic perspectives of "mental illness" and "human nature." To know that a form of rationality has a distinct history is to conceive of social reality being other than what it presently is. Hence, Foucault says, "experience has taught me that the history of various forms of rationality is sometimes more effective in unsettling our certitudes and dogmatism than is abstract criticism" (1988d: 83). In his selective appropriation of "modernity," Foucault abandons universals and preserves a critico-historical "attitude" that calls universals into question, challenging their status as givens. "All my analyses are against the idea of universal necessities in human existence" (Foucault 1988c: 11).

Foucault's histories are unique in their focus on topics most historians and revolutionaries thought unimportant. What previously were marginal topics for historians — madness, medical practice, punishment, sexuality — become central points of focus for Foucault. Where a historian like Collingwood tries to limit history only to the study of what is thought (1956: 304), a Nietzschean–Foucauldian genealogy greatly enlarges the boundaries of research to include previously excluded phenomena such as mechanisms of power, the body and its desires, and practices of the self. In place of hagiographic celebration of figures such as modern psychiatric reformers Tuke and Pinel, Foucault substitutes a critical analysis that exposes previously unseen forces of power suppressed by liberal, Whiggish histories as well as by Marxism.

Foucault's originality lies not in being the first to write micronarrative histories, or, certainly, to study mechanisms of power, but rather in combining emphasis on power and the local; in analyzing microhistories in relation to power networks; in theorizing power as a mechanism, tactic, and technology in its own right, rather than something wielded by a monarch or a class; in seeing power as a positive and productive force that does not simply inhibit, prohibit, and repress. By vividly alerting us to the "dangers" of rationality, and the increasing control of personal and social life by the processes of "governmentalization," Foucault successfully accomplishes one of his core objectives. He induces an important skepticism about the achievements of liberalism and democracy by showing that behind the rhetoric of increased freedom lies the mechanisms of detailed control and coercion. He points to ways in which "reason" is violence and "truth" is the concealment of power. He illuminates how, far before the "information society," modern society was based not only on the accumulation of capital, but also the "accumulation of knowledge"

(1991: 165) and how modern forms of knowledge have direct connections to power through the tactics of division, subjugation, confinement, and normalization.

Through detailed, concrete readings of the historical constitution of discourse and practices, Foucault convincingly challenges linear models that see history as a progressive continuum of concepts and action toward a culmination of freedom and knowledge. By appealing to the fundamental archaeological level of discourse, Foucault shifts attention away from the usual concern with the intentions of subjects or the influence of ideas to the more fundamental unconscious ground of discourse. This decenters the usual privileged figures of history to focus attention on more marginal figures. It allows a better understanding not only of historical discontinuity, but also of historical continuity, insofar as archaeology can delve beyond superficial difference among different thinkers to uncover the same underlying rules or codes to which their thought conforms. Where contemporary theory has done much to deconstruct modern notions like the subject, Foucault's works help to deconstruct History, to pluralize it as many histories with independent and unevenly developing trajectories, to recover the integrity and importance of microhistories that have been suppressed by monolithic macrohistories, and to recuperate a sharp sense of contingency lost in teleological Marxism. "The originality of Foucault amongst the great thinkers of this century has been that he does not convert our finitude into the foundation for new certainties" (Veyne quoted in O'Farrell 1989: 129)

While Foucault is weak on a dialectical analysis of modernity, he develops an important perspective on the emergence of modernity as a discursive order. The archaeology of the human sciences provides suggestive resources for understanding the metaphysical themes that can be found in much modern theory. Foucault's archaeological perspective provides a way to analyze the discursive dimensions of social reality that does not simply reduce them to ideology; his genealogical perspective establishes the importance of a historical critique of Western reason at the micrological levels of society; and his work on technologies of the self suggest new ways of theorizing historical agency and ethical self-constitution.

Foucault's works also have helped to deconstruct Marxism itself, by exposing its reductionist and essentialist dimensions, and by showing the extent to which it has assimilated problematic elements of Enlightenment and liberal–humanist thought that have helped to spread rather than destroy coercive forms of power. Foucault alerts us to the fact that modern discourse, even when "revolutionary," itself can help to expand the powers of reason over social life. Yet, rather than abandoning Marxist analysis, we need to contextualize it within a larger, multiperspectival framework, to replace its false claims to universality with the truth of its local or regional validity.[28] Marxism can illuminate production, labor, class, and state and other phenomena insofar as they are affected by capitalism, but it is not the only or the best means to analyze all those political, cultural, and personal phenomena it has marginalized as elements of the social "superstructure." What must be renounced is not Marxism itself, but the Marxist attempt to monopolize the historical and political terrain. Thus, one could conclude with Mark Poster that "The emancipatory interests promoted by historical materialism are sustained only with a detotalised stance such as that proposed by Foucault" (1989: 73).[29]

Yet, as Poster and many others have seen, despite his antitotalizing rhetoric, Foucault has his own totalizing dimensions. Specifically, these concern his homogenizing analyses of epistemes and his one-sided evaluations of modernity, truth, reason, and subjectivity. Much of the controversy centers around the totalizing periodization schemes in *Madness and Civilization* and *The Order of Things*. Sedwick (1982), Midelfort (1980), and others claim that in *Madness and Civilization* Foucault posits too sharp a break in history in terms of practices of normalization and confinement. They argue that the medieval and Renaissance eras were not always in dialogue with madness, just as the classical era did not only confine and normalize it. They point to historical evidence that the insane were imprisoned, treated in a cruel manner, and placed in therapy long before the "Great Confinement" — as early as the fifteenth century. While the classical era may have intensified such treatment, it was not the first period to initiate it. This evidence suggests that there is more continuity between the capitalist and precapitalist past than Foucault acknowledges and that his historical divisions are far too rigid and monolithic. Midelfort claims that Foucault's analysis of the "classical experience" is essentializing insofar as it assumes an essence of the age that applies to all countries, when in fact England, France, and Germany adopted different attitudes toward madness.

In *The Order of Things,* Foucault employs terms such as "classical thought,""modern thought," and "Western thought," all of which imply a homogenous framework. He denies that these terms represent undifferentiated monoliths or abstract totalities, but this qualification must be weighed against his claim that "in any given culture and at any given moment, there is always only *one* episteme that defines the conditions of possibility of all knowledge" (1973b: 168, my emphasis). This statement implies that discursive difference and plurality are only surface effects of a deeper archaeological unity, that there can be no overlapping of different epistemes, since they appear only in pure form and *en bloc,* and that there are no regional or even national differences in knowledge. It involves a structuralist-inspired attempt to find the one, ultimate structure of mind that underlies all consciousness of a given era. But as Midelfort notes,

"There is too much diversity in any one period, and too much continuity between periods, for the relentless quest for the elusive *episteme* to prove ultimately useful" (1980: 259). Similarly, Poetzl finds that Foucault's analysis in *The Order of Things* "eliminates almost all nonparadigmatic formulations. He also identified each episteme with a long period of time so that in spite of his claim to preserve differences he imposed a uniformity of thought on periods as long as a century and a half" (1983: 164–165). How can one isolate pure epistemes, as Foucault tries to do in this text, if continuities exist between them? Ironically, Foucault's notion of episteme is basically Hegelian in its attempt to resolve oppositions into the unity of a general structure and in its arrangement of the epistemes into a historical succession, albeit one devoid of Hegel's teleology.

Merquoir also has criticized *The Order of Things* for constructing epistemes as monoliths. He argues that in his selective focus on the human sciences, Foucault has ignored important continuities of knowledge that occur in the fields of physics and mathematics, such as the continued importance of mathematics from the Renaissance to the modern eras (1985: 58ff.). The lineage from Galileo to Einstein is far more continuous than that from Buffon to Darwin. While Merquior forgets that it was never Foucault's intention to analyze the mature sciences, it could be argued that they should have a more important role in an examination of theoretical knowledge, and it suggests that the theory of discontinuity may be relative to different branches of the sciences throughout different epistemes. For Merquior, Foucault ignores "transepistemic streams of thought," the ability of old ideas (e.g., phlogiston) to inspire new research, and the "epistemic lags" within a given episteme.

In his response to such critiques in *The Archaeology of Knowledge,* Foucault bemoans "the absence of methodological signposting [in *The Order of Things* that] may have given the *impression* that my analyses were being conducted in terms of a cultural totality" (1972: 16, my emphasis). His reply shows regret more for the style than for the substance of his work, but the problems here are not merely semantic. If the historical data Midlefort and others point to is correct, then Foucault has overstated his case and has produced too simplistic and monolithic accounts of the modern and premodern epistemes.

Yet in *The Archaeology of Knowledge* Foucault goes to great lengths to overcome any interpetation of his work as totalizing, and his actual analyses shift away from the totalizing use of epistemes employed in *The Order of Things*. While different fields are governed by the same rules, and therefore form a "perfectly describable system" (Foucault 1972: 62), each field has its own specificity that cannot be mapped through a universalizing approach; there are identities and differences. Foucault explains, "These groups of rules are specific enough in each of these domains to characterize a particular, well-individualized discursive formation; but they offer enough analogies for us to see these various formations form a wider discursive grouping at a higher level" (63). Foucault vehemently declares, "Nothing would be more false than to see in the analysis of discursive formations an attempt at totalitarian periodization, whereby from a certain moment and for a certain time, everyone would think in the same way, in spite of surface differences, say the same thing, through a polymorphous vocabulary, and produce a sort of great discourse that could travel in any direction. On the contrary, archaeology describes a level of enunciative homogeneity that has its own temporal articulations" (148).

While the critiques of Midelfort and others make valid points, they do not give an accurate picture of the overall thrust of Foucault's work, which is to identify both lines of continuity and discontinuity in history. In his later work, he made the disclaimer that he never proposed a "philosophy of discontinuity" (1988b: 149) and said that he sometimes exaggerated discontinuities in order to counter the traditional emphases on continuity. In *The History of Sexuality,* he states that historical breaks include some "overlapping, interaction, and echoes" (1980b: 149) between the old and the new. There are numerous instances in his works where he is careful to specify continuities and discontinuities, as when he analyzes the ways representation continues to be an important issue for modern philosophy and the human sciences, in a quite different way than it was for the classical era, or when he emphasizes continuity between medieval Christianity and modernity in terms of the constitution of the individual whose deep truth is its sexuality, or when he seeks "that [critical–historical] thread that may connect us [postmodern thinkers] with the Enlightenment" (1984: 42).

Interpretations of Foucault's works as either totalizing or detotalizing are themselves totalizing, since one finds both aspects in his work. As with Marx, what is needed is a more discriminating and contextualized analysis of the conflicting impulses at war within Foucault's work. The totalizing accounts of epistemes in *The Order of Things,* for example, contradict the more pluralizing emphases in *The Birth of the Clinic,* in which Foucault identifies different forms of clinical medicine coexisting in space and time (Poetzl 1983: 164). While the general thrust of Foucault's outlook is detotalizing, he occasionally falls into totalizing schemes that erase the very forms of plurality and differentiation he champions.

Nowhere is this more clear than in his attacks on the Enlightenment, modernity, reason, truth, and subjectivity. Typically, when Foucault and other postmodern theorists attack modern theory and the Enlightenment, they construct an ideal model that hardly fits the complexity and diversity of theorists. As pointed out by Walzer (1986), Taylor (1986), Habermas (1987a), and numerous other critics, Foucault reduces the complex dialectic of modernity, the historical creation of new forms of freedom and domination, to a caricatured distortion of a vast system of domination. He romanticizes the preclassical past as a time when difference was tolerated. The converse of this romanticization is a demonization of modern societies that exaggerates the evils of modern reform measures. Other historians (e.g., Doerner 1981) have argued that the reform measures of Tuke and Pinel had a genuine humanitarian and enlightened aspect to them. Evincing an attitude of *gauchisme* popular among the radical French intelligentsia in the 1960s, Foucault stigmatizes capitalism, rationality, and the Enlightenment without qualification. In his treatment of psychiatry as a "gigantic moral imprisonment" and a "moralizing sadism," Foucault does little justice to historical fact and evinces an inability to analyze modernity dialectically. Unlike Marx and Habermas, therefore, Foucault entirely occludes the progressive aspects of modern democracy, science, technology, and liberal individualism.

In addition to its totalizing aspects, historians have called into question the historical accuracy of Foucault's work. In his careful survey of historical literature on the history of madness, Midelfort shows how Foucault has misread or distorted the historical sources he used to construct his interpretation of madness. Among other errors, Midlefort claims that Foucault disregarded the way madhouses developed from medieval hospitals and monastaries, that he reproduced the false myth of the ship of fools and their pilgramage to reason (in fact, the mad were occasionally sent away on boats in order to be rid of them), that he ignored Pinel's debt to earlier English theorists and to classical antiquity, and that he neglected to show how Tuke used therapeutic methods besides moral authority and surveillance. Pierre Hadot (1992), whose work on ancient ethics was an important influence in Foucault's interpetations, argues that Foucault systematically misread ancient texts, leaving out the crucial fact that the self was cultivated not for its own sake, but it order to make connection with universal reason and nature. Foucault's interpretations, therefore, represent the Stoics and Platonists as more individualistic than they were. Pierre Vilar sums up such frustrations with Foucault's works by denouncing them as a confused collection of "authoritarian hypotheses," "mixed-up dates," "texts mistreated," "historical absurdities," and "errors so gross that we must believe them deliberate" (quoted in Megill 1985: 133).

Given these errors, some critics tend to dismiss Foucault as a bad historian and unreliable interpreter. Such critiques can be traced all the way back to the reception of Foucault's dissertation thesis, *Folie et déraison,* by Canguilhem and others. Setting the tone for subsequent receptions of Foucault's work, they admired his brilliance and originality, but criticized him for historical inaccuracies, cryptic rhetoric, and unwarranted interpretations that falsify texts to support idiosyncratic readings (see Eribon 1991: 108–115; Miller 1993: 103–105). Against such critiques, others came to Foucault's rescue, anticipating later defense of his work. Barthes, for example, saw *Folie et déraison* as "something other than a book of history" and read it instead as "something like a cathartic question asked about madness" (quoted in Eribon 1991: 118).

Foucault himself evinces contempt for the positivistic-inspired criticism directed at his thesis, as well as for conventional historiography, stating "I am not a professional historian" (quoted in Megill 1985: 117). He has insisted throughout his entire career that he is not engaged in historical study in any traditional sense that purports to be subserviently faithful to the "facts." Foucault claims that his books function more as experiences than as demonstrations of historical truth (1991: 36). For Foucault, the essential thing is not that his "experience books" function in a factual mode, in the language game of truth or falsehood, but whether or not they allow us to have a different experience, whether or not they "might permit an alteration, a transformation, of the relationship we have of ourselves and our cultural universe: in a word with our knowledge" (37).[30]

Foucault's defenders are well aware of such larger, unconventional purposes of his books. Hirst, for example, warns us that "one must be very careful of historians' criticism of Foucault precisely because they take their own practice as a privileged point of departure, which Foucault does not" (1985: 148). Hirst claims that Foucault's selection of historical material is governed by the kinds of problems he is trying to illuminate and does not attempt to provide a complete description of a given period. Dews holds that "Foucault is not a historian in the conventional sense but a spinner of philosophical allegories" (quoted in O'Farrell 1989: 27). For many critics, the real value of Foucault's works is not their literal historical truth, but his method and provocations. Hence, even Midelfort, one of Foucault's sharpest critics, says, "Historians . . . should not conclude that a catalogue of Foucault's errors vitiates his whole enterprise, for he still has much to teach us: namely, the necessity of reading omnivorously and of reading closely; the necessity of probing behind a verbal facade to the emotion or unconscious intention within; and the need for a history of mental structures that dares to imagine discontinuity as well as continuity" (1980: 259–260).

Miller (1993: 105–109), defends Foucault's style and images as crucial to the purposes of provoking new thought and experience. Connolly (1985) champions Foucault's rhetoric of disruption, which foregoes attempts to ground normative claims to focus on the genesis of social practices and how they limit us, hopefully inciting the reader to political action.

While critical of his evacuation of epistemological and normative concerns, Bernstein praises Foucault's ability "to expose instabilities, points of resistances, places where counterdiscourses can arise and effect transgressions and change" (1992: 299).

It is true that factual inaccuracies and textual misreadings do not refute Foucault's work. Foucault's works are meant to challenge our normal perceptions of the present, to show that power relationships are contingent and fragile, and to provoke new thought and action. Foucault might well say that the first task is to provoke new ways of thought and action and let others sort out the exact "facts." It is difficult, moreover, to accuse Foucault of misreading "texts" and "authors," since for him these terms imply a set of metaphysical assumptions that he rejects (i.e., the "meaning" of a text or the "intentions" of an author).

Indeed, Foucault eschews "responsibility" for "accurate" readings of texts in favor of using them for seemingly predetermined purposes. What he says of his favorite writers may be true for his research in general. "I prefer to utilize the writers I like. The only valid tribute to thought such as Nietzsche's is precisely to use it, to deform it, to make it groan and protest" (Foucault 1980a: 53–54). On this postmodern approach, aesthetic criteria are privileged over factual criteria. Yet, factual errors and textual misreadings pose a real problem for Foucault if he intends his works to have any credibility or claims to be offering better interpretations of modernity than other accounts. Of course, questions concerning what is and is not a "good" or "accurate" reading of history or a text implies some kind of evaluative criteria that must be specified and defended, a move Foucault refuses to make for fear of falling into foundationalist traps. One must ask, with McCarthy, "Can we write *history* in contrast, say, to fiction, propaganda, or rationalization without being oriented to the idea of truth?" (Hoy and McCarthy 1994: 234).

Ultimately, these hermeneutical problems require some attention to epistemology and metatheoretical issues that Foucault, like Marx, dismisses as irrelevant to the practical concerns of social change but that Habermas argues is of fundamental importance. Although they share some concerns and positions, Foucault and Habermas take diametrically opposed positions on fundamental issues. The encounter between Foucault and Habermas is a confrontation between vastly different outlooks, a clash of the leading representatives of French and German theory, a battle between postmodern and modern visions of theory and politics. Just before Foucault's death, these two thinkers had begun efforts at a dialogue that sought in a positive way to explore their similarities and differences. Although the face-to-face exchange can no longer take place, Foucault's works survive to make this important confrontation possible.

NOTES

1. Although there are clear postmodern moves in Foucault, he himself never used the term "postmodern." See Best and Kellner (1991).

2. For an excellent account of Foucault's relation to Bachelard and Canguilhem, see Gutting (1989).

3. As stated by Foucault himself, his works have grown out of his personal experiences: "Whenever I have tried to carry out a piece of theoretical work, it has been on the basis of my own personal experience, always in relation to processes I saw taking place around me. It is because I could recognize in the things I saw, in the institutions with which I dealt, in my relations with others, cracks, silent shocks, malfunctionings . . . that I undertook a particular piece of work, a few fragments of autobiography" (1988d: 156). Foucault describes his books, accordingly, as "experience-books" that not only articulate his experiences, but allow him to have new experiences, facilitate a change in himself, and prompt others to change as well (1991: 25–42). I return to this important concept below and in Chapter 4. Taking Foucault's own cue, one can clearly see Foucault's practical experiences in hospitals and prisons as a psychologist in the early 1950s as a key experiential stimulus for his studies on madness, medicine, and criminality. His homosexuality, which brought on profound depression and guilt feelings early in his life, helps to explain his theoretical studies on sexuality as well as his fascination with limit experiences. Some of those who knew Foucault personally believe that his obsession with psychology and abnormality stems from his own psychological problems and self-identity as a homosexual (Eribon 1991: 27). Both his early apoliticism and later militancy also must be understood in terms of his personal experiences (see below). Needless to say, Foucault's work cannot be reduced to his biography, for this would ignore, among other things, a host of important intellectual influences acquired from his reading (itself an important experience). But such biographical inquiries are both relevant and necessary for a thorough understanding of his work. Foucault asked us not to expect him to remain the same, but not to ignore the relation between his work and biography. For valuable biographical information on Foucault, see Eribon 1991, Miller, 1993, and Macey 1993.

4. As I show below, however, Foucault in his later work understands modernity more as a historical attitude, a mode of critique, than a historical period.

5. Foucault's various perspectives rehearse Aristotle's organization of the sciences around knowing (theoria), doing (praxis), and making (techne). It is difficult to be postmodern when one can hardly succeed in being post-Greek.

6. Foucault also lists Georges Dumézil, a historian of comparative religion and myths and colleague at the University of Uppsasla in the 1950s, as a major influence on his archaeology: "He is the one who taught me to analyze the internal economy of a discourse in a manner that was entirely different from the methods of traditional exegesis or those of linguistic formalism. It was he who taught me how to describe the transformations of a discourse and its relations to an institution" (quoted in Eribon 1991: 75–76).

7. For a summary of Foucault's debate with Sartre over this issue, see Eribon (1991: 163–165). Sartre is correct, however, in charging Foucault with evacuat-

ing praxis from his analyses and therefore with being unable to account for a key element in the specific forces behind historical change.

8. These are terms Foucault borrows from the *Annales* school of French historians. For Foucault's relation to this school, see Dean (1994).

9. The main example here comes from the *Grundrisse,* in which Marx recognizes that Greek culture develops in a manner autonomous from its economic mode of production and continues to attract the modern aesthetic sensibility even though its economic system has long since passed away (1973: 110–111).

10. Foucault continues his references to a new era in *The Archaeology of Knowledge,* speaking of "established positivities that have recently disappeared or are still disappearing before our eyes" (1972: 177). See also Foucault (1989a: 30) where he also delineates a postmodern era that begins around 1950.

11. See, for example, the nonevolutionist approach of Cuvier, discussed in Eiseley (1958). Cuvier rejects linear models of evolution and argues in favor of different life forms evolving along divergent paths.

12. As Foucault states, " 'archaeology' would be the appropriate methodology of the analysis of local discursivities, and 'genealogy' would be the tactics whereby, on the basis of the descriptions of local discursivities, the subjected knowledges which were thus released would be brought into play" (1980a: 85).

13. In *The Birth of the Clinic,* for example, Foucault's most abstract work outside of *The Order of Things,* he is concerned already with how the "medical gaze" targets the body as an object of knowledge, anticipating his later analysis of disciplinary power and the panopticon. Moreover he shows how medical knowledge was employed as a means of establishing norms of health and policing the social body, anticipating his later analysis of bio-power.

14. These charges stemmed from his refusal to work in a political movement (he did not, for example, take an active part in the antipsychiatry movement his work helped to spawn); his aversion to Communism and Marxism counterposed to his fascination with Sade, Bataille, and Nietzsche; and his work with the department of education to create reforms in the French school system. Foucault's removal from politics before 1969 should be understood in part to have resulted from his alienation from orthodox Communism, leftist sectarianism, and mainstream political parties. Foucault preferred the solitude of his studies on language to what he saw to be the sterile ideological battles and debates of "hyper-Marxism." His turn to militant politics was motivated by the 1968 student struggles that erupted for him not during May in France, but during March in Tunisia, where he was teaching (Foucault 1991: 136). Foucault felt compelled to support the students, who were risking their lives and freedom. At the end of 1968, he joined the faculty at the University of Paris, Vincennes, where he fought the police and pushed for radical changes in the university system.

15. For example, in 1972, Foucault spoke on behalf of the needs of exploited young French workers. In 1973 he proposed a regular column in *Libération* entitled "Chronicle of the Workers' Memory." As a part of this project, Foucault conducted an interesting interview with a Portugese worker at the Renault plant. He also demonstrated tirelessly in favor of Polish solidarity workers, and tried to create an organizational base of support between them and the French workers union, the Confederation Française des Travailleurs Démocratique (CFDT). For

Foucault, the point was not to bid *adieu* to the proletariat, but to expand the notion and terrain of politics and critique.

16. In the 1970s, in association with a group of French journalists, Foucault sought to produce a means of alternative information and images that would counter the dominant media powers. This project evolved into the creation of *Libération,* the Leftist daily, to which Foucault contributed a number of articles. Foucault's most sustained journalistic venture involved numerous trips to Iran in the 1980s as the revolution against the Shaw unfolded. Foucault thought this to be one of the most important political events of the contemporary world and wanted to study the events first-hand. His work led to a series of interesting articles published in the Italian daily *Corriere della sera* and the French paper *Le Nouvel Observateur.*

17. It is interesting that despite his theoretical condemnation of liberalism, Foucault made constant use of the liberal discourse of rights. He became increasingly interested in the liberal tradition and spoke of developing a "new form of right" (1980a: 108), which, unfortunately, he never fleshed out.

18. "[I]f I don't ever say what must be done, it isn't because I believe that there's nothing to be done; on the contrary, it is because there are a thousands things to do, to invent, to forge, on the part of those who, reocognizing the relations of power in which they're implicated, have decided to resist or escape them . . . I say certain things only to the extrent to which I see them as capable of permitting the transformation of reality" (Foucault 1991: 174).

19. Already in the late 1970s, Foucault saw that his dramatic rhetoric of the "death of man" obscured the perennial reality of human agency and changing forms of subjectivity: human beings "never ceased constructing themselves, that is, to shift continuously the level of their subjectivity, to constitute themselves in an infinite and multiple series of different subjectivities that would never reach an end and would place us in the presence of something that would [become historically constituted as] 'man' " (1991: 123–124).

20. The ambiguity in the word "identity" allows one either to condemn or praise it. In its negative connotation, "identity" suggests a static, imposed self-consciousness, a normalized mode of being to which one is to conform and that limits one's freedom. In its positive connotation, "identity" suggests a self-created, conscious relation to oneself that is dynamic and evolving. Until the 1980s, Foucault, following Nietzsche, operated only with the former sense of identity. Once we remove the normalizing and essentializing connotations of the term, to have an "identity" no longer seems a terrible thing; in fact, it is the lack of identity, selfhood, and stable (not static) ego that allows for the imposition of a normalizing selfhood and for the creation of a mentality predisposed to fascism.

21. Foucault defines technologies of the self as practices "which permit individuals to effect by their own means or with the help of others a certain number of operations on their own bodies and souls, thoughts, conduct, and way of being, so as to transform themselves in order to attain a certain state of happiness, purity, wisdom, perfection, or immortality" (1988c: 18).

22. For a similar exhaltation of endless becoming, see Deleuze and Guatarri (1983, 1987); for a critique of this position, see Best and Kellner (1991).

23. Such a quest, of course, conflicts with Foucault's claims that there is no pure space of freedom outside of power, that there is no essence that is not social-

ly constituted; the quest also betrays an emancipatory and utopian impulse that he otherwise wishes to renounce.

24. As clarified by Schmidt and Wartenberg (1994), this essay is not the first time Foucault confronted Kant. His engagement of Kant dates back to his (still unpublished) *Thèse compleméntaire* translation of Kant's *Anthropology*. In *The Order of Things*, of course, Kant plays a prominent role as the initiators of modern philosophical anthropology organized around "Man" and his doublets. In "What is Enlightenment?" Foucault offers a far more positive view of Kant not as the founder of humanism, but of the modern tradition of historical critique that Foucault himself draws from. Foucault engaged Kant's essay on the Enlightenment on at least two occassions prior to 1984, each time bringing out different, yet positive, aspects of it. That Kant's essay provided a model of critique for Foucault is an important fact in qualifying the "postmodern" nature of Foucault's work. As I show below, however, Foucault makes important changes in Kant's conception of criticism that relate more to a postmodern than a modern sensibility.

25. Foucault did not initially conceive his politics as reformist and rejected the dualism between radical and reformist. In his discussion with radical lycée students, "Revolutionary Action: Until Now" (1977), he employs the rhetoric of revolution and "radical contestation." He see radical change as emerging from local points of struggle and argues for the need to unify local actions so they are not isolated. He claims that minority struggles "are actually involved in the revolutionary movement to the degree they are radical, uncompromising and nonreformist" (216). After this time, however, Foucault increasingly moves toward more conservative positions and abandons all radical rhetoric, as is clear in the essay "What is Enlightenment?"

26. This was, in contrast, a crucial theme for Deleuze and Guattari (1987), who emphasized that the need to destroy the personal ego had to be done in a careful and measured way so that the individual achieved a "breakthrough" rather than a "breakdown."

27. Chomsky's experience with Foucault is illuminating here. After his televised debate with Foucault before a Dutch audience, where Foucault rejected any use of notions such as responsibility, justice, or law and advocated the position that might makes right ("One makes war to win, not because it's just"), Chomsky concluded: "I'd never met anyone who was so totally amoral" (cited in Miller 1993: 201).

28. In an acrimonious response to a young Maoist, for example, Foucault exclaimed, "Don't talk to me about Marx any more! I never want to hear anything about that man again. . . . I've had enough of Marx" (quoted in Eribon 1991: 266). As is made clear by comparing this remark with his statement that his work is deeply influenced by Marx (1980a: 52–53), Foucault retained an ambivalent attitude toward Marx(ism) after leaving the French Communist Party.

29. Throughout *Madness and Civilization*, *Power/Knowledge*, and *Discipline and Punish*, Foucault makes frequent references to Marxism and contextualizes his analyses within the framework of "capitalism," "class power," and "industrial society." Despite his denunciation of the "economic subordination" of power to a commodity logic and his insistence that power is a "complex domain" in its own right, he also states: "That is not to say that it is independent or could be made

sense of outside of economic processes and the relations of production" (1980a: 188). Clearly, he believes that Marx's work and his own analyses are compatible and complementary if employed intelligently.

30. Hence, Foucault insists his experiences not be solipsistic ones, but rather connect with, and help clarify, the experiences of others: "Starting from experience, it is necessary to clear the way for a transformation, a metamorphosis which isn't simply individual but which has a character accessible to others: that is, this experience must be linkable, to a certain extent, to a collective practice and way of thinking . . . it cannot have its full impact unless the individual manages to escape from pure subjectivity in such a way that others can—I won't say re-experience it exactly—but at least cross paths with it or retrace it" (1991: 38–39, 40). The commonality of experience is allowed by the fact that power itself is a generalizing force and targets different people in similar ways. That Foucault's own experiences indeed have spoken to others is clear from the fact that his "experience book" on madness helped to generate the antipsychiatry movement in England and Italy and his experience book on prisons helped to spawn the GIP and the prisoners' movement in France, to say nothing of the impact of his work on a worldwide readership.

3

HABERMAS' THEORY
OF SOCIAL EVOLUTION

Communicative rationality operates in history as an
avenging force.
                                    —HABERMAS (1982: 227)

Like Foucault, Habermas began his career within Marxism but eventually broke with Marxist assumptions to develop a new theory of society
and history. In both cases, this move was motivated by internal and external, logical and historical, concerns. In terms of its inherent theoretical deficiencies, Foucault and Habermas believe Marx's work is
reductionistic in its monological focus on material production. Each, consequently, attempts to escape the economistic heritage of Marxism and
to rethink history, society, and the subject within a new conceptual
framework.[1]
    In order to do this, each theorist draws on the resources of the "lin-
guistic turn" in philosophy and social theory, the transcontinental product
of Anglo-American philosophy and European semiotics and structuralism, which rethinks the traditional problems of consciousness as problems
of language. For Marx, language had only derivitive meaning in relation
to the primacy of productive activity.[2] Both Foucault and Habermas consider knowledge, discourse, and communication to be irreducible to the
determination of labor and social classes; both, subsequently, reject Marx's
base–superstructure model. As argued by Honneth (1991), each breaks
with the productivist concept of action developed by Marx and extended
by Adorno and Horkheimer to open up a new domain of social action
irreducible to the domination of nature; at the same time, they take this
turn in opposing directions.
    For Foucault, discourse analysis provides the tools for the study of
different systems of knowledge and how these form the epistemic spaces

in which individuals think, act, and speak. For Habermas, language is the key historical factor that separates humans from animals and is a fundamental medium for the production and reproduction of intersubjective life. Like Foucault, Habermas seeks to identify the anonymous rules that condition language and thought, but for Habermas these are rules of communicative competence that entail an active subject and have a crucial normative import. With Mead, Habermas sees action primarily as a process of communication and intersubjective understanding and defines societies as "networks of communicative action." He reworks the traditional Marxist theory of action, which focuses on the human transformation of nature, to include the processes of intersubjective understanding. Unlike Foucault, who regarded language and interaction primarily in terms of domination, Habermas sees them as the means of attaining a freely constituted social consensus. A central aspect of his project is to analyze the implicit and explicit nature of basic human competence required for such communication. Habermas does not, however, analyze language as a transparent medium; making the critique of ideology central to his version of critical theory, he redefines ideology as distorted communication rather than false consciousness. He also claims that in language one finds an innate human interest in emancipation, and so language provides the basis for the normative grounding of critique that he claims Marx and Foucault wrongly failed to provide.

Foucault and Habermas also think that Marxian theory needs to be rethought because of the significant historical changes since Marx's time. Where Foucault advances a new analysis of disciplinary power and marks the beginning of a new posthumanist, postmodern era, Habermas theorizes the historical shifts toward a postliberal, "late capitalism," in which the mechanisms of power, domination, and resistance have changed fundamentally since Marx's time. Like many theorists since Eduard Bernstein, Habermas attempts to respond to Marx's failed predictions that capitalism would fall due to its own internal contradictions, its technological development, and the formation of a revolutionary proletariat. Following Horkheimer, Adorno, Marcuse, and other Frankfurt School theorists, Habermas analyzes how capitalism has been able to regulate the market economy, control its crisis tendencies, and manage human consciousness through cultural means. Against the thesis of a one-dimensional or totally administered society, however, Habermas claims that capitalism continues to be vulnerable to economic crisis and has generated new crisis tendencies that relate to problems in securing loyalty and motivation.

According to Habermas, competitive capitalism has given way to monopolistic capitalism, where the state has assumed an enormously expanded role, with its primary function being to intervene in the economy, control its crisis tendencies, and supply rewards to the working class. With

the repoliticization of the economy–state relation in the political administration of the economy, Marx's base–superstructure model loses whatever
validity it once had; the ideology of advanced capitalism is no longer directly an economic matter derived from the exchange of "equivalents" in the
market. Morever, Habermas claims with Foucault that new forms of power
and resistance have emerged that are structured around issues of cultural
and psychological identity rather than exploitation, and hence that the
sources of power and political change no longer revolve around class struggle and the critique of political economy.

Furthermore, developments in late capitalism have called into question the validity of the labor theory of value and have thoroughly problematized the relationship between technological progress and social
emancipation. With the transformation of science and technology into the
leading productive forces of society, surplus value is no longer generated
solely from exploitation, and the rate of profit tends to increase rather
than decline. Science and technology have also become key sources of ideology. The development of science and technology, defined as the main
criterion of social progress, is seen to proceed according to neutral, objective laws or is accepted as the sole concern of experts. This is the ideological basis of a technocratic society that resolves ethical and political
questions into merely technical issues of system management and that dis-
sociates technical knowledge from public discussion and control. Because
of Marx's uncritical embrace of the growth of science and technology,
as a process deemed to have inherently progressive and democratic tendencies, Habermas claims that his work has become an unwitting support of technocratic ideology.

Hence, both Foucault and Habermas use the kind of historical consciousness that Marx tried to promote against capitalist ideology in order
to undermine the validity of Marxism itself, and to claim that the objective conditions sustaining Marxian theory and politics have undergone
massive changes. These changes have put Marxism, not capitalism, into
crisis and require extensive rethinking of radical theory and politics.

Both Foucault and Habermas, however, approach their reconstructive projects from entirely different theoretical orientations, each grounded in the intellectual traditions of his own country. Where Foucault's work
emerges primarily through contact with French literature and philosophy
of science, Habermas' work is influenced principally by Marx, Weber,
the Frankfurt School, and more contemporary German thinkers such as
Luhmann, Offe and Apel.[3] Despite these different traditions, the work
of Foucault and Habermas — following a trajectory that leads from
Nietzsche to Weber to Lukács through Horkheimer and Adorno and
Marcuse — converges around a critique of instrumental rationality and an
analysis of the growing technological control of life processes. The cri-

tique of instrumental reason that is central to the Frankfurt School and Habermas has obvious parallels with Foucault's critique of disciplinary power and his linkage of power to knowledge. But Habermas sees the critiques of the Frankfurt School and Foucault as too one-sided, as conflating different forms of rationality into one oppressive force that allegedly has colonized all of society.

For Habermas, the problem with modernity is not one of too much rationality, but of too little rationality. More precisely, in the modern world we find the hegemony of instrumental rationality, which seeks a technical mastery of nature and society over a communicative rationality that raises different validity claims requiring redemption under conditions of argumentation while seeking consensus over issues of social regulation. Habermas agrees with Weber, Horkheimer and Adorno, and Foucault that Enlightenment and capitalism produced domination instead of liberation, but he insists that there are also positive aspects of rationality and liberalism that still exist and can be further developed toward emancipatory ends. Habermas thereby breaks with the pessimistic tradition of social theory that stretches from Nietzsche through the Frankfurt School to postmodern theory, declaring modernity to be an "unfinished project."

Where Foucault develops postmodern alternatives to classical positions in modern philosophy, social theory, and historiography, Habermas attempts to reconstruct modern theory, while renouncing postmodern discourse as a counter-Enlightenment ideology injurious to the project of social critique and change. As Foucault wants to warn us of the "dangers of rationality" Habermas alerts us to the dangers of irrationality. For Habermas, postmodern theory is one of "the many symptoms of the destruction of practical reason" that involves a "retreat from universalistic demands, claims to autonomy, and expectations of authenticity" (1975: 124). All of these elements represent important advances in rationality that are wrongly jettisoned. Since Habermas accepts neither Marxism nor postmodern theory, he provides a significant foil to both Marx and Foucault and, more generally, to classical modern and postmodern theory. Habermas attempts a reconstruction of Marxism and critical theory without abandoning the emancipatory impulse of Marxism, the Hegelian-inspired theory of social evolution, and the Frankfurt School critique of instrumental reason. In his attempt to legitimate key modern values, particularly Enlightenment concerns with freedom, autonomy, democracy, critique, and the search for universal values and normative foundations, Habermas takes up arms against the relativistic positions embraced by Foucault and postmodern theory.

With Marx and against Foucault, Habermas has a Hegelian vision of history as fundamentally progressive in nature, as having definite developmental tendencies that lead toward a state of human freedom through a process of differentiation. For Habermas, differentiation involves the same technological, economic, and political dynamics that Marx analyzes, but Habermas also analyzes the differentiation of moral and practical consciousness, as a result of an evolutionary process, whereby objective, social, and subjective worlds are clearly delineated in addition to different logics of critique. This differentiation process leads to a state where cultural traditions, social systems, and value claims require rational justification in light of universal interests. Against Foucault's Nietzschean vision of history as a random succession of modes of power, Habermas, with Marx, constructs a metanarrative that charts the emergence of objective and subjective preconditions for human freedom that can be appropriated in a practical context.

At stake in this chapter is the validity of Habermas' critique of both Marx and Foucault, how well Habermas defends key Enlightenment and modern concepts as well as their postmodern repudiation, and whether or not he successfully achieves the goals of his project. Seeking normative foundations without conventional foundationalism, a universalistic perspective that has historical dimensions, a defense of Enlightenment reason without apologetics for scientism and technical domination, a critique of reification that does not succumb to neoconservatism, and an intersubjective theory of agency divorced from humanism, Habermas stakes out a middle ground between the essentialist formulations of the modern philosophical and sociological tradition and the radically deconstructive and relativistic aspects of postmodern theory. Where theorists such as Poster try to synthesize Marxian and Foucauldian positions, Habermas rejects both positions and claims that each theory is bound to the philosophy of consciousness and the subjectivist logic of the modern era. For Habermas, this means that neither Marx nor Foucault can analyze communicative rationality and employ the resources of this analysis to provide a philosophical foundation for critical theory. While Habermas develops important critiques of Marx and Foucault, I argue that he misreads each figure and wrongly tries to surpass or deny their core insights that must continue to inform contemporary theory, and that illuminate key problems in his own positions.

COMMUNICATION, RATIONALITY, AND DEMOCRACY

> A scientized society could constitute itself as a rational one only to the extent that science and technology are mediated with the conduct of life through the minds of its citizens.
>
> —HABERMAS (1970: 80)

Although Habermas has produced a complex, prolific body of work that has undergone a number of changes, he has pursued some constant, fundamental themes. At all times, Habermas is concerned with upholding the Enlightenment values of freedom, democracy, individuality, autonomy, criticism, and rationality; with analyzing their interconnections; with understanding how they have been threatened by developments within modernity; and with demonstrating how these values can be anchored in actual social institutions through advancing existing forms of "communicative action." The rationality that informs such action is based on raising and evaluating validity claims within an intersubjective context oriented toward achieving rational consensus over social values and policies. Like Marx and Foucault, Habermas embarks on a genealogy of modernity and believes that historical analysis is essential for a critical social theory and an oppositional politics. Where Marx is concerned primarily with the technical and economic bases of human evolution, and Foucault with the historical development of technologies of domination, Habermas focuses on the evolution of communicative rationality, on the moral–practical learning processes whereby human agents acquire skills in communication, debate, and evaluation.

Habermas' first major work, *The Structural Transformation of the Public Sphere* (1989a, orig. 1962), was a genealogy of the rise and decline of the public sphere in capitalist society. Habermas described the formation of literary societies in early bourgeois society where private individuals would meet in cafés, reading societies, lecture halls, and other public places, while creating numerous journals and newspapers, in order to engage in rational–critical debate. The existence of this vital public sphere began to decline, however, with the development of capitalism. The institutions of the public sphere were no longer focused on the criticism of political domination through the use of public reason, but rather became a means to manipulate individuals. The authentic public sphere in the world of letters was replaced by the psuedo-public world of consumer culture constituted by advertising and electronic media. These institutions worked to depoliticize and fragment individuals, robbing them of their potential for communicative rationality through propaganda and a barrage of images and symbols intended to substitute consumer behavior for critical thought.

Hence, unlike Foucault, Habermas sees media and advertising as key sources of power and control that distort communication and create a politics based on spectacle rather than active participation. Mass media isolate individuals into privatized modes of behavior, and create a "de-realized" public sphere.[4] On this point, Habermas' analysis has some affinities with Adorno and Horkheimer's critique of the culture industries (1972) and Baudrillard's analysis of hyperreality and the implosion of meaning in mass media (1983a, 1983b). Unlike Baudrillard, however, Habermas never relinquishes faith in the ability of individuals to regain the basic communicative competencies that inform their speech. Implicit in Habermas' largely descriptive analysis, explicitly brought out later, is a political vision of a revitalized public sphere where individuals assemble to debate political issues, to form and exercise a political will, to criticize social policy and developments, and to exert democratic control over the social conditions of their existence. Already, the key theme of Habermas' entire *oeuvre* is readily visible: democracy requires domination-free conditions of communication. The Habermasian political vision is one of an unconstrained public sphere where individuals unite in rational debate to achieve a democratic consensus about how society should be governed.[5]

While Foucault largely equated rationalization with domination, Habermas points to a positive aspect of modern rationalization whereby— unlike the dogmatic nature of premodern worldviews organized around myth and religion—critical norms emerge that allow for debate and critique and require rational legitimation of political power. Habermas is not unaware of the difficulties of forging a rational consensus in the face of two formidable obstacles, domination and social plurality, but he asserts that such consensus and the universal values it presupposes nevertheless can be attained (1989a: 234). On this count, as we will see, Habermas opposes the postmodern emphasis on the incommensurability of values, instead seeking a way to organize the cacophany of competing voices into a rational consensus, without lapsing into a repressive Comtean fetish of social order.

The analysis of the spread of communicative rationality into modern society as the result of historical developments would become Habermas' *idée fixe* in subsequent works. In *Toward a Rational Society* (1970, orig. 1968), Habermas analyzes the relationship between technology and democracy. Opposed to the separation between technical development and the social realm (an opposition he later terms "system" and "lifeworld"), he argues for the need to bring technical processes under conscious control and relate them to social needs. In capitalist society technology develops in alienated form, over and against human needs; Habermas believes it is imperative to subordinate technology to human needs, to the realm of "the communication of acting men" (1970: 56). He rejects the autonomous technology thesis as a mystification that occludes the fact that technological development is the result of conscious policy plans determined by capitalist and bureaucratic interests. In contemporary capitalist society, Habermas recognizes that the political will of depoliticized citizens is limited to a ritualistic acclamation of predetermined policies and goals. Democratic decision making is reduced to the formal appointment of elite rulers, while the important decisions of social organization are already made. Unlike ancient society—in which politics was indissociable from ethics, visions of the good life were promoted, and *phronesis* (practical wisdom) was distinguished from science—modern politics abandons all normative concerns, adopts the strictly negative goal of ensuring social order, and tries to establish practical rationality on a scientific basis to be organized by elites. Under the hegemony of positivism, moral and political issues are resolved into merely technical questions of efficient social organization.

According to Habermas, the technical development of societies has long proceeded apart from continuity with natural history and mere adaption to the environment, but it has not yet been rationally and democratically governed:

> Through the unplanned sociocultural consequences of technological progress, the human species has challenged itself to learn not merely to affect its social destiny, but to control it. This challenge of technology cannot be met with technology alone. It is rather a question of setting into motion a politically effective discussion that rationality brings the social potential constituted by technical knowledge and ability into a defined and controlled relation to our practical knowledge and will. (1970: 61)

By reference to common human needs, people could judge rationally "the direction and the extent to which they want to develop technical knowledge for the future" (61).

Thus, technical progress would not just be the result of the whims of specialists, but would be mediated through the conduct of social life. Scientific knowledge and practical concerns must interpenetrate and inform one another in a process where technical knowledge is employed to enhance human life. The construction of social policy concerning issues of economic planning and use of technology requires prior reflection of needs and values, and a discourse on the nature of human emancipation. The articulation of these needs and values, the enlightenment of the political will, requires hermeneutic self-understanding and public debate. It involves the recuperation of a practical rationality that raises and redeems validity claims, against the hegemony of a technical rationality that brackets value claims to seek only the instrumental control of society. But the clarification process needed for democracy "could be guaranteed only by the ideal conditions of general communication extending to the entire public and free from domination" (1970: 75). Thus, the existence of an authentic public sphere where citizens can determine social policy requires conditions of uninhibited, noncoerced, nonmanipulated discourse—what Habermas analyzes as the "ideal speech situation." Yet Habermas posits domination-free discourse as a normative ideal to strive for and he understands that under the best conditions this ideal may never be achieved.

In *Toward A Rational Society,* Habermas first posits his most distinctive — and most problematic — claim: that there is an inherent human interest in emancipation, in "the creation of communication without domination" (1970: 113). This appeal to autonomy as an *a priori* interest is fleshed out more fully in *Knowledge and Human Interests* (1971, orig. 1968). Whereas positivist forms of philosophy and science adhere to the "objectivist" belief in a pure knowledge untainted by theoretical presuppositions or external motivations and interests, Habermas argues that the construction of knowledge is indissociable from various human interests that serve as motives for action. He advances a hermeneutic and materialist claim that all cognitive processes are rooted in prescientific forms of experience, in "life structures" determined by distinct kinds of interests.

Habermas identifies three forms of human interest: a technical interest in controling objective processes, a communicative interest in forming an intersubjective world through linguistic symbols, and an emancipatory interest in becoming self-reflective, self-determining, and mature (*Mundigkeit*). Each interest informs a different human science. Hence, the "empirical–analytic" sciences are conditioned by an interest in technical control of external processes, and the "historical–hermeneutic" sciences are guided by an interest in consensus among actors within a shared linguistic tradition; in contrast, the "critical sciences," to which critical theory itself belongs, are determined by an interest in emancipating human beings from domination.

The idea that reason has an inherent interest in its own emancipation through self-reflection was first developed by Fichte who claimed that the ego seeks to become transparent to itself in the act of reflection.[6] For Habermas, this interest is the *a priori* of all ordinary linguistic acts and is thus reflected in language: "The human interest in autonomy and responsibility is not mere fancy, for it can be apprehended a priori. What raises us out of nature is the only thing whose nature we can know: *language*. Through its structure, autonomy and responsibility are posited for us. Our first sentence expresses unequivocally the intention of universal and unconstrained consensus" (1971: 314). Ordinary speech has an implicit *telos* that aims at clear, rational communication and the attainment of consensus. In his theory of "universal pragmatics," Habermas attempts a "rational reconstruction" of the universal "validity claims" inherent in ordinary speech. "We can reconstruct the normative content of possible understanding by stating which universal presuppositions have to be met for understanding to be achieved in an actual case" (Habermas 1982: 83). As Kant sought to uncover the preconditions of experience through analysis of the *a priori* structures of sense and cognition, Habermas seeks to reconstruct the "general and unavoidable" presuppositions of achieving understanding in language.

For Habermas, all individuals have an implicit knowledge of communication, whether or not they can give an explicit account of the structures and rules underlying their performances. This know-how belongs not simply to a particular group, culture, or historical period, but is a universal "species competence." In the midst of a strongly relativistic and nihilistic culture, Habermas advances "an outrageously strong claim . . . that there is a universal core of moral intuition in all times and in all societies" (1986: 206). According to Habermas' reconstruction, any speech act raises general validity claims that relate to "the comprehensibility of the utterance, the truth of its propositional component, the correctness and appropriateness of its performatory component, and the authenticity of the speaking subject" (1973: 18). Comprehensibility, truth, rightness, and sincerity are therefore the *a priori* norms of all communication, if only implicitly understood as such. Agreement is achieved through the implicit or explicit recognition of the validity of these claims. In all agreement, we find "a never silent although seldom redeemed claim to reason" (Habermas 1979: 97).

Thus, like Kant, Habermas relies on appeal to an *a priori* category to ground objective analysis, but this grounding relates to an inherent, prerational human interest rather than to categories of understanding. In the sense that these are universal and necessary presuppositions, and not relative to any one actor, culture, or historical era, Habermas terms them "transcendental" (pre)conditions of understanding or communication. But with Foucault and against Kant, Habermas claims that the presuppositions of (communicative) experience are historically shaped, and hence he initially describes human interests as "quasi-transcendental." These interests both *emerge out of* the laboring and communicative conditions of social existence and they also *condition* human knowledge and experience, thereby possessing a "doublet" nature that is suspect in the eyes of Foucault and has drawn much criticism (see below).

Because they have a universal, necessary, and *a priori* character, because they point to a basic human interest in emancipation, because they clarify what authentic communication is, and because reason and communication require adequate institutional settings, Habermas believes that the presuppositions of ordinary communication, as clarified in the ideal speech situation, provide the needed foundation for normative critique of undemocratic societies. The very nature of language and communication, in other words, has a normative thrust that needs to be unpacked and defended: "To this extent the truth of statements is based on anticipating the realization of the good life" (Habermas 1971: 314). By appealing to "the inherent telos of human speech" that seeks understanding and emancipation and that requires conditions of freedom and equality, Habermas thinks he can provide the noncontingent normative grounding for critique that Marx, the Frankfurt School, and Foucault did not and could not provide. Because Habermas emphasizes that the realization of the emancipatory impulse inherent in language presupposes conditions of unconstrained, undistorted communication, a key task of his social theory is to analyze distorted conditions of communication within capitalist society, to further the development of critical consciousness, and to help begin a movement that can deepen civic participation and democratize social institutions. In contradistinction to corrupted communication forms in capitalist society, Habermas employs the norm of the ideal speech situation, whereby communication and the redemption of validity claims can take place without distorting influences and the mediation of social hierarchy and power, as a counterfactual condition to guide his vision of social progress.

LABOR, LANGUAGE, AND SOCIAL EVOLUTION

> A theory of social evolution, although it must be the foundation of social theory, is today still scarcely at all developed.
>
> —HABERMAS (1979: 126)

Paradoxically, the positing of an *a priori* human interest in emancipation stimulates Habermas to further historical work, beyond the beginnings of the modern public sphere toward an evolutionary theory of the emergence of the human species itself. Habermas materialistically transposes Fichte's idea of the need for the ego to become transparent to itself into the idea of the human species reflecting on its own historical self-formation. The analysis of the human interest in emancipation, Habermas believes, requires a reconstruction of the conditions that lead to the possible emergence of human freedom and the conditions that thwart its realization. As I discuss below, Habermas' evolutionary theory involves a substantive critique of the Marxian narrative of history and a bold challenge to the postmodern rejection of metanarratives.

Since societies are not static, Habermas agrees with Marx and Foucault that a synchronic analysis of any social structure must be situated within the diachronic context of a larger historical process. Unlike Foucault, however, Marx and Habermas seek to grasp the historical conditions of emergence and the developmental tendencies of a given society. Since Habermas situates this analysis within the context of critical theory, the ultimate goal of a theory of social evolution is a diagnostic analysis of the present, with the practical intent of distinguishing between the positive and negative aspects of social rationalization in order to advance the former and contain the latter. The theories of social evolution and modernity require one another: a theory of social evolution is employed to contextualize modernity historically, and a theory of modernity is necessary to understand the developmental tendencies of social evolution. A theory of social evolution has immediate practical relavance insofar as it allows a historical diagnosis of developmental problems with a view toward resolving them in a future social situation. Surveying various contributions from the quarters of historical materialism, behavioralism, cognitive psychology, functionalist systems theory, hermeneutics, and social action theory, Habermas believes that no adequate theory of social evolution yet exists and so a major task of his work is to construct such a theory. Yet Marx's theory of history forms a key component of Habermas' account and it is on Habermas' differences with Marx's theory that I focus.

As noted in Rockmore's detailed account (1989), Habermas' analysis of Marx and Marxism is developed throughout numerous articles and books and over a period of three decades. It has evolved through various stages of development that Rockmore (1987) identifies as interpretation, critique, reconstruction, and abandonment. This development reflects the changes in Habermas' attitude from initial enthusiasm for historical materialism, to a more critical awareness of fundamental problems within Marxian theory, to an attempt to remedy these problems, and finally to a belief that the theory is inherently flawed and needs to be superseded in favor of Habermas' own theory of communication. In the process of reading Marx's work, Habermas develops various accounts of what kind of theory it is, emphasizing its status as philosophy, philosophical anthropology, empirically falsifiable theory of history, economic theory, social theory, and a theory of social evolution.

In *Communication and the Evolution of Society,* Habermas understands historical materialism not simply as Engels characterizes it, that is, as a heuristic method for the analysis of society, but rather primarily as a theory of social evolution, of the development of the human species as a result of its dynamic interaction with its natural environment. Habermas therefore emphasizes the diachronic and philosophico-historical aspects of historical materialism over its status as an economic theory. Habermas initially sees historical materialism as "a theory that needs revision in many respects but whose potential for stimulation has still not been exhausted" (1979: 95). Thus, rather than rejecting historical materialism, Habermas initially works to reconstruct it, to develop its critical resources in a more adequate fashion than did Marx himself. Habermas believes that Marx was unable to develop the critical potential of historical materialism because of the reductionistic nature of the work paradigm (see below).

Historical materialism must be redefined within a communicative framework informed by a Kantian epistemology that identifies universal foundations for critique. With Hegel and Marx, Habermas constructs a metanarrative that grasps the movement of freedom in history through the movement of alienation and differentiation. Following Marx, Habermas rejects Hegel's idealistic and deterministic interpretation of history that reduces human agency to a mere vehicle for the self-actualization of Reason. Both Marx and Habermas see history as a human product whereby human beings dynamically transform themselves as they transform their environment. Habermas agrees with Marx that while history is an active human creation, it has been created under alienated conditions and largely behind the backs of human actors, not subject to their conscious understanding and control. With Marx, Habermas rejects unilinear and determinist narratives that understand history as the progressive, uninterrupted realization of an inherent logic.[7]

Yet, like Marx and unlike Foucault, Habermas nevertheless holds that there is a discernible order and progressive learning movement in history that he tries to grasp through rational reconstruction. Habermas' theory of social evolution allows for contingency, discontinuity, and regressive developments in history, but he insists one can still identify a developmental process that leads in the direction of human emancipation (1976). For Habermas, "evolution" refers to "cumulative processes that exhibit a direction" (1979: 141). As with Marx, this direction can be analyzed in terms of a growing differentiation and complexity of social systems and forms of individuality, able to be periodized according to distinct stages of development that represent advances in a developmental logic, and that culminate in conditions that allow for human freedom and autonomy. Marx analyzes history primarily as the development of the productive forces, the division of social labor, and technical rationality; Habermas sees it mainly as the development of normative structures, moral and legal worldviews, identity formations, and communicative competencies. The contrast in their perspectives represents the differences between the paradigms of production and communication.

Through a focus on communication rather than production, Habermas rejects what Marx takes to be the fundamental criterion of the specifically human. According to Marx and Engels, "Men can be distinguished from animals by consciousness, by religion or anything else you like. They themselves begin to distinguish themselves from animals as soon as they begin to *produce* their means of subsistence, a step which is conditioned by their physical organisation" (1978: 150). Habermas notes that hominids, not just humans, reproduced their existence through social production involving rules for instrumental and communicative action (1979: 134). Since both labor and language predate the emergence of the human species, specifically human forms of social production begin only with the emergence of a family structure that employs role systems organized around intersubjective recognition of behavioral norms, and therefore that incorporates morality into action motivations. Human beings reorganize animal behavior according to imperatives based on morality

and validity claims. Marx understands language only as a mode of socialization whose basic dynamics involve material production. Habermas,
however, wants to separate language from labor, to grant far more importance to the role of language in social integration, and to argue that
language, with labor, forms the basis of social evolution.

Hence, Habermas substitutes a bidimensional for a unidimension-
al theory of evolution; both production and socialization are equally crucial for the reproduction of the human species.[8] These two dimensions
relate to the fundamental conceptual distinction in Habermas' work, the
difference between work and interaction. Habermas defines "work," or
"purposive–rational action," as activity governed by technical rules rooted in empirical knowledge designed to transform nature for human purposes.[9] He defines "interaction" as "communicative action," or
"symbolic action," which is governed by norms designed to achieve consensus on social issues through a process of articulating needs, defining reciprocal behavior expectations, and evaluating different validity
claims.

The distinction is meant to preserve the difference between "techne"
and "praxis," between technical and practical activity, between instrumental and critical reason, and thus between two different historical forms
of rationalization and emancipation. It also allows Habermas to follow
the lead of Dilthey, neo-Kantians, and hermeneutical theorists of the twentieth century in rejecting the unity of the sciences thesis and in separating
the logics of social and natural explanation, a distinction Habermas
preserves without ontologically divorcing the two approaches (see Chapter 4). Habermas claims that the distinction between work and interaction as irreducible categories first turned up in Hegel's early writings but
was subsequently abandoned by Hegel. Marx discovered the distinction
independently, but he also failed to preserve it. Where Marx allegedly conflated work and interaction under the category of social practice, Habermas separates them as two different forms of rationality, practice, and
integration, where "system integration" occurs in the realm of work, and
"social integration" occurs in the realm of communication.

The distinction between work and interaction roughly parallels Marx's
distinction between forces and relations of production, but since Marx
theorizes both in terms of *production,* and the subject–object,
human–nature, relation that entails, Habermas believes these terms are
locked into an economistic logic. The categories "forces" and "relations"
of production show that Marx clearly distinguished between work and
interaction, but, Habermas claims, he theoretically reduced the latter to
the former; the distinction thus has to be developed more consistently and
rigorously on another level through the categories of purposive–rational
action and communicative action. Habermas thinks the terms work and

interaction are "more suited for reconstructing the sociocultural phases of the history of mankind" (1970: 114) insofar as they allow for a non-reductionist analysis of normative structures and forms of social integration, apart from instrumental action and system integration.

The dual realms of work and interaction suggest that societies develop according to dynamics that relate to control processes over both outer and inner nature. The control of outer nature takes place in the realm of production. Here, human beings learn how to gain mastery over nature; throughout history they acquire and accumulate technical knowledge that is deposited in the productive forces of society. The control of inner nature takes place through socialization. Here, human beings develop competencies in communication and acquire practical knowledge that is deposited in worldviews (moral systems), in identity formations, and also in critical knowledge, the stages of reflection whereby social actors become aware of and work to dispel forms of domination operating within communicative action. Against the one-sided focus of Marx and Foucault on, respectively, the control of outer and inner nature, Habermas seeks to incorporate both perspectives into social theory and to achieve emancipation from both external and internal nature. Emancipation from external nature succeeds through the production of technically exploitable knowledge; emancipation from internal nature succeeds through the replacement of institutions based on force with institutions organized around communication free of domination. This achievement occurs not through the productive activity of labor, but the critical activity of intersubjective dialogue. The meaning of autonomy shifts from creative praxis to communicative competence.

The realms of work and interaction carry different kinds of validity claims. In the realm of work there are truth claims requiring verification; in the realm of interaction, there are normative claims requiring legitimation. It is a result of a historical learning process that claims are not accepted without sufficient conditions of argumentation. The rationalization of action, the dynamics of historical development, as well as human evolution and progress proceed through *both* kinds of knowledge, technical and moral–practical. In each area, development follows rationally reconstructable patterns. The social evolution of the human species, therefore, requires a double perspective that analyzes the realms of labor and symbolic interaction, and that can also analyze power structures derived from instrumental action that guide the "steering performances" of society. Habermas' attempt to reconstruct historical materialism, proceeding through the distinction between work and interaction, therefore allows him to account for key differences between technical progress and political emancipation, science and critique, and to recover the Aristotelian contrast between techne and praxis that he feels is lost in the Marxian tradition.

In the historical process, societies evolve from an undifferentiated organic unity organized around the family to a highly differentiated structure with complex social roles and forms of individual psychology and developed competencies in communication and moral reasoning. Historical development results in a gradual expansion of secular reason over the sphere of the sacred, a tendency toward increasing reflexivity and autonomy, and a movement from tribal particularism to universalism. With Marx, Habermas claims that there are clear developmental stages in the evolution of the human species, but he does not agree that the concept of a mode of production provides the best means for historical periodization. Rather, Habermas employs a new periodizing term, "principle of social organization," that differentiates stages in social development according to successive advances in the moral–practical learning process.[10] As Habermas defines it:

> By principle of organization, I understand those innovations which become possible through learning processes that can be reconstructed in a developmental logic, and which institutionalizes a new societal level of learning. The organizational principle of society circumscribes ranges of possibility. It determines in particular: within which structures changes in the system of institutions are possible; to what extent the available productive capacities can be socially utilized or the development of new productive forces can be stimulated; and thereby also to what degrees system complexity and steering performances can be heightened. A principle of organization consists of such abstract regulations that within the social formation determined by it several functionally equivalent modes of production are permitted. Accordingly, the economic structure of a particular society would have to be examined at two levels: firstly, in terms of the modes of production which have entered into a concrete connection within it; and then in terms of that formation of society to which the dominant mode of production belongs. (1979: 153–154)

By appealing to different principles of organization, Habermas attempts to trace progressive advances in the development of moral reflection, action competence, and ultimately, human freedom. By emphasizing the importance of learning processes as a determinant of social change, Habermas breaks with technological determinist accounts of social evolution, both narrow and broad. He agrees with the assumption (brought out by Cohen's "developmental thesis") underlying historical materialism—namely, that the impetus behind technological development is rational knowledge and the desire to implement it. Habermas states, "It is my conjecture that the fundamental mechanism for social evolution in general is to be found in an automatic inability not to learn" (1975: 15). No major social change is accomplished without employing normative resources toward resolving steering problems. But since Habermas insists that learning processes include not just technical knowledge, but also moral–practical knowledge, he also rejects a broader kind of technological determinism that functionally subordinates all social dynamics to production and technical knowledge.[11]

But there is also here an important break from the causal primacy Marx sometimes grants to the productive forces, or even to other endogenous factors such as war, for Habermas is privileging moral–practical forms of knowledge as the motor of history. Far from an epiphenomenon of the forces of production, learning processes in the domain of moral–practical consciousness function as "pacemakers" for social evolution. The evolutionary change of normative structures and forms of social integration is the *precondition* for further development of forces and relations of production. "New forms of social integration, and new productive forces, are due to the institutionalization and exploitation of new forms of knowledge" (Habermas 1986: 168). Rather than the main motor of history, Habermas interprets the development of the productive forces "as a problem-generating mechanism that *triggers but does not bring about* the overthrow of relations of production and an evolutionary renewal of the mode of production" (1979: 146).

In fact, Habermas is inconsistent on which realm has decisive causal importance. On the one hand, he grants the validity of the base–superstructure model (1979: 98) and the primacy of the productive forces (1970: 113), thereby making cultural phenomena and communicative action derivitive of technological and economic forces. He implies a functionalist subordination of communicative to instrumental action when claiming that while the rules of communicative action have their own logic, they "develop in reaction to changes in the domain of instrumental action" (1979: 148). There is a crypto-productivism here that limits the ultimate sources of change to the productive forces, a claim even Marx rejected in favor of a causal pluralism. Yet, on the other hand, as implied by the phrase "pacemaker," he rejects the base–superstructure thesis (1975) and overturns the primacy thesis by privileging normative structures. He does not deny that normative development sometimes can be causally conditioned by changes in the productive forces (12), but he believes that the major evolutionary changes in Western history "were not conditioned but followed by significant development of the productive forces" (1979: 146). Stages in social development, therefore, should not be distinguished according to advances in technology or as modes of production.[12]

Despite his inconsistencies, the thrust of Habermas' position is clearly directed away from the productivist thesis. Yet Habermas goes too far in the opposite direction by assuming that technical progress could not occur without progress at the normative level. Indeed, as Habermas himself would emphasize, the problem of modernity is that technical progress proceeds in almost complete autonomy from moral learning. Ultimately, Marx's understanding of the overdetermination of causal forces provides a more complex and plural account than can be found in Habermas, and it is fully compatible with Habermas' emphasis on the importance of normative developments. Moreover, although Habermas is aware in the abstract that history has so far been a largely unconscious creation of social actors, his concrete analyses and many of his general statements perhaps assume too much consciousness behind the process of social change, for he understands each social transition as the result of a reflexive employment of the learning resources deposited in collective worldviews. Where Marx says a great deal about the causal forces behind the historical transition to capitalism, Habermas says very little, although he does describe the current crisis tendencies in detail and tries to probe what learning resources exist today—such as universalistic and critical forms of consciousness—that could generate a new postcapitalist principle of organization.

Yet Habermas retains Marx's claim that societies rise and fall in response to inner dynamics, inherent social limits, and crisis tendencies. Habermas claims that a given social form remains stable until the point where its developmental tendencies generate "system problems" that disturb its reproduction. Such problems can result in a social "crisis" that arises when "the structure of a social system allows fewer possibilities for problem solving than are necessary to the continued existence of the system" (1975: 2). The crisis can be overcome and resolved in favor of an existing system, or its "solution" can require a whole new principle of organization.

Habermas outlines the following types of social formations: primitive, traditional, capitalist, late-capitalist, postcapitalist, and postmodern (see below). As he describes in detail (1975: 18ff.), each social formation has a different dominant subsystem and a different type of crisis in reproduction ability.[13] Perhaps the clearest example of social evolution he gives involves the transition from kinship to class societies. In the relatively simple and undifferentiated kinship society, system problems involving issues such as land scarcity or population density were unmanageable within its principle of organization. Drawing on the cognitive resources stored in collective worldviews, a new principle was institutionalized that tentatively arbitrated conflicts through an administration of justice on a conventional level of learning that broke with the uncritical nature of traditional norms. These new juridical forms became pacemakers of further social evolution. They allowed for the uncoupling of production from the limits of the kinship system in order to be employed on a larger level, such that "the intensification of cultivation and stock-farming, and the expansion of crafts were the results of the enlarged organizational capacity of class society" (1979: 163).

Habermas draws from the work of Piaget and Kohlberg in the genetic psychology tradition to reconstruct the stages of moral and reflective knowledge. Following their lead, he claims that the phylogeny of individual learning recapitulates the ontogeny of social learning; ego development is homologous to the development of worldviews and collective identities. In Habermas' view, "the basic conceptual structure of possible experience has developed phylogenetically and arises anew in every normal ontogenesis, in a process that can be analyzed empirically" (1979: 22). Each historically created cognitive structure represents the level of development a child can potentially acquire—the appropriation of historical advances is certainly not guaranteed and varies from individual to individual—in order to interact in its environment.

Habermas identifies three stages in the evolution of communication and moral consciousness: (1) symbolically mediated interaction, where speaking and acting coexist on the same undifferentiated plane of reality; (2) propositionally differentiated speech, where speaking and acting are separated such that actions are distinguished from norms; (3) argumentative speech, where norms and roles can be contested, are in need of legitimation, and assume a universal character binding to all social actors. These stages roughly overlap with Piaget's categorization of moral consciousness in preconventional, conventional, and postconventional stages. They parallel Kohlberg's more differentiated six stages (although Habermas added a seventh stage) in the development of moral consciousness, stretching from the initial stage of an undifferentiated self at one with its social and natural environment, to a rational, autonomous self critical of normative claims and choosing moral principles according to criteria of universalizability.[14]

This process at the level of individual development parallels the stages in the historical process of social development. Just as the representational schemes of paleolithic societies is homologous to the early development of the modern child in their lack of discrimination between natural and social phenomena, the rational character of modern society that subjects claims to the test of rational validity parallels the highest stage of ego development. The normal development of the ego identity of the modern citizen occurs in four stages that recapitulate the whole history of moral evolution: symbiotic, egocentric, socio-objective, and universalistic. In this process, the ego is gradually differentiated from both its natural and its social environment and becomes increasingly reflexive, to the point where it no longer accepts validity claims without rational basis and becomes self-determining. The process whereby propositions require rational justification represents an *advance* in the human learning process. Habermas claims that not just individuals but societies also can learn. The relation between individual and social learning is dialectical, since social learning is dependent on individual learning, which in turn draws from the moral–practical knowledge deposited in the worldviews and interpretive systems of society. These forms of learning are individually acquired, then deposited in collective worldviews, where they become resources that can be tapped by social movements engaged in political struggle.

We see that Habermas tries to work out a unified theory of evolutionary development both at the individual and social levels. Such correlations are vaguely suggested by Marx and Engels where they claim that developments in individuality follow developments in the productive forces of society (1978: 191), but they did not have the analytic resources to flesh these out and, Habermas believes, they ultimately conflated the two lines of development. While Habermas finds definite homological correlations between individual and social evolution (1979: 103–106), he also warns against drawing "hasty parallels" and points to important disanalogies between them (102ff.).

The major task of Habermas' genealogy is to identify progressive advances in learning whereby mythological worldviews and dogmatic forms of tradition gradually become rationalized and give way to validity claims in need of justification. Habermas' reconstruction of the learning process thereby resembles Comte's scheme of the progression of the mind from the theological and metaphysical stages to the positive stage dominated by reason and facts, although he rejects the linear and deterministic aspects of Comte's narrative along with his equation of progress with the development of scientific knowledge alone. The normative and political upshot of Habermas' theory of social evolution is that there presently exist advanced forms of moral–practical consciousness, the products of historical development, which could be employed to constitute a free and rational society, but which are blocked by capitalist economic and political powers. In other words, communicative competencies and conceptual resources are stored in our late-modern worldview that individuals and social movements can draw on to refashion their identities and societies toward greater autonomy, freedom, and democracy.

Like Marx, Habermas sees history as an evolutionary process of increasing complexity that is greatly stimulated through the emergence of class hierarchy, the state, and private property. Driven by structures of alienation and exploitation, history tends toward ever greater system complexity. Following Marx, Habermas claims that a new principle of organization only brings new steering problems, new forms of scarcity, and new crises. The more complex a society, the greater and more complex its steering problems and crisis tendencies. This raises an important problem: is system complexity compatible with social stability? If so, can this be achieved with democracy, or does it, as Weber argued, require bureaucracy? Habermas opts for the first alternative.

THE CRITIQUE OF MARX

> What today separates us from Marx are evident historical truths.
> —HABERMAS (1982: 221)

As we have just seen, Habermas claims that Marx subsumes the independent dynamics of intersubjective, communicative relations to the subject–object relation of human beings controlling nature. Habermas finds in Marx's work not only a reductionistic but also a related scientistic or technocratic impulse that leads him to abandon philosophy, equate knowledge in general with scientific knowledge, and undervalue the need for practical–moral reflection by granting too large a role to the development of the productive forces as bearers of social change. Habermas' conclusion is that these problems can only be overcome by replacing the paradigm of production with the paradigm of communication.

That Marx on occassion reduces social dynamics to production is clear from his claims that all forms of domination are modifications of class domination (1975a: 333), that all activity is a form of productive activity (349), or that "all history is nothing but the creation of man via labor" (357). But, as Habermas recognizes, Marx frequently uses general terms like "production" to designate related but independent dynamics of human action. In a narrow sense, the term "production" refers to the human–nature relation governed by instrumental logic; in a broader sense, it refers to all forms of human creation and "objectification" and includes language, social relations, forms of cooperation, morality, and art.

Properly understood, Marx's concepts of "production" or "social practice" refer to the dynamics of both work and interaction. The purpose of the forces/relations of production distinction was to differentiate the relations between human beings and nature and between different groups of human beings themselves. In his understanding that the human–nature relation is always mediated by specific social relations, Marx opened up an analytic space for theorizing the dynamics of communication, while insisting that one cannot separate production and interaction, since production is necessarily embedded in the context of interaction. It is, after all, specific social relations of production that structure different forms of the labor process as various modes of exploitation and that utilize scientific and technical knowledge for purposes of social and natural control.

Habermas' critique is not that Marx unambiguously reduced inter-action to work, but that his work has tensions and inconsistencies. The fundamental tension Habermas finds in Marx's work concerns what we have already identified as that between his general statements and con-crete investigations (see Chapter 1). For Habermas, this tension is between historical materialism as a general theory of history that grants primacy to purposive–rational action and the critique of political economy that implictly recognized the interdependence of purposive–rational action and symbolic interaction. As Habermas puts it,

> Self-constitution through social labor is conceived at the *categorical level* as a process of production, and instrumental action, labor in the sense of material activity, or work designates the dimension in which natural history moves. At the level of his *material investigations,* on the other hand, Marx always takes account of social practice that encompasses both work and interaction. The processes of natural history are mediated by the productive activity of individuals and the organization of their interrelations. (1971: 52–53)

Ultimately, however, Habermas claims that Marx *resolves* these ten-sions into productivist concepts of social life and technocratic concepts of historical change, as the dual dimensions of human evolution are dis-solved into the concept of social practice. A key clue to Marx's tendency to privilege technical over practical rationality is his call for a unified science that assimilates social dynamics to natural processes and his fetishization of scientific rhetoric.[15] Habermas wants not simply to broaden the ac-count of production to include socialization, but to develop an analyti-cally autonomous framework. Because Marx ultimately remains bound to a subject–object logic of production that fails to develop an explicit account of the intersubjective logic of communication, Habermas claims (1987a) that Marx remains wedded to the philosophy of the subject, despite his decentering of the individual producer to determining social relations.

With Habermas, I believe the main problem in Marx is not that he excluded interaction, but that he fails to provide an *explicit* account of the differences between work and interaction, and between technical and practical rationality. It is a significant virtue of Habermas' work to de-velop a specific account of these differences and to attempt a theory of the evolution of forms of moral–practical knowledge and the logic of cri-tique. By broadening the scope of a theory of evolution beyond the con-fines of system integration to account also for forms of social integration, by taking into account not only the development of technical knowledge but also moral–practical knowledge, and by theorizing the relative au-tonomy of communicative action from production, Habermas recovers the importance of consciousness and practical learning for political change and breaks with certain tendencies in Marx — rigidly absolutized by later mechanistic Marxists — to make the development of the forces of production the sufficient condition for human emancipation. By challenging the reductionistic tendencies of Marx's theory, Habermas is able to rethink the problems inherent in the Marxian base–superstructure model of analysis and its theory of crisis. The shift from mode of production to principle of organization recasts the material "base" of society such that it is no longer identical with its economic structure, but includes, more generally, a specific form of social integration, a dominant subsystem. Habermas makes a convincing case that culture and morality are not just "superstructural" phenomena, but are important components of social evolution that have an internal history of their own.

Habermas' better developed conceptual framework also helps to overcome a tendency in Marx toward a technocratic conception of historical change that on occasion led him to think the internal development of capitalism would generate the objective and subjective conditions of revolution. Here too Marx's work displayed competing tendencies. These emerge out of its dual character as both empirical/scientific and philosophical/critical. Marx is concerned both with an analysis and explanation of empirical phenomena in capitalist society and with a critique of its forms of distorted consciousness that seeks to initiate a critical class consciousness and a process of self-reflection (Wellmer 1971; Gouldner 1980). Since his earliest reflections, Marx was acutely aware of the need to emancipate critical consciousness from the distorting forces of ideology. A dominant theme of Marx's *Theses on Feuerbach* is the need for "practical-critical activity" that informs revolutionary practice. But in the *Grundrisse,* for example, Habermas finds conflicting tendencies toward both accepting and rejecting the view that advances in science and technology are sufficient for the liberation of those self-conscious subjects that democratically regulate their social life process (1971: 48–52).

Despite the critical nature of Marx's work, which implies the need for communicative rationality, Habermas claims that Marx ultimately privileged technical over moral–practical knowledge as the key source of social change. In the *Grundrisse,* for example, Marx envisaged the transition to socialism in terms of a growing technical command over society's productive forces: "The development of fixed capital indicates the extent to which general social knowledge has become *an immediate force of production,* and therefore the conditions of the social life process itself have come under the control of the general intellect" (Marx, quoted in Habermas 1971: 47). Habermas see here "a model according to which the history of the species is linked to an automatic transposition of natural science and technology into a self-consciousness which controls the material life-process" (1971: 48).

Habermas finds countervailing passages in the *Grundrisse* that deny that the transformation of science into machinery leads automatically to the liberation of self-conscious subjects.[16] In such alternative passages, he claims that for Marx the self-constitution of the species takes place both in the context of instrumental action upon nature and the dimension of power relations that govern social interaction. Habermas also maintains that Marx clearly distinguishes the self-conscious control of society by associated producers from the automatic regulation of production that is independent of individuals (1971: 51). Marx fully understands, in other words, that scientific–technical progress can be directed *against* the awakening of critical consciousness insofar as, for example, it binds the individual to the machine and its deadening repetitions. His vision of socialism entailed not only a quantitative extension of capitalist technologies but also their qualitative transformation, which requires a change in the form and social relations of production. The productive powers of society would no longer be deployed solely as the productive powers of capital, but as those of the workers' own powers. Habermas claims, moreover, that Marx abandoned this technocratic model after the *Grundrisse,* and that it does not therefore appear in *Capital* and other later works.

What Habermas criticizes, then, is a tendency in Marx to conflate technical with practical knowledge, to fail to see that the former does not guarantee the latter, that practical consciousness is separate from technical consciousness, that it involves a different learning process, and that it requires independent development and institutional forms. The consequence of the belief that the main learning mechanism for social change is found in technical knowledge is that "the relationship between theory to practice can only assert itself as the purposive–rational application of techniques assumed by empirical science" (Habermas 1973a: 254). Marx wrongly "localized the learning processes important for evolution in the dimension of objectivating thought — of technical and organizational knowledge, of instrumental and strategic action, in short, of *productive forces.*" He thereby failed to emphasize sufficiently the learning processes that also occur "in the dimension of moral insight, practical knowledge, communicative action, and the consensual regulation of action conflicts — learning processes that are deposited in more mature forms of social integration, in new *productive relations,* and that in turn first make possible the introduction of new productive forces" (Habermas 1979: 97–98). Marx therefore "eliminates reflection as such as a motive force in history" (1971: 44).

To put it in other terms, Marx sometimes exaggerated the extent to which capitalism was truly threatened by its economic crises alone, failing to emphasize adequately the independent need for moral–practical consciousness and political struggle. In some passages, Marx claimed that the economic crisis of capitalism would be so severe as necessarily to engender a lived crisis. But, as Habermas emphasizes, the economic and political crisis of the capitalist system was indefinitely postponed through systemic flexibility and was contained ideologically. While system and social crisis are interrelated, they are not identical and the latter is not a mechanical effect of the former. Abandoning the belief that technological development is inherently emancipatory, Habermas argues that rationalization at the level of purposive–rational subsystems must be accompanied by rationalization in the realm of symbolic interaction where human beings can assess validity claims and achieve consensus over the norms and procedures of social organization. To state it another way, social change requires that both forms of crisis—objective and subjective, system and lifeworld—exist and that lived crisis be generated through reflexive awareness, communication, debate, and a critique of domination. Unless communicative rationality is as developed as technological rationality, unless subjective crisis is as developed as objective crisis, there will be an insufficient basis for social transformation. As Habermas says, "*Liberation from hunger and misery* does not necessarily converge with *liberation from servitude and degradation,* for there is no automatic developmental relation between labor and interaction" (1973a: 169).

Marx himself emphasized the importance of class struggle and political consciousness. He insisted that critical consciousness does not come alone or automatically from production, but rather that workers would have to go through the long school of revolution. But Marx's focus was more on the economic–technological conditions of change and he sometimes spoke as though the transition to communism was guaranteed rather than contingent. Marx showed a tendency to believe both that immiseration would stimulate revolution and that there would be an automatic transposition of science and technology into critical self-consciousness. Marx conceived of the rational social world primarily in terms of the democratic technical control of use value. Since Marx's time, however, history has taught us "that even a well-functioning planning bureaucracy with scientific control of the production of goods and services is not a sufficient condition for realizing the associated material and intellectual productive forces in the interest of the enjoyment and freedom of an emancipated society. For Marx did not reckon with the possible emergence at every level of a discrepancy between scientific control of the material life conditions and a democratic decision-making process" (Habermas 1970: 58). Marx underestimated the phenomenon of power, in other words, which both Foucault and Habermas see to be a Hydra with many heads. For Habermas, technical knowledge does not constitute enlightenment and far from guarantees the creation of a vital public sphere engaged in the ongoing process of debate over needs, values, and the overall organization of society.

Habermas understands that the technocratic vision of social change implies a political technocracy that seeks authoritarian command over natural resources apart from furthering a general enlightenment and process of democracy. The epistemological result of conflating the social and natural sciences is that Marx succumbs to the positivist illusion of a presuppositionless theory and fails to justify adequately the validity of his own historical viewpoint. When historical materialism opposes itself to philosophy, understood merely as bourgeois ideology rather than epistemology, and establishes itself as science, it surrenders its radical character and itself becomes ideology by appropriating the scientistic understanding of theory and social life fostered by positivism and late capitalism. "That we disavow reflection *is* positivism" (Habermas 1971: vii). Against Marx, Habermas claims that social theory requires epistemological justification.

Seeking to break from the technocratic tendencies in Marx's analysis, Habermas explicitly distinguishes between technical and practical knowledge, between the capacity for control and the capacity for enlightenment, between the rational organization of science and technology and the democratic governing of social life, between the separate logics of the natural and social sciences. Habermas attempts to reconstruct the notion of praxis in a way that recovers the multidimensional meanings initially given to it by Aristotle—referring to speech, noble deeds, and ethical activity—but which Marx and the modern tradition beginning with Machievelli and Hobbes has drastically reduced (see Habermas 1973a).

Habermas also develops a more complex and multifaceted account of crisis pertinent to changing conditions of capitalism. Habermas finds capitalism vulnerable to four different crisis tendencies: an economic crisis of failure to produce sufficient quantities of goods, a rationality crisis in which the political system fails to administer economic imperatives adequately, a legitimation crisis generated by insufficient mass loyalty, and a motivation crisis resulting from a deficit in action-motivating meaning. For Habermas, crisis involves not only objective "system" factors that involve contradictions and malfunctions of the social structures, but also subjective "identity" factors that involve frustrated needs and dissatisfaction. Marx was aware of the difference and the need for both kinds of crisis to exist for a revolutionary situation, but he failed to integrate them into a coherent social theory and practice.

To sum up: in the case of Marx's reductive tendencies, Habermas' critique provides a necessary corrective; in the case of his nonreductive tendencies, Habermas' account serves to give a more explicit analysis of what is only implicit in Marx. I do not believe, however, that Habermas adequately understands the contextual nature of Marx's work (see Chapter 1), that he always situates specific passages in their proper framework, nor that he grasps the full complexity of the multiple modes of theory and practice that Marx develops. If Marx consistently analyzes the inseparability of work and interaction, of productive and interactive competence, of technical and critical knowledge, then it is misleading to claim that he has a technocratic or reductionist conception of history. The main problem in Marx's work is his undertheorization of the realm of interaction and the evolution and nature of moral–practical or critical knowledge.

While there are many theoretical advantages to Habermas' framework, there are also serious disadvantages and problems that frequently constitute a regression behind Marx's own analyses. In his attempt to separate work from interaction, Habermas fails to grasp the interrelationship between these two social realms as they develop historically and he moves from Marx's dialectical holism to a nondialectical dualism. Habermas claims that the distinction between work and interaction is only an analytic distinction and that empirically the two realms of social life overlap, but he nevertheless differentiates too sharply between these realms and does not concretely analyze important lines of overlap.[17]

The "strategic" action of class struggle, for example, clearly combines communicative and purposive–rational action. Ideally, its goal is not only control of natural resources and the social economy, but also the fostering of enlightenment and consensus oriented around norms of democracy and social justice. Similarly, workers' democracy movements use communicative rationality (in the form of dialogue, debate, and possibly consensus) to decide questions regarding instrumental rationality (the organization of the workplace). Sensat observes that because Habermas creates too strict a separation between work and interaction, he himself unwittingly succumbs to a technocratic conception that "presupposes that stages of scientific and technological development can be adequately individuated apart from their specific interactional (class-relational) contexts" (1979: 114). By contrast, Marx decisively overturned this view by analyzing the interaction between forces and relations of production.

Habermas' theory has other dualistic tendencies in the framework of ecology. Habermas claims that cognitive–instrumental rationality necessarily requires an observer and domineering attitude toward nature, while communicative rationality by nature overcomes this objectifying standpoint. Just as there can be an ecological science that understands the subject as a participant rather than a neutral observer and seeks to promote unity and harmony between human beings and nature, so the intersubjective standpoint of communicative rationality is compatible with an exploitative attitude toward nature, since nothing prevents dialogic participants from attaining consensus on the project of exploiting nature. There is no inherent ecological telos in any form of communicative rationality; moreover, the interdialogic "enlightenment" of human actors does not guarantee their socialization into an ecological sensibility. Habermas blocks the possibility of an "ecological science" that does not take a strictly instrumental attitude toward nature or reduce it to raw materials and resources for human use.[18] Habermas' critique is ahistorical, since it is only in capitalism that scientific practice developed such an attitude. As Keane points out (1975), Habermas' equation of work with instrumental rationality and efficiency transforms the capitalist organization of work into an eternal form and blocks alternative conceptions, such as Schiller, Marx, and Marcuse envisaged, that link work with spontaneity, play, or aesthetics.

Thus, Habermas has dualistic and ahistorical tendencies that Marx overcame in his analyses. Marx not only clearly analyzed the historical transformation of science and technology under the interests of capital, he also understood the interest in emancipation to be the specific product of the bourgeois democratic revolutions, rather than an innate norm given in language itself. Except for his early view of history as the unfolding of species being, Marx broke with the ahistorical and teleological view of a historical macrosubject retained by Habermas. Despite his theory of social evolution and his rejection of determinism, Habermas posits a developmental logic of history informed by a *telos* that seeks the optimization of a moral outlook that is realized in the universalism of postconventional thought. Rather than differentiating various historical actors and cultures, Habermas assumes a unified "human species." Marx, in contrast, had a far more plural and complex account of different historical groups and cultures; his narrative of history also contained significant ruptures lacking in Habermas' account.

In his eventual break from historical materialism, his transformation of historical specific forms of "work" into an invariant category of "purposive–rational action," Habermas abandons too much of the paradigm of production. To reject Marxism is to relinquish indispensable categories for the analysis of labor, exploitation, profit, accumulation, and commodification—core phenomena that continue to structure our present form of social existence and of which Marx had a far deeper understanding than Habermas. Moreover, the Marxian account of labor forms an indispensible precondition and context for any theory of communication. Marx showed how forms of consciousness and communication are distorted within socioeconomic forms and their ideologies. As Marx would insist, changes in the form and content of human communication must be understood in relation to general changes in the technical, economic, and political institutions of society, rather than as autonomous forms of development. Given the commodification of "communication" technologies, and the increasing historical tendency to eliminate interaction and communicative competence from the workplace through Taylorization and from the structures of everyday life through mass media, a Marxian perspective of political economy remains crucial for understanding key aspects of communication itself.

A decisive advantage Marx and Foucault have over Habermas is their direct focus on how power relations structure work, communication, and self-consciousness. To be sure, a key concern of Habermas' work is the relations of power embedded in "systematically distorted communication."[19] But Habermas tends to hypostatize power through abstract categories such as "steering performances" or "expansion of system autonomy." He doesn't adequately link normative structures to power relations and he rarely specifies concrete forces of domination and struggle. His account of the "socialization" of "inner nature" underplays the extent to which this involves a repression of needs, desires, and spontaneity, such as is emphasized by the Frankfurt School and Foucault.

In his parallel, but certainly not identical, category of purposive–rational action, Habermas fails to capture core aspects of the capitalist work process that are better illuminated through Marx. As Heller (1982) makes clear, Habermas reduced Marx's concept of work from its broad anthropological meaning to its most narrow meaning as instrumental activity. "Work" for Marx involves, inseparably, the transformation of both the internal and the external worlds. Habermas therefore misses the larger meaning of work as self-transformative activity. In this sense, "production" also involves communicative and aesthetic rationality. The early Marx's interpretation of history as the evolution of the senses, for example, is an insight into what Habermas refers to as advances in aesthetic–expressive rationality. Marx also saw attitudes toward nature that were not merely instrumental and dominating, but also aesthetic and sensuous (Roderick 1986: 157).

In addition, Honneth shows (1982) that Habermas' concept of work as instrumental action fails to retain Marx's distinction between alienated and unalienated labor. The distinction between free and distorted communication has no parallel in the realm of work, where the category of instrumental action subsumes the activity of the artisan as well as the factory worker disciplined by Taylorized management techniques. Consequently, Habermas drains the category of work of all critical import, failing to see that an important type of moral–normative knowledge and critique issues not only from the realm of communication, but from the realm of work as well, where the experience of degraded activity can prompt a serious questioning of the entire social system. Where Marx developed the concept of work not only as an economic category, but also as a normative category designating the potential for emancipatory self-development (*Bildung*), Habermas narrows the concept of work to the extent that it is emptied of all critical content. For Honneth, the fundamental flaw of

Habermas' communicative theory "is that its basic concepts are laid out from the beginning as though the process of liberation from alienated work relations, which Marx had in mind, were already historically complete" (1982: 54).

Habermas counters arguments in favor of the anthropological conception of work by addressing some of the problematic assumptions embedded in Marx's account (Habermas 1982: 223–226). Habermas finds it difficult to extend the economic concept of work into a generalized model of self-expression, especially under prevailing historical conditions of a Taylorized workplace that allegedly purges all normative content from the concept of work. Habermas also argues that after the *Economic and Philosophic Manuscripts* Marx himself abandoned the anthropological model of work as self-externalization and shifted the normative grounding to the labor theory of value.

Aside from his mistaken claim that the model of alienated labor is central only to one early text of Marx's, Habermas throws out the baby with the bathwater by dissolving the very concept of alienated labor with the allegedly problematic notion of work as self-expression. In its stead he substitutes a reified communication definition of alienation: "I explain the alienation phenomena specific to modern societies by the fact that spheres of communicatively structured life-world have increasingly been subjected to imperatives of adaption to autonomous sub-systems, which have been differentiated out through media such as money and power, and which represent fragments of non-free society" (1982: 226). Habermas obscures the very process of hyperalienated work to refute the self-expressive model of work. He uncritically accepts the recent trend where "the concept of labour has been purged of all normative content in industrial sociology" (225). Whatever the conditions of work today, Marx's normative vision of work as a type of craft activity remains crucial for recapturing a substantive notion of meaningful work, and should function as something like an ideal *work* situation. One could turn the tables on Habermas and argue that if the normative model of work is obsolete today, so too is the normative model of communication, for one sphere is no less colonized than the other.

It seems clear then that Marx and Habermas often provide useful supplements and correctives to each other's positions. Rather than following Habermas in his move toward a super-abstract communications framework, we can say, with Roderick, that "communication theory is most usefully construed as a supplement to the paradigm of production, and not as a replacement of it" (1986: 167). Just as Habermas' communication theory illuminates phenomena difficult to see through the lens of production, there are elements of Marx's analysis indispensible for a critical theory of society, such as the concept of alienated labor, that cannot be captured by a communication model. The analysis of the linguistic utterance is a poor substitute for that of the commodity form. In response to the objection that he seeks to supersede historical materialism rather than to provide complementary analyses, Habermas is evasive (1986: 213). He claims that he is incorporating the cognitive–instrumental aspects of action, while abandoning unteneable aspects of it such as the expressivist model of alienation and supplementing Marx by providing an account of developments of the social–integrative core of evolution. Yet, I have argued, Habermas has left behind key elements of the production framework and wrongly takes the turn to a whole new paradigm.

Before turning to Habermas' critique of Foucault and postmodern theory, we need to understand his critical defense of modernity and the Enlightenment, for Habermas' belief in the progressive tendencies of the modern world is the basis of his critique of postmodern theory.

MODERNITY AS UNFINISHED PROJECT

> Modern life-worlds are differentiated and should remain
> so in order that the reflexivity of traditions, the individ-
> uation of the social subject, and the universalistic foun-
> dations of justice and morality do not all go to hell.
> —HABERMAS (1986: 107)

A major goal of Habermas' theory is to overcome the pessimistic turn of critical theory initiated by Adorno and Horkheimer through the influence of Max Weber, and which reverberates powerfully in postmodern theories. Unlike Marx, who uncritically championed the emancipatory potential of modern rationality, science, and technology, Weber challenged the Enlightenment conception that the development of secular reason would lead to human freedom. For Weber, the rationalization of cultural and social life in the modern world resulted in greater forms of domination. Instrumental rationality carried a hidden logic that created a powerful form of bureaucratic and technical control which Weber likened to an iron cage of social life. For Weber, the kind of socialist society Marx envisioned, organized around technical imperatives, could only deepen the dynamics of domination further and therefore posed no emancipatory alternative to capitalism.

Lukács appropriated Weber's work to show how reification—the transformation of social relations into relations among things that leads to the occlusion of critical consciousness—was a form of rationalization. But Lukács ignored the fatalistic aspects of Weber and renewed Marx's optimism in the emancipatory tendencies in history that could be realized through a politically conscious working class. With the appearance of world wars, fascism, a culture industry, and a conservative working class, Adorno and Horkheimer found this optimism untenable and employed Weber's insights in an even more radical direction that traced the logic of domination all the way back to the beginnings of Western rationality. Anticipating Foucault's analysis of normalization, the *Dialectic of Enlightenment* theorized rationality as a repressive "identity logic" that seeks to extirpate difference and individuality. Hence, Adorno and Horkheimer abandoned the progressivist view of history, posited the existence of a totally administered society, and practiced a negative critique that only saw domination without positive possibilities for struggle or escape outside of the marginalized sphere of aesthetics.

Fully aware of the transformation of Marx's vision of revolution and emancipation into a philosophy of despair and resignation, Habermas attempts to rethink the foundations of critical theory and to develop a new vision of freedom and democracy. Habermas is deeply influenced by Weber's account of rationalization and takes into account the failure of rationalization to produce emancipation, but he nevertheless returns to Marx's practice of a dialectical theory, which sees both repressive and emancipatory tendencies in history and tries to advance historically created possibilities for human liberation.

Hence, Habermas seeks a theory of modernity that simultaneously is a theory of rationality that confronts the deformed realization of reason in history. This requires a theory of social evolution that analyzes the historical dynamics leading to the social pathologies of modernity, but also creates the possibility for their cure. The project here is to repair the damaged link between enlightenment and emancipation. Habermas intends to develop a sharp critique of modernity, but "without surrendering the project of modernity or descending into post- or anti-modernism, 'tough' new conservativism or [the] 'wild' young conservativism of Foucault and others" (Habermas 1986: 107).

Habermas draws from Weber to interpret modernity as a disenchanting, secularizing, and rationalizing process that destroys the philosophical basis of previous religions and worldviews and creates systems of purposive–rational action (1987a). Unlike the mythico-magical worldview, the modern worldview differentiates between objective, social, and subjective domains of reality, the different attitudes toward them, and the validity claims proper to each. Through his Kantianized reading of Weber, Habermas characterizes "cultural modernity" as a process of creating a rational worldview and differentiating reason into three separate fields of value—science, morality, and art—all of which were inseparably interwoven in traditional forms of life. Each branch of reason develops according to its own autonomous logic and has its own sphere of validity: truth, normative rightness, and authenticity and beauty. The rationality structures appropriate to these fields are cognitive–instrumental, moral–practical, and aesthetic–expressive. The discourses of science, morality and law, and art criticism were institutionalized in different spheres, where they became the province of cultural specialists isolated from the general public.

With Enlightenment philosophers, Habermas sees this differentiation as a positive effect of modernity, because it separates the cognitive potential of various spheres of life and makes possible a rational organization of everyday life. The differentiating logic of cultural modernity allows for questions of truth, justice, and taste to come into their own and promotes critical consciousness. Besides creating progressive advances in law, civil rights, and individual liberties, modernity releases forces of communicative rationality and establishes rational norms by which social institutions and ideologies can be assessed. For the first time, cultural norms lose their unquestioned character and require rational grounding.

But Habermas criticizes Weber for not seeing the *selective* nature of modernization processes that have given way to the disproportionate power of science and cognitive–instrumental rationality over other spheres of reason (1986: 111). It is only in modernity that the subsystems of purposive–rational action, economics and politics, burst through the normative fetters of cultural tradition to become independent ruling logics in the form of money and power. Habermas refers to the process of economic and political control over the social context from which they have been abstracted as the "colonization of the lifeworld." With the one-sided development of instrumental rationality, "ever more personal relations, services, and phases of life are being transformed into objects of administration, or into commodities" (141).

Habermas' analysis has important overlaps with Weber, in its reference to growing bureaucratization of life, with Marx, in its reference to expanding processes of comodification, and with Foucault, in its reference to the growing scientific and technological administration of life. But Habermas resists the postmodern descriptive claim (Baudrillard) that these various spheres have totally imploded and the postmodern prescriptive goal (Derrida) to collapse substantive distinctions among various spheres of value, such as between philosophy and literature. Habermas does acknowledge that in late capitalism there is a triumph of "system over lifeworld," as the result of the penetration of money, power, and instrumental rationality, but he does not accept the radical Baudrillardian thesis of total social implosion, a variation on Marcuse's thesis of "one-dimensional society." Habermas claims that the project of cultural modernity is still intact despite the growing complexity of modern society; he also argues that critical theory must try to rescue the remnants of communicative rationality and maintain the differentiation of spheres of rationality and their separate validity claims. He rejects all pessimistic philosophies, be they those of Luhmann or Baudrillard, that pronounce the assimilation of all conflict within a perfectly functional system.

The postmodern rejection of rationality and its field of differentiation replays surrealism's attempt to aestheticize all facets of social existence by conflating the boundaries between art and life. For Habermas, such a "terroristic" program is doomed to failure: "A reified everyday praxis can be cured only by creating unconstrained *interaction* of the cognitive with the moral–practical and the aesthetic–expressive elements. Reification cannot be overcome by forcing just one of those highly stylized cultural spheres to open up and become more accessible. Instead, we see under certain circumstances a relationship emerge between terroristic activities and the over-extension of any one of these spheres into other domains" (1983: 11–12, my emphasis).

Everyday life cannot be changed simply by transforming only one sphere; political programs must address and balance all three spheres. In a nonreified lifeworld one would find an autonomization and interaction of the three spheres of value and their appropriate forms of argumentation and validity claims. Just as instrumental rationality should not colonize aesthetics, aesthetics should not colonize instrumental rationality or the moral–practical sphere. The general solution Habermas proposes to cure the ills of the modern world is not to reject instrumental rationality, and with it science and technology, but to redress the balance between the various spheres of rationality and to increase the content of communicative rationality. Communicative rationality "is already embodied in the existing forms of interaction and does not first have to be postulated" (Habermas 1982: 227).

A Habermasian politics, therefore, turns on the distinction between instrumental and communicative rationality, on the critique of the colonization of the lifeworld by economic and political forces, on the attempt to salvage the remaining remnants of communicative rationality within a public sphere that can initiate greater democratic participation, and on the project of fostering moral–practical rationality that challenges the hegemony of science over ethics and politics. Where money and power have taken over the social integrative functions previously fulfilled by consensual norms, Habermas seeks to bring them back into the control of the lifeworld. The movement toward greater democratization begins with the revival of a public sphere organized around open discussion and the redemption of normative validity claims. From this, Habermas seeks to promote the gradual, nonviolent extension of democracy without advocating the overthrow of the social order.

Despite the typical picture in the United States of Habermas as an arid and apolitical intellectual, due to the highly abstract character of his main works, he is very much an *intellectual engagé,* and has a highly public profile in Germany.[20] For four decades, he has struggled against regressive tendencies in the Federal Republic and supported democratic alternatives. A key motivating factor of Habermas' politics is his own experience with fascism in Germany, since he grew up in the Hitler Youth movement (Habermas 1986). Beginning in the early 1950s, and again in subsequent decades, Habermas denounced Heidegger's fascism and the culture that influenced it. In the 1960s, he supported the German student movements, but condemned the ultrarevolutionary and surrealist factions that jettisoned the ideals of gradual reform or rational critique as "left-fascism" (a term he later withdrew). In the 1980s, Habermas took a progressive stance in the "Historian's Debate" over the issue of the moral responsibility of the German nation for the Holocaust (see Habermas 1989b, 1994). Whereas neoconservative historians wished to justify or whitewash the attempt at a "final solution" and to "normalize" the aberration of genocide, Habermas condemned Nazism and its historical revisionists. He insisted on the need of the German people never to forget this dark chapter in their history and to keep alive the memory of its victims so that the flames of fascism could never again burn. He also has supported the rights of asylum seekers in Germany and called for better immigration laws. Habermas did not support German reunification, because of worries over the loss of political and ethnic identities, but he did support the U.S. effort in the Gulf War, on rather unconvincing grounds (see Habermas 1994).[21]

In the 1980s, Habermas identified a new theoretical enemy, another species of conservativism, and he shifted the focus of his critique from the hyperrationalism of positivism to the irrationalism of postmodern theory.[22]

POSTMODERNITY AND THE CRITIQUE OF FOUCAULT

Habermas rejects both "postmodernism," as a cultural and philosophical project, and postmodernity, as an alleged new historical era that emerges from the ruins of modernity. Habermas identifies two different versions of the thesis that modernity and the Enlightenment have ended and given way to a postmodern or posthistorical condition (1983). The neoconservative version, as promulgated by Arnold Gehlen, holds that the ideals of the Enlightenment are dead, but live on in parodic, negative form. In Weber's terms, cultural modernity has collapsed and has been taken over by the irrevocable dynamics of social modernity; rationalization processes operate now only in instrumental, no longer in critical, form. The postmodern version, which Habermas claims is held by Foucault, also posits

the end of the Enlightenment, but bids farewell both to cultural and social modernity, since rationality is nothing but the will to power. For Adorno and Horkheimer, Foucault, Luhmann, and others, the end of the
Enlightenment also spells the end of the individual and its critical abilities, which prevent it from being completely assimilated by systems of
power.

Habermas denies that we are in a postmodernity where struggle, conflict, opposition, differentiation, and system crisis have been eliminated
in favor of a perfectly functioning cyberetic system. Instead, he claims,
we are in a late-capitalist society still determined by the capitalist state
and economy, still characterized by conflict and opposition, still crisis-
ridden, and still vulnerable to change through rational critique and political struggle. There remain objective possibilities for extending communicative rationality to more spheres of social existence, to create a rational
society that eliminates ideology and domination. Thus, all claims to a postmodern or posthistorical condition are false insofar as tendencies of Enlightenment and modernity remain alive and new historical events and
processes can still occur. Habermas readily admits that the "project of
modernity"—the attempt to preserve the different value spheres and to
promote moral progress, social justice, and human happiness—has so far
failed. But he refuses the postmodern rejection of this project as inherently flawed and he poses a fundamental choice: "Should we try to hold on
to the *intentions* of the Enlightenment, feeble as they may be, or should
we declare the entire project of modernity a lost cause?" (1983: 9–10).
Postmodern theorists pursue the latter choice, but they have prematurely
abandoned the project of modernity.

There are various indications, however, that Habermas believes that
a fundamentally new society is on the horizon and that we are reaching
the end of history, claims that I find to stand in tension with one another.
Habermas makes a reference to a "post-capitalist" society, but this is misleading because he uses the term to designate state-socialist societies (which
arguably are not significantly structurally different from capitalist societies) (1975). Habermas also posits a "post-modern society," but gives conflicting characterizations of it. He understands postmodern society as (1)
a society "characterized by a primacy of the scientific and educational systems" (1979: 165); (2) a society devoid of critical rationality and democracy
and overtaken by technical administration (1975: 133); and (3) "a historically new principle of organization and not a different name for the surprising vigor of an aged capitalism" (17). The first reference makes little
sense since it suggests no difference from late-capitalist society as Habermas characterizes it, the second reference he rejects, and third is left un-
specified. Despite the provocative quality of the third reference, there is
no evidence that Habermas departs from his main view that we remain

within a crisis-ridden late-capitalist society. In fact, rather than advancing an open-ended, continuously dynamic view of history, Habermas sees late capitalism as the end of history in a sense that coincides more with Fukuyama than with Baudrillard.[23] This occurs with the final stage in the development of ego identity and moral competencies, a process that culminates in the demands for autonomy, universal outlook, and postconventional learning. Habermas claims that "the logical space for evolutionarily new problems is exhausted with the reflexive turn of motive formation and the structural scarcity of meaning" found in capitalism (1979: 167).

Given Habermas' dialectical framework, his belief that progressive change can only come through an appropriation and development of communicative rationality, and his personal encounter with Nazism, it is not surprising he is hostile to attacks on modernity and Enlightenment reason and labels them "conservative." Habermas' shift from the critique of positivism to postmodern theory is perfectly logical: although positivists push everything nonempirical into the sphere of irrationality, and many postmodern theorists embrace the anarchic and irrational, both discourses equate rationality with instrumental rationality. This explains both why positivists denounce everything (such as moral and aesthetic language) except empirical knowledge as metaphysics, and why some postmodernists reject rationality per se as terroristic. Moreover, both camps reject normative critique, but for opposite reasons: positivists, because they seek a methodological separation between fact and value; postmodern theorists, because they believe political, legal, or moral norms are simply vehicles for domination, or because they no longer believe in the possibility for freedom.

While Habermas repudiates the irrationalism of postmodern theory, his work has important similarities with the postmodern critique of modern forms of reason. Beyond a shared understanding that modern forms of rationality have led to new modes of domination, Habermas and postmodern theorists reject the modern attempt to ground reason in a first philosophy whose foundation stands outside of historical and social existence. Like postmodern theory, Habermas claims that the subject and its modes of understanding are deeply embedded within social and historical existence, and he shares with postmodern theory a historical analysis of modes of rationality. Both Habermas and postmodern theorists argue that "there are no theory-neutral sets of 'facts,' no absolutely unblurrable distinctions, no unmediated 'givens'; no timeless structure of reason, no absolutely neutral standpoint for inquiry outside of the ongoing interpretations, values, and interests of the actual community of inquirers at work in our current social practices" (Roderick 1986: 8).

Like postmodern theory, Habermas rejects the classical totalizing project of philosophy. He describes how the traditional philosophical attempt to explain the unity of all reality through a comprehensive theory whose principles are discovered in reason has collapsed through advances in the empirical sciences. "Philosophy can no longer refer to the whole of the world, of nature, of history, of society in the sense of a totalizing knowledge" (Habermas 1984: 1). Subsequently, Habermas states that philosophical thought has withdrawn from speculative, metaphysical schemes and retreats into a metaphilosophy concerned with the formal conditions of knowledge. Habermas believes that "philosophy in its post-metaphysical, post-Hegelian currents is converging toward the point of a *theory of rationality*" (2), such as Habermas attempts to work out in his two-volume tome, *The Theory of Communicative Action*.

Habermas occludes the affinities between his work and postmodern theory and therefore posits too sharp a discontinuity between the two frameworks. Yet, among other things, Habermas' attempt to contextualize a historical critique of the present within a larger developmental–logical theory and to construct a positive theory of rationality that can ground critique marks a fundamental point of difference between his work and postmodern theory. For Habermas, postmodernists move from one false extreme to another when they replace a theory of rationality with a totalizing critique of rationality and when they leap from the rejection of absolutism to an embrace of relativism. For Habermas, the abandonment of foundationalism does not mean that no kind of foundations can be provided for normative critique. Rather than abandoning philosophy after the critique of its dogmatic and metaphysical adventures, Habermas seeks to employ it in conjunction with the empirical social sciences for normative critique and the reconstruction of normative learning processes. Rather than rejecting evolutionary theories as necessarily metaphysical and teleological, Habermas tries to redefine them in a nonmetaphysical manner. With Lyotard and Foucault, Habermas rejects the "philosophy of history" tradition for its metaphysical assumptions concerning teleology, continuity, rationality, and subjectivity, but unlike them he retains the historical metanarrative form in order to analyze actual historical continuities and possibilities for human freedom. Habermas seeks to abandon a speculative vision of history for an empirically falsifiable theory with practical intent.

Of the various postmodern theorists and counter-Enlightenment figures he criticizes, Habermas shows the most respect for Foucault. His reading of Foucault is far more nuanced and sympathetic than his reading of Heidegger and Derrida. He finds Foucault's work to be "more fertile, and simply more informative" for historical and sociological analysis than Heidegger's reflections on technology and enframing or Derrida's critique of metaphysics (1987a: 338). Nevertheless, Habermas lumps Foucault together with Derrida and others and denounces them as "young conservatives" or "anarchists" who surrender the progressive aspects of modernity and rationality and undercut the possibility for normative critique.

Habermas' attack on Foucault and postmodern theory begins in "Modernity as an Unfinished Project" and is developed further in *The Philosophical Discourse of Modernity*. Habermas distinguishes between the old conservatives who are traditional rationalists and antimodernists; the neoconservatives who embrace capitalism, science, and technology but blame a subversive modernism for the ills of modern society; and the young conservatives who attack modernity and the Enlightenment. The young conservatives "remove into the sphere of the far-away and the archaic the spontaneous powers of the imagination, self-experience, and emotion. To instrumental reason they juxtapose in Manichean fashion a principle only accessible through evocation, be it the will to power or sovereignty, Being or the Dionysiac force of the poetical. In France, this line leads from George Bataille via Michel Foucault to Jacques Derrida" (Habermas 1983: 14).

Habermas sees postmodern theory not as a rupture with modern theory *tout court,* but as an extension of the aesthetic modernity tradition that attacked reason and liberal discourse and valorized art as a radical other to the hegemony of rationality. Both the neoconservative and postmodern revolts against modernity are anticipated and inspired by preexisting modern critiques: "They are merely cloaking their complicity with the venerable tradition of counter-Enlightenment in the garb of post-Enlightenment" (Habermas 1987a: 5). Thus, overturning its claim to radical novelty, Habermas understands postmodern theory more as antimodern than as postmodern. Postmodern discourse is parasitic upon a line of questioning first made possible by Hegel's historical self-consciousness. Hegel's thought leads in various directions, to Marxism from the left-Hegelians, to neoconservativism from the right-Hegelians, and to postmodern theory from Nietzsche. Nietzsche's critique of metaphysics led to one line of postmodern thought that includes Heidegger and Derrida, and his unmasking of knowledge as the will to power led to another line established by Bataille and Foucault. Heidegger and Derrida seek the destruction of metaphysics, while Foucault allegedly seeks the destruction of historiography.

Whatever similarities one can find between the critique of metaphysics and traditional historiography in Foucault and Habermas, beneath these affinities one finds deep, irreconcilable differences that emerge in large part from their respective grounding in postmodern and modern paradigms. These differences relate principally to competing theories of rationality, modernity, history, and the question of a normative foundation for social critique.

Throughout his work, Habermas has criticized the damaging effects of an overextended instrumental rationality, and has shown how science and technology have subjugated rather than liberated human beings. Hence, he is in agreement with the critique of instrumental reason as made by Weber, the Frankfurt School, and Foucault. But Habermas believes that Adorno and Horkheimer and Foucault do not adequately account for the complexity and ambiguity of modernity, and that they level its multidimensionality to a simplistic one-dimensionality of domination. Habermas acknowledges that the Enlightenment project has failed, but he believes it is premature to abandon it, thus pursuing an "enlightened suspicion of enlightenment." In each differentiated logic of cultural modernity, Habermas finds a positive consequence of rationalization. Hence, he points to the employment of science for purposes other than technical manipulation, to the incorporation of universalistic foundations of law and morality within institutions of constitutional government, and to the critical consciousness promoted by developments in avant-garde art (1983: 113).

In *The Philosophical Discourse of Modernity,* Habermas claims that Foucault effects a number of "reductions" that undermine the project of critique and its rational justification. First, following structuralism, Foucault reduces the problem of the meaning of social practices as interpreted by conscious agents to that of explaining the conditions of possibility of discourse by the archaeologist. Subsequently, Foucault cannot account for his own interpretive standpoint; he is enmeshed in the "presentism" of his own position and cannot reconstruct the logic of historical development. Second, following Nietzsche, Foucault reduces truth–validity claims to mere power effects. Third, following positivism, Foucault reduces the problem of justifying critique to establishing pseudo-value-free historical explanations and thus conflates foundations with "foundationalism."

All three reductions subsume knowledge, truth, and value claims to power. With these reductions, Habermas thinks, Foucault paints himself into a relativist corner and disables the project of critical theory. If, as Foucault says, all truth claims are illusory and all discourse is power, then the same must be true of Foucault's own discourse and any other "critical" theory. Therefore, genealogy cannot unmask the power effects of the human sciences, since it has no base of truth from which to speak. In such a situation, "the validity claims of the counter-discourses count no more than those of the discourses in power—they too are nothing else than the effects of power they unleash" (1987a: 281). Genealogy cannot claim to be superior to the sciences to which it is opposed. By canceling the validity of its own standpoint in a radical perspectivism where everything is of equal value, genealogy destroys the foundations of its own research and defeats the very purpose of critique.

While Foucault makes pretense to value neutrality, his work, Habermas claims, is saturated with the values of oppositional politics. Foucault's terms "disciplinary society," "domination," "subjugation," and "power," are value-laden, normative terms that imply both negative judgment on the phenomena they describe and the possibility of freedom apart from such conditions. The partisan character of Foucault's work is even more obvious in his description of genealogy. The genealogist attacks all forms of history or science, be they mainstream or Marxist, that devalue and delegitimate the voices of suppressed groups in history. The avowed task of the genealogist is to raise these silenced voices to the level of audible discourse in order that their histories can be known and the knowledge attained from them inform present-day struggles against domination. The genealogist offers weapons for use by the dispossed and disenfranchized; far from neutral, he or she is thoroughly engaged.

Thus, Habermas claims that genealogy represents "the arbitrary partisanship of a criticism that cannot account for its normative foundations" (1987a: 276). This position is a "crypto-normativism" because it tries to deny its basic normative thrust. By combining detached analytic description of regimes of domination with suppressed normative values, Foucault's work is a "paradoxical linking of a positivistic attitude with a critical claim" (270). Foucault clearly opposes the present form of society and intends his ideas to have a political impact, but he simultaneously seeks a methodological detachment from normative commitments and questions of the legitimacy of his analyses. Such a result represents "the embarassment of a critique that attacks the presuppositions of its own validity" (127).

Habermas believes that the "postmodern" character of Foucault's work is more to be found in its rhetoric than its philosophical assumptions. This allows for a more complex understanding of Foucault than simply as a "postmodernist," a move I argue for throughout these chapters, but Habermas never identifies the conflicting elements—premodern, modern, and postmodern—in Foucault nor explicity states the substantively modern elements in Foucault. Yet, like Dreyfus and Rabinow (1982), Habermas believes that Foucault himself is caught within a transcendental–empirical doublet, and therefore has not himself escaped the metaphysical horizon of modern thought. According to Habermas, Foucault's genealogy of the human sciences assumes an empirical character in the analysis of the technologies of power and the political functions they perform as employed by the social sciences. But the same genealogy acquires a transcendental character when it tries to explain the conditions of possibility of the scientific discourse of man as they emerge within power relationships: "genealogical historiography is supposed to be both . . . functionalist social science and at the same time historical research into constitutive conditions" (1987a: 274). This results in a confused mixture of empiricist ontology with an idealist concept of transcendental synthesis.

For Habermas this means that even Foucault, like Marx and every other major nineteenth- and twentieth-century theorist, has not escaped the philosophy of the subject; the concept of power that unites both strains of genealogy is itself taken from this philosophy. Foucault's theory of power therefore does not lead him out of the aporias of the modern human sciences, as he hoped. The fact that Foucault's concept of power is basically subjectless, that it is a structuralist concept that denies the reality of subjective agency, means only that Foucault has reversed the terms of a subjectivist framework, which is by no means to escape from it. Such an escape, Habermas believes, requires direct reference to the communicative activity of an *intersubjective* lifeworld. Here, subjects adopt not only cognitive relationships regulated by the truth of judgments, and practical relationships regulated by the success of actions, but also communicative relationships guided by normative consensus. Since neither Marx nor Foucault take this turn—Marx decenters the subject in relation to social classes without explicitly reconstructing the logic of communication and Foucault destroys the subject without reconstructing it as a communicatively competent social being and then resurrects it in individualist form—they remain bound to the philosophy of the subject. Only a paradigm shift to a theory of communicative action can truly dispel the doublets haunting the philosophy of consciousness in its modern and postmodern forms. Habermas claims that doubling is unavoidable in the observer framework, since there is no possible intersubjective mediation between the transcendental and empirical "I." In the shift to a linguistically generated intersubjectivity, however, the ego stands in an interpersonal relationship with others and can thereby see itself from the point of view of the other (1987a: 297), a perspective that is crucial for Habermas' discourse ethics (see Habermas 1990).

Hence, Habermas executes a deconstructive, immanent critique of genealogy to show it is overtaken by the same problems that Foucault found to haunt the human sciences. "To the extent that [genealogy] retreats into the reflectionless objectivity of a nonparticipatory, ascetic decription of kaleidoscopically changing practices of power, genealogical historiography emerges from its cocoon as precisely the *presentistic, relativistic, cryptonormative* illusory science that it does not want to be" (1987a: 275–276). Like Nietzsche and Adorno and Horkheimer, Foucault also is trapped in the aporia of a totalizing critique of reason. When rational argument is employed to explain the corruption of all reason, and when demystified critical consciousness deplores the total mystification of thought, critique becomes fundamentally incoherent and reason turns against itself. Thus, from Habermas' perspective, neither Marx nor

Foucault, *prima facie* two of the most radical critics of modern thought, escape its fundamental problems, a move that Habermas thinks only he himself achieves through the framework of communicative action.

Although Habermas finds some value in Foucault's descriptions of modern power, he claims that Foucault's work is merely another false way out of the critique of subject-centered reason, a postmodern dead end. The failure of Foucault's theory points to the exhaustion of the philosophy of the subject and the need for a new communicative action framework. Habermas notes that Foucault admits to the incoherencies of his thought, but does not attempt to resolve them or draw any consequences from them. Consequently, he feels that Foucault cannot adequately address the substantive problems that arise with respect to key issues: the interpretation of social reality, the rejection of universal validity claims, and the normative justification of critique. Rather than deal with these issues, Foucault eliminates them through the effacement of the categories of meaning, validity, and value. The only way out of this impasse is to acknowledge the partisan character of all theory and to defend the normative basis of critical theory through metatheoretical means.

From Habermas' perspective, the totalizing condemnation of modernity that Foucault shares with Adorno and Horkheimer fails to do justice to its progressive aspects. Most generally, as we have seen, Habermas credits cultural modernity with separating and clarifying different logics of critique and with substituting standards of rational justification for dogma and prejudice. In each sphere of reason, therefore, Habermas finds a different contribution worth preserving: advances in science and technology; universalistic foundations of law and morality; and individualist patterns of identity formation along with advances in democracy and increasingly reflective worldviews. On the dialectical logic theorized by Habermas, none of these advances are possible without the dynamic effects of the detachment of instrumental rationality from traditional meaning complexes, yet this very abstraction of political and economic forces leads to the colonization of the lifeworld. The dialectic can only be redeemed in emancipatory fashion through bringing these forces back into the control of the lifeworld once their differentiating work has been done.

Habermas credits Foucault with some impressive analyses, but claims that his theory of power "is false in its generality" (1987a: 288) because it conflates the disciplinary and panoptic techniques of modernity with the whole structure of societal modernization. In his analysis of the modern criminological system, for instance, Foucault reduces law to an instrument of domination and consequently misses "the unmistakable gains in liberty and legal security, and the expansion of civil rights guarantees" (290). Similarly, Foucault sees the construction of modern sexual identities as nothing but vehicles of normalizing power, thereby "filtering out all the aspects under which the eroticization and internalization of subjective nature also meant a gain in freedom and expressive possibilities" (292).

Thus, from Habermas' perspective, Foucault reduces gains in moral–practical learning and complex processes of interiorization and individuation to an introjection of normalizing power. Against Foucault, Habermas believes that norms are not merely vehicles of domination; rather, they raise validity claims that require rational assessment and can be used to delegitimate the social system from which they originate. By equating individuation with subjectification, Foucault eliminates all aspects of self-determination and self-realization from socialization processes. This one-dimensional postmodern critique "levels down the complexity of societal modernization" (1987a: 290) and distorts its fundamentally ambiguous character. In the postmodern night where all cows are black, important distinctions are imploded:

> Enlightenment and manipulation, the conscious and the unconscious, forces of production and forces of destruction, expressive self-realization and repressive desublimation, effects that ensure freedom and those that remove it, truth and ideology — now all these moments flow into one another. They are not linked to one another as, say, conflicting elements in a disastrous functional context — unwilling accomplices in a contradictory process permeated by oppositional conflict. Now the differences and oppositions are so undermined and even collapsed that critique can longer discern contrasts, interests, shadings, and ambivalent tones in the flat, and faded landscapes of a totally administered, calculated, and power-laden world. (338)

An important source of the opposed attitudes of Foucault and Habermas toward modernity is their different assumptions about the nature of discourse. For Foucault, intersubjective communication takes place against the background of power struggles where discourse is constituted by truth claims that legitimate forms of power. Through discourse, different subjects and social groups vie for power over one another. Habermas acknowledges these forms of conflict and struggle, but claims that language is fundamentally oriented toward achieving clear, sincere, and truthful communication and reaching an understanding.

The different approaches of Habermas and Foucault over modernity are replicated on a larger scale in their conceptions of social evolution or history. They are equally unsympathetic to "philosophies of history" that seek a unifying principle that guides and unifies the whole process of history in a teleologically guaranteed movement toward emancipation. But while Foucault rejects all forms of historical metanarratives that attempt to discern a coherent pattern of historical development with progressive tendencies, Habermas seeks to construct a new theory of historical evolution that grasps the progressive development of technical and moral–practical knowledge. Thus, with the *philosophes,* Kant, Hegel, Marx, and the Western Marxist tradition, Habermas believes that the developmental patterns of history represent not simply blind movement, but *progress.* Like Hegel and Marx, Habermas understands this progress dialectically, that is, he sees the emergence of freedom in history to be inseparable from the dynamics of alienation and domination. Marx and Habermas nevertheless believe that the negative aspects of this movement, while historically necessary, eventually become obsolete and therefore can be historically superseded.

Thus, from Habermas' perspective, Foucault negates the progressive aspects of historical development. If Heidegger and Derrida attempt to destroy metaphysics; Foucault seeks to destroy historiography by dissolving history into a plurality of epistemes and power formations. For the image of a dialectical succession of progressive historical epochs, Foucault substitutes the image of a kaleidoscope of purely random patterns of movement (see Foucault 1977: 154). Attacking standard historiography and its linear narratives that emphasize continuity between eras, Foucault goes to the opposite extreme and adopts a "nominalism" that obliterates progress, evolution, and any form of historical pattern, continuity, and order. "History in the singular has to be dissolved, not indeed into a manifold of narrative histories [such as Habermas seeks], but into a plurality of irregularly emerging and disappearing islands of discourse . . . the space of history is seamlessly filled by the absolutely contingent occurrence of the disordered flaring up and passing away of new formations of discourse. No place is left for any *overarching* meaning in this chaotic multitude of past totalities of discourse" (Habermas 1987a: 251, 253). Foucault's theory prohibits the universality and developmental continuities Habermas thinks are necessary for the grounding of social theory and the advancement of human freedom.

MISREADINGS AND COUNTER-READINGS

The debate between Habermas and Foucault is one of the most important encounters in contemporary theory. At stake are crucial questions concerning whether or not critique can and should seek a normative grounding; the viability of modern ideals of truth, rationality, justice, and progress; and the possibility and desirability of creating a consensual, rational community that can overcome endemic social conflict and relations of hierarchy and domination.[24] While I find Habermas' framework superior to Foucault's in its detail, dialectical sensibility, and attention to methodological and normative issues that social theory ignores at great cost, I also think that Habermas himself has not sufficiently escaped the reductionist and metaphysical horizons of modern thought, and that many deficiencies in his work can be illuminated through Foucault's positions. Typically, readings of Foucault and Habermas are caricatured, one-sided defenses of one position over the other; I shall try to show here and in the next chapter that there are surprising similarities between their two positions and that there can be a productive *rapprochment* between their approaches, which is not to say an undisturbed synthesis.[25]

Foucault denies there can be any basis for objective descriptive statements of social reality or universal normative statements that are not socially conditioned and locally bound. He tries to show that all norms, values, beliefs, and truth claims are relative to the discursive framework within which they originate. Any attempt to write or speak about the nature of things is made from within a rule-governed episteme that predetermines what kinds of statements are true or meaningful. All forms of consciousness, therefore, are sociohistorically determined and relative to specific discursive conditions. There is no absolute, unconditioned, transcendental stance from which to grasp what is good, right, or true. Foucault refuses to specify what is true because he believes that there are no objective grounds of knowledge; he refuses to state what is good or right because he thinks there is no universal standpoint from which to speak. Universal statements merely disguise the will to power of specific interests; all knowledge is perspectival in character. For postmodern theorists like Foucault, the appeal to foundations is necessarily metaphysical and assumes the fiction of an Archimedean point outside of language and social conditioning.

Habermas rightly finds something puzzling in an approach that raises truth claims while destroying a basis for belief in truth, that takes normative positions while suppressing the values to which they are committed. For critique to be meaningful, it seems it must preserve at least one standard by which to judge and evaluate; Foucault's total critique turns against itself and calls all rational standards into question. Foucault's position appears to resemble the fool sawing off the branch on which he sits.

Habermas rightly concludes that Foucault, in dissolving all social phenomena in the acid bath of power and domination, prevents critical theory from drawing crucial distinctions, such as those "between just and unjust social arrangements, legitimate and illegitimate uses of political power, strategic and cooperative interpersonal relations, coercive and consensual measures" (McCarthy 1991: 54). One cannot say, for example, that one regime of power is any better or worse than another, only that they are different—"Another power, another knowledge" (Foucault 1979: 226). Since ruling powers attempt to erase such distinctions, or to present injustice as justice, falsehood as truth, and domination as freedom, Foucault's position unwittingly supports the mystifications of Orwellian doublespeak, now more rife than ever, and blocks the discriminations necessary for social critique. One cannot, at least with any force or authority, claim that the Gulf War was an unjust not a just war, as one has no means to set the record straight against the distortions of ideologues like Rush Limbaugh or Newt Gingrich. If there are no standards or right, then, with Thrasymacus and Hobbes, we can conclude might is as right as anything. There can be no ideology critique where there is no distinction between true and false. The normative character of Foucault's own work is not mitigated by his refusal to confront it explicitly. The problem becomes glaring in his later work, where he employs normative terms such as liberty and autonomy but cannot state what we should be free *for*. Foucault's antinormative stance therefore forces him into vague and cryptic formulations that are slogans at best.

As discussed in Chapter 2, a central reason why Foucault eschews normative positions is because he wishes to renounce the role of the universal intellectual who legislates values. For Foucault, the task of the genealogist is to raise problems, not to give solutions; to shatter the old values, not to create new ones. Any stronger, more prescriptive role, Foucault argues, can only augment existing relations of power and reproduce hierarchical divisions between rulers and ruled. While Habermas does not acknowledge these important concerns of Foucault, he is not unaware of the potential dangers of intellectuals taking normative positions. With the key difference that Habermas believes in universal values, he adopts a position similar to Foucault's "specific intellectual" in defining the role of the critical theorist as promoting enlightenment and critical thought without creating divisions between the theoretical specialist and the layperson. From Habermas' perspective, we can say that Foucault's error is to confuse provisional normative statements for dogmatic ones, to conflate suggestions to be dialogically debated with finalized creeds to be imposed, to fail to see that universal values can be the products not only of power or ideology but also of consensual, rational, and free choice.

In fact, there is evidence that Foucault holds a similar position, that his intention is not to renounce normative discourse in general, but only the normative pronouncements of *intellectuals,* or, more restrictively, of Foucault himself, in order to allow for individual and public choice and debate. Thus, while Foucault refuses to say whether or or not democracy is "better than" totalitarianism, he does not prohibit this distinction from being made by others: "I do not wish, as an intellectual, to play the moralist or prophet. I don't want to say that the Western countries are better than the ones of the Eastern bloc, etc. The masses have come of age, politically and morally. They are the ones who've got to choose individually and collectively" (1991: 172).

Foucault not only repudiates a Baudrillardian cynicism toward the masses, he approaches a Habermasian emphasis on communicative rationality within an intersubjective context. But to avoid the problems associated with speaking for others, we need not adopt a "crypto-normative" position, if we can now still accurately characterize Foucault's stance in such a manner. Within Habermas' democratically oriented communicative context, Foucault's concerns may not be applicable and the normative proposals of the specific intellectual may actually help to undermine power, promote new forms of thought, and engender new forms of freedom. There is no reason why prescriptive or normative statements need be anything but provisional statements, "tools" for further thought and struggle. How effective would a movement like the United Farm Workers be, for example, if Caesar Chavez (while not a self-described intellectual, certainly a leader of the people) refused to make normative pronouncements? How more more limited would have been his charismatic influence? How impotent his impassioned speeches about justice and workers' rights?

Habermas fails to see that Foucault is not only a "crypto-normativist," but is also a cryptorelativist. Habermas wrongly claims that Foucault reduced knowledge to power; rather, Foucault granted the possibility of objective analysis and distinguished between different kinds of knowledge. While Foucault sees knowledge and power as interlocking fields, it is a vulgar reading to argue that he reduces knowledge to power, to transform the mark between power/knowledge into a sign of identity. As Foucault stated, "When I read . . . the thesis, 'Knowledge is power,' or 'Power is knowledge,'" I begin to laugh, since studying their *relation* is precisely my problem. If they were identical, I would not have to study them and I would be spared a lot of fatigue as a result. The very fact that I pose the question of their relation proves clearly that I do not *identify* them" (1988d: 43).

While knowledge and power exist in a circular and mutually reinforcing relation, and even the most abstract of knowledges are ultimately connected to power formations (as physics and mathematics are indispensible to rocket science and hence to war), it does not follow that all forms of knowledge are directly reducible to mere power effects or domination mechanisms, that they have no truth status or objectivity whatsoever, and that some forms of knowledge cannot be deployed *against* systems of domination, as Foucault tries to do with his own genealogical studies. Foucault believes that highly formalized natural and mathematical theories can be sufficiently distant from politics to acquire a valid kind of objectivity. In *The Archaeology of Knowledge,* he states that while discourses such as political economy may be ridden with "ideology," "this is not a sufficiently good reason to treat the totality of their statements as being undermined by error, contradiction, and a lack of objectivity" (1972: 186). In one of his last interviews, he states that "mathematics is linked in a certain way and without impairing its validity, to games and institutions of power" (quoted in Gutting 1989: 276). He even grants fields of knowledge such as psychiatry a degree of "scientific validity." These qualifications in no way compromise Foucault's emphasis that forms of knowledge are related to forms of power, since he argues that knowledge can be both scientific and objective in character *and* be part of a disciplinary apparatus.[26] Foucault does not ask scientists to abandon "truth and method"; rather, he asks them only to acknowledge the political character of all knowledge and to be sensitive to the ways in which knowledge and truth effects are intertwined with power effects. Part of the problem results from the ambiguity of the term "power." Since Foucault defines power not simply as repressive but also as positive and productive, power/knowledge can inform practices of resistance as well as practices of domination; knowledge can lead to autonomy instead of a normalized identity. Most generally, power refers to the ability to act and effect changes driven by certain interests; depending on what these interests are, power can secure or impede freedom.

Thus, the problem in Foucault's work is not that he reduces knowledge to power, as Habermas claims, but that he does not develop the conceptual framework with which one could distinguish between different forms of knowledge and power. Habermas elides Foucault's distinction between power and domination and misrepresents his theory of power as something omnipotent, rather than as something ubiquitous but always contested. Habermas' characterization of Foucault as a relativist is accurate only if restricted to less formal modes of knowledge or to values, norms, and beliefs.[27] But Foucault doesn't provide an account for what constitutes objective knowledge or why the social sciences in general could not also achieve some degree of objectivity, as is established, for instance, in a pragmatic community of inquirers. Ironically, in granting objectivity to the more formal sciences, without analyzing the ways in which even "observational statements" are theory-laden, Foucault regresses behind the hermeneutic position and the self-understanding of contemporary science. Ultimately, he reproduces the old dualism of explanation versus interpretation.

It is a virtue of Habermas' work that it supplies a more differentiating account of various forms of rationality—some of which inform practices of domination and others of which have liberatory potential—and to develop a more adequate hermeneutic theory that applies to all the sciences. Like Foucault, Habermas sees that knowledge is not pure, but rather is informed by different "interests," is historically situated, and is employed in the service of power. But Habermas distinguishes between an instrumental rationality that seeks to dominate the social and natural world, a hermeneutic rationality that seeks to interpret past cultures, and a critical or emancipatory reason that seeks to raise validity claims and promote human freedom and autonomy. From Habermas' standpoint, we can see that Foucault's argument that modernity is characterized by a plurality of rationalities is only a pseudo-plurality of different institutional forms of instrumental reason itself. Foucault could have avoided the problems in his position with the Weberian distinction between social and cultural rationalization, which plays a major role in Habermas' work, in addition to a metatheory that identifies and justifies what counts as an advance in freedom rather than domination.

Foucault's initial totalizing rejection of reason prevents him from making such differentiations. Habermas correctly points out, for example, that Foucault does not account for the critical transformations in the social sciences in the 1970s, where "objectifying approaches no longer dominate the field [and] were competing instead with hermeneutical and critical approaches that were tailored in their field of knowledge to possibilities of application *other* than manipulation of self and others" (Habermas 1987a: 272–273). Habermas does not see, however, that Foucault did look favorably toward the emergence of the countersciences, insofar as they abandoned anthropologism and allowed for a posthumanist conception of the subject to emerge. Yet, here again, Foucault did not give any explicit substantive or positive appraisal of them because of the normative deficit of his theory. Foucault elides the distinction between norms and normalization; Habermas, by contrast, attempts to show how certain social norms make rational claims on a formally based democratic system that can be rationally assessed, used as critical tools in an immanent critique, and transformed into claims that demand redemption in a postnormalizing social order. But Habermas needs to absorb more of a Foucauldian emphasis on power in the medium of morality, knowledge, discourse, and communication.[28] Habermas' analysis of purposive-rational action yields the concepts of "instrumental action," oriented to control of the natural world, and "strategic action," oriented to following rules of rational choice with respect to influencing the decisions of rational opponents. Habermas also has a concept of "communicative action" to analyze interactions oriented to intersubjective understanding and consensus. Yet he does not have a concept for grasping interaction, norms, and communication themselves as forms of power. The general phrase "colonization of the lifeworld" comes close, but it is confined to the macrolevel of society and is vague in nature.

In other ways, however, Habermas' account of rationality is superior to both Marx and Foucault insofar as he overcomes Marx's uncritical attitude to instrumental rationality and science, while avoiding Foucault's conflation of rationality with domination. His differentiated analysis of spheres of rationality incorporates Foucault's appeal to the expressive–aesthetic dimension of cultural modernity, but without hypostatizing it in the dubious form of an emancipatory Other of reason or hyperindividualized self. Moreover, Habermas develops an account of the logic of communicative rationality suppressed by both theorists. It is Habermas' claim that neither Marx nor Foucault could grasp the normative content of modernity released by communicative rationality because they filter out all dimensions of reason except truth and efficiency (1987a: 320). Indeed, Habermas's theory of communicative rationality inescapably trumps any general argument postmodernists could make against it, since whoever strays into the realm of argumentative discourse *and* wishes to communicate and validate an argument cannot avoid at least implicit reference to the norms of argumentation itself, such as Habermas clarifies in his theory. Any serious argument is always already oriented to validity claims and the intersubjective recognition on which possible consensus relies.

As we have seen in the previous chapter, however, Foucault began to move away from a totalizing critique of modernity, rationality, and subjectivity in his later work. In affirming the critico-historical spirit of the modern era, the rational project of critique, the abilities of subjects to free themselves from oppressive values and practices and to constitute their own identities in a space of freedom, Foucault's analysis becomes less totalizing, more dialectical, and moves closer to Habermas' project. Unlike Baudrillard, Lyotard, and other radical postmodern theorists, Foucault ultimately does not seek to escape from Enlightenment and modern theory, but rather, like Habermas, attempts to work critically within it.

Foucault himself acknowledged the affinities between his work and that of the Frankfurt School.[29] He explicitly aligns his work with a broad tradition of modern critical theory that initiates historical reflection on the nature of the Enlightenment: "From Hegel through Nietzsche or Max Weber to Horkheimer or Habermas, hardly any philosophy has failed to confront this same question [*Was ist Aufklärung?*], directly or indirectly" (1984: 32). Foucault even chastises himself for his initial ignorance of the Frankfurt School:

If I had been familiar with the Frankfurt School . . . I would not have said a number of stupid things that I did say and I would have avoided many if the detours which I made while trying to pursue my own humble path—when, meanwhile, avenues had been opened up by the Frankfurt School. It is a strange case of non-penetration between two very similar types of thinking

which is explained, perhaps, by that very similarity. Nothing hides the fact
of a problem in common better than two similar ways of approaching it.
(1988d: 26)

Most likely, Foucault is referring to their shared concern with a critique of reason, the direct parallels between the notions of the disciplinary and one-dimensional or administered society, and the rejection of
progressivist views of history.[30] But while Foucault moved toward a
qualified analysis of rationality, he never developed a precise theory of
different aspects of rationality such as Habermas has attempted. And while
he came to align his work with the critico-historical outlook of modernity, he never offered any concrete dialectical analyses of modernity like
those of Marx and Habermas.[31] Foucault never renounced his earlier
characterization of modernity as a "disciplinary archipelago" and never
specified positive aspects of modern law, science, sexuality, and so on.
Hence Habermas' critique of Foucault's account of modernity is valid for
Foucault's later work also.

Ultimately, there is an extreme categorical poverty in Foucault's analysis of modernity, rationality, and subjectivity, resulting from the fact that,
unlike Habermas, he rejects important contributions of modern social theory. He consequently remains trapped, like Adorno, within the total and
negative critique that leads to critical reason renouncing its own efficacy.
Foucault opened up a logical space for a differentiating and positive account of modernity and its forms of rationality, but he did not fill it with
substantive and detailed analysis.

Habermas' account of history is superior to Foucault's insofar as he
can identify real advances in the human learning process that constitute
bona fide forms of "progress." With Marx, Habermas thinks that the vision of human freedom is not simply utopian because objective tendencies
exist in the present form of social existence that allow for democratization, autonomy, and emancipation. But while Foucault misses the extent
to which some developmental patterns in history suggest forms of progress
in democracy and the learning process, Habermas overlooks the dialectic
of historical continuity and discontinuity in Foucault's works. Foucault's
account of history is not as aleatory and nominalistic as Habermas believes.[32] There is a strong narrative component in Foucault's work that
tells the story of the emergence of normalizing and disciplinary mechanisms. From Greek to Roman to Christian and modern cultures, Foucault
describes how technologies of the self were overcome by technologies of
domination and how new technologies of the self again become possible
in a posthumanist, postmodern era. Foucault rejects "total history" in favor
of a "general history" that allows for historical continuities and regularities. These pertain, however, mainly to continuity in forms of domina-

tion and struggle, rather than developing tendencies of freedom. Yet, by identifying with the Enlightenment tradition of critique over premodern forms of thought rooted in tradition and religion, Foucault has an implicit theory of progress in history toward greater levels of learning and freedom, but he altogether lacks the means to contextualize and analyze such a development.

While Habermas is right to point to substantive continuities and emancipatory tendencies in history, his attempt to reconstruct these phenomena is highly flawed. As noted by numerous critics, there is a strong tension, if not contradiction, between the transcendental–logical and historical–empirical aspects of human interests that the phrase "quasi-transcendental" highlights but does not dispel (see McCarthy 1978, Thomas 1979, and Roderick 1986). For Habermas, knowledge-constitutive interests are both immanent and transcendent in character, they both mediate the historical self-constitution of the species and and are formed by it; they constitute our knowledge *a priori,* although they arose contingently in the natural development of the species. Human interests both mediate social activity and are formed by it; they are both "partially" transcendental and partially immanent in history.

This tension reflects the conflict between the Kantian and Hegelian/Marxian elements in Habermas' work. Despite his historical analysis of advances in learning, Habermas finds it necessary to postulate an ahistorical foundation for critique. Despite his claims to materialism and scientificity, his theory lapses into idealism by positing pregiven interests. Habermas' claim to an emancipatory interest is unfounded and dogmatic, since he never shows that such an interest actually exists. Given the fact (such as is theorized by Reich, Fromm, Adorno, and others) that human beings can prefer submission and domination to freedom, the burden is on Habermas is to prove that such claims are not counterfactual. Despite his confrontation with Freud, Habermas' theory is informed by a naive psychological rationalism articulated by Locke and other Enlightenment theorists that is overconfident about the ability of reason to influence individual life and social organization. The subrational logic that Foucault finds uncovered by Bataille and the countersciences provides a much-needed counterbalance to Habermas' rationalism. Habermas rejects "the fiction that Socratic dialogue is possible everywhere and at any time" (1971: 314), but he retains the Socratic myth that the attainment of rationality suffices to promote interests in emancipation and understanding and that conflicting values can be harmonized in the light of truth.

Against Habermas' essentializing claim for an innate interest in emancipation, McCarthy notes, "The interest in emancipation is not proper to reason as such, but only to a particular employment of reason: critical self-reflection" (1978: 101–102). Habermas later assented to this point

(1982: 233), but without seeing that critical self-reflection is a thoroughly historical phenomenon. As better seen by Marx, Dewey, and others, the "interest in emancipation" emerges only within modernity and hence is a relatively recent historical phenomenon. Through appeal to abstract, universal principles, rooted in a transhistorical subject, Habermas has hypostatized the historical forces underlying social systems and the cognitive interests they create, and himself succumbs to the philosophy of the subject.

This ahistorical move is explicit in Habermas. Rather than start with "concrete ideals immanent in traditional forms of life," he states that critical theory must proceed "reconstructively, that is unhistorically" (1987c: 383). Responding to criticisms of his quasi-transcendental claim, Habermas reformulated his theory in favor of an empirical reconstruction of "universal competencies" of communication. Yet, as Roderick (1986) notes, Habermas did not substantively modify the transcendental character of his theory. In general, the tendency of Habermas' work is to bury concrete social reality under the weight of abstract categories; his approach suffers from what Adorno has termed "conceptual fetishism" and "surplus of method" (1973: 8).

The core deficiencies of Habermas' theory—its ahistorical thrust, teleological biases, transcendental subject, hyperabstraction, naive rationalism, and overemphasis on communication—can be illuminated and, in some cases, overcome through Foucault's postmodern orientation. An important thrust of Foucault's work has been to deontologize and detranscendentalize Western theory, to show that alleged essences and universals are constituted in local and contingent historical contexts. Hence Foucault substitutes concrete sociohistorical analyses for ontologizing and universalizing schemes. Foucault too posits an *a priori,* but this is a "historical *a priori*" that analyzes how historically constituted rules of discourse shape different understandings of biology, work, and language, along with various historically shaped values and interests.

Habermas tries to implicate Foucault in the aporia of a transcendental–empirical doublet, but his critique only goes through with an equivocation on the word transcendental. This term can refer either to a Kantian attempt to escape history or a contextualist move to identify the historical preconditions of critique. Foucault's transcendentalism is the latter kind. Habermas is on safer ground when he points to the tension in Foucault between his positivist and critical attitudes. In fact, from a Foucauldian point of view, it is Habermas who is impaled on the horns of the transcendental–empirical. In trying to reconcile the transcendental and historical aspects of thought, rather than abandoning transcendentalism altogether in favor of a strictly historical analysis, Habermas remains within the metaphysical horizons of modern thought, trapped within its doublets.

Nor has Habermas altogether escaped the teleological framework of modern historiography. He claims that a "telos of mutual understanding is built into linguistic communication" (1986: 99) and that the telos of social evolution is toward rational autonomy. Moreover, he finds that "there is a universal code of moral intuition in all times and in all societies" (206), which stems from the unavoidable presuppositions of communication. The speculative, ahistorical, universalizing, and teleological logic of Habermas' theory leads him to homogenize the plurality of discursive and historical voices. He fails to give sufficient attention to the irreconcilable forms of conflict articulated through discourse, which cannot be forced into any easy "consensus" (or, certainly not through simple rationalist appeals to logic and argumentation), and to the vastly different linguistic and moral structures of various cultures such as are theorized by Sapir, Whorf, and others (see Whorf 1956).

Thus, some of the shortcomings of Habermas' work are illuminated by Foucault's critique. A postmodern critique can push Habermas' thought further in the direction of diversity, contingency, historical specificity, and concrete practice. Given the Hegelian character of Habermas' efforts to synthesize the insights of various philosophical theories, his own perspective should be open to the insights of postmodern critiques; instead, he reduces the postmetaphysical sensibility of postmodern theory to a species of conservativism. While there are important analogies between postmodern theory and the counter-Enlightenment (see Chapter 4), there are also important differences. Habermas' acute dialectical approach salvages nuggets of value in almost every theory he considers, even functionalism and positivism, *except* postmodern theory. His fear of irrationalist, counter-Enlightenment discourse is so great that it blinds him to a more balanced account of postmodern discourse that could grasp its positive and potentially progressive contributions to critical theory.[33] His critique of Foucault is as totalizing and one-dimensional as the postmodern positions he rejects. He fails to give a sufficiently complex account of Foucault's work that combines various elements into a new kind of critique that issues a strong challenge to modern theory and its transcendental impulses. In general, Habermas' tendentious strategy is to dismiss all positions that do not agree with his theory of communicative action.

By subsuming postmodern theory to conservativism, Habermas fails to grasp the ambiguity of postmodern theory itself. While there are indeed some conservative aspects to postmodern theory, such as its irrationalism and individualism, there are also important critiques that are similar to those of critical theory and that also add new critical perspectives to social theory and historiography. Habermas doesn't see that postmodern theorists are not all of one stripe and that the work of any one "postmodern" theorist (like Foucault) is itself ambiguous and multivalent in character. Where some postmodern theorists such as Baudrillard have the intention of subverting the project of critical theory, others such as Laclau and Mouffe (1985) share Habermas' goal of reconstructing modern discourse through postmodern insights (see Best and Kellner 1991).

THE HABERMASIAN VISION

> The pursuit of happiness might one day mean something different—for example, not accumulating material objects of which one disposes privately, but bringing about social relations in which mutuality predominates and satisfaction does not mean the triumph of one over the repressed needs of the other.
> —HABERMAS (1979: 199)

As is discussed above, there are various, interrelated narrative threads in Habermas' historical analyses: (1) a theory of social evolution that describes the development of both cognitive–instrumental and moral–practical reason; (2) a history of modernity that grasps the differentiation of spheres of validity and rationality and how the political, economic, and scientific subsystems of modernity colonize the lifeworld; (3) a genealogy of postmodern theory and other critiques of subject-centered reason in order to show how an intersubjective framework of communicative rationality was opened with Hegel and Marx, but was closed in favor of different variations on the modern philosophy of the subject.

Each narrative has a different purpose. The metanarrative of social evolution accounts for the growing autonomy of purposive–rational action from the communicative context in which it was initially embedded. It is necessary to grasp the developmental tendencies of contemporary society in order selectively to advance communicative over instrumental rationality and to regain proper balance, now in a differentiated way, between the different spheres of value. The genealogy of moral and normative consciousness inquires into the evolution of critical consciousness in general, as it moves from dogmatic to critical stages. Habermas shows that the political consciousness Marx and Foucault take for granted in their call for critique and enlightenment is the product of a long historical evolution that requires analysis and development in its own right. The genealogy of postmodern theory, finally, is intended to short-circuit the ideological spell of the most powerful contemporary rival of critical theory. Habermas tries to show that postmodernism is merely recycled counter-Enlightenment ideology that is devoid of conceptual coherence. By subsuming postmodern theory to modern subjectivism, Habermas tries to show that the paradigm of consciousness is bankrupt and that social theory requires a shift to communicative action.

Despite his critique of Marx, his encounter with postmodern thought, and his move to a postmetaphysical framework, Habermas retains, with Marx, a fundamentally Hegelian vision of history as a movement of freedom through differentiation. Habermas believes that this metanarrative is empirical, falsifiable, and so nonmetaphysical. Like Marx and unlike Foucault, Habermas has a keen vision of future community and solidarity. He foresees a realm of "undisturbed intersubjectivity" (1986: 125) and the generation of "new forms of solidaristic collective life . . . life-forms which offer a context within which one's own identity and that of others can be unfolded less problematically, and in a less damaged way" (144). Yet, through Weber's influence, Habermas thinks Marx was overly optimistic about the degree of democracy, reconciliation, and transparency possible in highly complex modern societies; he therefore qualifies the Hegelian vision of a perfect overcoming of contradictions and antagonisms. But Habermas is far from embracing Foucault's Nietzschean vision of history as the perpetuation of conflict and antagonism, and he rejects Foucault's individualism. Habermas believes that key oppositions must be eliminated, the most important being that between the general and the private interest. This can be accomplished through the recuperation of communicative rationality, which informs every speech act that seeks to communicate meaning and which provides the normative basis for the construction of a democratic social order.

In many ways, Habermas has advanced beyond Marx and Foucault. He undertakes an important defense of the Enlightenment that avoids Marx's uncritical acceptance of key tenets and Foucault's totalizing rejection of rationality. His shift to a communicative framework helps to overcome the philosophy of consciousness and to analyze the realm of symbolic interaction untheorized by Marx and denigrated by Foucault as nothing but a terrain of struggle and domination. But Habermas does not completely overcome problems associated with the Enlightenment such as ahistoricism, foundationalism, abstract universalism, and teleology. Although he undialectically repudiates postmodern theory, it is precisely that framework which offers important resources to overcome problems in Habermas and to advance more satisfactorily his goal of reconstructing and defending "the project of modernity." His genealogy of postmodern theory is a tendentious reading that sees only errors, irrationalism, and contradictions. Similarly, many of the flaws and excesses of his communication theory are corrected by returning to Marx's theory, which he attempts to transcend for a new paradigm.

In comparing the methods, visions, values, and politics of Marx, Foucault, and Habermas we see that no one theorist alone offers satisfactory positions and that each position has major strengths and weaknesses. We also see that there is no necessary opposition between modern and postmodern theories, that there is a great deal of diversity within each tradition, and that there are important continuities, as well as discontinuities, between both camps. My final discussion thus is concerned with the contributions and limitations of each thinker, and of modern and postmodern theories more generally.

NOTES

1. It needs to said, however, that Habermas' tenure in the Marxist tradition was longer and more profound than Foucault's. Habermas continued to identify himself as a Marxist at least until the late 1970s, whereas Foucault broke with Marxism by the early 1950s, well before his major books. Unlike Habermas, Foucault never characterized his project as trying to reconstruct historical materialism, and hence he could never be seen as a neo-Marxist. The degree of their respective allegiance to Marxist ideas is illuminated by the fact that Foucault praised the New French Philosophers, while Habermas denounced them (1986: 70).

2. "Language is as old as consciousness, language *is* practical consciousness that exists also for other men, and for that reason alone it really exists for me personally as well; language, like consciousness, only arises from the need, the necessity, of intercourse with other men" (Marx and Engels 1978: 158).

3. These do not, of course, exhaust the list of influences, nor do they remain within respective national boundaries. Just as Foucault is strongly influenced by Nietzsche, for example, so Habermas draws from Durkheim.

4. While Baudrillard (1987) is right that Foucault did not confront the most recent forms of power that devolved around media and images, Foucault did take up the hegemony of print mass media as a practical problem in his journalistic projects (see Eribon 1991). Foucault makes the false exclusive claim that modern society is one of surveillance, rather than one of hyperreality or spectacle (1977: 217). For a good example of Habermas' awareness of the problems with mass media, see (1986: 178, 1994: 6).

5. Here Dewey's work was also a decisive influence on Habermas. On the similarities and differences between Dewey and Habermas, see Antonio and Kellner (1992).

6. Habermas' initial failure to distinguish between reflection as analysis of the conditions of knowledge and as critical scrutiny of society brought him a great deal of criticism. For discussion of this point, see McCarthy (1981: 96ff.); for Habermas' own treatment of this distinction, see the introduction to *Theory and Practice* and the "A Postscript to *Knowledge and Human Interests*" (1973b).

7. See, for example, Habermas (1979: 139).

8. In fact, Habermas claims that evolution proceeds along three lines: production, socialization, and steering capacity (or power), which is the ability of society to maintain itself in the midst of internal and external changes. Below, I only focus on the first two lines of development, although I argue that the dimension of power is obscured.

9. Purposive–rational action is subdivided into instrumental and strategic action. Action is "instrumental" when it follows technical rules that can be appraised in terms of the efficiency of their intervention in the world; it is "strategic" when it follows rules of rational choice that can be appraised in terms of the efficiency of influencing the decisions of other individuals (see Habermas 1970: 92).

10. This term is meant to include stages in technical learning, but at a more abstract level. Where some theorists have tried to refine the notion of a mode of production by introducing distinctions relating to forms of private property or differences in exploitation, Habermas' fear is that this strategy will jeopordize historical materialism and the very idea of developmental tendencies in history: "These general sociological perspectives certainly permit a concrete description of a given economic structure, but they lead to a broader range rather than a deeper analysis. The result of this procedure would be a pluralistic compartmentalization of modes of production and a weakening of their developmental logic. At the end of this inductive path lies a surrender of the concept of the history of the species — and thus of historical materialism. We cannot exclude a priori that anthropological–historical research might one day make this necessary. But in the meantime, it seems to me that the opposite direction has not yet been sufficently explored" (1979: 153). Thus, Habermas is concerned to preserve the substantive narrative dimensions of diachronic analysis and to avoid a nominalist position that fails to see general patterns and progressive developments in history.

11. Habermas intends to grant communicative action more causal efficacy than has been granted by Marx or the Marxist tradition, without compromising the intended "materialist" character of his theory: "The analysis of developmental dynamics is 'materialist' insofar as it makes reference to crisis-producing systems problems in the domain of production and reproduction" (1979: 123). It is only that the causes for social change are sought now in a number of factors, in a wide range of contingent factors that include not only institutional systems organized around technology and economics, but also forms of moral–practical consciousness.

12. The inconsistencies and shifts in Habermas' work seemingly may be accounted for by the fact that the more he critically interrogates Marxism, the more convinced he is of the importance of interaction over work and the irredeemable deficiencies of Marxist theory. But this argument suffers from the fact that one finds such inconsistencies in the same essay (see 1979: 130–177).

13. Like Foucault, Habermas attempts to distinguish different social formations in terms of the abstract rules that allegedly condition thought, but he is even more vague than Foucault as to what these rules and their possible origins are.

14. To complexify this scheme, Habermas argues that different stages of consciousness exist at different levels of the same principle of organization (see 1979: 154–155).

15. "Natural science will eventually subsume the science of man just as the science of man will subsume natural science: there will be a *single* science" (Marx, quoted in Habermas 1971: 46). Habermas does not fail to emphasize the strong positivist overtones of this statement that sharply conflict with the "critical" dimensions of Marx's project and his critique of capitalist ideology that itself seeks to subsume human relations under natural laws (see Chapter 4).

16. Sensat (1979: 117) argues that, read in its proper context, such a passage criticizes technocratic ideology by underlining the contradictory nature of capitalism, such as is latent in the two-fold nature of the commodity as both use and exchange value (for a similar contextualizing argument see Cleaver [1979]). Such a passage, therefore, does not represent a departure from the demystifying tasks of the critique of political economy. From such a passage, Sensat denies the Habermasian–Wellmerian thesis that Marx's work is filled with tensions. Read

in their proper context, he argues, Marx never separates production and socialization, science and critique, and hence never succumbs to technocratic positions. But Sensat glosses over Marx's grosser positivistic remarks and hence does not give the complete story. Against Sensat, I side more with Habermas and Wellmer, but unlike Habermas and Wellmer I believe that Marx's technocratic "tendencies" are limited more to rhetoric and scientistic misrepresentations of his own work than to actual models or substantive positions.

17. As Habermas says, "I do not mind at all *calling* both phenomena [work and interaction] praxis. Nor do I deny that normally instrumental action is embedded communicative action (productive action is socially organized, in general). But I see no reason why we should not adequately *analyze* a complex, i.e., dissect it into its parts" (1973b: 186).

18. "So far nothing seems to suggest that alternative natural sciences can be developed in a non-objectifying attitude" (Habermas 1986: 177). While very little has developed in the realm of action, Habermas ignores an emerging paradigm of ecological science that belies his claim (see Griffin 1988a, 1988b; Best 1991b). In contrast to Habermas, Marcuse sought to articulate a new science and reason infused with a "new sensibility," a sensibility shaped by eros and utopia and aesthetic value. Habermas does not deny one can have an aesthetic, empathetic relation to nature (1982: 243–244), only that *science* can provide this. For a critique of Habermas' views on nature, see Whitebook (1979); for a critical comparison of the different views of Habermas and Marcuse on science, see Alford (1985).

19. In assent with Foucault, Habermas states, "I too think that relations of power are incorporated in the least ostensive forms of communication, and that analysis of systematically distorted communication yields results analogous to Foucault's analysis of discourses" (1986: 69).

20. Very little has yet been written or translated on Habermas' politics. Perhaps the best account of Habermas' political interventions is Holub's *Jürgen Habermas: Critic in the Public Sphere.* There is some discussion of Habermas' intellectual and political background in Dews' edited volume, *Habermas: Autonomy and Solidarity.* Some of Habermas' writing on the student movements can be found in *Toward a Rational Society.* During the 1980s, Habermas published several volumes of political writings, *Kleine politische Schriften,* many of which have been translated (see Habermas 1989b). For a collection of interviews that focus on Habermas' politics, see Habermas (1994).

21. For a far more critical and shrewd account of the Gulf War, see Kellner 1992.

22. Habermas' attack on the irrationalist aspects of postmodern theory was anticipated in his late 1960s critique of the German student movements who, he claims, had rejected not just technocracy, but science, technology, and reason as such. See Habermas (1970).

23. "Baudrillard has only been able to capture the attention of those with short memories. . . . As history goes over into another aggregate state, things get hotter, not colder" (Habermas 1994: 79–80). Thus, Habermas holds that momentous historical events and changes can occur, as always, while believing that the evolution of moral consciousness is largely complete, although not yet universally realized.

24. As Habermas describes (1987b), Foucault had asked him to meet with his American colleagues at a private conference in 1984 to discuss different interpretations of modernity based on Kant's essay, "*Beantwortung der Frage: Was ist Aufklärung?*" Foucault's death, however, made this event impossible.

25. See, for example, Rajchman's uncharitable critique of Habermas and uncritical defense of Foucault (1988). For a good example of a more balanced and nuanced approach, see Wolin (1990). Kelly (1994) has recently published an anthology of writings by Foucault, Habermas, and others that calls for an understanding of the theoretical and political issues uniting and dividing Foucault and Habermas. In his excellent concluding essay, Kelly shows that, once their positions are clarified, both Foucault and Habermas struggle with the problem of the self-referentiality of modern critique. Kelly claims, however, that Foucault's position trumps that of Habermas because of Habermas' failed transcendentalism. Kelly's defense of Foucault's pragmatism as nonrelativistic and "self-corrective" is unconvincing, however, because Foucault lacks the resources to tell us when one critique is "better" than another or when it is "corrected." Nor does Kelly see how historically constituted "universals" have an important function in social criticism (see Chapter 4), since, following Foucault, he limits them to an ideological function of legitimating contingency as necessity. Honneth (1991) provides a rigorous comparison of Foucault and Habermas as having different responses to the aporias of Adorno and Horkheimer's work. He emphasizes the strengths of each theorist, as well as their joint effort to overcome the philosophical concepts of labor that has hindered critical theory, but he favors Habermasian positions. Hoy and McCarthy (1994) square off in a fascinating, rigorous confrontation that dramatizes the core issues dividing supporters of Habermas and Foucault.

26. Formalization does not guarantee a lack of ideology since "the role of ideology does not diminish as rigour increases and error is dissipated" (Foucault 1972: 186). Foucault admits the validity of an ideology critique that shows how a form of knowlege serves the interests of a controlling group (185), but he does a different kind of ideology analysis than that of Marxism, one which operates "at the level of the positivity and the relations between the rules of formation and the structures of scientificity" (186).

27. For Habermas, relativists hold "that every possible description only mirrors a particular construction of reality that inheres gramatically in one of various linguistic worldviews. There are no standards of rationality that point beyond the local commitments of the various universes of discourse" (1992: 135). With postmodernists, Habermas holds that all claims are local and context-bound, but he argues that rational claims *also* have a potentially context-transcendent claim to discursively grounded truth. Theorists like Foucault or Rorty are not relativists in the extreme and untenable sense that holds that all views are equally sound. Pragmatists see relativism as a pure theoretical problem that is inapplicable to an approach that debates the merits of different views, test them in practice, defends them in a local context, and chooses one view over the other based on argumentation and results. Rorty therefore distinguishes between "philosophical theories" and "real theories," the formulations of which are directly applicable to practical problems in politics, the sciences, and so on. He denies that relativism is pertinent to issues of technical or practical concern (1982: 167–169). While Foucault and

Rorty can debate and experiment with different theories, Habermas believes that neither has any resources with which to legitimate the values that guide their practice, to defend ethical and epistemological issues that are not resolvable into action, or to raise claims that are valid beyond a merely local context. On Habermas' understanding, therefore, they do not escape relativism. Habermas' much stronger claim is that there are epistemic, not merely pragmatic, grounds for choosing between different interpretations.

28. The inadequate term "strategic action" is as close as Habermas' terminology comes to a Foucauldian emphasis on the forms of power and domination that operate within an intersubjective context itself. I use it while understanding its limitations. Habermas needs a new term that describes language and communication itself as a fundamental medium of domination, rather than idealizing it as essentialy concerned with reaching consensus. For his clearest attempt to delineate these various concepts, see Habermas (1982: 263–264).

29. In his brief remarks on Foucault's later lecture on Kant, Habermas (1987b) takes note of Foucault's new alignment of his work within the modern tradition, but only to reassert the nature of the contradictions in Foucault's thought and to forego any sustained reflection on the similarities between their projects. Indeed, the few occasions when one comments on the other's work, they misrepresent it. Foucault chastizes Habermas for seeking a utopian model of communication (1989), failing to see that Habermas is only using this as an ideal construct, and Habermas, as mentioned above, claims that Foucault reduces knowledge to power (1987a).

30. Foucault was not uncritical of the Frankfurt School, however. He claims that they adopted a traditional view of the subject tainted by Marxist humanism (1991: 120–122). Subsequently, he sees their goal to be that of recovering a lost identity, rather than producing a wholly new subject. Adorno is certainly exempt from the former critique, and I have argued in Chapters 1 and 2 that the latter critique does not adequately represent the intentions of Marx.

31. As Foucault makes clear, however, he refuses (in another misrepresentation of Habermas' position) the "intellectual blackmail of 'being for or against the Enlightenment'" (1984: 45). He also seeks "to move beyond the outside–inside alternative; we have to be at the frontiers" (45). Foucault also rejects the modern/postmodern distinction as too simple, and instead develops the distinction between the attitudes of modernity and countermodernity (39). It is clear that he himself has both.

32. There are passages supporting the aleatory reading of Foucault, such as where he states: "The world we know is not this ultimately simple configuration where events are reduced to accentuate their essential traits, their final meaning, or their initial and final value. On the contrary, it is a profusion of entangled events. . . . The true historical sense confirms our existence among countless lost events, without a landmark or point of reference" (1977: 155). Yet, Foucault also claims: "History has no 'meaning,'" though that is not to say that it is absurd or incoherent. On the contrary, it is intelligible and should be susceptible of analysis down to the smallest detail—but this is in accordance with the intelligibility of struggles, of strategies and tactics" (1980a: 114). Clearly, as his acutal analyses demonstrate, Foucault does find some order, pattern, or intelligibility to history,

although it is the result of his own assumptions and interpretive schemes, and not a meaning inherent in history as identified by Marx and Habermas.

33. As Whitebook observes, "There is something compulsively modernistic about Habermas' project. It is as though he cannot seriously entertain any objections to the project of modernity for fear of opening the Pandora's box of irrationalist regressivism" (1981–1982: 94).

4

HISTORY AS
CRITICAL THEORY

History is the most dangerous product ever concocted
by the chemistry of the intellect.
—PAUL VALÉRY

Despite their substantive differences, Marx, Foucault, and Habermas have important similarities as *critical* theorists, as writers who analyze history and society in order to criticize the prevailing social order, to further enlightenment and critical consciousness, and thereby to help bring about political change. All three break with the positivist goal of value-free theory by politicizing their work, by linking it to specific critical and political goals with liberatory intent. Even Foucault, heralder of the death of Man and slayer of utopian visions, came to adopt a discourse of freedom and liberty in order to speak more coherently about the *raison d'être* of the political resistance that he sought to promote.

The critical thrust of each theory is directed against the oppressive aspects of capitalism and modern rationalization processes. Each theorist looks past the liberal and democratic rhetoric of capitalist modernity to find underlying mechanisms of exploitation, coercion, and distortion. A historically based critique of capitalism and modern forms of rationality is central to the work of each theorist. Hence, Marx compares capitalism with precapitalist social forms to dramatize the uniqueness of capitalist forms of exploitation and alienation; Foucault undertakes a genealogy of modern power that carries his research back to ancient society; and Habermas analyzes the colonization of the lifeworld that threatens the liberatory differentiation of rationality and cumulative advances in moral–practical learning.

In their historical analyses, each theorist identifies both continuities and discontinuities of the present with the past. Marx underlines the evolution of the human senses, the progressive development of technology, the constancy of alienation, and the recuring dynamics of class struggle, while also portraying capitalism as a dramatic rupture from all precapitalist social forms. Foucault shows how technologies of the self were transformed

into technologies of domination and analyzes mutations in discursive formations and regimes of power. Habermas reconstructs the progressive advances in technical and moral learning processes while emphasizing the
singularity of the capitalist principle of organization and the decentered
worldview of modernity.

Through their use of a discontinuity perspective, all three employ
historical analysis of the present to shatter the entrenched sense that it
is given, necessary, or inevitable and to expose it as a contingent construct
that can be changed. In each vision of history, the past is employed to
disrupt the present; to show how reified economic, political, and technological imperatives rule over social life; and to allow an alternative future
where human freedom can become a reality. In each case, history is not
studied for its own sake; neither Marx, Foucault, nor Habermas adopt
the strictly past-oriented outlook that Emerson and Nietzsche attacked
for hindering action in the present and future. Rather, each writes a strategic history that applies a study of the past toward a critique of the present
in order to help effect an alternative future.

All, therefore, attempt to overcome the split between theory and practice characteristic of modern positivism. Each theorist, consequently, abandons the traditional conception of philosophy as a self-sufficient,
contemplative discipline that discovers eternal truths in the realm of theory while devaluing practice as the realm of the changing and false (see
Dewey 1979). Each seeks to break down disciplinary boundaries, to recon-
textualize philosophy within the broader context of critical social theory,
to historicize philosophy while philosophizing history, and to provide
philosophico-historical analysis with empirical and political content.
Hence, while all reject the "philosophy of history" tradition that seeks a
totalizing, speculative theory divorced from empirical analysis, each combines history and philosophy in a supradisciplinary critical theory.

Yet underlying the various similarities among these three theorists
at the abstract level of critical theory, we find substantive differences that
arise over different understandings of the nature of history, power, and
freedom; over what kind of social change is possible and desirable; and
over which methodological perspectives are best for analyzing history and
capitalist society.

SCIENCE, TRUTH, AND OBJECTIVITY

In exploring the differences among Marx, Foucault, and Habermas, let
us begin with some general issues regarding the epistemological status of
theory. While all three deny a version of science that seeks ahistorical laws,
that rigidly separates fact from value and theory from practice, and that

assimilates the social to the natural sciences, Habermas and Marx maintain a critical and positive relation to empirical and scientific standards that Foucault largely abandons for a postmodern standpoint.

Clearly, Marx is the most influenced by scientific norms; he alone retains the positivist rhetoric and ambition of a theoretical science that grasps "laws" of social change. Against all forms of idealist, speculative, and utopian theorizing, Marx defines historical materialism as a "science of history" that uncovers the general causal dynamics of social change, that penetrates through the false consciousness of ideology to grasp actual social processes, and that generates predictions about the future through empirical observation and inductive reasoning.

Positivist impulses are strong in Marx from his earliest "humanist" works. Already in the *Economic and Philosophic Manuscripts,* Marx attempts to articulate a conception of social and historical theory that is rigorous, empirical, and scientific. He seeks to establish a theory that begins from "real premises" and "actual economic fact[s]" through study of human beings in their social relations and activities. Yet this same text was filled with speculative thinking influenced by Hegel and Feuerbach that greatly conflicted with these empirical tendencies. In his quest for science, Marx accordingly jettisons these elements (although they never entirely disappeared) and moves toward a more rigorous scientific viewpoint in *The German Ideology.* Here, Marx and Engels advocate the eclipse of philosophy by science: "When reality is [properly] depicted, philosophy as an independent branch loses its medium of existence" (1978: 155). Philosophy, they claim, has no role in theory beyond summarizing empirically obtained results. This marks the end of Marx's philosophical anthropology and the beginning of his critique of political economy.

Yet the science of history Marx was struggling to develop was historical and critical in nature; he defined his materialism in opposition to all ahistorical, bourgeois theories. For Marx, all social phenomena are constituted within dynamic, changing social relations. He attacks bourgeois political economy for positing universal, ahistorical "laws" of social development that in fact only represent tendencies that vary according to different social formations. He claims that all forms of consciousness are historically relative and that even biology is socially mediated (1973: 92). As we saw, however, Marx did not adequately acknowledge the historical rootedness of his own theory: there is a tension in his work between philosophy and science, empirical explanation and ideology critique that reflects the intellectual climate of his time.

There is also tension in Marx's work regarding the question of the unity of the sciences. His scientific ambitions lead him to conflate the logics of the social and natural sciences (see Chapter 3) and thus to adopt a positivist-inspired misunderstanding of his own position, later replicated by Engels, Kautsky, Plekhanov, and others, which he undercuts in other ways. Marx's belief in the ability of human agency to change consciously the social environment prevents him from analyzing human beings as mere things. Where bourgeois thought tries to naturalize features of human experience by abstracting them from the social relations that constitute them (seeing, for example, capital as "a general and eternal relation of nature" [Marx 1973: 86]), Marx attempts to denaturalize them. Marx considered his most important scientific discovery the insight that the value of commodities is the expression of exploited labor power rather than the natural and inevitable operations of the market. He subverted the positivist attempt to limit analysis to mere surface appearances of reality in order to penetrate the underlying social relations that produce these appearances in fetishized form. He thereby undoes the Kantian distinction between essence and appearance to show how "social essence" (social relations) informs social appearace, and to claim that consciousness can grasp the noumenal as well as the phenomenal world.

Foucault and Habermas also underline the discontinuities between social and natural science, while effecting a more radical break with positivism. In *The Archaeology of Knowledge,* Foucault states "we should distinguish carefully between *scientific domains* and *archaeological territories:* their articulation and their principles of organization are quite different. Only propositions that obey certain laws of construction belong to a domain of scientificity" (1972: 183). Foucault distinguishes between different "thresholds" of knowledge according to their degree of coherence and formalizability. For Foucault, the so-called "social sciences" fall well below the "threshold of scientificity," where certain forms of knowledge can be formalized according to rigorous criteria and abstract propositional laws.

Foucault radically undermines the core tenets of positivism by analyzing the symbiotic relationship between knowledge, truth, and power. A key goal of genealogy is to show how science is employed for purposes of social control. This analysis is directed against positivist and Marxist theories that see knowledge as neutral, objective, or unproblematically emancipatory. Foucault attacks the very enterprise of science as normalizing by claiming that a wide range of "knowledges," such as those uncovered by the genealogist, are disqualified because they cannot meet formalist criteria of truth. As an "antiscience," genealogy seeks to recuperate marginalized, nonformalized, disqualified knowledges and to put them in the service of political struggles. Supplementing the Frankfurt School's analysis of the use of instrumental rationality in the domination of nature, Foucault shows how scientific rationality disciplines individuals through the imposition of normalizing identities. Where Marx was uncritical of the fundamental norms of science, Foucault forcefully shows that science and technical rationality are bound up with forms of power and that critique must therefore extend to science and technology themselves.

Yet, ironically, in some ways Foucault emulates positivist positions. Identifying himself as a "happy positivist" (in sardonic gesture to Nietzsche's "gay science"), Foucault eschews hermeneutics and normative values for an allegedly disinterested description of successive power/knowledge formations. In this light, it is no accident that Foucault not only refuses to defend normative values, but also brackets causal analysis since, according to positivism, causes are speculative, metaphysical entities. Both positivist and postmodern theories reject hermeneutic depth models and normative visions of the good life. In this sense, residues of a scientistic attitude inform Foucault's work.

As we have seen in Chapter 3, Foucault's critique of science does not mean that he denies the possibility of scientific objectivity. Compared to postmodern theorists like Baudrillard, Lyotard, Rorty, Feyerabend, or Seidman, Foucault is an epistemological moderate who grants objectivity to certain domains of knowledge. Yet, while Foucault does not reduce knowledge to power and sees the countersciences as a positive form of scientific knowledge, he does not incorporate scientific norms, moral categories, or truth claims into his own analyses to legitimate the implicit normative thrust of his work. "Truth" is reduced to "truth-games," to simulated contact with reality.

Adopting a postmodern aestheticist view, the only metatheoretical claims Foucault makes in reference to his analyses is to characterize them as "fictions" (1980a: 12, 1991: 33). Foucault claims that no one ever writes anything but fictions and in his work the search for truth gives way to the quest for experience. Examined carefully, however, Foucault's fictions are not defined in total opposition to truth. Foucault breaks down any firm distinction between fact and fiction and rewrites truth in a pragmatist context that speaks not of "truth," but "truth-effects":

> I have never written anything but fictions. I do not mean to say, however, that truth is absent. It seems to me that the possibility exists for fiction to function in truth, for a fictional discourse to induce effects of truth, and for bringing it about that a true discourse engenders or "manufactures" something that does not as yet exist, that is, "fictions" it. One "fictions" history on the basis of a political reality that makes it true, one "fictions" a politics not yet in existence on the basis of a historical truth. (1980a: 193)

This should be read not as a full-blown Sorelian construction of myth to engender political struggle, but rather as a break with realist notions of truth and as a suggestion that truth is a practical reality informed by a political vision. Despite occasional references to scientific and mathematical objectivity, Foucault demonstrates a postmodern sensibility (anticipated by many modern theorists) that "truth" is a perspective-laden construction, that the historian does not have an unmediated access to historical reality, that history is a text. With Marx, Foucault adopts a pragmatist attitude that truth is what works in practice. In Marx's words, "The question of whether objective truth can be attributed to human thinking is not a question of theory but is a *practical* question. Man must prove the truth, i.e. the reality and power, the this-sidedness of his thinking in practice. The dispute over the reality or non-reality of thinking that is isolated from practices is a purely *scholastic* question" (1975a: 422). The degree of truth, in other words, is dependent upon the power of vision and its practical consequences. Marx's and Foucault's own theories, therefore, become "true" to the extent that they change standard ways of thought and action and engender effective struggle and social change. Foucault's "reading" of social reality seeks to produce certain "effects of truth [that] could become implements within possible struggles" (1989: 189). But, since total fictions also can engender effective struggle, since "history" can be sheer lies and propaganda, and since there still remains the problem of adjudicating between competing factual and normative claims, such claims to truth beg the question. We need a more substantive sense of truth and normative validity.

This, of course, is Habermas' central preoccupation; he vehemently rejects postmodern attempts to erase boundaries between literature and philosophy and fiction and truth. The attempt to acknowledge the historical and context-dependent nature of validity claims without succumbing to relativism has been a characteristic aspect of Habermas' work from the start. Despite the interest structures guiding knowledge, Habermas holds that truth is still possible in two ways, which I call immanent and pragmatic. On the first model, the immanent claim, a norm is true if it conforms to the nature of language itself. Here, Habermas thinks that the emancipatory norms raised by critical theory are true, have normative correctness, because they are immanent within the nature of language itself, which seeks understanding and agreement within nondistorted conditions. As has been already suggested, this is a metaphysical model that is not successfully defended.

The second model, independent of the teleological assumptions of the first, holds that a claim is true if it can be successfully defended through argumentation within an intersubjective context. Under ideal conditions where all actors have equal chances to raise and defend validity claims, and where the conditions of communication are free of ideology and other disturbances, a claim is true when it can be successfully defended with good reasons. This is a pragmatic model of truth because it dispenses with the metaphysical assumptions of the immanent model and makes truth the result of a negotiated outcome among social actors. It challenges relativism on the grounds that not all claims are equally sound insofar as some will have the backing of better arguments—few would claim, for example, that the arguments of spokespersons from the Ku Klux Klan and the National Association for the Advancement of Colored People are equally valid. The better claim, the "truthful" claim, is the result of the "force of the better argument." Truth, then, is a matter of warranted assertability.

The pragmatic model is far more plausible than the immanent model because it dispenses with dubious metaphysical claims about innate interests and ties truth to nonarbitrary, falsifiable conditions of rationality. Habermas in fact, following Apel, makes a significant contribution to theories of truth by breaking the immanency of isolated subjects in quest of ahistorical truth through the unmediated, transparent medium of rational speech. This move links truth to a larger social context that includes not simply a community of actors, but ideals and conditions of freedom and justice. For how can a claim be "true," which implies accuracy and impartiality, under conditions where some have more power to speak than others and the conditions of communication are impaired from the start? The search for truth ultimately entails a free and just society.[1]

Yet Habermas' pragmatic theory remains problematic on at least two grounds. First, he has not provided an adequate account of the criteria of the "better argument," which would include, among other things, values of consistency and factual accuracy. Second, Habermas' argument appears to be circular: if truth is the result of a rational consensus, how do we judge this consensus itself as true, right, or accurate? If we answer because this consensus itself is validated by consensus, we are moving in a circle, or are trapped in an infinite regress. The fact that a community of actors freely consents to a claim does not guarantee that their consensus is not wrong or false. To the extent that certain claims will require assessment of factual accuracy in the way they relate to affairs in the world, one will also need a correspondence theory of truth that Habermas criticizes the Frankfurt School for not developing and holds is necessary for critical theory (1986: 99–100), but that he himself not yet developed.

Like Foucault, Habermas develops a strong critique of positivism by linking knowledge to action motivations, or "interests." Habermas deftly draws out the political implications of the positivist vision of society as a scientifically controlled field in the attempt to reduce the practical issues of enlightenment and democracy to mere technical issues of the command of resources by elites. But Habermas advances beyond Foucault's analysis in seeing that the interest structures of knowledge include not only the interest in power or strategic control, but also the interest in reaching an understanding and in attaining self-enlightenment. Since all three interests emerge from a prereflective lifeworld, hermeneutics has a priority in Habermas' work that it does not have in the theories of Marx or Foucault. For Habermas, hermeneutical approaches seek not only a method of interpretation, but also to promote "the intersubjectivity of mututal understanding in ordinary-language communication and in action according to common norms" (1971: 176).

Far more adequately than Marx, Habermas draws on hermeneutics to distinguish the separate logics of the social and natural sciences. But unlike someone such as Winch, who conceives of these differences as incommensureable, Habermas identifies important continuities since, on the one hand, both the natural and human sciences are fallible and hermeneutical in nature, and since, on the other, both can make legitimate empirical and causal claims. Far from denying the social sciences adequacy, Habermas sublates philosophy into the social sciences, where its proclivities toward ungrounded speculation are to be reined in by empirical logic.

Yet, amidst numerous cries of the "end of philosophy" (see Baynes et al. 1987), Habermas claims that philosophy is still important as a critical voice and defender of universal values. Despite valid attacks on the metaphysical illusions of the whole Western tradition, Habermas claims that philosophy remains "the hitherto irreplaceable representative of a claim to unity and universality" (1986: 32). These appeals to universality are not simply posited, but empirically discerned through historical study of past cultures. Drawing from Popper, Habermas insists that truth claims are falsifiable in nature, that they can be confirmed or proven wrong through the testing of hypotheses. In his project of rational reconstruction, Habermas employs procedures similar to those of the empirical sciences to gather data and test hypotheses; the purpose, however, is not to generate nomological hypotheses about observational events, but rather to reconstruct the intuitive knowledge of communicatively competent subjects. As first suggested by Horkheimer, Habermas believes that philosophy must abandon the claim that it alone represents reality, or that it has privileged access to truth, and instead must work with the reconstructive empirical sciences. A second role for philosophy here is to play the role of "stand-in," which mediates between layculture and expert knowledge in different realms (1986: 131–132, 1992: 28–51). In both cases, philosophy is "the guardian of rationality" (1990: 20) and it employs knowledge to raise public consciousness about the deformations of the lifeworld.

Thus, Habermas develops an interdisciplinary project that combines philosophy, social theory, psychology, empirical science, and history, and attempts to trace the development of cognitive learning processes while also clarifying the presuppositions of rationality inherent in the process of communication. He seeks a synthetic position that combines the logics of explanation (of empirical phenomena), interpretation (of traditional complexes of meaning), and critique (of ideologies, distorted forms of communication, and illegitimate forms of power). Positivists were right that causal logic can be used to explain social dynamics, but the hermeneuticists were also right that human beings are intentional subjects and there is no presuppositionless theory. Yet the hermeneutic tradition, such as represented by Gadamer, assumed language to be a transparent medium rather than a vehicle of ideology and domination, and so the perspective of critical theory is also required.

What Habermas develops, therefore, is a historically and hermeneutically informed mode of explanation with the aim of clarifying the presuppositions of communication and deploying their normative thrust to criticize ideology and deformed modes of interaction. Habermas seeks to pursue "the rigor of science" but without sacrificing the "practical intentions of classical politics" (1970: 144), and he thereby hopes to overcome the dualism between the ancient and modern political traditions. Where Marx abandons philosophy for science, and Foucault gives up science for historico-philosophical critique, Habermas seeks a position "between philosophy and science." With Marx and Foucault, Habermas eschews dogmatic, speculative, and metaphysical conceptions of philosophy, but he claims that both theorists have abandoned the epistemological resources of philosophy that are necessary to legitimate validity claims.

CAUSALITY, ABSTRACTION, AND GENERALIZATION

The attitudes of Marx, Foucault, and Habermas toward science directly bear upon their theoretical approach toward history as a general category. Unlike Foucault, Marx and Habermas seek to develop a "theory" of history, but in different forms where only Marx aims at a "science of history" and Habermas pursues a historically informed reconstructive science of communicative competence. A "theory of history" implies a comprehensive, explanatory analysis that seeks to grasp the main causal dynamics and outlines of the historical process as a whole. It attempts to discern basic laws or regularities of history and to construct some general narrative of historical development. While laws imply regularities, regularities do not imply laws, since there may be exceptions to the rule that the concept of "law" logically denies. Strictly speaking, a "law" holds only when an effect necessarily follows from a cause; but where there is contingency instead of necessity, freedom instead of determination, singularity instead of repetition, there can be no historical "laws."[2]

The distinction between law and regularity is important because, as the work of Dilthey shows (1962), one can deny the possibility of a "science" of history without denying that there are strong causal relations, regularities, patterns, developmental tendencies, and even "meaning" in history. The rejection of nomological science does not entail an acceptance of the empiricist–nominalist position that history is nothing but chaotic and random change that defies generalizing or developmental schemes. Marx, Foucault, and Habermas all attempt to analyze "history" as a general category with narrative import, while trying to avoid an essentializing or reductionistic approach that obscures historical differences and discontinuities.

Marx's theory of history breaks with metaphysics and idealism and develops a materialist theory that grasps the fundamental dynamics behind social change. As we have seen in Chapter 1, Marx tries to negotiate between empiricism and reductionism with his concept of rational abstraction. Empiricism is wrong because, at the synchronic level, it does not grasp the systemic interrelationship among different phenomena within a social totality structured by economics. It is wrong at the diachronic level because it fails to see important similarities among different forms of society insofar as they are governed by the dynamics of material production.

But, against reductionism and its search for universal laws of history, Marx insists that these basic dynamics operate in different ways in different societies. One cannot, therefore, identify any universal law of historical development that allows an *a priori* deduction of the basic characteristics of a given social form; rather, one must examine each society in an empirical, *a posteriori* way. A "rational abstraction" simultaneously grasps both what is general and particular about a given social phenomenon. It is because of the concern for specific historical differences in various modes of production that Marx claims that historical materialism is not an "*a priori* construction," a "lever for construction," or a "compulsory philosophical scheme of history." Except for his early Hegelian excesses and his misleading methodological summaries, Marx does not endorse seeking universal laws of historical development. Unlike his deterministic followers, Marx does not construct an *a priori,* linear model whereby social formations succeed one another through internal contradictions between forces and relations of production. Instead of the rigid primacy of the productive forces model that he articulates in theory, Marx analyzes a wide array of forces to explain social change. He employs a multicausal, contextualist approach that specifies different forces in different situations, showing how war, class struggle, technology, and other factors bring about social change. On this overdetermined logic, there are many engines of history that are nonreducible to the expansion of the productive forces.

Thus, Marx's appeal to historical "laws" requires a two-fold qualification. First, he believes that the task of science is to uncover the laws only of specific modes of production, and not laws that apply without restriction to history in general. Marx was careful not to generalize illicitly from capitalism to all other modes of production. The "laws" Marx identifies, in other words, are synchronic rather than diachronic. Second, because he rejects determinism, Marx intends these "laws" to refer to the *tendencies* of a society to function in a specific way. As "tendencies," they may be realized or blocked, depending on a number of contingent factors related to the dynamics of production, the market, and, most importantly, social struggle. Marx does frequently speak as if these laws were incontrovertible, as when he employs phrases such as "logical necessity" or "iron necessity," but he is guilty more of misrepresenting his actual position than adopting a rigid fatalism or teleology. The general rate of surplus value, for instance, is to be "understood only as a tendency, like all other economic laws" (Marx 1966: 213). When Marx speaks of "the absolute general law of capitalist accumulation," he then adds: "like all other laws, it is modified in its working by many circumstances" (Marx, quoted in Ruben 1979). Thus, as Ruben notes (1979), Marxian science is not incompatible with practice and does not obviate it, because if these "laws" are only tendencies which may or may not be realized, then it is crucial that the working class intervene to counter these tendencies (e.g., that lead toward greater exploitation). Thus defined, scientific knowledge facilitates rather than blocks revolutionary practice. Ultimately, Marx rejects functionalist analyses that dispense with human intentionality in favor of system autonomy, and he tries to show how human beings act within the structures that constrain them.

Like Marx, Habermas seeks a comprehensive theory of history that describes the main outlines and periods of history and tries to supply a causal analysis of the fundamental forces behind social change. Habermas too rejects both narrow and broad versions of technological determinism and grants an important role in history to subjective intention and knowledge. But where Marx speaks only of technical knowledge, Habermas argues that moral knowledge is equally or perhaps more important an evolutionary force. Thus, Habermas seeks to identify important historical continuities in the related, yet separate, dynamics of expanding technical–instrumental and moral–practical knowledge. In this emphasis, Habermas makes a decisive break with the determinist tendencies and scientistic language in Marx.

Traditionally, "causal analysis" signifies the attempt to link specific events to general laws in a universal and determined way that posits a simple relation of antecedent to consequence and arranges actions in a linear order. With the decline of determinism, causal analysis has fallen out of fashion and many see the job of the historian as being merely to describe events or construct narratives. If, with Leff (1969), we say the historian's task is to render the past intelligible, it would seem that this requires not simply narrating a random flow of events, but explaining the constituting forces of history, not just what happened, but also why. Casual explanation can be redefined in a postpositivist context that accounts for indeterminancy, overdetermination, subjective intentionality, unintended consequences of action, and the interpretive status of all historiography whereby the historian selects and arranges relevant facts in a narrative framework from a subjective point of view. The task is thus not to abandon causal analyis, but to complicate it, to renounce the old billiard-ball models of change (where B is explained through the determined force of A and only A), and to provide a more sophisticated, multicausal analysis.[4]

As we have seen, Foucault postpones causal analysis for the archaeological work he considers to be preliminary. Ultimately, however, he is not interested in explaining why things change, only in identifying points of discontinuity and describing various systems of power/knowledge.[3] Unlike Marx and Habermas, Foucault never attempted to explain why a change occurred from one historical era to another, only to show where the breaks occur and to describe their incommensurably different features. This leaves Foucault without the means to ask why such breaks occurred and the resources to identify and understand the constituting forces of society. Like normative assumptions, causal analysis and explanatory logic can be suppressed but not eliminated. Foucault's analyses covertly assume a functionalist viewpoint that explains the existence of discourses, knowledges, and actions according to their role in achieving power over individuals. These forces are therefore deterministic in character and preclude analysis of individual intention, motivation, or choice.

Like Habermas, Foucault rejects the science of history, but he also rejects Habermas' attempt at an explanatory theory of social evolution. Instead of a comprehensive "theory" of history in the Hegelian–Marxist tradition, Foucault seeks a detotalizing "analytics" of history that breaks with evolutionist narratives and the universal logics of "total history." Foucault's work is a good example of the postmodern gestalt shift from universalism to localism, from a systematizing general theory to specific and fragmentary analyses that abandon the "big picture." In place of a broad, macroscopic account of a social totality, Foucault substitutes microanalyses of particular social institutions informed by "local critique."[5]

Postmodern theories abandon all forms of universal narrative and general theory. Lyotard rejects metanarratives and the continuist vision of history they project. Foucault attacks "the inhibiting effect of global theory, *totalitarian theories*" (1980a: 80). Other theorists valorize local knowledges (Geertz 1983) or strictly regional analyses. While the postmodern attack on general theory rightly repudiates an ethnocentric Enlightenment universalism, and is helpful in pluralizing false totalities, such as Marx's assimilation of multiple historical subjects into the "universal working class," it produces a caricatured account of modern theory insofar as many modern theorists were themselves critical of totalizing, universal theories. Following Calhoun (1992), we need to distinguish between two kinds of general theory: one that seeks to produce universal, nomothetic statements applicable to all societies, and another which seeks broad and comprehensive accounts of the general forces structuring a given society, whose abstractions are empirically and historically grounded.

Similarly, Kellner (1988) draws an important distinction between "master narratives" that subsume all events and specific viewpoints into one totalizing theory and "grand narratives" that attempt to describe complex development patterns and trajectories. Kellner argues that in history we find continuous, long-term, general, and even universalizing processes such as the rise of capitalism, bureaucracy, or patriarchy that require general or large-scale theories to interpret them correctly. Even a radical postmodern theorist like Seidman (1991) recognizes the need for such general narratives. Seidman claims we should abandon metanarratives, but retain "general stories" and "broad social narratives" that can recount large-scale events and can offer critical alternatives to the dominant social narratives. As I argue below, even metanarratives can and should be reconstructed and have an important function in theory and politics.

The postmodern critique indiscriminantly discredits all forms of general theory through a critique of the most abstract and totalizing forms. Postmodernists evince a paranoid "aversion against universals" (Honneth 1985). They merely reverse the totalizing and essentializing logic of Enlightenment universalism by making everything into unrelated difference rather than abstract identity. Postmodern critiques fail to grasp the mediation of the local with the general or universal. Seidman (1992), for example, does not show how the analysis of a local issue such as homelessness is incomprehensible without a general analysis of capitalism as an international system whose effects reach into the most regional and private spheres of life.

Modern theories employ a systematic and comprehensive form of analysis that postmodern theories abandon in favor of partial and perspectival modes of analysis. Postmodern theorists like Foucault break up false continuities and totalities but leave things disconnected, failing to analyze systemic connections between economic, political, legal, cultural, interpersonal and personal domains. Where Marx and Habermas focus on the capitalist mode of production as a systematic whole, Foucault analyses modern society from numerous perspectives that, he believes, do not add up to a totality or "organic whole." Thus, Foucault claims that "'The whole of society' is precisely that which should not be considered except as something to be destroyed" (1977: 233). This approach, however, conflicts with Foucault's references to a "disciplinary society."

As Calhoun (1992) and Wagner (1992), argue a general theory of society is unavoidable. All social theory, if it illuminates anything at all, presupposes a general theory that integrates and guides the theoretical process. Even "local" theory issues general declarations about that nature of society and the proper role of theory. The denial of general theory leads to the aporia of renouncing the guiding assumptions of any local theory itself. Particular, local, or fragmentary analyses are blind when lacking a general context for reference, just as general theories are empty without concrete analysis, local reference, and specific application. Thus, it is no accident that Foucault himself issues general—indeed universal—statements about the nature of modern society as disciplinary and the ubiquity of power in all societies. Foucault acknowledges he is dealing with highly general problems—such as the nature of power or the constitution of the subject—but is trying to address them in strictly local and concrete forms. As he says, "Localizing problems is indispensible for theoretical and political reasons. But that doesn't mean that they are not, however, general problems. . . . What I take up is general, perhaps more so than anything else" (1991: 152–153, 165). Foucault's genealogies, therefore, are hardly theory-free; they are constructed from theoretically general frames and perspectives. The problem is not with general theory or holistic analysis per se, but rather with an approach insufficiently empirical; insensitive to the cultural specificity of different periods, societies, and regions; and unfalsifiable.

CRITIQUE AND NORMATIVE VALIDITY

> I don't like judgments. Frivolity should take the place of judgments.
> —KATHY ACKER

> We judge without criteria.   —LYOTARD

> This sucks.   —BEAVIS AND BUTT-HEAD

In the Middle Ages, there was little controversy about epistemological questions regarding the nature of reality and the legitimacy of claims to truth and rightness. It was universally assumed that God existed, that the scriptures conveyed his word and teachings, and that the Church correctly interpreted his voice. God provided an unchanging, infallible foundation for ontological and ethical claims. Although many thinkers in the Enlightenment tradition continued to believe in God, they agreed that traditional ways of justifying knowledge claims were inadequate to the extent that they were unfounded and dogmatic. All knowledge claims were to be criticized and subjected to the new tribunal of secular reason. Modernity can no longer appeal to the past to find the resources for critique, which has now become self-referential. In Habermas' words, "Modernity can and will no longer borrow the criteria by which it takes its orientation from the models supplied by another epoch; *it has to create its normativity out of itself*" (1987a: 7). Through appeal to rational principles discerned by enlightened minds, however early modern theorists thought one could find universal and nonarbitrary criteria for norms of truth and rightness, grounded in the natural order. Modern philosophy thereby embarked on its obsessive concern with epistemology and with the foundations—as well as the limits—of knowledge; "self-referential" critique quickly became a new form of foundationalism.

Following waves of critical reactions that began with Vico, Montesquieu, Montaigne, and others, the nineteenth and twentieth centuries brought a host of challenges to Enlightenment rationality and modern foundationalism. From a variety of perspectives, two key assumptions of Enlightenment thought have been questioned and overturned: that reason is a progressive, liberating force; and that it provides us with the means for an objective apprehension of reality and a legitimation of its own epistemological and normative claims. A key departure point for these critiques—from Heidegger to the Frankfurt School to feminism and postmodern theory—has been Nietzsche's claim that reason is limited to a perspectival apprehension of reality and that it is informed by a will to power. Such critiques show that while the Enlightenment initiated a process of demystifying reason through grounding it in secular values, many modern theorists created new myths about the universality, objectivity, and neutrality of reason.

Influenced by the critical attitude of the Enlightenment, Marx, Foucault, and Habermas all develop critical theories that attempt to unmask the ideologies of capitalist society, to undo the distortions of thought in order to free critical consciousness, to facilitate the extrication of the body from disciplinary regimes, and to expose the forms of power and domination in modern society that limit human freedom. For any critical theory, the inescapable problem is the legitimacy of criticism itself, the validity of the claims it makes, explicit or implicit. Critical theory has to show that its perspective is the "right" or "true" one that is better than those of the social system it denounces; it has to show that its own perspective is not tainted by the norms and ideology it rejects. The *raison d'être* of critical theory, therefore, is its ability to distinguish between legitimate and illegitimate forms of power, true and false propositions, and right and wrong actions. Critical theory must prove as well that these distinctions are not arbitrary, but rather have some basis in rationality or empirical fact.

The question, then, concerns what kind of foundations or forms of objectivity are possible for normative critique. Is there a universally valid criterion of truth and rightness to which we can appeal to adjudicate competing claims? If not, is the extreme relativist position correct in its thesis that all claims are equally arbitrary? Or is there some alternative conception of foundations and objectivity possible that allows us to discriminate among different kinds of claims and to defend some as better than others? Are pluralism and relativism the same things?

Marx's critical method involves an immanent critique, whereby he exposes the glaring contradiction between capitalist ideals of freedom and justice and the actual reality of social life. Marx wishes to expose the inequalities behind the fiction of equality in the wage contract and to show that liberty, equality, and fraternity were nonexistent ideals in a society organized around the rule of private interests and and class power. Marx does not attempt to ground his critique in any extrahistorical foundation; rather, he claims that values are historical in nature and therefore relative to their time. What is "just" in ancient, capitalist, and communist society will greatly differ without any notion corresponding to an essence of "justice." Marx therefore does not confront the normative underpinnings of communism and the question of how his own critical perspective could transcend the ideological horizon of its historical perspective to achieve normative validity or factual truth. In his appropriation of Hegel's dialectical method, Marx jettisons its ontological underpinnings (truth as the development of Reason in history), and does not construct a materialist normative foundation. Thus, while Marx's immanent critique implies the legitimacy of a standpoint not purely context-bound and a positive normative vision of free and creative individuals interacting within a democratic polity, the issue of the rational justification of critique is not addressed.

Foucault too fails to clarify the normative dimensions of his critique, but his critical attitude is far more muted than Marx's. Foucault eschews Marx's moral rhetoric and diatribes and lacks even an immanent critique of modern power, since, unlike Marx, he finds no progressive or rational content in bourgeois norms. Against Marx and Foucault, Habermas takes as a central concern the epistemological status of theory and the question of the validity of normative claims. For Habermas, the main problem with Marx, Adorno and Horkheimer, and Foucault is the lack of reflection on the epistemological status of theory. Habermas rejects Marx's scientism, Adorno and Horkheimer's total critique, and Foucault's crypto-normativism. In contrast, Habermas employs philosophy to reconstruct the epistemological foundations of critical theory and to defend universal values. While rejecting traditional forms of absolutism, Habermas also wishes to avoid relativism by providing a foundation for critique.

For Habermas, postmodern theory is the culmination of a long process of decline of critical theory and its emancipatory vision. Beginning with the loss of the proletariat as the bearer of emancipation, and continuing with historical movements stabilizing capitalism and disqualifying socialism, as well as philosophical developments overturning transcendental, foundational, and universal perspectives, the project of critical theory was in danger of being snuffed out. In the hands of Adorno and Horkheimer, critical theory abandoned a political standpoint and limited itself to mere gestures of resistance confined to the realm of aesthetics. The emancipatory norms informing critical theory required rehabilitation; Habermas attempts this massive undertaking through a revival of Kantian transcendentalism and the construction of an immense, eclectic philosophical framework.

As Roderick (1986) shows, Habermas employs the method of immanent critique in his early works. In *The Structural Transformation of the Public Sphere,* he critically contrasts the bourgeois ideal of a free and democratic public sphere with the historical reality of capitalist control over and distortion of communication and political discourse. In *The Logic of the Social Sciences,* as well as in *Theory and Practice,* he continues to use this method, but in a more Adornoesque manner, focusing on internal contradictions within various philosophical positions in order to move toward a satisfactory, comprehensive theory. This method is still employed in *Knowledge and Human Interests,* but where the earlier work of Habermas implicitly relies on Hegelian–Marxist dialectics, he now adopts a Kantian-inspired search for the necessary and universal preconditions of critique. In this framework, the standard for critique is located not in the truth of the Absolute or in the worker's movement, but rather within communication and the cognitive interest in emancipation. Although Habermas replaces the timeless transcendental ego with a linguistically and historically constituted subject, he follows Kant in seeking the conditions of possibility for experience, in this case, for speech and action, that can provide an objective grounding for ethical norms.

This move is prompted by Habermas's awareness of the limitations inherent in the method of immanent critique. Habermas notes that the strategy failed since bourgeois consciousness has become "cynical" (1979: 97) and no longer acknowledges its revolutionary values, trading them in for a legitimation secured through a technologically secured rise in material well-being. Moreover, while immanent critique can demonstrate how capitalism falls short of its own emancipatory ideals, it cannot supply any positive concepts of what is right or state why there is rational and progressive content in capitalist norms such as freedom, democracy, and justice. Nor can immanent critique escape relativism, since it can appeal only to the values of a given culture and historical era. Thus, to provide critical theory with a foundation for critique, Habermas leaves behind the historicism of Hegel and Marx for the universalist and foundationalist approach of Kant. "The critique of ideology can no longer set out directly from concrete ideals intrinsic to forms of life, but only from formal properties of rationality structures" (Habermas 1982: 254).

While Habermas identifies a key weakness in Foucault's refusal to defend his supressed normative committments, he fails to see other options available to Foucault.[6] Rather than admitting to any contradiction between what his critique assumes and what it does, Foucault has at least two strategies available to him. First, he can take the Nietzschean position that he is only offering a perspective for consideration, another instrument for the toolbox of knowledge, without granting any special privilege to genealogy, and without burdening the theorist with the weight of justification. The task of genealogy is simply to problematize what is presented as necessary and eternal without needing to legitimate any positive visions or values. Second, he can give a pragmatist response and claim that the "truth" of his analyses are verified through their results; a theory is "right" or "true" if it works, if it facilitates struggle and empowers individuals against coercion.

This pragmatism is common to postmodern theory. Richard Rorty and Steven Seidman, two theorists whom Foucault's work has inspired, both formulate important challenges to Habermas' foundationalism. Following Foucault, Rorty finds justification of critical norms unnecessary and rejects universalism in favor of a historicist position that frankly characterizes critique as ungrounded. Rorty believes that the role of philosophy is not to lay the groundwork for a new metaphysics, ontology, or epistemology, but simply to develop new ideas and discover new social possibilities without providing them with a metatheoretical justification: "What is needed is a sort of intellectual analogue of civic virtue — tolerance, irony, and a willingness to let spheres of culture flourish without worrying too much about their 'common ground,' their unification, the 'intrinsic ideals' they suggest, or what picture of man they 'presuppose'" (1985: 168).

Freed from abstract epistemological concerns, analysis can focus on concrete historical studies. "Detailed historical narratives of the sort Foucault offers us would take the place of philosophical metanarratives. Such narratives would not unmask something created by power called 'validity' or 'emancipation.' They would just explain who was currently getting and using power for what reasons, and then (unlike Foucault) suggest how some other people might get it and use it for other purposes" (Rorty 1985:

173). On Rorty's aestheticist position (1989), no argument is better than another on logical grounds; rather, all the theorist—the "ironist"—can do is to counter one "description" of the world with another. This might be accepted because it is more new, interesting, attractive, or useful, but not because it is "true."

From a similar postmodern standpoint, Seidman (1991, 1992) has advanced a vigorous political critique of foundationalism. According to Seidman, the concern with foundations and metatheoretical justification makes social theory obscure, marginal, and irrelevant to social struggles and everyday life. The obsessive concern for rigor and justification shifts focus from immediate practical struggles to technical discourse and theoretical vocabulary. Theory becomes increasingly distant from the conditions it is designed to illuminate. Critical theory itself reflects contemporary trends toward increasing professionalization of discourse that only specialists can understand. An elite culture emerges around the production and consumption of theory. This actually contributes to the decline of citizenry and the depoliticization of the public sphere by promoting a culture of experts and transfiguring moral and practical struggles into analytical and metatheoretical battles. On Nietzschean grounds, epistemology is another expression of the ascetic ideal; we should be suspicious of attempts to privilege abstract ideals such as truth over concrete values that directly contribute to human well-being. Because of these unfortunate consequences, Seidman concludes that foundationalism should be abandoned and that modern metatheory should be replaced with a postmodern pragmatism that seeks strategic intervention at local levels without concern for analytical truth and ultimate justification.

The postmodern pragmatism espoused by Foucault, Rorty, and Seidman has definite advantages. It allows theory to stay close to concrete social and historical analysis and prevents it from bogging down in abstract metatheoretical issues. It is perhaps for similar reasons that Marx also rejects abstract epistemological concerns in order to focus on empirical issues and concrete political struggles. In the case of Habermas, despite his numerous political essays, we see a clear example of how the concern for providing foundations for critique has overtaken the initial goal of theory, which was to engage in social critique and political analysis. When reading Habermas' political essays, such as his intervention in the German historians' debates, little connection between these more concrete concerns and his massive theoretical apparatus is apparent, throwing into question the extent to which the metatheoretical emphasis is needed or helpful.[7] All too often, Habermas' political "addressee" is not the new social movements or citizens, but rather fellow academics. The Habermas industry has engendered a new form of scholasticism that rivals medieval Aristotelianism in its arid, obtuse jargon.

Seidman articulates a serious problem with modern theory, along with a hope that social criticism would become more socially relevant as it becomes more local, pragmatic, and accessible. But Seidman fails to see that postmodern theory itself has become as specialized as any modern metatheory and even more esoteric—witness the work of Derrida, Lacan, or Kristeva, and their followers. More importantly, the postmodern positions advocated by Foucault, Rorty, and Seidman inescapably beg crucial questions. If, for example, we believe that all values and voices are equally valid, then we must also embrace those that espouse the suppression of conversation and liberal pluralism—a true "performative contradiction." To reject this conclusion requires some means of discriminating between which values are legitimate and which illegitimate, and thus to make normative claims in need of rational defense. The more voices awakened from silence, the more social heterogeneity and complexity, the greater the need to weigh and adjudicate among competing claims and interests. If, with Foucault, we speak of coercion, domination, discipline, and normalization and intend theory to create new forms of subjectivity and liberty, we need to know which forms are desirable and why. While Foucault technically can wriggle out of the performative contradiction, this escape comes at a great cost. In Bernstein's words, Foucault's "rhetoric of disruption forces us to raise questions and at the same time appears to deny us any means for effectively dealing with these questions" (1992: 395).

Thus, to the extent postmodern theorists wish their analyses to have any kind of truth status or political efficacy, they cannot avoid epistemology, metatheory, and foundationalist issues. Correctly understood, the postmodern position is not incompatible with normative justification. In addition to pragmatic appeals, the postmodern theorist can claim that adjudicating criteria can be found immanent within a specific sociohistorical context. For Seidman, "moral inquiry can be socially compelling only in a historicist, pragmatic mode. If offering universal principles carries no epistemic authority or (to put it differently) if the invocation of those principles has little or no social efficacy, moral inquiry must take the form of appeals to cultural tradition or current social conventions and ideals to justify social practices or norms" (1992: 73).

Within a given culture, the postmodernist can argue, there are prevailing standards of right and wrong, truth and falsehood, beauty and ugliness, which allow nonarbitrary factual, moral, and aesthetic judgments. For the postmodernist, unlike Habermas, there are no "foundations" of values that lie within the world itself, outside of language, social convention, a community of inquirers, and historically changing conceptions of logic and rationality. Criticism has to proceed immanently within a given culture and its standards. Within the culture of advanced capitalist nations, for example, prevailing liberal values allow people to criticize certain practices as being racist or sexist. By appealing to the ideals of autonomy, rights, and liberty, oppressed people can cry foul and unjust actions can be rectified.

Yet the appeal to immanent norms collapses from severe problems. It assumes a cultural homogeneity that does not exist anywhere outside of tribal communities. It therefore has no means to deal with the very conflict and diversity of voices it celebrates. Moreover, it prevents taking any critical position toward cultural tradition, as if all traditions were positive or emancipatory. What response can Seidman give if the prevailing cultural norms are evil or oppressive, if the culture he finds himself in is that of Wall Street, the Mafia, the New Right, or the Third Reich? Clearly, we need some critical, moral standards that transcend a merely local context and attempt to define a standpoint outside of some given principles in order to evaluate them. Strictly speaking, this is a "transcendental" — or better, transcontextual — standpoint, but it should not be confused with an ahistorical Kantian transcendentalism, since it acknowledges the historical character of all legitimating norms.

Thus, the problems Habermas and others find in Foucault's work are not imposed on it from the outside, as a kind of blackmail, as Bernstein (1992) suggests might be the case; rather, they arise unavoidably from the critical goals Foucault sets for his own writing. Against the ahistorical thrust of much modern theory, Habermas agrees with Foucault and postmodern theory that reason is historical and immanent to the cultural context from which it emerged. Yet Habermas believes that reason *also* has a transcendental quality insofar as it raises validity claims that can be criticized, defended, and revised beyond a merely local context, a specific point of view, or a particular historical set of circumstances.

But as we have seen, Habermas never successfully overcame a metaphysical standpoint. His quasi-transcendentalism combines contradictory logics, it is informed by unfounded teleological claims, and it does not fully overcome an ahistorical transcendentalism. Ultimately, Habermas provides no convincing argument for the factual reality of the alleged universality of ideal speech presuppositions and inherent interests in emancipation. His argument, therefore, cannot dispel a Foucauldian critique that such universal appeals are gained ficticiously and at the expense of real cultural differences.

But to disagree with Habermas' own attempt to provide foundations for critique does not disqualify the non-relativist argument itself. Habermas' error does not lie in seeking an objective or universal standpoint per se, but rather in seeking it ahistorically. Habermas is right to say, "I cannot imagine any seriously critical social theory without an internal link to something like an emancipatory interest" (1986: 198). But this interest is not given; it must be formed. Rather than grounding norms in the ideal speech situation or inherent emancipatory interests, we can only appeal to historically constituted norms that, after rational consideration, are recognized as a valid court of appeal. Since this kind of foundation is historical, it has no fundamental, Archimedean point outside of any historically conditioned presupposition or human interest.

Democratic values are derived from the cultures of ancient Greece and the modern liberal tradition. These values can only be "grounded" within the assumptions of democratic discourse, having no external basis in God, natural law, *Geist,* language, or human nature. They are defensible to the extent that it is rational to believe that no person or group has a right to infringe on the freedom of any other person or group, that one's race, gender, nationality, or sexual orientation are wholly irrelevant to moral considerations, and that power and domination have no nonutilitarian justifiability (since one may argue against democracy through appeal to the values of security or efficiency).

Ultimately, we can do no more than agree on the importance of autonomy and liberty as basic values, try to define their meaning, draw proper conclusions from them, specify their institutional requirements, provide them with legal guarantees, and struggle to realize them in concrete form. Not all people will agree with these values (since some people will be elitist, sexist, racist, or homophobic), but they must specify the reasons why they disagree and be open to the possibility that their position is not well founded. Habermas rightly claims that the only means of adjudicating competing claims is through the "force of the better argument," but the norms behind this force are not given in language itself. Rather, different values, norms, and policies have to be debated and chosen within conditions of a public discursive will formation. This scheme presupposes that people are rational and can be motivated by rational arguments, which cannot in fact be assumed and which raises important problems about dealing with dissent and the possibility of genuine democracy.

I draw three important conclusions from what I have discussed above. First, some appeal to universal values remains necessary. Normative claims for freedom lack progressive content unless they mean freedom and democracy for all, not just for some. If legally instituted by a court of deconstruction, postmodern theories could not guarantee the rights and liberties of all people. An appeal to universality is also necessary in order to criticize double standards that political leaders and representatives establish, applying legal regulations to everyone except themselves. As Marcuse said in 1937 (in reference to Heidegger, but he might as well have been addressing Derrida, Lyotard or Foucault):

> That man is a [potentially] rational being, that this being requires freedom, and that happiness is his highest good are all universal propositions whose progressive impetus derives precisely from their universality. Universality gives

them an almost revolutionary character, for they claim that all, and not merely this or that particular person, should be rational, freed, and happy. In a society whose reality gives the lie to all these universals, philosophy cannot make them concrete. Under such conditions, adherence to universality is more important than its philosophical destruction. (1989: 70)

Thus, the appeal to universals need not be merely obfuscatory and ideological; it may also have a utopian content and progressive function.

Second, the denial of objectivism does not entail the truth of relativism. Postmodern theory commits us to an either/or fallacy that blocks a third alternative to absolutism and relativism. This alternative provides a nonarbitrary, extralocal means of grounding normative claims, without appealing to any ahistorical criteria. Nevertheless, the postmodern critique of a totalizing modern universalism is important, and to preserve its validity we need to distinguish between an abstract universalism that dissolves important differences among diverse phenomena (at the same time presenting contingent phenomena as necessary and immutable) and a concrete universalism that carefully draws such distinctions while acknowledging contingency and upholding conditions that are binding for all. Postmodern theories help to recuperate important differences lost by universalizing, essentializing, and foundationalist modern theories, but they are unable to contextualize these differences within a more general framework that also grasps formal moral and legal conditions that need to apply to all individuals within a given society.[8] Thus, against Habermas, postmodern theories do not necessarily destroy the attempt to provide foundations for critique, rather they can help to reconstruct them better. Habermas fails to recognize the difference between pluralism and relativism—both posit the incommensureability of values, but pluralism allows for shared understanding and potential accord.[9]

Third, while postmodern theorists wrongly deny good reasons to worry about epistemological, metatheoretical, and foundational questions, they are right that such concerns should not become so obsessive, detailed, and abstract that theory takes precedence over practice and degenerates into a specialist language removed from and irrelevant to concrete social issues. We need to formulate a means of sensible mediation between the metatheoretical silence of Foucault and the loquaciousness of Habermas. When arguments about the status of claims and rationality become self-reflexive, metatheory is useful and necessary. But if we have to wait for the perfection of metatheory, or if metatheory overwhelms both theory and practice, then it is better—to borrow a phrase from Camus—to live a life without appeal. We would then be like musicians who could play the tune without needing to read the music.

Rorty believes that society carries on well enough without existence of foundations; it seems certain that sound moral judgments can be made without having read Habermas' *The Theory of Communicative Action.* Perhaps, as Nicholson (1992) suggests, relativism is less a theoretical question than a practical problem of fragmented communities and divided practical interests. While the construction of a rational community of free social actors cannot take place without a theoretical critique of the prevailing social forms and an articulation of alternative forms, it also requires forging emotional bonds and common interests such that what Kant or Weber say about spheres of rationality or how Searle or Austin define speech acts ultimately is of no consequence.

IN DEFENSE OF METANARRATIVE

As can be seen from the foregoing discussion, the theories of Marx, Foucault, and Habermas have a coherent narrative character. From the immense complexity of history, each constructs a narrative that imposes meaning and order on past events. Hence, Marx tells the story of the development of class society and the transition from the realm of necessity to the realm of freedom; Foucault describes the transformation of technologies of the self into technologies of domination; and Habermas reconstructs the development of moral consciousness in stages of social evolution.

But while each theorist utilizes a narrative form, only Marx and Habermas articulate metanarratives. The ultimate goal of their theories, unlike that of Foucault, is to identify actual historical possibilities for human emancipation. The metanarratives of Marx and Habermas attempt to discern and help realize the possibilities for human freedom as they develop throughout history. For Marx and Habermas, human freedom is not a metaphysical property of human nature, but a historical property that evolves through time and can be actualized under certain social conditions. Their metanarratives attempt to locate past and present emancipatory dynamics that can be further advanced in a future state. Their visions of future freedom are inseparably linked with their dialectical evaluation of the past and present.

Despite their differing emphases on productive and communicative activity, both Marx and Habermas follow the basic Hegelian insight into history as an evolutionary process and synthesis of particularity and universality. In their theories of social evolution, each traces the progressive complication and differentiation of social and individual forms of existence. Marx's narrative describes the negation of abstract sociality in the form of primitive communism through the development of the productive forces and the division of labor and the subsequent emergence of class society.

Within class societies, particularity develops in the form of class-based interests and emerging individualism. In capitalism, however, these dynamics lead to a new form of universality, a global capitalist culture, and the possibility of overcoming class divisions and private interests in a new form that combines sociality and individuality in a concrete unity and mediated universality.

Similarly, Habermas describes a relatively undifferentiated, primitive social form that develops with the evolution of its subsystems and the emergence of the state and social classes. As Habermas characterizes it, the shift from the mythic to the modern worldview involves a differentiation of spheres of rationality with their respective validity claims and modes of argumentation. The universal conditions in modernity that Habermas focuses on involve the postconventional moral consciousness that allows for the redemption of validity claims, the attainment of social consensus, and the realization of rational autonomy.

For Marx and Habermas, progress is defined in terms of advances in freedom. Freedom is understood as freedom from external constraints and ideology, as well as freedom to pursue creative activity, to develop one's individuality, and to communicate with others under distortion-free conditions. For both, external constraints on freedom include those of nature, in the form of want and need, and those of society, in the form of domination and exploitation. For Marx, the key historical dynamic that creates the preconditions of freedom is the development of the productive forces. Marx holds that human freedom requires an advanced technological apparatus to overcome need and the drudgery of work. From his understanding of freedom, Marx can argue that capitalism is a progressive historical form compared to feudalism insofar as it develops the productive forces of society, creates more democratic social conditions, and allows for greater differentiation of individual being. Whatever its shortcomings, bourgeois democracy is "a big step forward" (Marx 1975a: 221) toward human emancipation. But Marx argues that capitalism, initially a revolutionary force, quickly became a conservative force, and restricted its democratic elements to a formal level. Communism, on the other hand, has the goal of developing the democratic dynamics capitalism initiated abstractly in concrete institutional forms.

For Habermas, progress relates to both "capacities for cognitive–instrumental mastery of natural processes and for consensual resolution of morally relevant conflicts of action" (1982: 228). Communicative rationality develops to the point where individuals can democratically debate the practical and normative issues that arise in the governing of their lifeworld, and can formulate a consensus under conditions free of domination. In their ability to distinguish among different "worlds" and in their reflective, postconventional forms of learning, Habermas claims that modern cultures are superior to early cultures. As he understands it, the evolution of theoretical and practical knowledge involves a transition from nonreflective to reflective forms of learning. Only in modernity does the possibility of a "rational society" and a rational "conduct of life" emerge, once validity claims are no longer naively accepted, are subject to rational scrutiny, and are accepted or rejected on the basis of argumentation. Habermas claims that the formal features of bourgeois institutions "demonstrate a conceptual structure or moral–practical thought and interpretation which must be considered superior in relation to the built-in moral categories of traditional legal and political institutions" (1986: 101). Thus, he adopts a kind of Hegelian or Comtean scheme that traces the development of rationality from cultural traditions organized around myth, religion, philosophy, and ideology, to those organized around moral and factual truth claims that require intersubjective redemption.

Foucault's abandonment of a progressivist vision of history is symptomatic of the "postmodern condition" diagnosed by Lyotard (1984), which finds metanarratives to be implausible. Foucault rejects metanarratives because he believes they rely on (1) essentialist notions of subjects whose freedom exfoliates from their inner essence; (2) continuist, linear time schemes that posit a rectilinear march toward rationality and autonomy; (3) a teleological logic whereby history moves toward this predetermined goal; and (4) a totalizing vision of the good life that implies coercive social engineering.

Marx and Habermas are indeed vulnerable to some of these objections. Each makes references to a unified "species subject" or "human species" that obscures fundamental cultural differences. Both lapse into teleological positions. In the *Economic and Philosophic Manuscripts,* Marx posited a unified macrosubject that unfolds its potentiality throughout history, and he saw communism as the "goal of history" (1975a: 365). In *Capital,* he abandoned the notion of human essence, but spoke as though the demise of capitalism were inevitable. Such rhetoric aside, Marx's actual position, shared by Habermas, is that there are *tendencies* in history toward progress, toward establishing the preconditions of freedom, toward a liberatory mediation of the universal and concrete. The realization of these tendencies, however, is entirely dependent on the contingencies of social action. While Habermas abandons a teleology of history, he advances a teleological conception of language as striving toward mutual understanding and consensus and as the carrier of an innate interest in emancipation.

Both Marx and Habermas, however, reject a logic of linear development and claim that the subject is socially and historically constituted. For both, subjectivity and freedom are historical constructs, not essences, which have evolved throughout history, although Habermas confuses the picture by also assuming transhistorically given human interests and moral intuitions. As Marx says, "Liberation is a historical and not a mental act, and it is brought about by historical conditions, the [development] of industry, commerce, [agri]culture, the conditions of intercourse" (1975a: 169). Autonomy, freedom, and maturity are possible only with the evolution of society, technology, and individuality itself, "within the wealth of previous periods of development" (348). Neither Marx nor Habermas push dogmatic normative positions defining the nature of the good life. Marx refuses to speculate on the concrete nature of communist society, which he thinks is the task of future generations, and Habermas argues that normative values should be developed through debate and consensus within a rational community rather than dictated *ex cathedra* by intellectuals.

Where the postmodern critique would throw out a theory of social evolution along with teleology, a theory of social evolution is defensible on a nonteleological basis that may speak of a developmental logic, but that harbors no internal goal such as the optimization of rationality. Such a theory would describe developmental dynamics that result from contingent means of structural adaption, and that lead to advances in rationality and to moral and legal institutional forms that facilitate human freedom and individual development. For someone like Schmid, however, if "reconstructed developmental logics *appear* to us as cumulative sequences, this is *only the result of the reconstruction itself*" (1982: 179). Any reconstruction of a developmental logic is "theoretically arbitrary." Schmid illuminates the unfounded philosophical underpinnings of Habermas' allegedly empirically rooted theory, but his argument reduces the progressive–developmental *tendencies* of history to the Eurocentric biases of the interpreter, and thereby discounts the possibility that such tendencies may actually exist. The "reconstruction" of such tendencies can lay claim to the universalizing, rationalizing, individualizing, and differentiating dynamics of Western history. Against some poststructuralists, history is not simply a "text."

While postmodern theory offers effective critiques of linear, essentialist, and teleological metanarratives, the rejection of all forms of metanarrative disables emancipatory theory and practice. We must distinguish between plausible and implausible notions of progress. If we reject the idea (held by Comte, Spencer, Condorcet, and others) of progress as a necessary and invariable development in human knowledge from primitive to modern societies that leads to enlightenment and freedom, we can recast the notion as a sum of contingent, successive changes in which patterns and tendencies for freedom can be discerned, appropriated, and advanced in a new social form, but that carry no guarantee of realization.

The abandonment of teleology does not mean that history has no order, meaning, or direction. One clear tendency in Western history, however halting or broken, is the development of individuality, rationality, and democratic ideals. Hegel was not completely wrong in characterizing history as progress from the freedom of one, the oriental despot, to freedom of many, Greek and Roman citizens, to freedom for all in the modern world. As Marx forcefully showed, however, the ideal of universal freedom and democracy was a reality only at a formal level, and true historical progress requires that these ideals receive concrete reality through institutional embodiment. Yet the ideals of democracy, however abstract, distorted, or incomplete, are difficult to contain because they inflame the passions of the exploited and underprivileged. They tend to spread and assume an increasingly universal character. In the modern tradition itself, they have become increasingly inclusive, incorporating women and minorities, and inspiring social change in non-Western countries such as China. Moreover, there have been important tendencies in the last two decades toward extending the ideals of rights, democracy, and community to animals and the earth. Despite false starts, wrong turns, reversals, repetitions, and betrayals, progressive ideals continue to advance.

A theory of progress—far from "an unhelpful distraction from what Dewey calls 'the meaning of the daily detail' " (Rorty 1986: 175)—provides a normative yardstick with which to assess the legitimacy of the present era and possible future social forms by analyzing the ways in which it is or is not creating conditions of freedom. One era constitutes "progress" over another insofar as the conditions of human freedom are more developed in that era than the ones preceding it. Without a theory of progress, we cannot say that one society is better than another; rather, one is led to the conclusion that all are of equal value and thus no society is worth struggling for. The rejection of progress, therefore, has quietistic and conservative implications. The rational principles called into being by capitalist modernity can be used to judge the inadequacy of capitalist social forms themselves and to assert the necessity for further advances in rationalization, democratization, and individualization processes.

A valid theory of progress of course will have to specify what it means by freedom (such as gains in critical rationality, individuality, and social harmony); to construct a plausible account of this notion; to provide empirical evidence supporting the claim that conditions of freedom have developed cumulatively (which is not the same as linearly) throughout history, or at least from one society to another; and to establish clear criteria for differentiating stages of social development. An adequate theory of progress must capture the complexity and ambiguity of historical developments. Since there is no single criterion for human freedom, one must look at multiple levels of social development—economic, technological, political, moral, and so on—and avoid a simple linear narrative. As Marx makes clear, progress and regress occur simultaneously in history and are inseparably connected. Increased differentiation of individuality, for example, occurred concomitant with the loss of communal values and a renewal of slave labor in capitalism. Increases in scientific and technical rationality come at the expense of a holistic relation between human beings and nature and the destruction of the environment. Because societies develop unevenly and history is marked by gains and losses, Habermas claims that he is only reconstructing certain aspects of social evolution (1986: 169).

As Vico, Herder, Montesquieu, and other anti-Eurocentrists argued, each human culture has its own form of value beyond what it contributes to the teleological triumph of rationality in modernity, and therefore needs to be assessed on its own terms. On Berlin's metaphor, "winter is not a rudimentary spring; summer is not an undeveloped autumn" (1982: 108). Marx did not respect this principle when he justified the British colonization of India as necessary for the advance of history. Habermas, similarly, tends to view the value of premodern societies mainly in terms of what they contribute to subsequent developments in rationality. We see that a key danger in progressivist theories of history, whether teleological or not, is that they can reduce the value of a particular culture to an abstract historical whole, which can easily justify imperialism and aggressive modernization policies. But the pluralist conception of culture does not preclude a narrative account of progressively developing tendencies in history, for any culture could in fact, whatever its autonomous value, contribute in different ways to a multifaceted developmental process.

Finally, an adequate theory of progress must also justify its own hermeneutic standpoint as adequate; it must defend the normative assumptions it starts out with and show that it has correctly grasped or reconstructed the nature of historical developments without falsely projecting present forms of understanding onto the past. This last necessity brings us to our next topic.

THE HERMENEUTICS OF HISTORIOGRAPHY

> Life can only be understood backward but it must be
> lived forward.
> —KIERKEGAARD

The attempt to analyze the specificity of past historical eras raises difficult problems: how can one comprehend past history from the standpoint of the present? How can one successfully understand past cultures standing on this side of a historical discontinuity? How is it possible to reconstruct the past as intelligible without imposing one's own values and perspectives? Are all theories of history necessarily ethnocentric? Is objective historical description ever possible?

Unless we actually live in another culture, obviously impossible in many cases, the only way to understand it is to construct an interpretation from textual sources. Dilthey thought that the interpreter could bridge cultural gaps and recreate the original intelligibility of a culture through an empathetic process. Employing a similar move, Gadamer spoke of a "fusion of horizons" where one field of meaning intersects with another. Whatever the problems with their hermeneutics, Dilthey and Gadamer are correct that historical writing requires that the historian try to enter into the lifeworld under study to render it intelligible for readers from another culture.

Such historical understanding cannot be perfectly objective, since the historian can never fully overcome the presuppositions and prejudices of his or her existential situation (one's racial, sexual, class, and national identity). Unless one seeks the fictitious standpoint of the Husserlian epoche that pretends to bracket the natural attitude and remove any finite historical constraints through a methodological sleight of hand, one can do nothing but write history from the standpoint of the present, from a local cultural situation, from within a more or less prejudiced preunderstanding. Unlike the object of natural science, historical data are not known through observation or experience, but rather through the interpretation of documents, inferential reasoning, and imaginative reconstruction. Although historical writing is always a rewriting, the hermeneutical distance between the present and the past can be lessened with careful and sensitive intepretation aware of the cultural and temporal barriers that may lie between the historian and his or her object. As Trevalyan insisted, history is as much an art as a "science."

Thus, good historiography requires hermeneutical sensitivity, empathetic and imaginative reconstruction, and reflexive methodological sophistication. Both Marx and Foucault suppress the hermeneutical dimension of historiography that Habermas foregrounds as an important epistemological issue. Marx buries the methodological problems concerning the validity of his own historical standpoint under positivist rhetoric. In similar bad faith, Foucault rejects hermeneutics because he believes it relies on a metaphysical surface–depth model that assumes essential or ideal meanings and because he adopts the position of a detached observer. In contrast to both theorists, Habermas frankly acknowledges the hermeneutical character of theory and takes on the difficult philosophical problems of interpretation, critique, and justification.

Despite their different emphases, both Marx and Habermas believe that there are substantive continuities in history that allow one to reconstruct a developmental logic from the standpoint of the present. In other words, we do not need a Diltheyian empathy of historical otherness if we can read our own historical dynamics accurately enough and work backwards from the present to see how they have developed since then.[10] If, as Hegel says, the owl of Minerva only flies at dusk, Marx and Habermas both believe world history is now in the twilight period where the main developmental logics of history are either completed or sufficiently developed such that they can be accurately reconstructed. Hence, Habermas repeats Marx's claim that "the anatomy of bourgeois society is a key to the anatomy of premodern societies; to this extent the analysis of capitalism provides an excellent entry in the theory of social evolution" (Habermas 1979: 123).

But the obvious danger of the retrospective method, besides the seduction of teleology, is the temptation to overemphasize the continuities of the present with the past and thereby to project onto the past dynamics that apply only to the present. All too often, historical narratives are the product of a distorting hindsight that arbitrarily selects specific phenomena from a welter of facts to tell the story it wants and to give a misleading impression of a linear development. Despite their sensitivity to this problem, both Marx and Habermas lapse into Eurocentric positions that fail to grasp the full degree of difference between capitalist and precapitalist societies and forms of consciousness. Marx, as I have argued (see Chapter 1), illegitimately abstracts economics from other precapitalist social dynamics, fails to grant noneconomic phenomena sufficient importance, and naturalizes bourgeois logic by reading all human modes of exchange as utilitarian. Habermas overcomes Marx's productivism by emphasizing that, until capitalism, the dynamics of production were inextricably embedded in tradition and were not of primary importance in premodern societies, even in "the last instance."[11]

Yet where Marx falsely projected a utilitarian logic onto premodern societies, Habermas does the same with communicative rationality. Given his distinction between mythic and modern worldviews, Habermas is aware that the ability to distinguish among and redeem different validity claims and their respective "worlds" is not universal. His argument is that the communicative competence evident in the modern West represents the realization of a species-wide potentiality for discursive rationality whose development culminates in postconventional liberal morality.[12] Rather than creating a new logic characteristic of its own time, modernity universalizes and makes explicit the logic implicit in all forms of communicative action through a process of increasing reflexivity (1986: 209). Despite this qualification, Habermas projects a uniform logic of communicative rationality—if only implicit—throughout history and obliterates fundamental differences between modern and premodern forms of communication. Any attempt to substantiate the claim that *all* acts of human communication employ the presuppositions of the ideal speech situation will reveal a huge empirical deficit. To the extent that Habermas employs empirical research at all, he uncritically relies on the work of Piaget and Kohlberg, whose "universal" claims have been shown to be biased and incomplete.[13] Habermas' search for the "general and unavoidable" presuppositions of communicative action turn out to be specific and contingent aspects of rationality in the modern West. His Kantian analogy of early cultures as the childhood of humanity is a biased reduction of cultural sophistication and complexity to simple technical and moral forms of knowledge. Habermas falls behind the contribution of Claude Lévi-Strauss (1966), who showed that premodern cultures have highly developed analytical capacities but employ them in different ways than modern cultures. Overall, Habermas fails to do justice to the historical plurity of incommersurable standards of rationality, reducing them to a single universal form.[14] Habermas' universal individual looks less like humanity in general than like a tenured liberal academic in a tweed jacket debating a colleague near the departmental coffee pot.

Foucault's discontinuity perspective frees us from the notion of a singular history and breaks up the linear narrative pattern that accompanies the conception of Humanity as unified, in order to untangle history in its complex differences. Foucault exposes the unwarranted metaphysical assumptions behind progressivist and teleological visions of history, including the assumption of a unifying subject — such as Habermas' "human species" — of history. The liberation of different histories from the straightjacket of universal history, in which each stage of history is allegedly better than the preceding stage allows a less prejudiced and more dialectical evaluation of different historical eras and cultures. Postmodern theories such as Foucault's provide resources to criticize Eurocentric theories that privilege the modern West as the telos of history. Postmodern history and ethnography seeks to free premodern, non-Western histories from colonial narratives in order to appreciate their difference and value.[15] These postmodern theories side with the oppressed, the marginal, and the subaltern against the dominant powers of the world.

Foucault avoids the Eurocentrism of Marx and Habermas because he refuses a theory of social evolution and universal proclamations about the meaning of history. Foucault's problem is a different one. While his postmodern suspicion of metanarratives and universal values and his emphases on historical differences and discontinuities provide an important counter to teleological and evolutionist theories, he fails to grasp other important lines of continuity involving developmental tendencies toward technological advances, differentiation of rationality, individuation of subjective experience, and democratization of social life. Except for the qualifications of his later work on ethics, Foucault constructs a metanarrative in reverse which, in Nietzschean fashion, describes a progressive movement toward more effective forms of domination with the expansion of Western rationality and disciplinary technologies. Although his later work acknowledges historical gains in cognitive learning, unlike Marx and Habermas, he has no evolutionary framework to contextualize them as progressive advances.

THEORY AND POLITICS

> Without the imagination, all philosophical knowledge
> remains in the grip of the present or the past, severed
> from the future, which is the only link between
> philosophy and the real history of mankind.
> — MARCUSE

> Man's self-esteem, his sense of freedom, must be
> re-awakened.
> — MARX (1975a: 201)

We have seen that Marx, Foucault, and Habermas all break with positivist notions of value-free theory and attempt to connect theory with practice and political change. Marx and Habermas operate from Enlightenment assumptions that social subjects can employ rationality to become conscious of their social and historical existence, to understand the conditions of their domination, to criticize and overthrow illegitimate forms of power, and to conceive of alternative forms of social existence. Despite a postmodern orientation toward theory and politics that devalues rationality, Foucault becomes modernist enough to hold with Marx and Habermas that knowledge and critique are important for social change. For all three theorists the general purpose of critical theory is to expose the operations of domination and reveal the arbitrary and contingent character of modern institutions and practices. As Foucault says, "Knowledge can transform us" (1988d: 4) through defetishizing social conditions presented as neutral, inevitable, or the best of all possible worlds. Foucault's differences with Marx and Habermas result from his rejection of the universal standpoint, of generalizable interests suppressed by domination, of teleological dimensions to rationality or history, and of a foundational grounding of social critique.

Habermas and Foucault theorize from a contemporary standpoint where the organic connection between theory and practice that once existed for Marx is decisively broken. Marx's optimistic tendencies for the possibility of revolutionary change and his privileging of the working class as the universal subject of history have been abandoned by successive generations of the Frankfurt School and by postmodern theorists. Before the postmodern embrace of new social movements, Marcuse (1969, 1989) argued that the sources of change would come not from the working class but rather from various marginalized groups such as students, blacks, and women, who were not as absorbed into the system as the proletariat. With its emphasis on plurality, there was a natural affinity between postmodern theory and new social movements. Postmodern theories articulate a "politics of limits" that abandons teleology, metaphysical guarantees, and the norm of revolution; a "politics of margins" that validates the political potential of groups excluded by Marxism; and a "politics of identity" that seeks to foster different political and cultural identities essential for the self-recognition and autonomy of different social groups and individuals. Postmodern theorists attempt to link totalizing theories to totalitarian politics and they challenge what they think to be the elitist values and authoritarian core of modern theories.[16] For postmodernists, the theoretical project of subordinating differences to a system or conceptual center has its ominous political analogue in the repressive and centralizing aspects of the modern state. Similarly, the Marxist theoretical privileging of production inevitably entailed the political primacy of the working class and the subordination of racial and sexual politics to class struggle.

For both Habermas and Foucault, the starting point for theory and politics today is skepticism for grand schemes of social change and a politics of limits. This new sensibility is fostered by developments in philosophy that undermine confidence in truth, progress, and teleology and by sociopolitical conditions characterized by the decline of the industrial working class and the extension of domination throughout social life. In reference to the contemporary situation, Habermas states that both *"revolutionary self-confidence* and *theoretical self-certainty* are gone"* (1982: 222). Claims to truth are abandoned or tempered, and ontological guarantees for revolutionary norms are replaced by a "new arbitrariness in the relation of theory to practice" (223). Politics can no longer take as sufficient the critique of political economy and the task of developing working class consciousness. Two key facts of the twentieth century are that the development of technology has not had emancipatory effects, and that the working class has become neither unified nor revolutionary.

Theoretically, Habermas evinces a new awareness of fallibility that requires empirical verification of theory and skepticism toward totalizing philosophical schemes of analysis and change. With this skepticism, he is in agreement with Foucault. Politically, Habermas finds uncertainty about the possibility of revolution and the very concept of revolutionary change. Both he and Foucault reject the norm of "revolution" on the grounds that the cure may prove worse than the disease by bringing about social upheaval favorable for breeding a political system even more oppressive than capitalism. For Habermas, Marx's ideal of revolution is imaginable now only as a long-term process that allows for " 'acclimatization' to new democratic forms of life, through a gradual enlargement of democratic, participatory and discursive action" (1986: 68).

With Marx, Habermas emphasizes a need for enlightenment and political consciousness, but he rejects tendencies in Marx to privilege intellectuals and the working class. Habermas sees scientific rationality itself to be an ideological force that thwarts the democratic process by legitimating expert knowledge and elite rule. Building on the Frankfurt School critique of instrumental rationality, Habermas analyzes the ways in which scientific rationality has been used for purposes of domination rather than emancipation. He opposes all forms of elite engineering of consciousness, be it through an intelligensia or a technocratic elite. For Habermas, enlightenment and democratic social change can only come through a collective process of rational discussion of social values and public policy that privileges practical over technical rationality.

This requires breaking the power of technocratic elites over the political process, revitalizing the public sphere, and appropriating the "avenging force" of communicative rationality for purposes of social change. Habermas believes that once the distorting influences of power and money are eliminated from communication, individuals will be able to act from their shared interest in emancipation and to articulate the social conditions necessary to bring it about. Within this process the philosopher or critical theorist assumes a modest role as an engaged citizen along with others. The role of intellectuals is to influence public debate with critical viewpoints that promote democratic change. From Habermas' perspective, Marx begged important questions as to how the working class could attain enlightenment if the conditions of communication were distorted from the start, a fact recognized by Marx as he lost faith in the demystifying effects of bourgeois rule and analyzed the new phenomenon of commodity fetishism.

Habermas emphasizes that current social conditions are drastically different from Marx's time and that the class struggle model is obsolete. Because of the welfare-state compromise, class conflict is defused and institutionalized. With the colonization of the lifeworld, the capitalist economy and state have penetrated further into social and personal existence and created new forms of domination. Like Foucault, Habermas holds that in advanced capitalism struggles have shifted toward the "margins" of society where they involve groups and issues that do not directly relate to the exploitation of labor. Both see the new social movements—feminism, people of color, gay and lesbian coalitions, ecology and antinuclear movements, and so on — as critical responses to the growing administration of social and personal life.[17] While Habermas finds that these movements unleash "new potentials for protest" (1986: 105), he argues they must not fragment into competing projects that obscure the need for reorganizing society around the identification of general interests. Moreover, he embraces them as potential challengers to the extension of instrumental rationality that is destructive to social life so long as they do not falsely generalize their critique into a rejection of reason *tout court*.

Clearly, there are strong political affinities between the post-Marxist approaches of Foucault and Habermas. In many ways Habermas has a postmetaphysical, postmodern conception of politics that acknowledges the collapse of teleological guarantees for politics, rejects ontological grounding for critique, and abandons a workerist standpoint. Both Foucault and Habermas develop a politics of limits that seek a more modest conception of political change than the Marxian revolutionary tradition. Both attempt to overcome the antidemocratic legacy of Marxism and embrace the more pluralistic politics of the new social movements. Habermas is in agreement with Foucault that the nature of power in contemporary society cannot be understood solely through a critique of political economy and that it involves forms of political, administrative, and cultural control that Marx did not, and to some extent could not, analyze. Their different theories converge on the general point that the development of modernity represents the increasing domination of administrative structures over social and personal existence. As Habermas says, "The power of technical control made possible by science is extended today directly to society" (1970: 56). Habermas therefore acknowledges the validity of Foucault's insight that power involves normalization and surveillance (1987a: 362). Both break with the pretension of the theorist to know the real interests of oppressed groups. For both, the task of theory is not to impute needs and interests to the public, but rather to break the bonds stifling thought and initiate a process of critical reflection.[18] Both, therefore, promulgate versions of what Foucault calls the "specific intellectual" and reject the authoritarian assumptions of the Leninist model whereby an enlightened avant garde will lead the masses to truth. As I have argued, this also characterizes Marx's position.

But the political differences between Habermas and Foucault are substantial. Habermas acknowledges the validity of a microanalysis of power (1986: 69–70); like Marx, however, his focus is macroanalytic and he interprets modernity in terms of expanding political and economic subsystems. For Habermas, advances in power come from macrostructural forces, from the expansion of the economy and state. Foucault, in contrast, insists on the primacy of disciplinary power that originates at the micrological levels of society and is subsequently concentrated at the level of the state. Habermas' postmetaphysical orientation to theory and politics stops short of a postmodern rejection of core values and tenets of modern philosophy and politics. His emphasis on progress, his teleological conception of a historically developing rationality, his search for general interests and foundations for critique, his belief that the goal of communication is agreement and consensus, and his attempts to deepen the democratic content of bourgeois social life through an appropriation of liberal values and institutions put him at odds with Foucault and much postmodern theory.

Although Foucault in his later work lays claim to the Enlightenment tradition, he initiates a more radical break with Enlightenment values than Habermas. Where Habermas proposes an "enlightened suspicion of the enlightenment," Foucault abandons the search for universal values, the discourse of progress, and a dialectical critique of modernity that attempts to redeem the progressive content of bourgeois law and morality. Given his belief in the efficacy of knowledge and in some possibility for greater individual freedom, Foucault's pessimism does not match that of Baudrillard, who declares that all meaning has imploded in the masses (1983b), but it runs deep enough to reject normative visions and any positive conception of collective change, social justice, or the good life. Foucault's later embrace of Enlightenment critique retains links to the modern tradition, but it hardly amounts to a Habermasian theory of communicative rationality. Habermas attempts a far more positive and systematic defense of the liberal tradition than do either Marx or Foucault, both of whom dismiss the language of rights, justice, and liberty as bourgeois ideology or normalizing discourse.

Unlike Habermas, Foucault thinks that the central political objective is to break from the grip of normalization and disciplinary power and to recreate one's own identity and desiring existence in a creative, self-chosen manner. While Foucault's theoretical positions regarding the plurality of forms of power are directly compatible with a postmodern politics of new social movements, and while he himself intervened on behalf of different political groups and causes, the thrust of his political remarks is toward the highly individualized project of creative self-transformation. Foucault appropriates and redirects concepts from Greco–Roman ethics and aesthetic modernism to decenter the role of collective struggle, moral consciousness, and critical awareness in favor of individualist and aestheticized modes of being. Foucault's politics of identity, which rejects normalized identities in order to recreate one's own self and desires as different from others, sharply contrasts with Habermas' discursive politics, which emphasizes rationality and intersubjectivity.

Marx, Foucault, and Habermas all understand that power and domination engender struggle. Marx understands class struggle as the key to history, Foucault sees power and resistance as inseparable, and Habermas claims that disturbances to the lifeworld inevitably engender conflict and protest. While Marx worried about the ability of capitalism to absorb conflict and retain its ideological power over the working class, he did not relinquish the belief that capitalism was an inherently crisis-ridden system. Habermas concurs with Marx on this point and tries to develop further the concept of crisis in order to address not just economic crisis, but also political, legitimation, and motivational crises.

Despite Foucault's abstract remarks about resistance, he is extremely parsimonious in his concrete references to actual struggles, tending to paint modern disciplinary society as a totalizing, one-dimensional system that maintains near-complete control over its subjects. Foucault's work gives the impression, explicitly argued for by Luhmann and other systems theorists, that advanced modern societies are largely self-reproducing and innoculated against crises, that they are no longer held together by normative structures and intersubjective communication. Such cybernetic claims assume, as argued by both Luhmann and Foucault, the "end of the individual"—no longer the critical, autonomous actor championed by Goethe, Kant, Rousseau, and other Enlightenment theorists, but the totally conforming subject. As I have claimed, Foucault abandoned this position after paying greater attention to Greek and Enlightenment ideas.

Habermas is keenly aware that advanced capitalism is approaching a cybernetic state of self-reproduction unchallenged by critical rationality, a condition where "the steering imperatives of highly complex societies could necessitate disconnecting the formation of motives from norms capable of justification [such that] legitimation problems *per se* would cease to exist" (1975: 122). In such conditions, Habermas sees that, in Foucault's language, norms could become *solely* vehicles for normalization. But Habermas argues that these processes have *not* advanced so far as to negate individuality and preclude persistant motivational and legitimation crises.[19]

Habermas feels that as long as subjects retain vestiges of communicative rationality, norms will always require justification and capitalism will generate needs it cannot satisfy. Because of its system dysfunctions and ideological deficits, capitalism remains prone to legitimation crisis; because it has irretrievably dismantled the cultural traditions it has been dependent on and has failed to create new ones, capitalism is still vulnerable to motivation crises. "Only if motives for action no longer operated through norms requiring justification, and if personality systems no longer had to find their unity in identity-securing interpretive systems, could the acceptance of decisions without reasons become routine, that is, could the readiness to conform absolutely be precluded to any degree" (Habermas 1975: 44). Habermas finds, therefore, not only external limits to economic and technological expansion, such as cause disturbances to ecological balance, but also internal limits to socialization that result in "violation of the consistency requirements of the personality system" (41).

Unlike Habermas, Foucault fails to appreciate that all social orders, particularly those that develop past the kinship form and its blood ties, require legitimation and are subject to legitimation crisis when the systems function poorly, cannot justify asymmetrical power distribution, and cannot meet human needs. Foucault could hardly analyze legitimation and motivation crises given his initial rejection of the individual and his later failure to flesh out the psychological conditions of autonomy, to articulate a theory that would discuss human needs, values, and interests such as was developed by Maslow, Fromm, and others.[20] Foucault's work, however, is of enormous value in that it shows how normalization processes tend to destroy communicative rationality. Where Habermas does not sufficiently show how norms *also* function in a process of normalization, Foucault does not see that norms can be used to challenge and delegitimate a social order. The status of norms, in other words, is ambiguous, and neither Habermas nor Foucault adequately brings this out, although each supplies the needed corrective for the other.

Foucault's and Habermas' differing conceptions of the nature of discourse provide important contrasts for their overall political positions. While each theorist understands the centrality of language and discourse in the constitution of social reality and individual identity, as well as the direct connection between power and discourse, they diverge in their conception of the nature of communication. Where Foucault finds language to be the medium of disagreement and conflict, Habermas sees it as a vehicle for agreement and consensus, steered by an innate interest in emancipation. Habermas acknowledges social diversity, but thinks that rational discussion can nevertheless produce consensus about democracy, justice, and basic social goods. Against Habermas, Foucault sees consensus as a normalizing mechanism designed to suppress social plurality. He is in agreement with Lyotard (1984) that the telos of consensus does violence to the heterogeneity of language games and leads to social conformity.

This critique points to potential problems with the concept of consensus, but it more accurately represents the position of someone like Comte than Habermas. Given his critique of distorted forms of communication, Habermas is hardly unaware of the connection between power and language. Nor does Habermas see the ideal speech situation or the rational society as anything but values to be approached as far as possible. Unlike Foucault, however, Habermas sees the possibility of uncoupling communication from power in order to produce a rational consensus. For Habermas, the point of consensus is not to homogenize different viewpoints around specific ethical or political viewpoints, but to provide the preconditions for rational discussion and nondebilitating forms of disagreement.[21] Where Comte sought to eliminate criticism and dissent in favor of order and conformity, Habermas states that the ideal of consensus "does not exclude conflict, rather it implies those human forms through which one can survive conflicts" (1986: 126). Consensus is not a way of denying social complexity, but of coordinating it toward positive ends that are shared. The main thing that plural viewpoints need to agree on is the value of plurality itself, and creating the institutional forms that ensure it. For Habermas, the telos of agreement is only the goal of the specific language game of mutual understanding, and not the aim of all normative discourse.

Thus, Habermas claims that unity and diversity, solidarity and autonomy, rational agreement and dissent, are compatible values. He believes he can retain what is positive in the postmodern emphasis on individuality and difference, while also rectifying its deficit on community and consensus.[22] Universal values and intersubjective agreement are necessary for genuine individuality to emerge. The assumption behind Habermas' vision of social unity is that there are identifiable general interests lurking beneath the "impenetrable pluralism of apparently ultimate value orientations" (1975: 108), but which are suppressed under conditions of distorted communication. A key function of ideology is to mask particular interests as allegedly general interests, to create false general interests that advance the cause of specific private interests. Through a collective process of reflection and argumentation, social members can uncover this mystification, challenge the legitimacy of power interests, interpret their actual needs and values, and identify authentic general interests that can preserve the validity of different individual aspirations.

In this conception of discourse, the demands for sincerity and truth prevail, along with formal conditions of argumentation that allow one to raise and evaluate different claims. The telos of this process is consensus oriented around the ascertainment of a common interest, an interest to which all can assent, the intersecting point where individual and general interests overlap. No claim is legitimate unless it is advanced under conditions of distortion-free reflection and communication and is universalizable. Following the basic move of moral theorists like Kant and Rawls, Habermas seeks to eliminate personal bias and prejudice from the sphere of morality. An interest is valid only if it is generalizable, and it is generalizable only if it equally advances the interests of all rather than an individual or a minority. This requires bracketing one's own preferences, adopting the perspective of others, and formulating a claim, value, or policy that gives equal weight to all possible viewpoints. But unlike Kant's test of noncontradiction, or Rawls' veil of interests, Habermas does not simply employ a logical device for testing generalizable claims. These claims are determined instead through a collection process of inquiry and are redeemed through "discourse ethics" under conditions of undistorted communication (see Habermas 1990: 43–115).[23]

Not unlike Marx and Foucault, Habermas is well aware of the political implications of theories that lay claim to ideals of objectivity or universality. Marx claims that a core aspect of ideology is that of masking specific interests through general theories, demonstrating how bourgeois conceptions of justice or democracy mystify capitalist hegemony over the working class. Foucault attacks the norms of truth and objectivity and studies the circular relationship between power and knowledge, where power employs knowledge and knowledge is implicated in techniques of domination. He shows how humanism and discourses of truth work to ensnare individuals within normalizing regimes and values presented as universal and eternal. Habermas analyzes the interests and practical orientations informing different theories. His critique of scientism attempts to reveal the technical interest in controlling natural processes that is obscured through the rhetoric of objectivity. But while Foucault abandons the notion of general interests, and Marx redefines it from the false general standpoint of the proletariat, thereby merely resituating its ideological claims, Habermas tries to reconstruct it as the rational outcome of a public discussion process. Habermas claims that bourgeois forms of universalistic consciousness are not merely ideological, but rather are also the result of a collective learning process that can be employed toward progressive ends. Where Foucault equates universals with the logic of necessity, Habermas shows that, in his framework, they have a status of contingency, fallibility, and are context bound.

Habermas' attempt to ferret our forms of distortion, power, and manipulation that preclude autonomous action, authentic interaction, and genuine universality is commendable, but his formulation of this project is problematic. I do not doubt that there are in fact important common interests that all individuals share, such as the need for freedom, a safe community, and a clean natural environment, but it is not clear that the identification of authentic general principles can produce any concrete principles of social organization. It is hard to imagine which political, economic, cultural, and moral arrangements would be satisfactory to all social groups. General values such as freedom generate a welter of conflicting interpretations—such as one finds between Adam Smith, Bakunin, and Marx—with divergent and contradictory practical implications.

This takes us to the heart of the problem: Habermas' underestimation of political and cultural diversity and his overestimation of the efficacy of rationality. Despite his rhetorical acknowledgement of social plurality, Habermas gives too little weight to the incommensureability of different social voices. Even a social sector as small and self-contained as the Left—ranging from black nationalists to lesbian separatists to surrealist-inspired anarchists—has so far been unable to achieve unity on fundamental positions. How can one then expect to reach a general social consensus when the other political voices—including conservative fundamentalists, liberal technocrats, dixie democrats, and so on—are added to the "conversation"? To gauge the magnitude of the problem of building consensus, one need only look at the immense difficulties Gandhi and King faced in trying to build unified, nonviolent resistance to divisive, violent forms of power. Their respective national and racial movements eventually disintegrated into chaos and factionalism, with some elements practicing the very tactics of violence against which Gandhi and King had tried to unite. If the differences among various individuals and social groups run deeper than Habermas grants, then mass-based consensus is difficult if not impossible to achieve.

Moreover, if human beings are motivated more by bias, prejudice, and self-interest than by reason and concern for others, communication would continue to be distorted and consensus thwarted even under adequate—"nondistorted"—institutional conditions. Habermas has uncritically assimilated the Western tendency, from Socrates to Locke to cognitive ethics, that sees the only obstacle to truth and social harmony to be a lack of rationality, believing that truth and reason can resolve all moral conflicts. But if personal and social pathologies run deeper than Socratic dogma allows, emancipatory projects will not only have to foster communicative rationality, an important project indeed, but will also have to address human emotions, desires, fears, and insecurities, and find ways of appealing to subconscious sources of motivation in ways that do not undermine the value of individual autonomy. Unless citizens are somehow already predisposed toward argumentation, truth, and compassion for others communicative action will remain isolated and marginalized. Whatever his qualifications, Habermas' reconstruction of the ideal speech situation is far too idealized a model to comprehend human interaction: it reduces prejudice, bias, and deception to nothing more than accidental, contingent, or derivitive aspects of speech. A more accurate model, such as that developed by Goffman (1959), would address the centrality of dodging, feigning, simulation, theatricality, self-deception, and illusion in our everyday discourse, which, as Habermas acknowledges, all too rarely is sincere or motivated by a search for truth.[24] Communication need not imply understanding, just as understanding does not presuppose agreement.

Habermas is insufficiently critical of the Enlightenment claim that all value conflicts will disappear once human beings attain a rational standpoint. The compelling challenge to this position, as argued by Machiavelli, Montesquieu, along with various postmodernists, is that the different ends human beings choose are ultimately incompatible, that no single universal standard of action can settle the question of which ends are ultimately superior or best (see Berlin 1982). I do not see that Habermas has successfully refuted this skeptical claim. If the various moral ends of life are ultimately incommensureable and if consensus is difficult to attain through the identification of general interests that translate into actual social policy, then we should be prepared in many instances to accept the more modest endeavor of constructing compromises between different points of view. Habermas acknowledges the need for compromise, but sees it as involving only nongeneralizable interests and acceptable only when there is a balance of power among different parties (1975: 111–112).

The postmodern embrace of diversity and nonconformity provides a necessary counter to Habermas' idealization of social existence as a potential unified harmony of rational voices, but it falls into the opposite error of privileging individualism, difference, and antagonism over unity and solidarity.[25] It abandons the possibility that at least some conflicts can and should be harmonized through reason. The postmodern position is self-refuting since it implicitly seeks consensus over the value of dissent and plurality. Foucault's politics would seem to imply the possibility and desirability of articulating a general interest (such as defending basic human rights) and reaching a political consensus, but he subverts this notion in theory.

Despite their opposing conceptions of discourse, both Foucault and Habermas reduce a plurality of language games to a basic linguistic essence. As Wittgenstein argued, no universal theory of language can successfully capture the "general and unavoidable" presuppositions of communication on a species-wide level, because these are irreducibly plural in nature. Habermas' theory of universal pragmatics has to be relativized to apply to the language game of rational discourse itself; in this regard it is quite helpful in drawing out the presuppositions of argumentative speech as a particular language game. Rather than valorize unity or difference as a general principle, we should see that the two values are compatible, that they demand one another, and that in different contexts either difference or unity might be desired and privileged (see Best and Kellner 1991).

Postmodern theorists fetishize difference to the point where community and shared needs and interests are impossible to identify and construct. The emergence of new social movements as autonomous interests separate from a generalized working class has been extremely important, but these movements have fragmented into a cacophony of groups and subgroups, all competing for their specific claims to rights and justice. The tyranny of the fragments is as oppressive as the dictatorship of the universal. Just as ethics demands some kind of universal standpoint, social policy requires some notion of general interests.

Unlike both Marx and Habermas, Foucault at no point has a vision of a future community life, of shared goals, interests, and values. The ideal of collective social transformation is abandoned in the postmodern politics of Foucault, Lyotard, Rorty, Baudrillard, Deleuze and Guattari, and others. Foucault rejects the idea of common interests and develops a politics based on values of difference, conflict, struggle, and fragmentation. Unlike Habermas, Foucault abandons the attempt to regenerate intersubjective communication and opts instead for the aestheticization of individual modes of being.

While Habermas gives a reductionistic critique of postmodern theory, he rightly points out the regressive political implications of much postmodern theory. Through his early totalizing critique of modernity and Enlightenment rationality, Foucault forfeits a critical appropriation of the progressive achievements of modernity that allow for gains in freedom and individuality. Implicitly, his defense of critical reason requires what Habermas theorizes as a postconventional identity, but he lacks the conceptual means to historically contextualize his notion of modernity. This move follows from a conflation of cultural and social modernization processes. Unable to deepen the progressive content of bourgeois culture, many postmodern theorists can only turn to the counter-Enlightenment, Romanticism, and existentialism to valorize antirational and antimodern principles. Such theorists try to escape domination through valorizing madness, language, desire, the body, or art, and by seeking a hypostatized Other of reason. These moves stifle the rational critique of an unjust social order—precisely when it is most needed—and substitute easily coopted fragmented modes of self-expression for the collective struggles that alone can effect large-scale social transformation and personal freedom. Habermas can accomodate the postmodern appeal for new modes of desire and self-expression through defense of the aesthetic dimension of cultural modernity (1986: 59), while avoiding a debilitating aestheticism by connecting this with a communicative rationality that articulates and defends critical norms and promotes an undamaged intersubjective life.

While Foucault and Habermas advance beyond Marx in their understanding of the complexity of power and domination in the capitalist world, they fall behind him in the replacement of a systemic conception of social change with a piecemeal scheme of pragmatic reform that concedes legitimacy to the most irrational and destructive aspects of the capitalist mode of production: its profit imperative, grow-or-die logic, and centralized state apparatus. Foucault rejects radical change as being totalitarian and espouses small-scale transgressions at the individual and microlevels of society. Foucault may rightly be suspicious of large-scale, transformative programs, at least in certain forms, but he also prevents any substantive transformation of the basic dynamics of capitalism. His position is "modest" to the point of debilitating apprehension and paralysis of political vision.

Habermas' project is that of a "radical reformism" which attempts to overcome the dichotomy between reform and revolution. He renounces the ideal of a sudden, convulsive transformation of social life and instead calls for gradual extension of democractic control to the point of qualitative transformation of social life. He promotes democratic changes "even and especially if they have consequences that are incompatible with the mode of production of the established system" (Habermas 1970: 48–49). With Marx, Habermas correctly challenges the false opposition between reform and revolution, but he is hesitant and inconsistent in pursuing its consequences. At various places in his writings he sees the incompatibility between capitalism and democracy (e.g., 1973: 4), and links problems such as uncontrolled growth to the very logic of capitalism (1975: 42). Yet his political stance is at best vague on whether one should strive for a postcapitalist society and how this might be achieved. He condemns the capitalist labor market, but does not specify what to put in its place, also remaining vague as to whether he adheres to socialism or market capitialism (1986: 187).[26] Nor does Habermas, like Foucault, even contest the rule of the state itself. Marx wanted to smash the bourgeois state, but only to resurrect it in the form of a worker's state without challenging the very logic of centralization. Foucault's attack on hierarchies and "governmentalization" fails to call into question the need for a state. Habermas uncritically adopts the conservative claim that the modern lifeworld is too complex to change its centralized, bureaucratic structure in any profound way and that attempts to do so would be a worse "cure" than the disease itself (1982: 23). Habermas too quickly accomodates himself to gigantism, sprawling urbanization, and the status quo in politics and industry.

Habermas replicates the fantasy that all conflicts can be overcome through rational discussion that leaves intact the social institutions and structures that in fact *cause* irreconcilable differences between different individuals and groups. A key political implication of Habermas' vision of undistorted communication is his undervaluation of the important role of force—which need not entail violence—in bringing nonresponsive parties into a communication process.[27] As Heller notes (1982), dominating groups do not listen to reason unless forced to do so. Such force could take the form of a strike, for example, rather than violence, and its goal should be to further a process of argumentation, not to replace it.

The inadequacy of Foucault's postmodern politics and Habermas' post-Marxist politics turns on the absence of a discontinuity model at the political level. Since Marx's political vision involves a dialectic of continuity and discontinuity, a politics of appropriation and transformation, in addition to a contextualist approach that does not seek violence as a necessary tool of revolution, and a democratic conception of the intellectual's role, he does not after all advance the intoxicated, wild-eyed, apocalyptic radicalism that Foucault and Habermas fear. But Marx insists that the progressive achievements of history cannot be salvaged without their reconstruction in a postcapitalist social order that destroys the institutions and values based on anarchic growth, unimpeded accumulation, and rapacious drives for profit. Marx rightly sees that a politics of fulfillment is bankrupt without a politics of transfiguration.

Yet, ultimately, neither Marx, Foucault, nor Habermas have an adequate vision for social transformation. Each theorist has a glimpse of a potential future, but it is dim and clouded. Habermas foresees a rational community and a realm of "undisturbed intersubjectivity," Marx projects a democracy of associated producers and individual creativity, and Foucault envisions a non-normalized social order that allows for a full play of differences among individuals. Yet all lack a concrete sense of the kind of philosophical, moral, and institutional changes necessary for building a society that eliminates domination and exploitation.[28]

This concrete vision of the future requires a utopian sensibility. In the current philosophical climate, of course, the concept of utopia is less than fashionable. On Berlin's understanding (1992), utopian vision has played a crucial role throughout the history of Western thought. Berlin finds, however, that the Western utopian vision—from Plato to More and Bacon to St. Simon and Owen—has been articulated in a highly problematic form, which assumes that a perfect society can be created, that this can be accomplished through rational methods, that there is an invariant human nature, and that all conflicts can be overcome through universal assent to timeless rational laws. "All the Utopias known to us are based on upon the discoverability and harmony of objectively true ends, true for all men, at all times and places" (Berlin 1992: 211). Berlin rightly rejects this form of utopian vision as both illusory and dangerous: it projects a false optimism about the possibility for the total eradication of suffering and conflict, it is rooted in the fallacious concepts of a universal human nature and timeless rational laws, and it denies the incommensureability of values, the unresolvable conflicts over different rational conceptions of the good life. Any "utopian" attempt to end suffering and conflict through ultimate solutions and a zealous vision of the human good can only multiply the amount of suffering and conflict it seeks to eradicate.

Hence, for postmodern figures like Foucault and Lyotard, utopian schemes for an orderly and harmonious social world imply a social engineering process that eliminates heterogeneity. But clearly the postmodern critique of utopian vision is not new. Utopian schemes were seriously challenged by pluralist modern thinkers like Machiavelli, Vico, and Herder. Numerous nineteenth-century writers like Tolstoy or Baudelaire, to say nothing of twentieth-century figures like Kafka and Beckett, rejected the vision of an ideal world (Berlin 1992). Marx himself denounced all socialistic utopias that attempted dogmatically to prefigure the future. Habermas acknowledges that a utopian dimension of the concept of communicative rationality lies in his vision of undamaged intersubjectivity, but he limits it to delineating the merely formal conditions of a rational way of life—characterized by phenomena such as a universalistic moral and legal consciousness and a reflective collective identity—and does not extend it to concrete details of possible paradigmatic life forms.[29]

While dogmatic, universalistic, perfectionistic, and naively rationalistic utopian visions should be rejected, postmodernists wrongly abandon all utopian and radical visions. Given the crisis of historical imagination, utopian visions are indispensible to shattering the pessimistic or complacent sense that the present is the best or last of all possible worlds. More and more, the legitimacy of radical schemes of social change require not simply abstract, rhetorical appeals for a postcapitalist order, but a concrete vision of how things could be different in every facet of social organization, from education and health care to sexual relations and the workplace. On this point, Fourier's utopianism is more liberatory than the scientific socialism of Marx and Engels.[30] While the postmodern critique of attempts to dictate universal norms of the "good life" is well founded utopian visions, properly conceived, should stimulate, not stifle, alternative ideals and social settings, and should increase rather than reduce social plurality.

Along this line, Wolin draws a useful distinction between a strong utopianism informed by eschatological yearnings and dogmatic principles and a weak utopianism that merely seeks to change habits of thought and perception (1992: 76–77). Bookchin (1986, 1991) advocates something like a weak utopianism since he believes that utopian thought is properly concerned with the necessary preconditions of the future rather than the allegedly sufficient conditions, but he also provides some suggestive visions of a possible "post-scarcity" future. In fact, Bookchin, along with Marcuse (1969), argues that "utopian" vision is a misnomer because positive proposals for the future are based on empirical analysis of real tendencies present in history. Materialist utopian theories try to grasp present potential for human freedom or, in Bloch's terms, the "not yet" embedded in the present. Thus, we can speak, paradoxically, of a "utopian realism."

TOWARD A MULTIPERSPECTIVAL VISION

Every vision of history functions as a specific lens or optic that a theorist employs to iluminate some facet of human reality. Each perspective is both enabling, allowing a strongly focused study, and limiting, preventing consideration of other perspectives. While a theorist may utilize numerous perspectives on history, most have a privileged perspective. As should be clear by now, Marx, Foucault, and Habermas each make important and distinctive contributions to historical and social theory, but each has their particular blind spots and reductionistic tendencies.[31]

For Habermas, society reproduces itself along three different axes: labor, language, and power. We can see the work of Marx, Foucault, and Habermas, with their distinctive focuses, as contributing to a general theory of history along these lines. Marx focuses on production, technology, economics, and class as the key causal forces in history, but leaves out detailed analysis of culture, morality, language, communication, and political institutions. Habermas tries to broaden materialism to analyze both technical and practical rationality, both labor and language. He attempts to incorporate themes from the empirical, hermeneutical, and critical sciences. He develops a complex, eclectic framework that synthesizes an astonishing number of research programs, ranging from cognitive psychology to historical materialism to systems theory. This diversity, however, is employed toward an abstract, one-sided analysis of communication. Foucault concentrates on regimes of power/knowledge, microforms of power, and modes of subjectification and self-transformation. Each methodological focus — archaeology, genealogy, and ethics — represents a different perspective adopted when he became aware of limitations in his prior work. Foucault intends these perspectives to be incorporated into a coherent framework that criticizes normalizing power, but the different focuses were never successfully integrated and he largely neglects analysis of the state, the economy, and various cultural (rather than specifically moral or normative) mechanisms of control such as mass media and entertainment.

It is also instructive to compare different theories of the subject. Postmodern theories reject the essentialist view of the subject that is employed by some modern theories, but rejected by Marx and Habermas (although not wholly sucessfully). The continuist narratives of modern theory often depend on a theory of human nature, a conscious subject, or an evolving macrosubject, a unified humanity. In his archaeological works, Foucault defines his task as purging history of all anthropological influences and eliminating the category of the subject. In his early and middle works, Foucault did not so much "solve" the problem of the subject as dissolve it by merely rejecting it as an active, substantive agency. His structuralist dismissal of the subject reduces it to an empty category and essentializes it as a pure nothingness, a product of discourse and power. Instead of developing an account of ways in which subjects can influence the course of events through knowledge and conscious intervention, Foucault reifies history as a pregiven result that occurs entirely behind the backs of subjects. Rather than analyzing a dialectic of intended and unintended consequences, Foucault sees no consequences to action at all because there are no agents of action. In his later works he abandons this view to acknowledge agency and the potential for autonomy, and thereby moves closer to the kind of modern (hermeneutic or pragmatic) account of the subject given by Marx and Habermas. But Foucault's later account moves toward the individualist–voluntarist side; at no time does he adequately balance the two perspectives of structure and agency. Ultimately, he never grants the full importance of social relations for subjective freedom, and tends to define individuality and sociality in opposition to one another.

Marx and Habermas, by contrast, give a more satisfactory account of the subject, both descriptively and normatively. Rejecting Foucault's essentialist determinism, each constructs a theory of the historical constitution of the subject within evolving social networks of action and interaction. For Marx and Habermas, the individual has different values, needs, and modes of consciousness in different societies; individuals evolve with the evolution of their social forms. Hence, both see individuation as a process of socialization and differentiation, as the work of history. The rich individual requires rich forms of sociality. Against postmodernists, but in agreement with Hegel, Sartre, Mead, and others, Habermas holds that self-identity is achieved only in and through others.

From this perspective, the postmodern call for a radically free individuality is impossible given its negation of social relations and community. Postmodern theorists tend to see only the coercive aspects of "subjectification" that implode individuals into a normalized mass, and not the emancipatory aspects that differentiate the individual from others and allow for the rich aesthetic–expressive attitude postmodernists celebrate. Postmodern theorists fail to grasp progressive tendencies in history toward greater forms of freedom and individuation. Where Marx and Habermas seek to build on the achievements of bourgeois subjectivity and the whole process of history, Foucault has a nondialectical, discontinuous vision of a new subject "entirely different" than the modern subject, a "total innovation" (Foucault 1991: 122). His belated acknowledgement of the positive aspects of modern subjectivity is severed from a theory that connects historical–critical attitudes from an institutional framework and a larger appreciation of the historical development of subjectivity.

Although Marx acknowledges the reality of agency, he does not theorize it. Drawing from Piaget and Kohlberg, Habermas goes much farther than Marx or Foucault in fleshing out the psychological and moral dimensions of individual existence. His develops a detailed and comprehensive theory of the subject in the form of a theory of action. His differentiation among different types of action allows him to incorporate a distinctly Foucauldian perspective on ("strategic") action, while also going beyond the limitations of Foucault's theory, which focuses only on conflict and struggle and denies subjects an active role.

Yet while Habermas' work provides the logical space for Foucault's interpretation of action oriented to power and control, he does not fill it with the empirical detail that characterizes Foucault's work. Foucault's genealogies, therefore, provide an important contribution to a theory of strategic action and a corrective to Habermas' overly idealized focus on consensus and agreement. Contrariwise, Foucault's genealogical politics assume a theory of communicative action insofar as it requires that actors criticize validity claims and reach intersubjective agreement on the need to resist domination and create new social forms. Needless to say, Foucault does not develop an account of communicative rationality. Rather, as I have argued, he tends to subsume the model of communicative action that is implied in his work to a model of aesthetic–expressive behavior where "politics" involves isolated individuals seeking the goals of creative self-transformation.

But Foucault's genealogical emphasis on the body and Marx's early emphasis on sensuous activity help to overcome Habermas' overly abstract conception of communication and the self. There is little indication in Habermas' works that subjective being and social existence is anything beyond dispassionate logic, argumentation, and rational articulation of goals and values. Even when Habermas acknowledges the importance of art, as in the case of Peter Weiss, it is only for its potentially cognitive value.[32] As Agnes Heller observes, "Habermasian man has . . . no body, no feelings; the 'structure of personality' is identified with cognition, language, and interaction . . . one gets the impression that the good life consists solely of rational communication and that needs can be argued for without being felt" (1982: 223). While Heller's critique fails to acknowledge how Habermas incorporates sensuous and expressive forms into his conception of rationality and praxis, Habermas' overall account tends toward disembodied abstraction.[33]

Marx's emphasis on human agents as sensuous beings and Foucault's understanding of the subject as a desiring body help to correct Habermas' limited conception of agency. Foucault introduces the body into social theory through a powerful analysis of the methods of normalization and discipline. He draws the political implications, however vaguely and inadequately, that individuals need to generate new desires and modes of bodily experience in order to attain subjective freedom. Habermas' separation of rationality from desire and the body prevents him from analyzing a crucial form of power that normalizes the body and from grasping the physiological determinants of consciousness. In a regression to a pre-Freudian theory of consciousness (and Spinoza and Nietzsche before Freud), Habermas assumes that undistorted social communication media guarantee the desire for emancipation and secure the means of accomplishing it. The consequence of Habermas accepting a fuller, less abstract account of subjectivity would be accepting more contingency and heterogeneity into his theory than he allows.

We see that the different theoretical approachs of Marx, Foucault, and Habermas each provide a necessary yet limited perspective on the issue of the subject. Marx shows how subjects develop within processes of social labor; Habermas analyzes the evolution of individual being within the context of communication and the moral regulation of life; and Foucault shows how subject identities emerge through technologies of domination that constrain individual freedom. An adequate social theory requires a multiperspectival approach to agency that has the resources to analyze work, communication, and disciplinary power, while also seeing how subjective existence is historically differentiated and potentially self-constituting.

While each theory has a metatheoretical critique of totalizing epistemology in addition to a multiperspectival outlook, each succumbs to totalizing positions of one sort or another. Marx fails to differentiate adequately work and interaction, Foucault reduces rationalization and individuation to domination, and Habermas tends to reduce production to communication and communication to rational discourse. The standard view of Marx as the great totalizer and Foucault as the radical pluralist and perspectivist needs serious qualification. Just as Marx provides a complex and differentiated analysis of social change and capitalist society, Foucault has strong totalizing impulses in his archaeological and genealogical analyses of Western society. In general, modern theory is far more complex, differentiating, and critical than postmodern theory allows. Postmodern theorists themselves are totalizing in reducing the diversity of modern positions to a caricatured ideal type that embraces naive realism, teleology, essentialism, and other flawed positions. In fact, the "modern tradition" contains within it pro-, anti-, pre-, and even "post-" modern elements.

As I argue above, postmodern theory also collapses important distinctions among phenomena, such as the distinction between legitimate and illegitimate power, truth and falsehood, instrumental and critical rationality, and science or philosophy and literature. From a Habermasian point of view, postmodern theory reverts to a "mythical–magical" worldview that levels different domains of reality, the different attitudes toward them, and different validity claims. To advance their critiques of a totalizing rationality, postmodern theorists draw upon the very achievements of modernity that they try to negate, whereby forms of rationality are differentiated. Postmodern critiques operate from a postconventional stage of learning that is the result of a long historical process that they try to erase.

In contrast to Foucault, Habermas is far more sensitive to differences and distinctions. Habermas differentiates between the positive and negative aspects of modernity, among the different spheres of rationality and their distinct validity claims, among different human interests, and so on. Foucault only identifies one mode of rationality, cognitive–instrumental rationality, and reduces other dimensions to this. While Habermas can agree with Foucault and others on the negative consequences of social modernity, he wishes to reclaim the positive consequences of cultural modernity, which consists in "detaching the formal structures of reason from the semantic contents of traditional world interpretations, that is, in letting reason come apart into its different moments" (1982: 251).

In the case of all three theorists, we see that historical vision can inform practice in an emancipatory way by breaking the grip of the present, by developing a countermemory that recalls positive forms of past life and past freedoms, and by projecting the norm of human liberty into an alternative future. In continuity with Voltaire, all three believe that the purpose of history is to impart instructive truths about the world and to educate. But as critical theorists, their work transcends Voltaire in a crucial way. History for them is not a form of entertainment, an idle collection of facts, an abstract scheme of explanation, a mode of understanding past cultures, or even a means of enlightenment per se. Rather, their histories apply knowledge strategically and seek to politicize actors, to stimulate social change, and do so by calling attention to the oppressive effects of systems of power on our lives. For them, we are not unhappy simply because we are ignorant or unenlightened, but because hostile social forces exploit, alienate, and coerce us, blocking our potential for creativity, cooperation, and autonomy.

Marx's anatomy of the capitalist mode of production revealed profit, accumulation, and commodity production as the heart of the system. Marx showed how the inherent dynamics of capitalism has led to the commodification of everything natural, social, and personal in their reduction to mere exchange value. Marx had prescient insight into the commodification of culture and everyday life and the globalization of capitalism, which would transpire fully only in the twentieth century. He struggled to preserve historical knowledge in the face of deepening capitalist fetishization of history and social relationships and the positivist methods seeking universal laws of history. Yet Marx also remained mired in the assumptions of his time and did not adequately break from the economistic and scientistic logic of capitalism. He universalized the primacy of production characteristic only of capitalism throughout history; he falsely reduced multifaceted forms of power and struggle to the battle between capitalists and the working class; he was too uncritical of science, technological values, and instrumental rationality; and he failed to appreciate the ability of capitalism to manage its crisis tendencies.

Following the lead of Weber, Adorno and Horkheimer, and Marcuse, Foucault and Habermas begin where Marx left off and create a critical theory in many ways more relevant for our contempory world. They problematize what Marx took to be unproblematic, demonstrating how science, technology, and instrumental rationality have become crucial forces of domination in late modernity. In breaking from economism, without losing sight of the economic, both highlight the expanded role of science, technology, and political administration in the rationalized control of everyday life. Through his genealogies, Foucault analyzes how mechanisms of domination based on discipline and normalization pervade modern society through interlocking matrices of power/knowledge. Habermas' theory of social evolution empasizes the colonization of the lifeworld by detailing how science, technology, economic imperatives, and bureaucratic structures undermine communicative rationality and democracy. Each, therefore, uncovers important dimensions of a coercive regulation of social life that goes far beyond the fetishization of commodities described by Marx. Yet while each uncovers crucial flaws in Enlightenment theories, Foucault rejects too much of the Enlightenment and Habermas too little.

Of course the multiperspectival theory I am advocating should not be limited only to the contributions of Marx, Foucault, and Habermas. Nor am I proposing a harmonious "synthesis" of their viewpoints, since there are fundamental points of incompatibility among all three. Foucault's work in particular is a troubling ingredient to add to the pot since he rejects fundamental aspects of radical theory, including the notions of repression, alienation, mystification, emancipation, revolution, as well as the project of normative theory.[34] In general, however, I am suggesting that social theory avoid both dogmatic insulation from contemporary theoretical developments (still derided as ephemeral shifts in fashion), as well as appropriating new postmodern theories in a facile manner that assumes the bankruptcy of the modern tradition or is ignorant of a larger historical context where we find fundamental continuities between modern and postmodern theory.

TWILIGHT OF A DUALISM

> If there is an age that desparately needs the humane
> aims and the critical methods of the Enlightenment, it is
> certainly our age.
>
> —PETER GAY

At a general level, the differences among Marx, Foucault, and Habermas can be analyzed through the modern/postmodern distinction, where Marx and Habermas are paradigmatic figures of an Enlightenment tradition of thought that Foucault rejects in important ways. Both Foucault and Habermas define their work, in part, as correcting the aspects of Marx's analysis that they find to be analytically reductive and historically obsolete. While Habermas was far more critical of rationality, science, and technology than Marx, he never abandoned the core rationalist and progressivist assumptions of Marx's thought. But it is Habermas' modernist assumptions, however critically reconstructed, that Foucault rejects in order to theorize from a postmodern standpoint. Foucault eventually acknowledged the importance of critical and historical rationality, but renounced the systemic methodology of dialectics and Habermas' appeals to universal values, foundationalism, transcendental structures, and normative epistemology. As we have seen, Foucault eventually embraced some of the modern themes that had informed his work from the start. But he attempted to engage the "critico-historical attitude" of the Enlightenment in a new postmodern context that breaks with humanism and universal values. Since there are substantive premodern, modern, and postmodern elements to his work, it is misleading—and essentializing—to unqualifiably characterize Foucault as a "postmodernist"; rather, it is better to say there are important postmodern characteristics in Foucault's work that are employed toward rethinking key modern and premodern principles and values.

At the most general level, however, the differences separating Marx, Foucault, and Habermas are best characterized according to two major competing tendencies within *modern* thought: the Hegelian and the Nietzschean visions of history, the former opening the philosophical horizons of modern thought and the latter closing them. Marx and Habermas advance Hegelian visions of history that emphasize historical continuities, progressive tendencies of social development, emerging forms of rationality and subjectivity, the role of the individual within society, freedom as a social construction and relationship, and the reconciliation of conflicts and opposites. Foucault, in contrast, propounds a Nietzschean vision of history as a random succession of modes of violence and power that leaves antagonisms intact (such as between general and private interest), strives to create differences without unity, defines freedom as an individual accomplishment, attacks Enlightenment rationality, and finds no progressive movement in history. With Hegel, against Nietzsche, we must continue to be guided by the vision of reconciliation of objective and subjective worlds, of reason and freedom, of rational laws that promote both community and individual freedom. In its deconstructive impulses, however, the Nietzschean vision helps to detranscendentalize the Hegelian

262   THE POLITICS OF HISTORICAL VISION

vision of history, to curb its metaphysical proclivities, and to maintain the tension between opposing values.[35] Neither Marx nor Habermas in any case accept Hegel's belief that the owl of Minerva flies too late, that philosophy can only interpret the world retrospectively, once events have transpired and it is too late to change them. But the Nietzschean vision is still useful in its focus on the future, on the need for a revaluation of values, and on maintaining an optimistic outlook, a joyful wisdom, that is lacking in postmodern theory except as textual play divorced from life concerns.

In this context I read postmodern theory less as an absolute rupture with modern theory, irreconcilably opposed to it, than as a critical response to the problems with and failures of modern theory that can be appropriated in a positive way. The concept of "postmodern theory" is valid not in the sense of something new and radical that comes *after* modern theory, since almost all of its key ideas were anticipated or developed already in the counter-Enlightenment, critical quarters of modern theory, and in avant-garde art; it is valid also in the sense of being *against* modern theory or, more precisely, certain features of modern theory and the Western philosophical tradition. As against the modern, it represents the coalescence of previous skeptical and antirationalist currents of thought in a focused and dramatic way that seems to allow for at least a provisional use of the term "postmodern."

Modern theory challenged the dogmatic and metaphysical basis of premodern worldviews and initiated a rationalizing, secularizing movement in theory. But the modern revolution was incomplete and retained a number of metaphysical beliefs, such as in a teleology of history, natural law or rights, or an unchanging human nature. Some versions of modern theory—those of Weber, Marx, Dewey, and others—challenged foundationalism, ahistoricism, essentialism, and other problems, but did not fully overcome them, as Marx did not overcome scientism or Eurocentrism and Habermas remained mired in teleology and transcendentalism. In large part, the exhuberant optimism, simplifications, and naiveté of much modern theory must be understood against the background of stupendous advances in science, rationality, technology, and medicine, in addition to the desire to overcome the hegemony of medieval forms of ignorance, superstition, hierarchy, and religious intolerance. This crucial historical context is ignored in most postmodern critiques of Enlightenment and modern theory. In many ways, the modern rationalist tradition overcompensated for previous deficits in rationality, just as postmodern theorists frequently overcompensate for the problems in modern positions and jettison important theoretical and political advances. In Nietzsche's framework, the nihilism of postmodern theory represents the failure of the highest ideals of humanity as embodied in Enlightenment values. The "recovery of nerve"

(Gay 1969) gained by the *philosophes* against forces of oppression and ignorance led in time to a new failure of nerve registered by postmodernists who evince a renewed sense of human impotence, who display a lack of vision for social change, and who channel their energies into destroying without recreating.

Yet in his undialectical negation of postmodern theory, Habermas fails to grasp the ways in which postmodern theory itself represents an advance in a cognitive learning process. In this case, the learning involves a realization that core claims of modern philosophy and social theory are philosophically untenable and politically problematic. Postmodern theory is a radicalization of the historicizing, detranscendentalizing impulse of Enlightenment rationality. Postmodern theory represents a critical, antimetaphysical attitude—one that begins within modern theory itself—that seeks a more sophisticated and complex understanding of social and historical reality than that provided by crude modern accounts such as are epitomized by Comte and Spencer. We can therefore read postmodern theory as continuing the revolution modern theory began by criticizing the metaphysical residues in modern theory and by pushing further some of its key critical themes. Postmodern theories are effective for historicizing, localizing, concretizing, and differentiating ahistorical and overly abstract aspects of modern theory, and thus for reconstructing modern theory in more satisfactory form.

Thus, while I see the modern emphases on developmental and progressive tendencies in history, systemic interrelatedness, macroanalysis, and normative criticism on behalf of emancipatory change to be principles worth preserving, I find important value in postmodern critiques. Specifically, there are things to be learned from the postmodern critiques of linear and Eurocentric models of progress and emancipation; the emphasis on the dangers of science, technology, and rationality; the focus on historical difference, heterogeneity, and discontinuity over identity, unity, universality, and linear continuity; the substitution of contingency and indeterminancy for rigid law, determinism, and teleological guarantees; the insistence on the interpretive and constructed nature of historical narratives; the sensitivity toward the relation between power and knowledge and hence the dangers of replicating domination within critical discourses themselves; the emphasis on theory with practical and moral dimensions over esoteric abstractions; and the subsequent rejection of the universal intellectual in favor of the specific intellectual engaged in concrete struggles.

Yet we cannot understand the transition from the modern to the postmodern as itself representing a linear, unambiguous path of progress. For while postmodern theory has often advanced beyond modern theory in its critique of dogmatic assumptions and metaphysical residue clinging to secular theories, it also *regresses* behind the best aspects of modern theory by frequently adopting irrationalist, individualist, nondialectical, and cynical positions that militate against appropriating existing possibilities for social change and progress. While postmodern theories effectively deconstruct the contradictions and metaphysical tenets in modern theory, they tend toward an undialectical negation of modern theory and cannot reconstruct the contributions of modern historiography and social theory. On the rare occasions that a postmodernist attempts to develop positive ethical or political positions, he or she does not, and cannot, avoid substantive reference to the concepts and values of the modern tradition.[36]

Foucault vituperated against the "enlightenment blackmail" that forces one to take a stand either for or against rationality without adopting a critical attitude. We must also acknowledge the *postmodern blackmail* that tries to force a choice between one extreme position or another, between humanism or structuralism, objectivism or relativism, determinism or indeterminism, linear progress or aleatory movement, universalism or localism, rationalism or irrationalism. In succumbing to the black or white fallacy that denies important options to extreme positions, postmodern theorists reject as metaphysical what can be reconstructed as rational — concepts such as agency, normative foundations, or historical progress.

At the turn of the century, pragmatists like James and Dewey were already engaged in the project of seeking a middle road between allegedly opposing theories such as idealism and empiricism.[37] This project needs to be reinvigorated today, especially with regards to the opposition between modern and postmodern theory. To the extent that theory is useful for criticism and practical change, we need new theories that combine aspects of both modern and postmodern theories and that have political relevance for the contemporary era.[38] Important linkages and mediations still need to be made between explanation and interpretation, structure and agency, macro- and microanalysis, absolutism and relativism, voluntarism and determinism, universalism and nominalism, community and individuality, global and local politics, capitalism and disciplinary power, class politics and new social movements, naive optimism and cynical pessimism. As we move into the next century, we need general theories that are sensitive to differences, that are aware of the limits of abstraction, and that are grounded in specific empirical analyses, while being critical, hermeneutic, and normative in content and vision.

Rather than seeing Foucault's work, or postmodern theory in general, as a new paradigm of critical theory to be appropriated in a wholesale manner, we should see it as providing important tools for the reconstruction of modern theory. The very nature of any "post-" theoretical discourse militates against a balanced and critical dialogue between older and newer work. Rather than abandoning every fundamental aspect of modern historiography and social theory, as radical postmodernists propose, it is better to salvage and critically reconstruct modern theories in light of valuable postmodern critiques. After Voltaire, after Marx, after Foucault, and after Habermas, the projects of enlightenment and democracy remain incomplete and worth struggling for.

NOTES

1. This is an argument on behalf of the full normative import of the ideal of truth. It does not imply that isolated individuals could not make true empirical discoveries about the nature of reality, nor that even under distorted conditions of communication, true claims could not made.

2. Since the application of scientific models on history and society constitutes a category mistake, it is not surprising that positivists have failed to identify any invariant laws. There is nothing in historiography equivalent to laws of gravity or conservation. The historical "laws" propounded by positivists either have been so general and vague they become tautological or so qualified and diluted they lose explanatory force (see Leff 1969, Walsh in Gardiner 1959). The contingent, transient, and irreducibly unique character of each historical culture precludes the formation of abstract laws. In Leff's words, "There is no conceiveable principle by which [different histories] can be reduced to a common meaning and procedure, beyond being regarded as the activities of men" (1969: 4). Even hard-core positivists like Hempel have been forced to retreat to nonuniversalistic phrasings of historical "laws," seen more like tendencies or dynamics limited to specific eras.

3. Foucault is unapologetic about this approach: "After all, mathematical language since Galileo and Newton has not functioned as an explanation of nature but as a description of its processes. I don't see why non-formalised disciplines such as history should not undertake the primary tasks of description as well" (quoted in O'Farrell 1989: 58).

4. For an excellent defense of more complex causal models, see Ricoeur (1984).

5. As I argue in chapter two, however, Foucault does provide some account of the capitalist state and economy.

6. For examples of sympathetic defenses of Foucault against Habermas on this issue, see Connolly (1985), Bernstein (1992), and Dean (1994). For reasons I have already stated, I find these defenses unsuccessful.

7. Yet, the general theoretical concerns of Habermas, if not their obsessive detail, are certainly relevant to such concrete issues. The historians' debates in Germany provide a good example of the need for a theory of truth and objectivity because, otherwise, the revisionists' attempts to deny facts about the Holocaust could not be refuted.

8. Whether these similarities can apply cross-culturally or not is a different and more difficult problem and attempts to make cross-cultural moral judgments risk the danger of ethnocentric arrogance.

9. This suggestive argument is made in detail by Berlin (1992), who claims

that Vico and Herder are properly understood as pluralists not relativists because they allow for the possibility of imaginative sympathy between very different cultures through historical investigation. One need only extend this position to differences within a given society to hold open the possibility that some common ground could be found beneath the welter of conflicting values, that different visions of the good life might find points of overlap like a Venn diagram.

10. For a valuable study of Marx's retrospective method, see Ollman (1993).

11. From the fact that capitalism is the most developed of historical structures, Habermas argues, "one cannot derive a demand that 'the logic of capital' be utilized as the key to the logic of evolution. For the way in which disturbances of the reproduction process appear in capitalist economic systems cannot be generalized and transposed [unqualifiably] to other social systems" (1979: 124). For Habermas, the forces and relations of production scheme only applies to class-structured societies and kinship structures dominate prior to that time. Until the end of the mesolithic period, purposive-rational actions were intimately tied, and subordinated, to the sphere of communicative action. The separation between them occurs with the emergence of class societies and the constitution of technical knowledge deployed independent of premodern mythical and religious worldviews. " 'Traditional societies exist as long as the development of subsystems of purposive-rational action keep within the limits of the legitimating efficacy of cultural traditions" (Habermas 1970: 95).

12. For relevant quotes see an untranslated essay by Habermas, in McCarthy (1991).

13. See, for example, Carol Gilligan's critique that Piaget's categories of moral development are male biased (1982).

14. For debates on this topic see Wilson (1970) and Hollis and Lukes (1982).

15. See Marcus and Fischer (1986) and Clifford and Marcus (1986).

16. For a critique of the poststructuralist attack on the concept of totality, see Best (1988).

17. One must certainly add to this the, by human beings, increasing domination of nature, as a motivating force for new social movements.

18. See Habermas (1973: 43, 39, 40). Yet Habermas perhaps is not true to his own intention: he imputes an alleged emancipatory interest to all social members and tries to instigate social change on that basis. It seems just as logical to conclude that there is no such interest and that people are better off left completely alone by the critical theorist. Roderick underscores the tension in Habermas' position: "Habermas' 'general and unavoidable' critical standards contain the implicit danger of being imposed upon social actors who do not have the 'competencies' of their leaders. This is a subtle form of the danger faced by all 'scientific' Marxism" (1986: 166).

19. For Habermas' extended response to the end of the individual concept, see *Legitimation Crisis* (1975: 117–143).

20. For a good example of an analysis of human needs, see Fromm (1955).

21. In McCarthy's words, "Habermas's discourse theory of validity is not meant to *define* either truth or moral rightness but to offer an account of what is involved in 'redeeming' or '*justifing*' truth and rightness claims" (Hoy and McCarthy 1994: 239). Habermas seeks consensus, therefore, only on abstract matters

of procedural rationality as outlined in the ideal speech situation. "The more abstract the agreements become, the more diverse the disagreements with which we can *nonviolently* live" (Habermas 1992: 140).

22. Rajchman (1988) gives a typical misreading of Habermas on this point and is corrected by Wolin (1990). But where Wolin insists that there are no dogmatic elements in Habermas insofar as he does not seek to prescribe the content of agreement, he fails to see what Rajchman identifies as dogmatism on the formal level, where Habermas prejudges correct procedures of rationality and argumentation.

23. Hence, Habermas rejects the argument that social actors as he conceives them are abstract, since they must bring all their concrete being into the discursive situation (1986: 255).

24. Michael Ryan uncovers the potentially repressive consequences of the ideal norm of rationally transparent speech: "A speech in which error and misunderstanding, the possibility of nontruth, are purged entirely could function only by establishing absolute univocal meaning for words and by rigorously determining contexts so that a displacement of truthful meaning by a contextual shift would no longer be possible. . . . The establishing of the conditions necessary for ideal speech (as the ideal goal of the removal of all distortion) requires measures that contradict the emancipatory impulse of Habermas' project" (1982: 113).

25. Here it is instructive to compare Rorty (1989) who emphasizes values of solidarity with Foucault's more radical individualism.

26. As a marker of the current decline in radical vision, Habermas states: "I'm rather careful these days about using the expression 'emancipation' beyond the realm of biographical experiences. Rather, concepts like 'reaching understanding' and 'communicative action' have moved to the center of my thinking" (1994: 104).

27. Habermas acknowledges the phenomenon of force as the alternative to the failure of communication action (1982: 269), but he does not distinguish between different kinds of force (violent and nonviolent) and he does not see how force may be necessary to achieve communicative action in the first place.

28. Of course, no theorist can have an "adequate" vision of change that provides solutions to all problems and envisages all aspects of a new society, even if this were desirable. To refuse to speculate on the nature of the future is one thing, to lack a theory of how to build alternative values and institutions is another. Some theorists do much better than others at attempting to imagine how to get, in Bookchin's phrase, "from here to there." Bookchin's work provides an admirable example of a concrete and nondogmatic attempt to articulate political strategies and envisage new forms of social life.

29. See Habermas, (1982: 228, 262; 1984: 174; 1986: 146, 171, 210, 213). The wrong place to find utopian elements in Habermas work is in his notion of the ideal speech situation. He has explicitly stated that he upholds this only as a regulating ideal and he rejects the idealist fiction of transparent communication. Moreover, against Marx, he does not believe that it is possible in a postcapitalist order to fully integrate the economic and political subsystems into the lifeworld. Habermas claims instead that modern social orders are too complex to fully avoid partial systems (1986: 91).

30. Despite his proscriptions of utopian thinking, Marx nevertheless had at least a general vision of what communist society and its values might be like. A key aspect of his vision of the future projected a society based on creative activity rather than alienated labor, on a shortened work day, and on the well-rounded development of individuals. For details, see Ollman (1979: 48–98).

31. For further analysis and application of the concept of multiperspectivalism, see Best and Kellner (1991).

32. Yet, as Jay notes (1986), Habermas also realizes the limitations of communicative rationality and sees art as crucial to the human quest for happiness.

33. The narrow and abstract character of Habermas' theory of communication can be illuminated through a comparison with someone like Dewey, who developed a radical historicist position and who understood communication as a multifaceted process involving boldily senses, emotions, and feelings of empathy, and not merely written and spoken symbols (see Antonio and Kellner 1992).

34. Perhaps the best treatment of this issue is Rajchman (1985).

35. For example, the metaphysical tendencies in Marx's "melting vision" of the history (Berman 1982) of social reality is powerful and profound, but it inexplicably solidifies in his vision of a future communist society that has resolved complex social, cultural, psychological, and philosophical differences into a stable society no longer beset by conflict and contradiction. These problems allegedly disappear with the destruction of their material basis. It is with such a position in mind that we can better appreciate Habermas' insistence on "system complexity" or Weber's analysis of the autonomy of social rationalization dynamics. No different from Hegel, Marx brings history to a premature close. Marx has not adequately shed the rationalist faith of the Enlightenment that human differences are ultimately commensurable; he has simply relocated its basis from rational moral principles to rational social institutions. While there should be no doubt that a just and egalitarian social order would eliminate many debilitatiating and unnecessary forms of human conflict, no one social order, however utopian, can satisfy the needs and values of all its citizens or eliminate the stubborn and irreducible heterogeneity of values.

36. For an excellent illustration of this aporia, see McCarthy's analysis (1990) of Derrida's efforts to construct a positive ethics or politics.

37. For a superb analysis of this project and its politics, see Kloppenberg (1986).

38. Fortunately, there are many examples of such an approach and this trend seems to be growing. See Wolin (1992), Bernstein (1992), and Best and Kellner (1991).

ECOLOGY AND
THE END OF HISTORY

History is a nightmare from which we are trying to awaken.
　　　　　　　　　　　　　　— JAMES JOYCE

We are still a curse on natural evolution, not its fulfillment.
　　　　　　　　　　　　　　— MURRAY BOOKCHIN

There is a widespread belief today that Marxism, radical social theory, and the metanarratives of the Enlightenment are in shambles and should be relegated to the storehouse of historical errors and myths. A major aspect of the postmodern outlook is extreme skepticism toward the ideals of revolution, emancipation, freedom, rationality, truth, utopia, normative justification, and progress. Within this climate the ideological heartbeat of Marxism has been flatlined into a stasis that signifies coma or death. Any declaration today that history is tending toward communism, that the growth of the productive forces is bringing liberation, or that the working class is the subject of history is met with justifiable laughter. The specter of communism has been replaced by the specter of fascism, universalized capitalism, social engineering, global warfare, and ecological collapse.

　　Liberalism too is a moribund ideology. Under the hegemony of conservative ideologies of the last two decades, in which George Bush's sneers turned liberalism into a dirty "L-word" that Michael Dukakis and other spineless democrats could not utter, the classic tradition of Mill and others has mutated into a laissez-faire economics with strong Social Darwinian overtones that defends only the freedom to accumulate wealth. With the boundaries of political discourse pushed so far to the right, liberalism is conflated with socialism and both are rejected as foreign to the values of "mainstream America" (as underscored by Newt Gingrich's smear of Bill Clinton as a "countercultural McGovernite"). One thing the liberal and radical traditions have in common is that their metanarratives have met the same fate: the utopia of an enlightened, rational, free society has become the dystopia of institutionalized domination. What we witness today is not simply a justifiable skepticism toward modern visions of progress and freedom, but a bitter cynicism that renounces the best aspects of the Enlightenment and legitimates narcissism and quietism. Ours is an age devoid of emancipatory vision.

In numerous quarters of modern and postmodern theory we have heard siren songs of the end of history Claims of the end of history are as old as the apocalyptic consciousness itself. As J. D. Bury notes, "at all times men have found a difficulty in picturing how the world could march onward ages and ages after their own extinction. And this difficulty has prejudiced their views" (1973: 218). In our current environmental crisis, however, such a difficulty seems justified for the first time. The only potentially valid meaning the end of history has today is the end of *homo historicus,* the literal ending of human life, if not through nuclear annihilation, then through the collapse of the earth as an inhabitable ecosystem. If the end of history is near, it is the result of the triumph of history, the Pyrrhic victory of human control over nature. The "humanization of nature" celebrated by Marx has developed to the inconceivable point that human beings have begun to destroy the protective shield of ozone and have thereby started a disastrous process of global warming that is only one facet of systemic environmental degradation.

The dual sources of our current crisis lie in the modern scientific worldview, which has deep roots in the logocentric tradition of Western thought beginning with Plato and Aristotle, and in the capitalist economic system with its inexorable growth imperative. Together, the conceptual objectification of nature as a machine and the practical exploitation of nature as a resource for private profit have overdetermined the possibility of ecological collapse. The modern ideal of progress has taken a bad beating in this century of global wars, concentration camps, genocide, ecological catastrophes, and nuclear annihilation, but it is this ideal itself that has informed the manifold catastrophes of modern life. As developed by its main architects—Descartes, Bacon, Smith, Locke, and others—progress has been defined principally in terms of untrammeled industrial growth, unlimited economic expansion, and uncompromising technical control over "dumb nature."

If the forms of life inhabiting this planet and the earth's natural "resources" are to be sustained beyond the next few decades, this concept of progress, the worldview to which it belongs, and the economic and political systems it informs, will have to be dismantled. Perversely, we have in effect defined progress as the alienation of humans from nature, the dependency of culture on ever greater quantities of resources and energy, the creation of massive bureaucratic structures that rule over individuals, the increase in hitherto unknown diseases such as cancer and heart disease, the production of increasingly lethal technologies of war and destruction, the advance of ideological control over the human mind, and the ruination of the environment.

Yet, rather than renounce the notion of progress as intrinsically pernicious, we should reconstruct it in a rational and sane form that can guide our vision of a better world. The concept of progress can legitimately involve growth in instrumental knowledge and technical reason, but it can no longer abstract such advances from the evolution of moral–practical reason. The social and ecological crisis in global capitalism today can be traced to the fact that there has been immense progress in the technical realm without parallel achievements in communicative competence, moral consciousness, and democracy. Such "progress," as Martin Luther King observed, has created a state where misguided men control guided missiles.

Social theory has to begin examining the relationship between the domination of human beings and nature. As Murray Bookchin has argued for decades, the hierarchical relationships within the human realm and the human endeavor to dominate nature are interconnected. Marx's work is profoundly ambiguous with respect to ecology. There is a productivist ethos that seeks the mastery of nature, but there is also a critique of the destruction of nature through capitalist industry and a philosophical naturalism that sees human beings as natural beings while seeking to overcome the contradiction between humanity and nature. This is a Hegelian move that can be interpreted as reintegrating human beings into nature in a harmonious, nonantagonistic, differentiated way.[1] If ecological vision is dim in Marx, it is blind in postmodern theory. Postmodern theories see human beings as embedded in systems of semiotics, technology, and social power, but not in the natural world; they lack a philosophical anthropology and an ecological ethics, to the point that there is almost no reference to ecology in any of the major postmodern thinkers.[2] Foucault's notion of power, for example, is applied only to interhuman relationships. The focus on the domination of nature inherent in Western rationality that characterizes Adorno and Horkheimer's *The Dialectic of Enlightenment,* a text that has helped to generate a postmodern mood, has not been pursued by postmodern thinkers.

A key virtue of Habermas' work is that it emphasizes the gains in moral–practical learning processes as indispensible preconditions for historical progress, and thereby overcomes the reified technocratic outlook of modernity. But Habermas himself does not sufficiently call into question the very idea of "cognitive–instrumental *mastery* [my emphasis] of natural processes" to which he makes such easy reference. Despite the lead of earlier Frankfurt School theorists and his own critique of a domineering egological reason, Habermas too fails to take an ecological turn. Advances in moral–practical learning must include not only gains in communicative rationality, but also an ecological sensibility that overturns the dualism of culture and nature. On Habermas' account, advances in moral–practical reasoning involve the gradual separation of the ego from its natural and social environment in order to develop a postconventional, critical attitude. Yet this process of differentiation and separation has developed to the point that the ego is totally divorced and alienated from other species and the natural conditions of life.

Habermas' claim that the postconventional stage of ego development is the last stage in moral development legitimates the domineering sensibility of Descartes and Bacon as the summit of human consciousness. The next logical stage in moral development that Habermas bypasses in his cognitive psychology must involve the overcoming of anthropocentrism, speciesism, and the dualism of culture/nature. As Bookchin warns us, however (1991), the dialectical unity of humanity and nature must be a mediated unity, eschewing the reversion to a reductionistic worldview that collapses important differences between human beings and other forms of life. It must be premised on developing a new ecological vision where human beings learn to see themselves as members of a vast biotic community and assume responsibility for maintaining nature and its diverse life-forms. But Habermas can only imagine the unity of internal and external nature as a regression to enchanted, animistic thinking, rather than as a differentiated unity where human beings interact harmoniously with their natural environment.

In order for this shift to occur, the modern worldview based on values of control, domination, cold "objectivity" centralization, competition, and separation must give way to a new worldview informed by alternative values of yielding, empathy, decentralization, cooperation, unity, and balance. Such a paradigm shift would truly merit the designation of a *post-modern* worldview or a genuine "age of Enlightenment." Resources for this shift can be found not only in the cultural traditions of the East, where some ecologists locate them (see Devall and Sessions 1985), but also in the dialectical traditions of the West (see Bookchin 1995).

Far from living in a lost or frozen moment, stranded at the end of history, we now stand at a crucial historical crossroad where what we do, or fail to do, will decide the fate of all future life on this planet. Our futures lie open before us, but neither conservativism, liberalism, nor Marxism, can guide us out of the current impasse. Neither classical forms of modern social theory nor postmodern social theories have generated the paradigms needed for developing a radically different alternative to the mechanistic and anthropocentric modern worldview that deeply informs even "radical" theories. Recent theories of postmodern science have made progress in this area, but they have failed to develop the critical social theory necessary for ecological visions to have practical relevance or political import (see Best 1991b).

Social change today demands a radical ecological vision and a politics that seeks the regeneration of nature through the reconstruction of society along ecological lines. An uncompromising ecological politics challenges the fundamental logic of the global system based on profit, growth, accumulation, and the manipulation of needs. With Marx, we must continue to envision the end of one kind of history — organized around hierarchy, exploitation, and alienation — and the beginning of another, based on equality, freedom, democracy, and individuality. But the new vision requires not only that we be citizens within a reinvigorated polis, but also responsible participants within the ecosphere. Human history can only advance through a new relationship to the natural world from which it originated.

NOTES

1. For arguments that Marx's vision of history is fundamentally antiecological, see Balbus (1982) and Clark (1989).

2. To my knowledge, the only "postmodern" text that deals with ecological issues, and only perfunctorily at that, is Guattari and Negri (1990).

BIBLIOGRAPHY

Adamson, Walter (1985). *Marx and the Disillusionment of Marxism.* Berkeley: University of California Press.

Adorno, Theodor W. (1973). *Negative Dialectics.* London: Routledge.

Adorno, Theodor W., and Horkheimer, Max (1972). *Dialectic of Enlightenment.* New York: Continuum.

Alford, C. Fred (1985). *Science and the Revenge of Nature: Marcuse and Habermas.* Tampa and Gainesville: University of Florida Press.

Althusser, Louis (1979). *For Marx.* London: New Left Books.

Althusser, Louis, and Balibar, Etienne (1979). *Reading Capital.* London and New York: Verso.

Anderson, Perry (1979). *Lineages of the Absolute State.* London and New York: Verso.

Anderson, Perry (1984). *In the Tracks of Historical Materialism.* London and New York: Verso Books.

Antonio, Robert, and Kellner, Douglas (1992). "Communication, Modernity, and Democracy in Habermas and Dewey." *Symbolic Interaction,* 15(3): 227–297.

Antonio, Robert, and Kellner, Douglas (1994). "Modernity and Critical Social Theory: The Limits of the Postmodern Critique." In David Dickens and Andrea Fontana (eds.), *Postmodern Social Theory,* pp. 127–152. Guilford Press.

Armstrong, Timothy J. (ed. and trans.) (1992). *Michel Foucault: Philosopher.* New York: Routledge.

Balbus, Isaac D. (1982). *Marxism and Domination.* Princeton, NJ: Princeton University Press.

Baudrillard, Jean (1975). *The Mirror of Production.* St. Louis: Telos Press.

Baudrillard, Jean (1983a). *Simulations.* New York: Semiotext(e).

Baudrillard, Jean (1983b). *In the Shadow of the Silent Majorities.* New York: Semiotext(e).

Baudrillard, Jean (1984). "On Nihilism." *On the Beach,* 6(Spring): 38–39.

Baudrillard, Jean (1987). *Forget Foucault.* New York: Semiotext(e).

Baudrillard, Jean (1988). "The Year 2000 Has Already Happened." In Arthur Kroker and Marilouise Kroker (eds.), *Body Invaders: Panic Sex in America,* pp. 35–44. Montreal: The New World Perspectives.

Baynes, Kenneth, Bohman, James, and McCarthy, Thomas (eds.) (1987). *After Philosophy: End or Transformation.* Cambridge, MA: MIT Press.

Becker, Carl L. (1964). *The Heavenly City of the Eighteenth-Century Philosophers.* New Haven and London: Yale University Press.

Benhabib, Seyla (1986). *Critique, Norm, and Utopia: A Study in the Foundations of Critical Theory.* New York: Columbia University Press.

Berlin, Isaiah (1957). *Historical Inevitability.* Oxford, England: Oxford University Press.

Berlin, Isaiah (1982). *Against the Current.* New York: Penguin Books.

Berlin, Isaiah (1992). *The Crooked Timber of Humanity.* New York: Vintage Books.

Berman, Marshall (1982). *All That is Solid Melts Into Air.* New York: Simon and Schuster.

Bernauer, James (1992). "Beyond Life and Death: On Foucault's Post-Auschwitz Ethic." In Armstrong (1992), pp. 260–279.

Bernstein, Richard (1985). *Philosophical Profiles: Essays in a Pragmatic Mode.* Cambridge: Polity Press.

Bernstein, Richard (1992). "Foucault: Critique as Philosophical Ethos." In Axel Honneth et al. (eds.), *Philosophical Interventions in the Unfinished Project of Enlightenment,* pp. 280–310. Cambridge, MA: MIT Press.

Best, Steven (1988). "After the Catastrophe: Postmodernism and Hermeneutics." *Canadian Journal of Political and Social Theory,* Vol. 12 (no. 3): 87–100.

Best, Steven (1991). "Chaos and Entropy: Metaphors in Postmodern Science and Social Theory." *Science as Culture, #11:* 188–226.

Best, Steven, and Kellner, Douglas (1991). *Postmodern Theory: Critical Interrogations.* New York: Guilford Press.

Blumenberg, Hans (1983). *The Legitimacy of the Modern Age.* Cambridge, MA: MIT Press.

Bologh, Roslyn Wallach (1979). *Dialectical Phenomenology: Marx's Method.* Boston and London: Routledge, and Kegan Paul.

Bookchin, Murray (1982). "Finding the Subject: Notes in Whitebook and 'Habermas LTD.' " *Telos, #52*(Summer): 78–98.

Bookchin, Murray (1986). *Post-Scarcity Anarchism.* Montreal: Black Rose Books.

Bookchin, Murray (1991). *The Ecology of Freedom: The Emergence and Dissolution of Hierarchy.* Montreal: Black Rose Books.

Bookchin, Murray (1995). *The Philosophy of Social Ecology: Essays on Dialectical Naturalism.* Montreal: Black Rose Books.

Breisach, Ernst (1983). *Historiography: Ancient, Medieval, and Modern.* Chicago: University of Chicago Press.

Brown, Richard Harvey (1992). "Social Science and Society as Discourse: Toward a Sociology for Civic Competence." In Seidman and Wagner (1992), pp. 223–243.

Buckle, Thomas (1973). "General Introduction" to *The History of Civilization in England.* In Stern (1973), pp. 121–137.

Bury, J. D. (1973). "The Science of History." In Stern (1973), pp. 209–223.

Butterfield, Herbert (1957). *Origins of Modern Science: 1300–1800.* New York: Free Press.

Calhoun, Craig (1992). "Culture, History, and the Problem of Specificity in Social Theory." In Seidman and Wagner (1992), pp. 244–288.

Clark, John P. (1989). "Marx's Inorganic Body." *Environmental Ethics,* vol. 2 (#3): 243–258.

Cleaver, Harry (1979). *Reading Capital Politically.* Austin: University of Texas Press.

Cleaver, Harry (1992). "The Inversion of Class Perspective in Marxian Theory: From Valorisation to Self-Valorisation." In *Open Marxism,* Vol II, ed. Werner Bonefeld, Richard Gunn, and Kosmas Psychopedis, pp. 106–144. London: Pluto Press.

Clifford, James, and Marcus, George E. (eds.) (1980). *Writing Culture: The Poetics and Politics of Ethnography.* Berkeley: University of California Press.

Cohen, G. A. (1978). *Karl Marx's Theory of History: A Defense.* Princeton, NJ: Princeton University Press.

Collingwood, R. G. (1956). *The Idea of History.* Oxford: Oxford University Press.

Connoly, William E. (1985). "Taylor, Foucault, and Otherness." *Politcial Theory, 13*(August): 365–375.

Comte, Auguste (1973). *The Catechism of Positive Religion.* Clifton, NJ: Augustus M. Kell Publishers.

Comte, Auguste (1974). *The Essential Comte,* ed. S. Andreski. New York: Barnes and Noble.

Comte, Auguste (1988). *Introduction to Positive Philosophy.* Indianapolis and Cambridge: Hackett Publishing Co. Inc.

Debord, Guy (1983). *The Society of the Spectacle.* Detroit: Red and Black Press.

Debord, Guy (1990). *Comments on the Society of the Spectacle.* London and New York: Verso.

Dean, Mitchell (1994). *Effective and Critical Histories: Foucault's Methods and Historical Sociology.* London and New York: Routledge.

Deleuze, Gilles, and Guattari, Felix (1983). *Anti-Oedipus: Capitalism and Schizophrenia.* Minneapolis: University of Minnesota Press.

Deleuze, Gilles, and Guattari, Felix (1987). *A Thousand Plateaus.* Minneapolis: University of Minnesota Press.

Devall, Bill, and Sessions, George (1985). *Deep Ecology: Living as if Nature Matters.* Salt Lake City: Peregrine Smith Books.

Dewey, John (1979). *The Quest for Certainty.* New York: Paragon.

Dilthey, Wilhelm (1962). *Pattern and Meaning in History: Thoughts on History and Society,* ed. H. P. Rickman. New York: Harper and Row.

Doerner, Klaus (1981). *Madmen and the Bourgeoisie: A Social History of Insanity and Psychiatry.* Oxford: Blackwell.

Dreyfus, Hubert L. (1894). "Beyond Hermeneutics: Interpretation in Late Heidegger and Recent Foucault." In Gary Shapiro and Alan Sica (eds.), *Hermeneutics,* pp. 66–83. Amherst, MA: University of Massachusetts Press.

Dreyfus, Hubert L., and Rabinow, Paul (1982). *Michel Foucault: Beyond Structuralism and Hermeneutics.* Chicago: University of Chicago Press.

Eiseley, Loren (1958). *Darwin's Century: Evolution and the Men Who Discovered It.* New York: Anchor.

Elliot, George (1986). The Odyssey of Paul Hirst," *New Left Review, 159:* 81–105.

Engels, Frederick (1976). *Anti-Duhring.* New York: International Publishers.

Eribon, Didier (1991). *Michel Foucault.* Cambridge: Harvard University Press.

Featherstone, Mike (1988). "In Pursuit of the Postmodern," *Theory, Culture, and Society,* vol. 5 (nos. 2–3): 195–216.

Fleischer, Helmut (1973). *Marxism and History.* London: Allen Lane.

Foster, Hal (ed.) (1983). *The Anti-Aesthetic: Essays on Postmodern Culture.* Port Townsend, WA: Bay Press.

Foucault, Michel (1972). *The Archaeology of Knowledge.* New York: Pantheon.

Foucault, Michel (1973a). *Madness and Civilization.* New York: Vintage.

Foucault, Michel (1973b). *The Order of Things.* New York: Vintage.

Foucault, Michel (1975). *The Birth of the Clinic.* New York: Vintage.

Foucault, Michel (1977). *Language, Counter-Memory, Practice.* Ithaca, NY: Cornell University Press.

Foucault, Michel (1979). *Discipline and Punish.* New York: Vintage.

Foucault, Michel (1980a). *Power/Knowledge.* New York: Pantheon.

Foucault, Michel (1980b). *The History of Sexuality.* New York: Vintage.

Foucault, Michel (1980c). *Herculine Barbin, Being the Recently Discovered Memoirs of a Nineteenth Century French Hermaphrodite.* New York: Pantheon.

Foucault, Michel (1982a). "The Subject and Power." In Dreyfus and Rabinow (1982), pp. 208–226.

Foucault, Michel (1982b). "On the Genealogy of Ethics." In Dreyfus and Rabinow (1982), pp. 229–252.

Foucault, Michel (1983). "Preface." In Deleuze and Guattari (1983), pp. xi–xiv.

Foucault, Michel (1984). "What is Enlightenment?" In Paul Rabinow (ed.), *The Foucault Reader,* pp. 32–50. New York: Pantheon.

Foucault, Michel (1986). *The Use of Pleasure.* New York: Vintage.

Foucault, Michel (1988a). *The Care of the Self.* New York: Vintage.

Foucault, Michel (1988b). *The Final Foucault,* ed. James Bernauer and David Rasmussen. Cambridge, MA: MIT Press.

Foucault, Michel (1988c). "Technologies of the Self." In *Technologies of the Self,* ed. Luther M. Martin, Huck Gutman, and Patrick H. Hutton, pp. 16–49. Amherst, MA: University of Massachusetts Press.

Foucault, Michel (1988d). *Michel Foucault: Politics, Philosophy, Culture,* ed. Lawrence D. Kritzman. New York: Routledge.

Foucault, Michel (1989a). *Foucault Live.* New York: Semiotext(e).

Foucault, Michel (1989b). "Introduction," *The Normal and the Pathological,* pp. 7–24. New York: Zone Books.

Foucault, Michel (1991). *Remarks on Marx.* New York: Semiotext(e).

Foucault, Michel, and Sennet, Richard (1982). "Sexuality and Solitude." In D. Rieff (ed.), *Humanities in Review,* vol. 1, pp. 3–21. London: Cambridge University Press.
Fromm, Erich (1955). *The Sane Society.* New York: Henry Holt.
Fukuyama, Francis (1992). *The End of History and the Last Man.* New York: The Free Press.
Gardiner, P (ed.) (1959). *Theories of History.* Oxford: Oxford University Press.
Gay, Peter (1966). *The Enlightenment: An Interpretation: The Rise of Modern Paganism.* New York: Norton.
Gay, Peter (1969). *The Enlightenment: An Interpretation: The Science of Freedom.* New York: Norton.
Geertz, Clifford (1983). *Local Knowledge.* New York: Basic Books.
Germino, Dante (1972). *Machiavelli to Marx: Modern Western Political Thought.* Chicago: University of Chicago Press.
Giddens, Anthony (1981). *A Contemporary Critique of Historical Materialism.* Berkeley: University of California Press.
Gilbert, Alan (1981). *Marx's Politics: Communists and Citizens.* New Brunswick, NJ: Rutgers University Press.
Gilligan, Carol (1982). *In a Different Voice: Psychological Theory and Women's Development.* Cambridge, MA: Harvard University Press.
Goffman, Erving (1959). *Presentation of Self in Everyday Life.* Garden City, NY: Anchor.
Gouldner, Alvin W. (1980). *The Two Marxisms.* New York: Oxford University Press.
Graff, Gerald (1973). "The Myth of the Postmodernist Breakthrough." *Triquarterly, 26:* 383–417.
Griffin, David Ray (ed.) (1988a). *The Re-enchantment of Science: Postmodern Proposals.* Albany: State University of New York.
Griffin, David Ray (ed.) (1988b). *Spirituality and Science: Postmodern Visions.* Albany: State University of New York.
Guattari, Felix, and Negri, Toni (1990). *Communists Like Us.* New York: Semiotext(e).
Gutting, Gary (1989). *Michel Foucault's Archaeology of Scientific Reason.* Cambridge, England: Cambridge University Press.
Habermas, Jürgen (1970). *Toward a Rational Society: Student Protest, Science, and Politics.* Boston: Beacon Press.
Habermas, Jürgen (1971). *Knowledge and Human Interests.* Boston: Beacon Press.
Habermas, Jürgen (1973a). *Theory and Practice.* Boston: Beacon Press.
Habermas, Jürgen (1973b). "A Postscript to *Knowledge and Human Interests.*" *Philosophy and the Social Sciences, 3:* 157–189.
Habermas, Jürgen (1975). *Legitimation Crisis.* Boston: Beacon Press.
Habermas, Jürgen (1976). "History and Evolution." *Telos, #39:* 5–44.
Habermas, Jürgen (1979). *Communication and the Evolution of Society.* Boston: Beacon Press.

Habermas, Jürgen (1981). "Modernity versus Postmodernity." *New German Critique,* 22: 3–14.

Habermas, Jürgen (1982). "A Reply to my Critics." In Thompson and Held (1982), pp. 219–283.

Habermas, Jürgen (1983). "Modernity: An Incomplete Project." In Foster (1983), pp. 3–15.

Habermas, Jürgen (1984). *Theory of Communicative Action,* Vol. 1. Boston: Beacon Press.

Habermas, Jürgen (1986). *Habermas: Autonomy and Solidarity,* ed. Peter Dews. London: Verso.

Habermas, Jürgen (1987a). *Lectures on The Philosophical Discourse of Modernity.* Cambridge, MA: MIT Press.

Habermas, Jürgen (1987b). "Taking Aim at the Heart of the Present." In Hoy (1987), pp. 103–108.

Habermas, Jürgen (1987c). *Theory of Communicative Action,* Vol. 2. Boston: Beacon Press.

Habermas, Jürgen (1989a). *The Structural Transformation of the Public Sphere.* Cambridge, MA: MIT Press.

Habermas, Jürgen (1989b). *The New Conservatism.* Cambridge, MA: MIT Press.

Habermas, Jürgen (1990). *Moral Consciousness and Communicative Action.* Cambridge, MA: MIT Press.

Habermas, Jürgen (1992). *Postmetaphysicial Thinking: Philosophical Essays.* Cambridge MA: MIT Press.

Habermas, Jürgen (1994). *Jürgen Habermas: The Past as Future: Interviewed by Michael Haller.* Lincoln and London: University of Nebraska Press.

Hacking, Ian (1979). "Michel Foucault's Immature Science." *Nous, 13:* 39–51.

Hadot, Pierre (1992). "Reflections on the Notion of 'the Cultivation of the Self.' " In Armstrong (1992), pp. 225–232.

Hampson, Norman (1968). *The Enlightenment: An Evaluation of its Assumptions, Attitudes, and Values.* Middlesex, England: Pelican Books.

Hawthorn, Geoffrey (1987). *Enlightenment and Despair: A History of Social Theory.* Cambridge, England: Cambridge University Press.

Hempel, Carl (1942). "The Function of General Laws in History." *Journal of Philosophy, #39,* 35–48.

Heller, Agnes (1982). "Habermas and Marxism." In Thompson and Held (1982) pp. 21–41.

Hertsgaard, Mark (1989). *On Bended Knee.* New York: Schocken.

Hindess, Barry, and Hirst, Paul (1975). *Pre-Capitalist Modes of Production.* London: Routledge & Kegan Paul.

Hindess, Barry, and Hirst, Paul (1977). *Modes of Production and Social Formation: An Auto-Critique of Pre-Capitalist Modes of Production.* London: Macmillan.

Hirst, Paul (1985). *Marxism and Historical Writing.* London: Routledge, & Kegan Paul.

Hollis, Martin, and Lukes, Steven (eds.) (1982). *Rationality and Relativism.* Cambridge, MA: MIT Press.

Honneth, Axel (1982). "Work and Instrumental Action." *New German Critique,* #26(Summer): 31–54.

Honneth, Axel (1985). "An Aversion Against the Universal." *Theory, Culture, and Society,* vol. 2, (no. 3): 147–157.

Honneth, Axel (1991). *The Critique of Power: Reflective Stages in a Critical Social Theory.* Cambridge, MA: MIT Press.

Hook, Sidney (1933). *Towards the Understanding of Karl Marx.* New York: John Day.

Hoy, David Couzens (1986). *Foucault: A Critical Reader.* Oxford and New York: Basil Blackwell.

Hoy, David Couzens (1988). "Foucault: Modern or Postmodern?" In Jonathan Arac (ed.), *After Foucault: Humanistic Knowledge, Postmodern Challenges,* pp. 12–41. New Brunswick, NJ: Rutgers University Press.

Hoy, David Couzens, and McCarthy, Thomas (1994). *Critical Theory.* Oxford and Cambridge: Blackwell.

Hume, David (1955). *Enquiries Concerning the Human Understanding and Concerning the Principles of Morals,* ed. L. A. Selby-Bigge. Oxford: Claredon Press.

Huyssen, Andreas (1986). *After The Great Divide: Modernism, Mass Culture, Postmodernism.* Bloomington and Indianapolis: Indiana University Press.

Jameson, Fredric (1991). *Postmodernism, or the Cultural Logic of Late-Capitalism.* Durham: Duke University Press.

Jay, Martin (1986). "Habermas and Modernism." In Richard Bernstein (ed.), *Habermas and Modernity,* pp. 125–139. Cambridge, MA: MIT Press.

Keane, John (1975). "On Tools and Language: Habermas on Work and Interaction." *New German Critique,* #6(Fall): 82–100.

Kellner, Douglas (1983). "Science and Method in Marx's *Capital.*" *Radical Science Journal,* #13: 39–54.

Kellner, Douglas (1984). *Herbert Marcuse and the Crisis of Marxism.* Berkeley: University of California Press.

Kellner, Douglas (1988). "Postmodernism as Social Theory: Some Problems and Challenges." *Theory, Culture, and Society,* vol. 5 (nos. 2–3): 239–270.

Kellner, Douglas (1992). *The Persian Gulf TV War.* Boulder, CO: Westview Press.

Kelly, Michael (1982). *Modern French Marxism.* Baltimore: Johns Hopkins University Press.

Kelly, Michael (ed.) (1994). *Critique and Power: Recasting the Foucault/Habermas Debate.* Cambridge, MA: MIT Press.

Kloppenberg, James T. (1986). *Uncertain Victory: Social Democracy and Progressivism in European and American Thought, 1870–1920.* Oxford and New York: Oxford University Press.

Kroker, Arthur, and Cook, David (1986). *The PostModern Scene: Essays in Excremental Culture.* New York: St. Martin's Press.

Laclau, Ernesto, and Mouffe, Chantal (1985). *Hegemony and Socialist Strategy: Toward a Radical Democratic Politics.* London: Verso.

Laclau, Ernesto (1988). "Politics and the Limits of Modernity." In Andrew Ross, (ed.), *Universal Abandon,* pp. 63–82. Minneapolis: University of Minnesota Press.

Larrain, Jorge (1986). *A Reconstruction of Historical Materialism.* London: Allen and Unwin.

Leff, Gordon (1969). *History and Social Theory.* New York: Anchor.

Lefort, Claude (1978). "Marx: From One Vision of History to Another." *Social Research, 45*(4): 615–666.

Lenin, V. I. (1981). *Philosophical Notebooks,* Vol. 38. *Collected Works.* Moscow: Progress Publishers.

Lévi-Strauss (1966). *The Savage Mind.* Chicago: University of Chicago Press.

Little, Daniel (1986). *The Scientific Marx.* Minneapolis: University of Minnesota Press.

Löwith, Karl (1949). *Meaning in History.* Chicago: University of Chicago Press.

Lukács, Georg (1971). *History and Class Consciousness.* Cambridge, MA: MIT Press.

Lyotard, Jean-Francois (1984). *The Postmodern Condition.* Minneapolis: University of Minnesota Press.

Macey, David (1993). *The Lives of Michel Foucault.* New York: Pantheon Books.

Manicas, Peter (1987). *A History and Philosophy of the Social Sciences.* Oxford: Basil Blackwell.

Marcus, George E., and Fischer, Michael M. J. (1986). *Anthropology as Cultural Critique.* Chicago: University of Chicago Press.

Marcuse, Herbert (1969). *An Essay on Liberation.* Boston: Beacon Press.

Marcuse, Herbert (1989). "Philosophy and Critical Theory." In Douglas MacKay Kellner and Stephen Eric Bronner (eds.), *Critical Theory and Society: A Reader,* pp. 58–74. New York: Routledge.

Markus, George (1978). *Marxism and Anthropology.* Assen, The Netherlands: Van Gorcium.

Marx, Karl (1963). *The Poverty of Philosophy.* New York: International Publishers.

Marx, Karl (1965). *Pre-Capitalist Economic Formations.* New York: International Publishers.

Marx, Karl (1966). *Capital,* Vol. III. Moscow: Progress Publishers.

Marx, Karl (1972). *Theories of Surplus Value,* Vol. 3. London: Lawrence and Wishart.

Marx, Karl (1973). *Grundrisse.* New York: Vintage.

Marx, Karl (1975a). *Early Writings.* New York: Vintage.

Marx, Karl (1975b). "Letter to Otechestvenniyc Zapiski, November 1877." *Marx-Engels: Selected Correspondences,* Moscow: Progress Publishers.

Marx, Karl (1977). *Capital,* Vol. I. New York: Vintage.

Marx, Karl, and Engels, Friedrich (1975). *The Holy Family.* Moscow: Progress Publishers.

Marx, Karl (and Engels, Friedrich) (1978). *The Marx-Engels Reader,* ed. Robert Tucker, New York: Norton.

Mauss, Marcel (1967). *The Gift: Forms and Functions of Exchange in Archaic Societies.* New York: Norton.

McCarthy, Thomas (1978). *The Critical Theory of Jürgen Habermas.* Cambridge, MA: MIT Press.

McCarthy, Thomas (1990). "The Politics of the Ineffable: Derrida's Deconstructionism." In Michael Kelly (ed.), *Hermeneutics and Critical Theory in Ethics and Politics,* pp. 146–168. Cambridge, MA and London: MIT Press.

McCarthy, Thomas (1991). *Ideals and Illusions: On Reconstruction and Deconstruction in Contemporary Critical Theory.* Cambridge, MA: MIT Press.

McMurtry, John (1978). *The Structure of Marx's World-View.* Princeton, NJ: Princeton University Press.

Megill, Allan (1985). *Prophets of Extremity.* Berkeley: University of California Press.

Merquior, J. G. (1985). *Foucault.* Berkeley: University of California Press.

Midelfort, H. C. Erik (1980). "Madness and Civilization in Early Modern Europe: A Reappraisal of Michel Foucault." In Barbara C. Malament (ed.), *After the Reformation: Essays in Honor of J. H. Hexter,* pp. 247–265. Philadelphia: University of Pennsylvania Press.

Miliband, Ralph (1977). *Marxism and Politics.* Oxford: Oxford University Press.

Miller, James (1993). *The Passion of Michel Foucault.* New York: Simon and Schuster.

Miller, Richard W. (1984). *Analyzing Marx.* Princeton: Princeton University Press.

Mills, C. Wright (1959). *The Sociological Imagination.* New York: Oxford University Press.

Mouffe, Chantal (1988). "Radical Democracy: Modern or Postmodern?" In Andrew Ross (ed.), *Universal Abandon,* pp. 46–62. Minneapolis: University of Minnesota Press.

Nicholson, Linda (1992). "On the Postmodern Barricades: Feminism, Politics, and Theory." In Seidman and Wagner (1992), pp. 82–100.

O'Farrell, Clare (1989). *Foucault: Historian or Philosopher?* New York: St. Martin's Press.

Ollman, Bertell (1976). *Alienation.* Cambridge, England: Cambridge University.

Ollman, Bertell (1979). *Social and Sexual Revolution: Essays on Marx and Reich.* Boston: South End Press.

Ollman, Bertell (1993). *Dialectical Investigations.* London: Routledge.

O'Neil, John (1976). "Critique and Remembrance." In John O'Neil (ed.), *On Critical Theory.* New York: Seabury Press.

Poetzl, Pamela Major (1983). *Michel Foucault's Archaeology of Western Culture:*

Toward a New Science of History. Chapel Hill: University of North Carolina Press.

Popper, Karl (1961). *The Open Society and its Enemies,* 2 vols. Princeton, NJ: Princeton University Press.

Poster, Mark (1975). *Existential Marxism in Postwar France.* Princeton, NJ: Princeton University Press.

Poster, Marx (1989). *Critical Theory and Poststructuralism: In Search of a Context.* Ithaca, NY: Cornell University Press.

Rader, Melvin (1979). *Marx's Interpretation of History.* New York: Oxford University Press.

Rajchman, John (1985). *Michel Foucault: The Freedom of Philosophy.* New York: Columbia University Press.

Rajchman, John (1988). "Habermas' Complaint." *New German Critique #45*(Fall): 163–190.

Randall, John (1976). *The Making of the Modern Mind.* New York: Columbia University Press.

Ranke, Leopold Von (1973). "The Ideal of Universal History." In Stern (1973), pp. 54–62.

Rader, Melvin (1979). *Marx's Interpretation of History.* New York: Oxford University Press.

Reinfelder, Monica (1980). "Introduction, Breaking the Spell of Technicism." In Philip Slater (ed.), *Outlines for a Critique of Technology,* pp. 9–37. London: Inks Links.

Renier, G. J. (1965). *History: Its Purpose and Method.* New York: Harper and Row.

Ricoeur, Paul (1984). *Time and Narrative,* Vol. 1. Chicago: University of Chicago Press.

Rochlitz, Rainer (1992). "The Aesthetics of Existence: Post- Conventional Morality and the Theory of Power in Michel Foucault." In Armstrong (1992), pp. 248–259.

Rockmore, Tom (1987). "Theory and Practice Again: Habermas on Historical Materialism." *Philosophy and Social Criticism,* 13(3): 211–225.

Rockmore, Tom (1989). *Habermas on Historical Materialism.* Bloomington: Indiana University Press.

Roderick, Rick (1986). *Habermas and the Foundations of Critical Theory.* London and New York: Macmillan and St. Martin.

Rorty, Richard (1982). *The Consequences of Pragmatism.* Minneapolis: University of Minnesota Press.

Rorty, Richard (1985). "Habermas and Lyotard on Postmodernity." In Richard J. Bernstein (ed.), *Habermas and Modernity,* pp. 161–175. Cambridge, MA: MIT Press.

Rorty, Richard (1989). *Contingency, Irony, and Solidarity.* Cambridge, England: Cambridge University Press.

Rosdolsky, R. (1977). *The Making of Marx's Capital.* London: Pluto.

Rotchlitz, Ranier (1992). "The Aesthetics of Existence: Post-Conventional Morality and the Theory of Power in Michel Foucault." In Armstrong (1992), pp. 248–259.

Rotenstreich, Nathan (1971). "The Idea of Historical Progress and its Assumptions." *History and Theory,* vol. X (no. 2): 197–221.

Ruben, David-Hillel (1979). "Marxism and Dialectics." In John Mepham and D. H. Rubin (eds.), *Issues in Marxist Philosophy,* pp. 37–85. Atlantic Highlands, NJ: Humanities Press.

Ryan, Michael (1982). *Marxism and Deconstruction: A Critical Articulation.* Baltimore and London: Johns Hopkins University Press.

Sahlins, Marshall (1972). *Stone Age Economics.* New York: Aldine.

Sahlins, Marshall (1976). *Culture and Practical Reason.* Chicago: University of Chicago Press.

Schaff, Adam (1970). *Marxism and the Human Individual.* New York: McGraw-Hill.

Schmid, Michael (1982). "Habermas' Theory of Social Evolution." In John B. Thompson and David Heid (eds.), *Habermas: Critical Debates,* pp. 162–180. Cambridge, England: MIT Press.

Schmidt, James, and Wartenberg, Thomas E. (1994). "Foucault's Enlightenment: Critique, Revolution, and the Fashioning of the Self." In Kelly (1994), pp. 283–314.

Sedwick, Peter (1982). *Psycho Politics.* London: Pluto Press.

Seidman, Steven (1991). "Postmodern Anxiety: The Politics of Epistemology." *Sociological Theory,* Vol. 9 (No. 2): 180–190.

Seidman, Steven (1992). "Postmodern Social Theory as Narrative with a Moral Intent." In Seidman and Wagner, pp. 47–81.

Seidman, Steven and Wagner, David G. (1992). *Postmodernism and Social Theory: The Debate over General Theory.* Oxford and Cambridge: Blackwell.

Sensat, Julius, Jr. (1979). *Habermas and Marxism: An Appraisal.* London: Sage.

Shaw, William H. (1978). *Marx's Theory of History.* Stanford, CA: Stanford University Press.

Smart, Barry (1985). *Michel Foucault.* New York: Tavistock.

Solomon, Robert (1988). *Continental Philosophy Since 1750: The Rise and Fall of the Self.* Oxford and New York: Oxford University Press.

Solomon, Robert C. (1993). *The Bully Culture: Enlightenment, Romanticism, and the Transcendental Pretense.* Lanham, MD: Rowman and Littlefield.

Steiner, George (1971). *In Bluebeard's Castle.* New Haven: Yale University Press.

Stern, Fritz (1973). *The Varieties of History: From Voltaire to the Present.* New York: Vintage Books.

Taylor, Charles (1986). "Foucault on Freedom and Truth." In Hoy (1987), pp. 69–102.

Thomas, Paul (1979). "The Language of Real Life: Jurgen Habermas and the Distortion of Karl Marx." *Discourse, #1*(Fall): 59–81.

Thompson, John B., and Held, David (1982). *Habermas: Critical Debates*. Cambridge, MA: MIT Pres.

Toulmin, Stephen (1990). *Cosmopolis*. New York: Free Press.

Trevelyan, George Macauly (1973). "Clio Rediscovered." In Stern (1973), pp. 227–245.

Tucker, Robert (1961). *Philosophy and Myth in Karl Marx*. Cambridge, England: Cambridge University Press.

Vico, Giambattista (1968). *The New Science of Giambattista Vico*. Ithaca and London: Cornell University Press.

Von Ranke, Leoplod (1973). "The Idéal of Universal History." In Stern (1973), pp. 55–62.

Wagner, David G. (1992). "Daring Modesty: On Metatheory, Observation, and Theory Grauth." In Seidman and Wagner (1992), pp. 199–220.

Walzer, Micheal (1986). "The Politics of Michel Foucault." In Paul Rabinow (ed.), *The Foucault Reader*, pp. 51–68. New York: Pantheon.

Wellmer, Albreacht (1971). *Critical Theory of Society*. New York: Continuum.

Wellmer, Albrecht (1976). "Communications and Emancipation: Reflection on the Linguistic Turn in Critical Theory." In John O'Neill (1976) (ed.), *On Critical Theory*, pp. 231–263. New York: Seabury Press.

Wolin, Richard (1986). "Foucault's Aesthetic Decisionism." *Telos, #67:* 71–86.

Wolin, Richard (1990). "On Misunderstanding Habermas: A Response to Rajchman." *New German Critique, #49*(Winter): 139–154.

Wolin, Richard (1992). *The Terms of Cultural Criticism: The Frankfurt School, Existentialism, Poststructuralism*. New York: Columbia University Press.

Wolin, Sheldon S. (1960). *Politics and Vision: Continuity and Innovation in Western Political Thought*. Boston: Little, Brown.

White, Hayden (1973). *Metahistory: The Historical Imagination in Nineteenth-Centruy Europe*. Baltimore and London: Johns Hopkins University Press.

White, Hayden (1978). *Tropics of Discourse*. Baltimore: Johns Hopkins University Press.

Whitebook, Joel (1979). "The Problem of Nature in Habermas." *Telos, #40:* 41–69.

Whitebook, Joel (1981–1982). "Saving the Subject: Modernity and the Problem of the Autonomous Individual." *Telos, #50:* 79–103.

Whorf, Benjamin Lee (1956). *Language, Thought, and Reality*, ed., John B. Carroll. Cambridge, MA: MIT Press.

Wilson, Bryan (ed.) (1970). *Rationality*. Oxford: Basil Blackwell.

INDEX